Library of
Davidson College

DANTE'S POETS
TEXTUALITY AND TRUTH IN THE *COMEDY*

DANTE'S POETS

TEXTUALITY AND TRUTH IN THE *COMEDY*

Teodolinda Barolini

PRINCETON UNIVERSITY PRESS
PRINCETON, NEW JERSEY

Copyright © 1984 by Princeton University Press
Published by Princeton University Press, 41 William Street,
Princeton, New Jersey 08540
In the United Kingdom: Princeton University Press,
Guildford, Surrey

All Rights Reserved

Library of Congress Cataloging in Publication Data will be
found on the last printed page of this book

ISBN 0-691-06609-4

This book has been composed in Linotron Aldus

Clothbound editions of Princeton University Press books are printed
on acid-free paper, and binding materials are chosen for strength
and durability

Printed in the United States of America by
Princeton University Press
Princeton, New Jersey

IN MEMORY OF
ANTONIO BAROLINI

forse non pur per lor, ma per le mamme,
per li padri e per li altri che fuor cari
anzi che fosser sempiterne fiamme

CONTENTS

ACKNOWLEDGMENTS ix
EDITIONS AND TRANSLATIONS xi
PREFACE xiii

I Autocitation and Autobiography
Prelude: the *Inferno* 3
Textual History 14
"Amor che ne la mente mi ragiona" 31
"Donne ch'avete intelletto d'amore" 40
"Voi che 'ntendendo il terzo ciel movete" 57

II Lyric Quests
Historiography Revisited: " 'l Notaro e Guittone e me" 85
Fathers and Sons: Guinizzelli and Cavalcanti 123
The Poetry of Politics: Bertran and Sordello 153
The Lyric Picture: Patterns of Revision 173

III Epic Resolution
Prelude: the *Opere minori* 188
Vergil: "Poeta fui" 201
Statius: "Per te poeta fui" 256
Dante: "ritornerò poeta" 269

APPENDIX. Dante's Poets 287
INDEX 299

ACKNOWLEDGMENTS

I wish to take this opportunity to thank, for their past and present counsel, Joan M. Ferrante, W.T.H. Jackson, and Joseph Anthony Mazzeo of Columbia University, and Nicolas J. Perella and Ruggero Stefanini of the University of California, Berkeley. My appreciation goes also to the University of California and the American Council of Learned Societies for their generous support, and to Narriman Casati Shahrokh for her preparation of the manuscript. My deepest and most unreferential gratitude is reserved for my family and in particular for Douglas Caverly, my husband.

EDITIONS AND TRANSLATIONS

Citations of Dante's texts are from the following editions:

La Commedia secondo l'antica vulgata, ed. Giorgio Petrocchi, 4 vols. (Milan: Mondadori, 1966-1967).
Dante's Lyric Poetry, ed. Kenelm Foster and Patrick Boyde, 2 vols. (Oxford: Oxford U. Press, 1967).
Vita Nuova, ed. Domenico De Robertis (Milan-Naples: Ricciardi, 1980).
Il Convivio, ed. G. Busnelli and G. Vandelli, 2d ed. rev. Antonio Enzo Quaglio, 2 vols. (Florence: Le Monnier, 1964).
De Vulgari Eloquentia, ed. Pier Vincenzo Mengaldo, in Dante Alighieri, *Opere minori*, tomo II, vol. 5 of *La letteratura italiana: storia e testi* (Milan-Naples: Ricciardi, 1979).
Monarchia, ed. Bruno Nardi, in Dante Alighieri, *Opere minori*, tomo II.
Epistole, ed. Arsenio Frugoni and Giorgio Brugnoli, in Dante Alighieri, *Opere minori*, tomo II.
Egloge, ed. Enzo Cecchini, in Dante Alighieri, *Opere minori*, tomo II.

All translations are my own, although I have greatly benefited from existing translations of the authors cited herein.

PREFACE

Misguided though he was by the pre-humanist stirrings that circulated in the scholarly milieu of his day, Giovanni del Virgilio is responsible for two eminently accurate observations regarding his illustrious correspondent: in the verse epistle that initiates their correspondence he calls Dante a "most free judge of poets," and in his responsive eclogue he hails him the next Vergil, or indeed Vergil reborn (*Egloge* I, 19; III, 33-34). If the first of these labels, Dante *censor liberrime vatum*, provides the starting point for this study, the second illuminates its goal, which is to trace, by deriving the implications of this censorship, the itinerary Dante designs for himself, the self-definitions that take him from being the *primo amico* of Guido Cavalcanti to being Giovanni's *Alter . . . aut idem*—the new Vergil.

The self-reading that this study aims to delineate is built upon Dante's reading of others: the poets of the *Comedy*. These poets, sign-makers, are themselves transformed into signs in the crucible of Dante's text; like the souls in the heaven of Jupiter, who obligingly form a sentence of thirty-five letters for the pilgrim to read (thus confirming the identity of souls and signs), the poets of the *Comedy* constitute a carefully fashioned narrative that may be deciphered and read. We begin with the observation that they are differentiated by Dante according to genre. The epic poets, Vergil and Statius, move in geographic and discursive space, i.e. physically and in their discourses, which cover a broad range of topics from the nature of free will to the generation of the human soul. Lyric poets, on the other hand, are restricted in both these spheres, more confined than their brethren in their movements and in their speech, since

Preface

their discourses generally reflect their primary poetic concerns on earth.

An attempt to draw significance from Dante's treatment of the poets in his poem necessarily begins by investigating his most overt treatment of himself as poet, in the *Comedy*'s three autocitations. Thus, Chapter I deals with Dante's retrospective appraisal of earlier poetic selves; Chapter II charts the intricate maze of his relations with vernacular precursors, while Chapter III traces his handling of classical antecedents, especially Vergil. Since the focus of this study is dictated by Dante's placement and treatment of the poets within his text, it does not seek to be a comprehensive catalogue of the *Comedy*'s sources; the intertextual currents of the *Comedy* are explored in detail, but always with the goal of illuminating less Dante's poets than Dante himself, the only poet present from the poem's beginning to its end, its textual alpha and omega. In short, this is an inquiry into Dante's beliefs on textuality: its limits, purposes, and—most crucially—its relation to truth.

New York
December 1983

DANTE'S POETS
TEXTUALITY AND TRUTH IN THE *COMEDY*

I

Autocitation
and Autobiography

Prelude: the *Inferno*

In a text that functions largely through a dialectical process of revision and appropriation, the moments in which the poet looks to his own poetic past, through autocitation, acquire a peculiar significance; indeed, in a study of the *Comedy*'s poets, one must begin by examining Dante's retrospective treatment of his poetic self. Nowhere can this palinodic self-analysis that permeates the *Comedy* be more tellingly isolated than in the episodes in which Dante quotes from his earlier literary achievements. In this chapter I propose to approach these episodes as a unified and continuous autobiographical meditation purposely inscribed by the poet into the text of his poem.[1]

[1] Scholars dealing with autobiography or autoexegesis in Dante have adopted a variety of approaches. The critic who has most illuminated the dialectical intersecting of the *Comedy* with its poetic past is Gianfranco Contini, who comments that "la *Commedia* è, dopo tutto, anche la storia, stavo per dire l'autobiografia, di un poeta" ("Dante come personaggio-poeta della *Commedia*," *L'Approdo letterario*, 4 [1958], 19-46, repr. in *Un'idea di Dante* [Turin: Einaudi, 1976], pp. 33-62; the quotation is from *Un'idea di Dante*, p. 40). Giovanni Fallani, *Dante autobiografico* (Naples: Società editrice napoletana, 1975), reconstructs Dante's biography on the basis of his texts. Marziano Guglielminetti, *Memoria e scrittura: l'autobiografia da Dante a Cellini* (Turin: Einaudi, 1977), places the *Vita Nuova* and *Convivio* in a historical framework (see in this context the questions raised by Paul Zumthor, "Autobiography in the Middle Ages?" *Genre*, 6 [1973], 29-48). William C. Spengemann discusses the *Vita Nuova*

Autocitation and Autobiography

There are three autocitations in the *Comedy*: two in the *Purgatorio* and one in the *Paradiso*. All are incipits of canzoni, all from love poems. The fact that none occurs in the *Inferno* is relevant to this discussion, representing as it does a deliberate omission. Autocitations appear in the *Comedy* as integral parts of larger deliberations on textuality; the very nature of Dante's infernal commentary on this issue precludes the possibility of quotation, since the mimesis of the first canticle is dedicated to reproducing instances of textual distortion. Textually, the governing principle of the *Inferno* is misuse, which is objectified into a series of misquotations operating at all levels of textual activity, from the religious hymn, in the case of *"Vexilla regis prodeunt inferni"* (*Inf.* XXXIV, 1), to the secular lyric.

The most explicit evocation of love poetry in the *Inferno* occurs in canto V, where the dense fabric of literary reminiscences, ranging from Vergil and Augustine to Boethius and the vernacular traditions, is intended to sustain an investigation into the status of authoritative texts.[2] The material for Dante's in-

---

from an autobiographical perspective in *The Forms of Autobiography* (New Haven and London: Yale U. Press, 1980), as does Jerome Mazzaro, *The Figure of Dante: An Essay on the Vita Nuova* (Princeton: Princeton U. Press, 1981). The *Convivio* and Epistle to Cangrande della Scala are situated within the tradition of medieval exegesis by L. Jenaro MacLennan, "Autocomentario en Dante y comentarismo latino," *Vox Romanica*, 19 (1960), 82-123, and Gian Roberto Sarolli, "Autoesegesi dantesca e tradizione esegetica medievale," *Convivium*, 34 (1966), 77-112, repr. in *Prolegomena alla Divina Commedia* (Florence: Olschki, 1971), pp. 1-39. John Freccero has written on the role of the Augustinian model in shaping the *Comedy* as a confessional narrative; see especially "Dante's Novel of the Self," *Christian Century*, 82 (1965), 1216-1218, "Dante's Prologue Scene," *Dante Studies*, 84 (1966), 1-25, and "Dante's Medusa: Allegory and Autobiography," in *By Things Seen: Reference and Recognition in Medieval Thought*, ed. David L. Jeffrey (Ottawa: U. of Ottawa Press, 1979), pp. 33-46. A recent proposal for reading the *Comedy* in an autoexegetical key is provided by Amilcare A. Iannucci, "Autoesegesi dantesca: la tecnica dell' 'episodio parallelo' nella *Commedia*," *Lettere italiane*, 33 (1981), 305-328.

[2] The following studies focus on textuality in *Inferno* V: Paget Toynbee, "Dante and the Lancelot Romance," in *Dante Studies and Researches* (London: Methuen, 1902), pp. 1-37; Gioacchino Paparelli, *"Galeotto fu il libro e chi lo scrisse"* (Naples: Conte, 1954), repr. as "Ethos e pathos nell'episodio di Fran-

Prelude: the *Inferno*

quiry is provided by Francesca, whose monologue can be conveniently divided into two parts: the first (88-107) contains her celebrated anaphoric invocation of Love; the second (121-138) responds to the pilgrim's question regarding the specifics of her fall. In this latter, more representational phase of her discourse Francesca relies on the authority of the *Lancelot du Lac*; in the first preparatory phase she draws on the tenets of the established amatory code, explaining that love flourishes in the noble heart and that reciprocity in love is obligatory. Here commentators uniformly point not only to the presence of Andreas Capellanus, but also to that of the Italian, specifically stilnovist, lyric.[3]

cesca da Rimini," in *Ideologia e poesia di Dante* (Florence: Olschki, 1975), pp. 171-200; Renato Poggioli, "Tragedy or Romance? A Reading of the Paolo and Francesca Episode in Dante's *Inferno*," PMLA, 72 (1957), 313-358, repr. in *Dante: A Collection of Critical Essays*, ed. John Freccero (Englewood Cliffs, N.J.: Prentice-Hall, 1965), pp. 61-77; Gianfranco Contini, "Dante come personaggio-poeta della *Commedia*," esp. pp. 42-48; Roger Dragonetti, "L'Épisode de Francesca dans le Cadre de la Convention courtoise," *Romanica Gandensia*, 9 (1961), 93-116; Daniele Mattalia, "Moralità e dottrina nel canto V dell'*Inferno*," *Filologia e letteratura*, 8 (1962), 41-70; Antonino Pagliaro, "Il canto di Francesca," in *Ulisse: ricerche semantiche sulla Divina Commedia*, 2 vols. (Messina-Florence: D'Anna, 1967), vol. I, pp. 115-159; Lanfranco Caretti, "Il canto V dell'*Inferno*," *Nuove letture dantesche* (Florence: Le Monnier, 1968), vol. I, pp. 105-131; Anna Hatcher and Mark Musa, "The Kiss: *Inferno* V and the Old French Prose *Lancelot*," *Comparative Literature*, 20 (1968), 97-109; Robert Hollander, *Allegory in Dante's Commedia* (Princeton: Princeton U. Press, 1969), esp. pp. 106-114; Nicolas J. Perella, *The Kiss Sacred and Profane* (Berkeley-Los Angeles: U. of California Press, 1969), pp. 140-157; D'Arco Silvio Avalle, ". . . de fole amor," in *Modelli semiologici della Divina Commedia* (Milan: Bompiani, 1975), pp. 97-121; John A. Scott, "Dante's Francesca and the Poet's Attitude towards Courtly Literature," *Reading Medieval Studies*, 5 (1979), 4-20; Giuseppe Mazzotta, *Dante, Poet of the Desert* (Princeton: Princeton U. Press, 1979), esp. pp. 160-170; Stephen Popolizio, "Literary Reminiscences and the Act of Reading in *Inferno* V," *Dante Studies*, 98 (1980), 19-33; Susan Noakes, "The Double Misreading of Paolo and Francesca," *Philological Quarterly*, 62 (1983), 221-239; Karla Taylor, "A Text and Its Afterlife: Dante and Chaucer," *Comparative Literature*, 35 (1983), 1-20. See also Baldo Curato, *Il canto di Francesca e i suoi interpreti* (Cremona: Editrice Padus, 1963).

[3] Contini points out that Francesca's verse, "Amor, ch'a nullo amato amar perdona," draws on two of Andreas' Rules of Love: Rule IX, "Amare nemo potest nisi qui amoris suasione compellitur" ("No one can love unless he is

Autocitation and Autobiography

The first of Francesca's precepts regarding the god of Love, "Amor, ch'al cor gentil ratto s'apprende" ("Love, which is quickly kindled in the noble heart" [100]), is far from original; Contini points out that it is in fact a conflation of two verses from Guinizzelli's programmatic canzone "Al cor gentil," considered a manifesto for the poets of the *dolce stil novo*.[4] Onto the canzone's incipit, "Al cor gentil rempaira sempre amore" ("Love always returns to dwell in the noble heart"), which formulates a necessary and causal relationship between love and inborn—rather than conferred—nobility, is grafted the first verse of the second stanza, "Foco d'amore in gentil cor s'aprende" ("The fire of love is kindled in the noble heart"), which introduces the element of love as a kindling fire. But for the addition of the adverb "ratto," an intensifier characteristic of Francesca's speech patterns, the result is pure—albeit misquoted—Guinizzelli.

The density of line 100 is further augmented by the fact that it also echoes the first verse of a sonnet from the *Vita Nuova* in which Dante is openly imitating his precursor Guinizzelli. The young poet formulates the relation between love and the gentle heart in terms of identity (they are "one thing"), and ascribes his beliefs to his Bolognese predecessor, the *saggio* of the sonnet's second verse: "Amore e 'l cor gentil sono una cosa, / sì come il saggio in suo dittare pone" ("Love and the noble heart are one thing, as the wise man claims in his verse"

---

compelled by the persuasion of love"); Rule XXVI, "Amor nil posset amore denegare" ("Love can deny nothing to love") ("Dante come personaggio-poeta della *Commedia*," p. 46). The theme of love and the noble heart in its various transmutations from Andreas to Guittone, Guinizzelli, and Dante is discussed by D'Arco Silvio Avalle, "Due tesi sui limiti di amore," in *Ai luoghi di delizia pieni: saggio sulla lirica italiana del XIII secolo* (Milan-Naples: Ricciardi, 1977), pp. 17-55. On Dante's relation to Andreas, see also Maria Simonelli, "Il tema della nobiltà in Andrea Cappellano e in Dante," *Dante Studies*, 84 (1966), 51-68, and Antonio Viscardi, "Andrea Cappellano," *Enciclopedia Dantesca*, 6 vols. (Rome: Istituto dell'Enciclopedia Italiana, 1970-1978), vol. I, pp. 261-263.

[4] "Dante come personaggio-poeta della *Commedia*," p. 43. For the poetry of Guinizzelli and his peers, the edition used throughout, unless otherwise noted, is Contini, *Poeti del Duecento*, 2 vols. (Milan-Naples: Ricciardi, 1960).

Prelude: the *Inferno*

[*Vita Nuova*, XX]). The love poetry of Dante's early years, as inherited from poets like Guinizzelli, would therefore seem to be implicated in the condemnation of literature that critics have discerned as a primary theme of *Inferno* V. But although Dante is undoubtedly alerting readers of the *Comedy* to the perils inherent in the lyric tradition, *Inferno* V cannot be seen as positing a final damnation of the genre; its practitioners—including Guinizzelli and the poet of the *Vita Nuova*—are firmly lodged in the *Purgatorio*, where they figure in the review of contemporary poetry that runs through the second canticle.

Moreover, Dante is careful to draw immediate attention to the positive as well as negative dimensions of the lyric. To this end he devises the stilnovistic discourse between Vergil and Beatrice in *Inferno* II, a canto imbued with the kind of morally unambiguous lyric atmosphere that characterizes the final cantos of the *Purgatorio*. Indeed, canto II anticipates not only the *Purgatorio*'s later positive treatment of the lyric, but also—by contrast—the negative treatment of *Inferno* V. There are a number of intriguing correspondences between the two cantos, correspondences intended, I believe, to proleptically defuse and unmask the values underlying Francesca's discourse. Both cantos are, for instance, unusually verbal. Canto II consists almost entirely of referred speech, from the pilgrim's to that of the heavenly intercessors. Beatrice's speech is mediated through Vergil, who repeats it to Dante, using his "parola ornata" (67) and "parlare onesto" (113).[5] Like Francesca (whose word is as ornate but less honest), Vergil draws on both the lyric and romance registers in his account, thus anticipating her discourse and establishing the stylistic complementarity of the cantos.

[5] The high incidence of language relating to speech supports the notion that *Inferno* II is a markedly verbal canto; besides the various forms of *dire* employed to relate what one person said to another, we note the frequent iteration of "parlare" and "parola": "S'i' ho ben la parola tua intesa" (43), "Or movi, e con la tua parola ornata" (67), "amor mi mosse, che mi fa parlare" (72), "com' io, dopo cotai parole fatte" (111), "fidandomi del tuo parlare onesto" (113), "e 'l mio parlar tanto ben ti promette" (126), "a le vere parole che ti porse" (135), "sì al venir con le parole tue" (137). The court of heaven seems to rely heavily on words. For more on this issue, see Chapter III, note 100.

7

Autocitation and Autobiography

Vergil's use of the lyric register is especially apparent in his initial description of Beatrice's arrival, a passage whose stilnovist flavor has been remarked:

Io era tra color che son sospesi,
  e donna mi chiamò beata e bella,
  tal che di comandare io la richiesi.
Lucevan li occhi suoi più che la stella;
  e cominciommi a dir soave e piana,
  con angelica voce, in sua favella

I was among those who are suspended, and a lady called me, so blessed and so beautiful that I requested her to command me. Her eyes shone more than the stars, and she smoothly and softly began to speak, with angelic voice, in her tongue

(*Inf*. II, 52-57)

The paired adjectives "beata e bella" and "soave e piana" remind us of the synonymic reduplication typical of the early lyric.[6] Her angelic voice and the likening of her eyes to stars are reminiscent of stilnovist developments in the lyric; we think for instance, of Guinizzelli's comparison of his lady to the *stella diana* or morning star.[7] The tone of the passage matches the description of Beatrice; it is "smooth and soft," like the praise

---

[6] For examples of synonymic reduplication in the early Dante and the relation of this stylistic feature to the Italian poetic tradition, see Kenelm Foster and Patrick Boyde, *Dante's Lyric Poetry*, vol. II: *Commentary*, p. 35. Regarding the stilnovist resonance of Canto II, Sapegno comments that "L'atmosfera in cui si colloca questa prima presentazione di Beatrice è tipicamente stilnovistica, anche nei particolari, e prima di tutto in questo gesto di 'omaggio' di Virgilio" (Natalino Sapegno, comm., *La Divina Commedia*, 2d ed., 3 vols. [Florence: La Nuova Italia, 1968], vol. I: *Inferno*, p. 22.

[7] See the sonnet "Vedut' ho la lucente stella diana," where the poet not only compares his lady to the morning star, but also refers in line 6 to her "occhi lucenti," thus anticipating both terms of Dante's "Lucevan li occhi suoi più che la stella." Other comparisons to the *stella diana* appear in line 3 of Guinizzelli's "Io voglio del ver la mia donna laudare" ("più che la stella diana splende e pare"), and in the second line of Cavalcanti's "In un boschetto trova' pasturella" ("più che la stella—bella").

8

Prelude: the *Inferno*

sonnets of Dante's high *stil novo* phase, in which he aimed precisely at creating a *stilus planus*.

The presence of the romance register is less explicit in canto II than in canto V, if only because canto II does not contain a protagonist-text like the *Lancelot du Lac*. Instead, the canto's words and actions are superimposed onto a backdrop of romance conventions: Vergil is the chivalrous knight, begging Beatrice to command him; she is the anxious romance heroine, concerned for her lost friend. Indeed, the context of romance relations, with their prerequisite courtly network, helps to explain Beatrice's promise to praise Vergil to her lord, a remark that has puzzled critics because it seems so gratuitous: is Beatrice suggesting that she can alter Vergil's fate?[8] Her words, "Quando sarò dinanzi al segnor mio, / di te mi loderò sovente a lui" ("When I am before my lord, I will praise you frequently to him" [73-74]), suggest a secular context, in which *il segnor mio* takes on the connotations of a secular lord. Like the repeated commands and "recommendations" that run through the canto, they belong to the courtly register to which we are introduced in line 17, where the description of God as *cortese* implicitly likens Him to a beneficent king. This adjective, etymologically connected to "court," will reoccur twice: in Beatrice's opening words to Vergil ("O anima cortese mantoana" [58]), and again in the pilgrim's words of gratitude to his guide ("e te cortese

---

[8] The sixteenth-century commentator Lodovico Castelvetro sums up the perplexity of the critics in his question "Questo che monta a Virgilio che è dannato?" ("How does this help Vergil, who is damned?"). The quotation is from Guido Biagi, ed., *La Divina Commedia nella figurazione artistica e nel secolare commento*, 3 vols. (Turin: Unione Tipografico-Editrice Torinese, 1924-1929), vol. I, p. 68. The commentators closest to Dante tend to do away with the problem by reading the passage allegorically; for instance, Benvenuto comments: "Hoc autem significat quod theologia saepe utitur servicio rationis naturalis" ("this moreover signifies that theology often makes use of the services of natural reason"). See Benvenuti de Rambaldis de Imola, *Comentum super Dantis Aldigherij Comoediam*, ed. J. P. Lacaita, 5 vols. (Florence: Barbèra, 1887), vol. I, p. 93. With the exception of Benvenuto, who will be cited according to Lacaita, all quotations from the early commentators will be taken from Biagi's edition.

ch'ubidisti tosto" [134]). *Inferno* II is the only canto in the poem where *cortese* appears more than once, as part of a calculated stress on courtliness; in the *Convivio* Dante explicitly links the word *cortesia* to the notion of the court, saying "si tolse quello vocabulo da le corti, e fu tanto a dire cortesia quanto uso di corte" ("that word was taken from the courts, for to say courtesy was as much as to say the practice of the court" [II, x, 8]). The canto's insistence on courtliness reaches its metaphoric peak when Vergil, toward the end, refers to the domain of the assisting luminaries as the "court of heaven": "tre donne benedette . . . ne la corte del cielo" (124-125).

Dante, then, goes to great lengths to create the ambience of a court in *Inferno* II. Whereas the canto's lyric echoes may be accounted for by the poet's desire to introduce Beatrice to the *Comedy* in a stylistic environment consonant with the last text in which she figures prominently, the *Vita Nuova*, the creation of the "court of heaven" is less easily explained. I would suggest that it belongs to an associative network designed with an express purpose: Dante intends us to recall this evocation of a courtly scenario when, a few cantos later, we encounter a similar figurative construct. Francesca too invokes an imagined court in which God is king, also in order to offer her protection to the pilgrim: "se fosse amico il re de l'universo, / noi pregheremmo lui de la tua pace" ("if the king of the universe were a friend, we would pray to him for your peace" [*Inf.* V, 91-92]). This remark is curiously analogous to Beatrice's offer to Vergil, with the difference that Francesca—an exile from the court of heaven—uses a conditional mode that contrasts sharply with Beatrice's self-assured use of the future tense: "di te mi loderò sovente a lui" (*Inf.* II, 74).

Similarly, much of the diction of *Inferno* V can be seen as an inverse reflection of that of *Inferno* II. *Talento* in *Inferno* II refers to Beatrice's desire to save the pilgrim (81); in *Inferno* V it occurs in the definition of the carnal sinners, "che la ragion sommettono al talento" ("who submit reason to desire" [39]). *Disio* and its derivatives in *Inferno* II refer to Beatrice's desire to return to heaven (71), or to the pilgrim's desire to move

Prelude: the *Inferno*

forward on his journey (136), whereas in *Inferno* V they occur four times and always in the context of physical passion (82, 113, 120, 133). "Eyes" in the second canto are either Beatrice's shining eyes or Beatrice's tearful eyes (55, 116); in the fifth canto they are the medium through which passion is first expressed (130). A lady in *Inferno* II is a "donna di virtù" (76; cf. also 94, 124); in *Inferno* V she is immediately coupled and—more dangerously—romanticized (in the most literal sense of the word: she becomes a heroine of romance): "le donne antiche e ' cavalieri" (71). *Amor*, so over-invoked in canto V (in various forms, we find 13 occurrences), is used in canto II with a deliberately chaste infrequency (only twice). And finally, the first words spoken by Beatrice and Francesca offer an interesting contrast. Francesca's "O animal grazïoso e benigno" (*Inf.* V, 88) syntactically parallels Beatrice's "O anima cortese mantoana" (*Inf.* II, 58); both statements are direct addresses consisting of a vocative preceded by "O," followed by a noun and two adjectives. The similarity underlines the shift from *anima* in one case to *animal* in the other. In a context where the poet has already indicated the difference that changing one letter can make, in reference to Semiramis' legalization of lust ("che libito fé licito in sua legge" "she made lust licit in her law" [*Inf.* V, 56]), the contrast is suggestive of the larger difference between these two ladies and their two "courts."

Dante's analogous treatment of cantos II and V, his drawing in both cantos on the same genres in order to create a similar textual environment, points to an implied comparison; the two "courts" of these cantos illustrate in fact the two possible outcomes for courtly literature. Dante's statement regards especially the lyric, the courtly genre in which he conducted his own early poetic experiments and whose development he traces throughout the *Comedy*. In *Inferno* V the lyric is criticized for its tendency to conceptual banality; its philosophical underpinnings are susceptible to being reduced to the level of Andreas Capellanus' maxims. The same lack of sufficient critical self-awareness that afflicts the genre also afflicts the youthful Dante, whose willingness to defer to a *saggio* finds its precise echo in

Francesca's deference to authorities (and, even verbally, in her naming of " 'l tuo dottore" in line 123). If misquotation in a broad sense is the issue of this episode, there is nonetheless also a strong implication that these particular texts are unusually capable of misrepresenting themselves, of creating traps for the inattentive reader, and of generating the occasions for their own misquotation and misuse.

Inferno V represents one possible outcome for the love lyric; *Inferno* II points ahead to the other. The general rebirth of the *Purgatorio* does not leave poetry unaffected: "Ma qui la morta poesì resurga" ("But here let dead poetry rise up again" [*Purg.* I, 7]), from the poet's invocation to the Muses at the beginning of the canticle, is emblematic of the renewal that the *Purgatorio* works at all levels of textuality. The redemption of the love lyric, in particular, is signified in the second canto by the verbatim citation of a verse of love poetry, no longer misquoted but faithfully transcribed. The lyric surfaces on the shores of the mountain in much the same condition as the pilgrim, functioning in fact like all other newcomers to this realm: in need of purgation, refinement, but definitely saved.

The love lyric is a major theme of *Purgatorio* II as it is of *Inferno* V; indeed, one could say that *Purgatorio* II stands as a corrective to *Inferno* V, and that Casella is in this sense a new version of Francesca. "Amorous song," as the lyric is dubbed in *Purgatorio* II, is a key component of both episodes; its reception is in both cases a paradigm for the relation to textuality obtaining in each canticle. Whereas in the *Inferno* tension is generated from the interplay between the "subjective" sinners who view themselves as victims and the "objective" structure (mirrored by the "objective" text) that views them as recipients of justice, in the *Purgatorio* tension results from the dialectic between the souls' conflicting desires, rendered in the purgatorial topos of voyagers who are not sure whether they are more drawn to what lies ahead or to what they leave behind. The dialectic of the *Purgatorio* derives its power from the fact that the sentiments that must be put aside are not, from an earthly perspective, wrong per se; rather, we are dealing here with the

Prelude: the *Inferno*

highest of earthly loves: love of friends, love of family, love of one's native city and country, love of poetry and poetic masters.

Art, as mankind's supreme collective accomplishment, pervades the *Purgatorio*. Like the women who are insistently invoked throughout this canticle, art is the emblem of the *Purgatorio*'s fundamental problematic: the transcending of an object of desire that is intrinsically worthy but earthbound and subject to time. All aspects of artistic endeavor are represented and find expression in the *Purgatorio*: music, the pictorial and plastic arts, poetry. Of these, however, poetry is the most thoroughly explored; this one canticle contains the episodes of Casella, Sordello, Statius, Forese Donati, Bonagiunta da Lucca, Guido Guinizzelli, and Arnaut Daniel, to mention only those episodes that may be categorized by name. Poetry has a central role in the *Purgatorio* because this is the canticle where even poets must rearrange their priorities; by the same token, this is the only one of the three realms where poetry can truly come into its own as a theme. In the *Inferno* it is only valuable in so far as it is exploitable; in the *Paradiso* it is out of place, surpassed.

In the first two cantos of the *Purgatorio* Dante rehearses the canticle's theme of detachment with respect to a woman (Cato's wife, Marcia), a friend (Casella), and the *amoroso canto* that Casella sings. All three inspire a love that is in need of being redirected upward, away from the earthly catalyst. Of particular interest is Casella, the first of many "old friends" in this canticle, and his song, "Amor che ne la mente mi ragiona," which, as the *Comedy*'s first autocitation, also establishes Dante as the first lyric poet of the *Purgatorio*. If we look at the three episodes that contain autocitations in the *Comedy*, we notice that they are all linked to encounters with friends: in *Purgatorio* II Casella sings "Amor che ne la mente"; in *Purgatorio* XXIV the recital of "Donne ch'avete intelletto d'amore," although executed by Bonagiunta, is part of the larger episode of Forese Donati; in *Paradiso* VIII "Voi che 'ntendendo il terzo ciel movete" is quoted by Charles Martel. Autocitations, or poetic reminiscences, are thus linked to personal encounters, or biographic reminiscences, so that the literary and literal moments of the poet's life are fused together in a highly suggestive pattern.

In the same way that the personal encounters of the *Comedy* have furnished clues to Dante's actual biography—for instance, by allowing us to date the canzone "Voi che 'ntendendo" with respect to the year in which Charles Martel visited Florence—so the *Comedy*'s autocitations may furnish clues to a more internal poetic biography.[9] The linking of all three self-quotations to episodes that relate to Dante's previous life is a signpost; as those meetings reflect an experiential history, so the autocitations reflect a poetic history. In that they are depositories of a poetic past, deliberately inscribed into a poetic present, the autocitations are markers of a space in the text, a space defined as the relation between their previous existence outside the poem and their new existence within it. Why did Dante choose these specific poems for inclusion in the *Comedy*? Why did he place them where he did? Such questions face us with authorial decisions whose unraveling yields a definitive autobiography of the poet's lyric past, Dante's final statement regarding the way he wants us to perceive his poetic development, from its origins to the engendering of the great poem.

Textual History

The complexity of the issues raised by the choice of these particular incipits becomes apparent when we consider their provenance: one from the *Vita Nuova* and two from the *Convivio*. Thus, each of the major stages in Dante's poetic devel-

---

[9] Following the evidence of *Paradiso* VIII, the *terminus ante quem* of this canzone has been placed by most critics as March of 1294, the date given by Villani for Charles Martel's three-week visit to Florence; Foster and Boyde accept Santangelo's suggestion that the canzone could not have been written substantially later than the spring of 1294 (*Commentary*, pp. 345-346). See their Appendix, "The Biographical Problems in 'Voi che 'ntendendo,' " *Commentary*, pp. 341-362, for a lucid exposition of the debate surrounding the dating of this canzone and the other poems to the *donna gentile*.

opment before the *Comedy* is involved. The *Vita Nuova* and the *Convivio* are both texts in which Dante overtly reassesses his previous performance and seeks to revise his audience's perception of his poetic production. Indeed, these texts are both primary examples of Dante's tendencies toward autoexegesis, for the genesis of each can be located in an act of revision.

Dante's quintessential authorial persona first manifests itself in the reflexivity that generates the *Vita Nuova*: circa 1292 to 1294 the poet looks over the lyrics he has already composed, which run the gamut from those in his earliest Guittonian mode of a decade earlier to more recent poems of the most rigorous stilnovist purity, and he chooses some of them to be set in a prose frame. The lyrics thus chosen undergo not only a passive revision in the process of being selected for inclusion, but also an active revision at the hands of the prose narrative, which bends them into a new significance consonant with the poet's "new life." The violations of original intention that occur result in certain narrative reversals; poems written for other ladies in other contexts are now perceived as written for Beatrice. The prose is the chief witness to the author's revised intentions, since through its agency poems composed as isolated love lyrics are forced into a temporal sequence that places them in a predetermined and significant relation to each other. In such a context, "Donne ch'avete intelletto d'amore," for example, is no longer a beautiful canzone that develops the themes of its precursors in some striking ways, but is emblematic of a moment described in the prose: the moment in which the poet finds his own voice and creates the "new style."

This line of reasoning is even more applicable to the *Convivio*, for whereas the *Vita Nuova* is the result of an implicit revaluation of the *rime*, the *Convivio* finds its pretext in an explicit revaluation of the *donna gentile* sequence of the *Vita Nuova*. In chapter XXXV of the *libello*, after the anniversary of Beatrice's death, Dante sees in a window a "gentile donna giovane e bella molto" who looks pityingly at him. He writes the next two sonnets to her (chaps. XXXV and XXXVI): in both she is characterized by her "pietate," and in the prose of XXXVI he

Autocitation and Autobiography

comments that her appearance is reminiscent of Beatrice's, thus linking her to the *gentilissima*. Subsequently, the pendulum begins to swing back to his first love: in chapter XXXVII he rebukes his eyes for taking pleasure in the *donna gentile*; in chapter XXXVIII his heart, defending the newcomer, is in litigation with his soul, which represents Beatrice. Beatrice herself then appears to Dante in a "forte imaginazione" in chapter XXXIX, prompting him to regret his temporary inconstancy and to return his thoughts entirely to her. The *donna gentile* episode thus extends from chapter XXXV, when he first sees the new lady, to chapter XXXIX, where he reconverts to Beatrice.

This brief sequence from the *Vita Nuova* has become the subject of much critical speculation because Dante, true to his pattern of autoexegesis, returns to it in the *Convivio*. At the treatise's outset, in the first chapter of Book I, Dante places his new work in relation to its predecessor, explaining that where the *Vita Nuova* was "fervida e passionata," the *Convivio* will be "temperata e virile" (I, i, 16). He further explains that the treatise will consist of fourteen previously written canzoni which will be expounded according to both their literal and allegorical senses. The first of these canzoni, commented on in Book II, is "Voi che 'ntendendo il terzo ciel movete"; it describes the same struggle between the new love for the *donna gentile* and the old love for Beatrice previously described in the sonnets of the *Vita Nuova*. Indeed, the canzone is essentially an expansion of the sonnet "Gentil pensero che parla di vui," from *Vita Nuova* XXXVIII, in which the heart defends its new attraction to the disapproving soul. The key difference between the sonnet and the canzone is, of course, that the sonnet is followed by a return to Beatrice, while in the canzone the new love triumphs.

In his commentary to the canzoni of the *Convivio*, Dante begins with the exposition of the literal meaning. Regarding "Voi che 'ntendendo," therefore, he begins with the identity of the new love, who is specifically introduced as the *donna gentile* of the *Vita Nuova*. She is presented, moreover, not in a temporal vacuum but in strict chronological relation to Beatrice, whom she will supplant; we learn that Venus had completed two revolutions after the death of Beatrice when the *donna gentile* first appeared to him: ". . . quando quella gentile donna, cui feci menzione ne la fine de la Vita Nuova, parve primamente, accompagnata d'Amore, a li occhi miei e prese luogo alcuno ne la mia mente" ("when that gentle lady whom I mentioned at the end of the *Vita Nuova* first appeared to my eyes, accompanied by Love, and occupied a place in my mind" [II, ii, 1]). Continuing, Dante describes the psychomachia waged within him between the thoughts supporting the *donna gentile* and those supporting Beatrice. This image of mental combat, deriving from *Vita Nuova* XXXVIII where "la battaglia de' pensieri" was the subject of the sonnet "Gentil pensero," is dramatized and escalated in "Voi che 'ntendendo."

The three central stanzas of the canzone take the form of an internalized *tenzone* in which the Beatrician thought is the first to state its case, only to be overcome by the thoughts of the *donna gentile*. Before being vanquished, Beatrice is memorialized in precisely the terms in which she last appears in the *Vita Nuova*. In the *libello*'s final sonnet, "Oltre la spera che più larga gira" (chap. XLI), Dante's thoughts (specifically, his sighs) follow Beatrice beyond the farthest of the circling heavens to the presence of God. The fortunate *sospiro* witnesses Beatrice in splendor:

> Quand'elli è giunto là dove disira,
> vede una donna, che riceve onore,
> e luce sì, che per lo suo splendore
> lo peregrino spirito la mira.
>
> When he arrives there where he desires, he sees a lady who receives honor, and gives off such light that for her splendor the pilgrim spirit gazes at her.
>
> (5-8)

In "Voi che 'ntendendo" the Beatrician thought is described as undertaking just such a journey:

Suol esser vita de lo cor dolente
un soave penser, che se ne gìa
molte fiate a' piè del nostro Sire,
  ove una donna gloriar vedia,
di cui parlava me sì dolcemente
che l'anima dicea: 'Io men vo' gire.'

The life of my sorrowing heart used to be a sweet thought, who would go many times to the feet of our Lord, where he would see a lady in glory of whom he would speak to me so sweetly that my soul would say: "I wish to go to her . . ."

(14-19)

Here the celestial vistas are described in better detail; where the *Vita Nuova*'s pilgrim-sigh simply saw the lady in glory, the canzone specifies that the location achieved by the poet's envoy, the "soave penser" of line 15, is "a' piè del nostro Sire" (16). However, this recapitulation and expansion of the *Vita Nuova*'s last sonnet is not the canzone's final statement; "Voi che 'ntendendo" ends not with the pursuit of Beatrice "oltre la spera" but with her defeat, and with an injunction to accept the newcomer as his lady: "e pensa di chiamarla donna, omai!" ("and resolve to call her your lady from now on!" [48]). The narrative overlap between the *Convivio*'s beginning and the *Vita Nuova*'s ending makes the later text's reversal of the former all the more striking.

The transfer of allegiance from Beatrice to the *donna gentile* is complete in the *Convivio*'s next canzone, "Amor che ne la mente mi ragiona," expounded in Book III. This is a song of praise dedicated to the triumphant new lady, not a debate like "Voi che 'ntendendo" but an unqualified celebration. It is interesting that Dante removes Beatrice from his treatise in the course of the prose commentary of Book II, before achieving the victorious stasis of "Amor che ne la mente." In chapter viii of Book II Dante suggests that he deliberately inserts his last mention of Beatrice into a digression on the immortality of the soul, because this lofty topic is an appropriate one with which to commemorate her final appearance: "perchè, di quella [la immortalità de l'anima] ragionando, sarà bello terminare lo parlare di quella viva Beatrice beata" ("it will be beautiful to terminate our speaking of that living blessed Beatrice while discussing the immortality of the soul" [II, viii, 7]). Although tactfully accomplished, the implication nonetheless remains that there is no place for Beatrice in a text dedicated to another lady: ". . . quella viva Beatrice beata, de la quale più parlare in questo libro non intendo per proponimento" ("that living blessed Beatrice, of whom I do not propose to speak further in this book" [II, viii, 7]). Shortly after this dismissal Dante completes the literal exposition of "Voi che 'ntendendo" and begins, in chapter xii, to explain the poem's allegorical significance; it is here that we first learn that the *donna gentile* is to be identified with Lady Philosophy.

When, in chapter xii of Book II, Dante finally reveals the true identity of the *donna gentile*, the context is overtly Boethian. He recounts that, finding himself inconsolable after the death of Beatrice, he turned to philosophy as a form of comfort that had revived others in similar straits. Thus, he begins to read Boethius ("e misimi a leggere quello non conosciuto da molti libro di Boezio" "and I began to read that book by Boethius not known to many" [II, xii, 2]) and Cicero's *De Amicitia* ("E udendo ancora che Tullio scritto avea un altro libro . . . trattando de l'Amistade" "and hearing further that Tully had written another book . . . touching on Friendship" [II, xii, 3]). Although both texts are of great importance to the *Convivio*, Dante's treatise is more explicitly modeled on the *Consolatio Philosophiae*; in fact, in Book I he justifies his first-person confessional narrative by invoking Boethius and Augustine (I, ii, 13-14).[10] If the *Consolatio Philosophiae* influenced Dante's

---

[10] On the importance of the *De Amicitia* and its medieval epigones for Dante, see Domenico De Robertis, *Il libro della Vita Nuova*, 2d ed. rev. (Florence: Sansoni, 1970), pp. 21-24 and 93-115. De Robertis links Cicero's notion of disinterested friendship with the *Vita Nuova*'s elaboration of a disinterested love. See also Alessandro Ronconi, "Cicerone," *Enciclopedia Dantesca*, vol. I, pp. 991-997. Marziano Guglielminetti, in "Dante e il ricupero del 'parlare di

adoption of alternating prose and verse in the *Vita Nuova*, we should remember that the *Convivio* too is a modified form of *prosimetrum*. Most significantly, Boethius offers Dante, in the topos of the consoling lady, the way out of his impasse with the *donna gentile*.

The critical controversy surrounding the *donna gentile* may be reduced to essentially the following question: are we to believe Dante when he claims that she is Philosophy? Scholars are to be found at all points of the critical spectrum: the realists believe that the *donna gentile* is real (or conceived as real) in the *Vita Nuova* and that all the poems written about her, including "Voi che 'ntendendo" and "Amor che ne la mente," were originally composed with a real woman in mind; the allegorists believe that the *donna gentile* was always a symbol of philosophy, even in the *Vita Nuova*, and that all poems about her, including "Voi che 'ntendendo" and "Amor che ne la mente," were originally composed with allegorical intentions.¹¹ Perhaps the single most authoritative position on this issue has been Barbi's, endorsed by Pernicone in his commentary to the *Rime*

___

se medesimo,' " chap. 2 of *Memoria e scrittura: l'autobiografia da Dante a Cellini*, stresses the role of Boethius as Dante's confessional model in the *Convivio* over that of Augustine, esp. pp. 74-75 and 97-99. For Dante and Boethius, see Rocco Murari, *Dante e Boezio* (Bologna: Zanichelli, 1905); Marie Thérèse D'Alverny, "Notes sur Dante et la Sagesse," *Revue des Études Italiennes*, 11 (1965), 5-24; Francesco Tateo, "Boezio," *Enciclopedia Dantesca*, vol. I, pp. 654-658.

¹¹ Perhaps the most conspicuous among the allegorists is Bruno Nardi, who argues that the *donna gentile* was born allegorical; for an explicit formulation see "Le figurazioni allegoriche e l'allegoria della 'donna gentile,' " in *Nel mondo di Dante* (Rome: Edizioni di Storia e Letteratura, 1944), pp. 23-40. Another strong advocate of this view is James E. Shaw, *The Lady "Philosophy" in the Convivio* (Cambridge: Dante Society, 1938). Among the realists are Fausto Montanari, *L'esperienza poetica di Dante*, 2d ed. (Florence: Le Monnier, 1968), esp. chap. III, "Tra la Vita Nuova e il Convivio"; also Amerindo Camilli, "Le prime due canzoni del *Convivio* di Dante," *Lettere italiane*, 4 (1952), 70-91. De Robertis offers a cogent dismantling of Nardi's position in "Il libro della Vita Nuova e il libro del Convivio," *Studi urbinati*, 25 (1951), 5-27. For a survey of the critical positions, see Giorgio Petrocchi, "Donna gentile," *Enciclopedia Dantesca*, vol. II, pp. 574-577, repr. in *L'ultima dea* (Rome: Bonacci, 1977), pp. 97-104.

Textual History

as well as by Foster and Boyde in theirs; Barbi argues for a middle course, claiming that the original *donna gentile* of the *Vita Nuova* was indeed conceived as flesh and blood, but that, by the time Dante came to write the later poems in the sequence devoted to her, he had already come under the sway of Lady Philosophy.[12] With regard to "Voi che 'ntendendo" and "Amor che ne la mente," therefore, he suggests that we accept the statements of the *Convivio*, reading them as allegorical lyrics composed for Philosophy.

Barbi's thesis is doubtless correct at least with regard to the *Vita Nuova*; an impartial reader of that text would be hard pressed to make a case for the *donna gentile* as Lady Philosophy.[13] The *Vita Nuova* does not admit the type of personification allegory employed by Dante in the *Convivio*, where he refers

[12] Barbi states his position in his Introduction to the *Convivio*, ed. G. Busnelli and G. Vandelli; his insistence that we distinguish the problems inherent in the *Vita Nuova* from those of the *Convivio* ("Bisogna risolverci . . . a intendere ciascun'opera di Dante secondo la reale ispirazione del momento" [I, xxiii]) is picked up and endorsed by De Robertis, who stresses the disjunction between the two texts in his title "Il libro della *Vita Nuova* e il libro del *Convivio*." This line of reasoning eventually leads, however, to sundering what Dante deliberately conflated, and thus bypassing the problem altogether; as an example of this tendency, see Maria Simonelli, " 'Donna pietosa' e 'donna gentile' fra *Vita Nuova* e *Convivio*," in *Atti del Convegno di studi su aspetti e problemi di critica dantesca* (Rome: De Luca, 1967), pp. 146-159.

[13] In order to support his thesis Nardi was forced to defend Pietrobono, who had postulated the existence of a first version of the *Vita Nuova* in which the *donna gentile* was victorious; accordingly, we possess the second version, to which the author returned after the experience of the *Convivio* with the intention of providing a new ending (Beatrice victorious) that would be consonant with the *Comedy*. See "Dalla prima alla seconda *Vita Nuova*," in *Nel mondo di Dante*, pp. 3-20; "Filosofia dell'amore nei rimatori italiani del Duecento e in Dante," in *Dante e la cultura medievale*, 2d ed. rev. (Bari: Laterza, 1949), esp. pp. 49-51; "Sviluppo dell'arte e del pensiero di Dante," *Bibliothéque d'Humanisme et Renaissance*, 14 (1952), 29-47; "Dante e Guido Cavalcanti," in *Saggi e note di critica dantesca* (Milan: Ricciardi, 1961), pp. 190-219. This theory of two redactions of the *Vita Nuova* (which unfortunately runs through all of Nardi's work on the subject) never gained general acceptance and was laid definitively to rest by Mario Marti, "Vita e morte della presunta doppia redazione della *Vita Nuova*," in *Studi in onore di Alfredo Schiaffini*, 2 vols. (Rome: Edizioni dell'Ateneo, 1965), vol. II, pp. 657-669 (= *Rivista di cultura classica e medioevale*, 7 [1965]).

Autocitation and Autobiography

to it as the allegorical mode used by the poets (II, i, 4); instead the *libello* adumbrates, perhaps unwittingly, the figural allegory of the *Comedy*, in which a literal reality is revealed to be miraculous.[14] The historical level—i.e. Beatrice—exists in the *Vita Nuova*; the poet's task is to discover that she is a signifier, that she has come "from heaven to earth to show forth a miracle," that she is the number nine. Once he has discerned her significance, he must hold fast to his knowledge without the assistance of her presence, a presence from which he is weaned gradually through the revoking of her greeting. Like Christ, whose analogue she is, she makes the invisible visible; after her death the poet assumes this responsibility for himself. It is in this context, as a lapse into an opaque nonsignifying but visible and literal reality, that the *donna gentile* episode fits into the *Vita Nuova*. As an alternative to Beatrice, the *donna gentile* must possess an equally historical identity.

Dante's concern regarding the public repercussions of his inconstancy is already evident in the *Vita Nuova*, where he worries that the *donna gentile* episode may continue to reflect negatively on him even after his return to Beatrice, and says that the sonnet of chapter XXXIX is intended to lay the matter to rest once and for all.[15] In the *Convivio* this concern for his

[14] Singleton stresses the analogical rather than allegorical nature of the *Vita Nuova* in *An Essay on the Vita Nuova* (1949; repr. Baltimore: Johns Hopkins U. Press, 1977), esp. pp. 22-24 and 110-114. In "Dante Theologus-Poeta," *Dante Studies*, 94 (1976), 91-136, repr. in *Studies in Dante* (Ravenna: Longo, 1980), pp. 31-89, Robert Hollander argues that "Had Dante assigned a designation to the mode of signifying of the *Vita Nuova*, using the same two possibilities he set before us in the *Convivio*, he would not have hesitated to have told us that the *Vita Nuova* was written in the allegory of theologians" (p. 56). At this point I should like to alert the reader to my fundamental agreement with Singleton as regards Dante's use of the so-called allegory of theologians in the *Comedy*; for bibliography on this subject, see Hollander's *Allegory in Dante's Commedia* and "Dante Theologus-Poeta," and Jean Pépin, *Dante et la Tradition de l'Allégorie* (Montréal: Institut d'études médiévales, 1971).

[15] "Onde io, volendo che cotale desiderio malvagio e vana tentazione paresse distrutto, sì che alcuno dubbio non potessero inducere le rimate parole ch'io avea dette innanzi, propuosi di fare uno sonetto ne lo quale io comprendesse

reputation and the impulse to present the *donna gentile* episode in a less derogatory light are recurrent: from the start of the treatise, Dante treats the *Vita Nuova* as a product of his youth whose evidence, it may be inferred, is suspect; moreover, his insistence that he does not wish to detract from the *Vita Nuova*, but only to promote the *Convivio*, does little to enhance the credibility of the earlier work. He openly states his fear that the content of the canzoni will brand him as one who passes lightly from one passion to the next: "Temo la infamia di tanta passione avere seguita, quanta concepe chi legge le sopra nominate canzoni in me avere segnoreggiata" ("I fear the infamy of having yielded to and having been conquered by such passion, as will be conceived by him who reads the above mentioned canzoni" [I, ii, 16]); he believes that the treatise will restore his integrity by revealing that the motive force behind the canzoni is "non passione ma vertù" ("not passion but virtue"[I, ii, 16]). It seems noteworthy that such sentiments are consistently followed, in the *Convivio*, by an appeal to allegory; to show that the canzoni deal not with passion but with virtue he must uncover their true—allegorical—significance: "Intendo anche mostrare la vera sentenza di quelle, che per alcuno vedere non si può s'io non la conto, perchè è nascosa sotto figura d'allegoria . . ." ("I intend also to show their true meaning, which no one will see if I do not explain it, since it is hidden under the figure of allegory" [I, ii, 17]).

The *Convivio* owes its existence to a convergence of new interests, concentrated primarily in the areas of classical culture and philosophy. The countless citations from philosophical and religious authors, the opening sentence under the sign of Aristotle, the new prominence of classical poets—all testify to the extent of Dante's development away from the primarily vernacular and courtly world of his earlier texts. To this philo-

---

la sentenzia di questa ragione" ("Wherefore I, desiring that such a wicked desire and vain temptation would appear to be destroyed, so that no doubts could be adduced with respect to the rhymed words I had composed heretofore, proposed to write a sonnet which would include the essence of this discourse" [*Vita Nuova*, XXXIX, 6]).

sophical inclination, we may add an interest in the formal properties of allegory which overtakes Dante at this stage in his career; it is not fortuitous that *Convivio* II, i contains Dante's only discussion of the four modes of allegory outside of the Epistle to Cangrande, nor that he should use the treatise to formulate his distinction between the allegory of poets and the allegory of theologians. Dante is, moreover, consistent in his application of the allegory of poets throughout the *Convivio*, from his Fulgentian reading of the *Aeneid* to his interpretation of his own poems. Indeed, "Voi che 'ntendendo," whether or not originally written as allegory, stands as Dante's first nonimitative allegorical work.[16] Finally, a third factor to be considered in the genesis of the *Convivio* is the urge, demonstrated by Dante throughout his career, to reconcile his narratives. These three factors—an interest in philosophy and in allegory combined with a pattern of self-correction—add up to the solution of the *Convivio*: the *donna gentile* as Lady Philosophy.

The *Convivio*'s position along the itinerary of Dante's development is an ambivalent one. In its essential historicity, its insistence on a sign-bearing reality, the *Vita Nuova* is the *Comedy*'s truer precursor. The promise of a new text for a new lady with which the *Vita Nuova* ends ("io spero di dicer di lei quello che mai non fue detto d'alcuna" "I hope to say of her that which has never been said of another" [XLII, 2]) is a promise fulfilled

[16] The qualification is intended to leave room for the *Fiore* as possibly Dante's first allegorical venture, in imitation of the *Roman de la Rose*. The attribution of the *Fiore* to Dante is now widely accepted in the wake of the internal evidence demonstrated by Gianfranco Contini; see his "La questione del *Fiore*," *Cultura e scuola* 4, nos. 13-14 (1965), 768-773, and his article in the *Enciclopedia Dantesca*, vol. II, pp. 895-901. A recent book that takes Dante's authorship of the *Fiore* for granted is that of Luigi Vanossi, *Dante e il Roman de la Rose: Saggio sul Fiore* (Florence: Olschki, 1979). The *Fiore* is not discussed at greater length in this study because it lacks explicit literary references; although the text is a sustained tribute to the *Roman de la Rose*, and although it names philosophers (Socrates in XLIII, Sigier of Brabant in XCII, Ptolemy in CLXX), kings (Solomon in LXV and CIX, Justinian in CX), and literary lovers (Tristan and Isolde in CXLIV, Dido and Aeneus in CLXI, Jason and Medea in CXLI and CXC), it names no precursor poets.

only by the *Comedy*. On the other hand, although the *Convivio* cannot claim newness (both personification allegory and Lady Philosophy have long and venerable histories), the fact remains that the Beatrice of the *Comedy* is in many ways a synthesis of the *Vita Nuova*'s heroine with the *Convivio*'s. Thus, certain descriptions of Lady Philosophy, "la sposa de lo Imperadore del cielo" ("the bride of the Emperor of heaven" [III, xii, 14]), prepare us for the Beatrice of Paradise, "O amanza del primo amante, o diva" ("O beloved of the first lover, o divine one" [*Par.* IV, 118]). In fact, the *Comedy* as a whole cannot be imagined without the prior existence of the *Convivio*; not only does the treatise rehearse the poem's philosophical, linguistic, and political ideas, but it is also the first text to articulate fully the *Comedy*'s indispensable supporting metaphors of pilgrimage and voyage.[17]

Even in its dependence on the allegory of poets, the *Convivio* represents a detour that is simultaneously an essential forward step in Dante's poetic journey. From the love poems of the *Vita Nuova*, Dante passes to the allegorized love poems of *Convivio* II and III; here the allegory permits him to add a moral dimension he considers lacking in love poetry, to show that the canzoni treat "non passione ma vertù." This progression toward an overt moral content continues; the fourth and last book of the *Convivio* glosses a canzone, "Le dolci rime d'amor ch'i solia," which no longer requires an allegorical commentary because it is a straightforward moral discussion of the nature of true nobility. Because the canzone's ethical concerns are not hidden under a "beautiful" (i.e. amorous) exterior, allegory is not required to decipher its "vera sentenza." Book IV is an

[17] One of the most striking features of the *Convivio* is its adumbration of the *Comedy*'s metaphors, in the "pane de li angeli" (I, i, 7), the "selva erronea di questa vita" (IV, xxiv, 12), and especially in the recurrent images of wayfaring, by land and by sea, that run through the treatise. The sustained metaphorization of life as a pilgrimage in *Convivio* IV, xii, 14-19 renders explicit what in the *Vita Nuova* is implied by the pilgrims who pass through the city. On the *Convivio* as the most important source of the *Comedy*, see the article on the treatise by Maria Simonelli, *Enciclopedia Dantesca*, vol. II, pp. 193-204.

indication of the direction in which Dante was moving; "Le dolci rime" is but one of a number of moral poems that cap Dante's lyric career, poems like "Poscia ch'Amor" on the chivalric virtue *leggiadria* and "Doglia mi reca" on avarice. By mirroring the social and ethical concerns of the contemporaneous prose treatises, these late lyrics are an important part of Dante's preparation for the *Comedy*.

The essential fact, then, regarding the *Convivio*'s first two canzoni, is that they eventually receive an allegorical dress. Although this fact is finally more significant than the question of Dante's original intentions, the basic arguments on either side of the debate should be noted. There are cogent reasons for questioning Dante's retroactive assertions regarding the two canzoni: first, they belong stylistically, like the *Vita Nuova* sonnets to which they are thematic sequels, to the climax of Dante's *stil novo* period, i.e. they are written in a style appropriate for love poetry. Second, they repeat the same erotic hyperbole that had heretofore been addressed to Beatrice and they function admirably as love poems, an assertion that Dante himself corroborates by dedicating lengthy glosses to their literal senses and expressing concern lest they tarnish his reputation. Dante's very preoccupation with disjoining the *Convivio* from the *Vita Nuova* strengthens one's impression that he was casting about for a way to change his image, and that he found it in allegory.[18]

---

[18] This view is shared by Montanari, *L'esperienza poetica di Dante*, p. 118, and De Robertis, "Il libro della *Vita Nuova* e il libro del *Convivio*," p. 20. For the stylistic homogeneity of these canzoni with Dante's *stil novo* phase, see De Robertis, p. 11; Foster and Boyde comment as follows on the style of "Voi che 'ntendendo": "There are no describable innovations in style with respect to the preceding sonnets: this and the following poems represent the climax of Dante's *stilnovo* period" (*Commentary*, p. 161). Dante himself essentially admits that his canzoni do not *appear* allegorical, for instance when he writes "E con ciò sia cosa che la vera intenzione mia fosse altra che quella che di fuori mostrano le canzoni predette, per allegorica esposizione quelle intendo mostrare" ("And since my true intention was other than that revealed by the surface of the aforementioned canzoni, I intend to reveal them through an allegorical exposition" [*Convivio* I, i, 18]).

On the other hand, one cannot categorically discount the allegorical potential harbored by the texts of the canzoni themselves. In the case of "Voi che 'ntendendo," allegorists point especially to the *congedo*, where the poet alludes to the difficulty of his poem and distinguishes between its abstruse content and beautiful form. Also interesting is the characterization of the new lady as "saggia e cortese ne la sua grandezza" ("wise and courteous in her greatness" [47]); it has been noted that Beatrice is never called *grande*, and that *grandezza* does not belong to the lexicon of the conventional love lyric.[19] Regarding "Amor che ne la mente," the pro-allegory arguments are based on the contention that certain verses go beyond the domain of erotic hyperbole and cannot designate a real woman, no matter how miraculous. The verses most often singled out are those in which the poet paraphrases or translates passages from Scripture referring to Sapientia: for instance, "però fu tal da etterno ordinata" ("for this she was established from eternity" [54]) echoes Sapientia's words about herself, "ab aeterno ordinata sum," from Proverbs viii, 23.[20]

"Voi che 'ntendendo" and "Amor che ne la mente" are also noteworthy for their textual situation prior to the *Convivio*. They belong to an interlocking sequence of lyrics, which consists, besides the two canzoni, of a *ballata*, "Voi che savete ragionar d'Amore," and two sonnets: "Parole mie che per lo mondo siete" and "O dolci rime che parlando andate." "Voi che 'ntendendo" initiates the series by announcing the sovereignty of a new lady, whom, in the *ballata* "Voi che savete," the poet renounces because of her cruelty. This renunciation is then retracted in the *congedo* of "Amor che ne la mente," where

---

[19] Foster and Boyde, *Commentary*, p. 167. On the other hand, *grandezza* need not have allegorical implications; it could serve merely as a means of distinguishing the new lady from Beatrice.

[20] Other verses seized on by the allegorists are "Ogni Intelletto di là su la mira" ("All the Intelligences from above gaze on her" [23]) and "costei pensò chi mosse l'universo" ("He who moved the universe thought of her" [72]). In his gloss to line 72 (*Convivio* III, xv, 16) Dante makes the connection to Sapientia, citing Proverbs viii, 27-30.

the poet asserts that the *ballata* (referred to as the "sorella" of the canzone) is mistaken in its harsh judgment:

> Canzone, e' par che tu parli contraro
> al dir d'una sorella che tu hai;
> ché questa donna, che tanto umil fai,
> ella la chiama fera e disdegnosa.
>
> Canzone, it appears that you speak contrary to the words of one of your sisters, because this lady, whom you consider so humble, she calls harsh and disdainful.
>
> (73-76)

This first cycle of contradiction and resolution is then followed by a second; in the sonnet "Parole mie" Dante again repudiates the new lady. The opening quatrain of this sonnet is interesting because it specifically names "Voi che 'ntendendo" as the starting point of this spasmodic textual love affair:

> Parole mie che per lo mondo siete,
> voi che nasceste poi ch'io cominciai
> a dir per quella donna in cui errai:
> 'Voi che 'ntendendo il terzo ciel movete',
>
> andatevene a lei . . .
>
> Words of mine who are throughout the world, you who were born when I began to write for that lady in whom I erred "Voi che 'ntendendo il terzo ciel movete," go to her . . .
>
> (1-5)

This sonnet is in turn retracted in the following sonnet, "O dolci rime," where the poet denies "Parole mie" and recommits himself to the service of his new love.

The two complete cycles of renunciation and recommitment described by these poems are ultimately resolved in the first stanza of the canzone "Le dolci rime," which effectively brings this series to a close. Here too the poet refers to the hardness of the lady, not as a motive for renouncing her but as an explanation for his shift to explicit didacticism; her coldness has prompted him to temporarily put aside love poetry for the brisker pleasures of polemical verse. In the *Convivio* gloss, Dante explains this statement in terms of the allegory of Lady Philosophy, saying that he had not been able to penetrate certain metaphysical problems and had therefore turned to the more accessible ethical issue of *gentilezza*. The opening of "Le dolci rime" is thus the final scene in a drama that extends from the episode of the *Vita Nuova* to Book IV of the *Convivio*, from the pale and pitying countenance of the *libello* to the social concerns of the treatise. This series of poems, linked by a complex system of palinodic recalls and further related by the adoption of genetic terminology ("sorella" in "Amor che ne la mente" [74]; "vostre antiche sore" in "Parole mie" [11]; "nostro frate" in "O dolci rime" [4]), testifies to the textual importance of the *donna gentile* and to her resilience as an imaginative construct.

Due to the circumstantial nature of most of the evidence, the debate over the canzoni of the *Convivio* is not likely to be resolved. For our purposes, however, the issue of Dante's original intentions vis-à-vis the canzoni is not crucial. From the perspective of the *Comedy* and Dante's overall development, the significant fact is that he did, at a certain point in his career, choose to read (or write) selected love poems allegorically. In so doing, he effects a transition from one stage of his career to the next, moving from poems that function only as love poems to poems that function only as doctrine. The allegorized lyrics of the *Convivio* mark a precise moment in Dante's development in that they mediate between the exclusively erotic and the exclusively moral, thereby pointing to the eventual fusion of the affective with the intellective that will characterize the *Comedy*.

Dante's poetic career achieves such absolute retrospective coherence—a coherence whose emblem is the proleptic ending of the *Vita Nuova*—that we are perhaps tempted to endow his early poetic shifts with too much teleological significance. Nonetheless, if the *Comedy* returns to Beatrice and to the *Vita Nuova* for its point of departure, resuming in fact where the final sonnet of the *libello* leaves off, the departure itself would not be conceivable without the mediating experience of the *Convivio* and the poems to Lady Philosophy. Thus, although retrospectively all the texts written before the *Comedy* and after the *Vita Nuova* could be similarly classified as mistaken but necessary, the *Convivio* is in this respect first among equals: it is the most necessary of the erring prerequisites for the *Comedy*. For, unlike the *De Vulgari Eloquentia* and the *Monarchia*, which address themselves (albeit sweepingly) to single issues, the *Convivio* knows no limits; it sets itself the *Comedy*'s task, and fails.

In one of the sonnets in which he temporarily renounces the *donna gentile*, Dante calls her "quella donna in cui errai." Although "errai" is variously translated as "I erred," "I suffered," "I was deceived," *errare* conserves its primary meaning of "to wander," hence "to stray."[21] This use of *errare* with respect to a poetic mistake reinforces our sense of a textual *selva oscura*, a poetic wandering which only from the providential perspective of the *Comedy* could be retrospectively arranged as a *diritta via*. From this point of view, the strange shifts and turnabouts of the *donna gentile* poems begin to fall into place as signs of textual stress, external indicators of a profound uneasiness. Indeed, Dante's restlessness during this period is confirmed by his irresolution; the unfinished status of two major works from these middle years, the *Convivio* and the *De Vulgari Eloquentia*, indicates his recognition of being textually on the wrong path. And, of course, from the perspective of the *Comedy*, the substitution of another for Beatrice would constitute an unparalleled failure; for the later Dante any lady who is not Beatrice

---

[21] Numerous possibilities for "errai" are listed in M. Barbi and V. Pernicone, eds., *Rime della maturità e dell'esilio* (Florence: Le Monnier, 1969), p. 461. Contini notes that the verse is usually interpreted as referring to the lady "in whom I erred" ("nella quale presi errore"), but prefers Barbi's suggestion "because of whom I suffered" ("per la quale soffersi"); see his edition of the *Rime* (1946; repr. Turin: Einaudi, 1970), p. 107. Although Foster and Boyde translate the verse with "the lady in whom I was deceived," they note that "the sense could be 'through whom I went astray' " (*Commentary*, p. 184).

"Amor che ne la mente" is "quella donna in cui errai," as any poetic path not directed toward her is, by definition, a false one.

The issues raised in the above discussion are all implicit in the *Comedy*'s autocitations. Thus, a problem facing decipherers of *Purgatorio* II is whether Dante intends us to view "Amor che ne la mente" as an allegorical poem. Two points should be borne in mind: (1) the central fact regarding the canzoni of the *Convivio* is that they are not dedicated to Beatrice; (2) the poet who places these incipits in the *Comedy* surely expects us to know that they have a history of being singled out. As "Donne ch'avete" was selected for the *Vita Nuova*, so "Voi che 'ntendendo" and "Amor che ne la mente" were placed in the *Convivio*. We may reasonably believe, therefore, that Dante intends us to read these incipits in the light of their previous histories; indeed, it seems not unlikely that he chose these poems precisely for the archeological resonance they afford.

"Amor che ne la mente mi ragiona"

The autocitation of *Purgatorio* II has received considerable attention of the kind we are here concerned with; Casella's song has been studied in the context of the episode and in the light of its past associations.[22] The canto has also generated a great deal of speculation regarding such issues as the reasons for Casella's delay on the banks of the Tiber, his identity, and whether a "doctrinal" song like "Amor che ne la mente" may be sung—this despite the fact that in *Purgatorio* II it is sung. Marti answers this last question by drawing on musicological data which shows that the canzone form was still set to music

[22] Two studies meriting particular attention are John Freccero, "Casella's Song (*Purg*. II, 112)," *Dante Studies*, 91 (1973), 73-80; and Robert Hollander, "*Purgatorio* II: Cato's Rebuke and Dante's *scoglio*," *Italica*, 52 (1975), 348-363, now repr. in *Studies in Dante*, pp. 91-105. Gian Roberto Sarolli, "*Purgatorio* II: dal *Convivio* alla *Commedia*," in *Prolegomena alla Divina Commedia*, pp. 55-74, does not deal with "Amor che ne la mente," but with general thematic convergences between the canto and the prose treatise.

in Dante's time; he also points out that Casella would in any case have few qualms about singing "Amor che ne la mente," since he would be unlikely to consider it a doctrinal poem.[23] Indeed, the poem makes its appearance in canto II in two guises. Vis-à-vis Casella, a musician who died before the composition of the *Convivio* and whose sphere of interest seems to have been far removed from that work's concern with transforming eros into ethos, the canzone "Amor che ne la mente" functions according to its literal sense in the *Convivio* gloss, as a love poem. Thus Casella, who is unacquainted with the *Convivio*, sings the canzone in response to a specific request from the pilgrim for an "amoroso canto":

E io: "Se nuova legge non ti toglie
    memoria o uso a l'amoroso canto
    che mi solea quetar tutte mie voglie,
di ciò ti piaccia consolare alquanto
    l'anima mia, che, con la sua persona
    venendo qui, è affannata tanto!"
'*Amor che ne la mente mi ragiona*'
    cominciò elli allor sì dolcemente,
    che la dolcezza ancor dentro mi suona.[24]

And I: "If a new law does not take from you memory or practice of the amorous song which used to quiet all of my desires, with this let it please you to console my soul

---

[23] Mario Marti, "Il canto II del *Purgatorio*," *Lectura Dantis Scaligera* (Florence: Le Monnier, 1963). On the performance value of "Amor che ne la mente" and Dante's other texts, see John Ahearn, "Singing the Book: Orality in the Reception of Dante's *Comedy*," *Annals of Scholarship* 2, no. 4 (1981), 17-40. Also useful on this canto is the reading of Vittorio Russo, "Il canto II del *Purgatorio*," in *Esperienze e/di letture dantesche* (Naples: Liguori, 1971), pp. 53-99.

[24] Although Petrocchi replaces the customary "voglie" of line 108 with "doglie," I have followed Singleton in preserving a variant that, in my opinion, is more consonant with the voluntarist emphasis of the episode and of the *cantica* whose paradigm it is; see Charles S. Singleton, trans. and comm., *The Divine Comedy*, 6 vols. (Princeton: Princeton U. Press, 1970-1975), *Purgatorio*, 2: *Commentary*, p. 40.

"Amor che ne la mente"

somewhat, which coming here with its body is so wearied!" "Amor che ne la mente mi ragiona" he began then so sweetly, that the sweetness still rings inside of me.
(*Purg.* II, 106-114)

The emphatic presence of "dolcemente" and "dolcezza" in lines 113-114 further underscores the status of "Amor che ne la mente" as a love lyric, since, from the canzone "Le dolci rime d'amor" to the discourses of *Purgatorio* XXIV and XXVI, "sweetness" is considered by Dante to be the external sign and stylistic prerequisite of love poetry as a genre. The inclusion of the code word *dolce* thus confirms that Casella has complied with the pilgrim's request; he sings what he presumes to be nothing more than a love song.

This stress on the love lyric serves to place *Purgatorio* II in direct contrast to *Inferno* V, opposing the present verbatim citation of the *amoroso canto* to its former misquotation. A number of textual correspondences—the simile of the doves with which *Purgatorio* II ends, the use of expressions that echo *Inferno* V ("persona" for "body" in line 110 is a Francescaism; "affannata" in line 111 recalls 'O anime affannate"), and especially the reference to the love lyric as "that which used to quiet all my desires" (108)—evoke the lovers of *Inferno* V and put them into purgatorial perspective. As—erotically—fulfillment of desire at the level of canto V is a narcissistic illusion ("lust") that leads to the *bufera infernal*, so—textually—love poetry at the level of canto V lacks the upward momentum that will redeem its physical point of departure. With respect to Dante's poetic autobiography, *Inferno* V represents a stage in which the poet operates entirely within the confines of a tradition and its authorities, a stage of nonexploratory stasis in which desire is prematurely satisfied.

If desire in the *Inferno* is eternally misplaced, in the *Purgatorio* it functions dialectically as both the goad that keeps the souls moving upward and the source of the nostalgia that temporarily slows them down. *Purgatorio* II is a paradigm for the rest of the canticle in this respect, dramatizing both these aspects of purgatorial desire in the lull created by the song and Cato's subsequent rebuke. Whereas formerly scholars tended to underline the idyllic qualities of the interlude with Casella, effectively ending their readings with the poet's strong endorsement in line 114 (where he says that the song's sweetness still reverberates within him), recently they have stressed Cato's rebuke as a correction—and indeed condemnation—of previous events. Thus, Hollander judges Casella's song severely, as a secular poison in contrast to the canto's other song, the Psalm "In exitu Isräel de Aegypto."[25] Freccero, on the other hand, views the episode in a more positive light, claiming that "The 'Amore' celebrated here marks an advance over the 'Amore' of Francesca's verses in the same measure that the *Convivio* marks an advance over the *Vita Nuova*."[26] These views should be integrated as two facets of the same problematic within the dialectical structure of the canto: the quotation of "Amor che ne la mente" does indeed mark an advance over the misquotation of *Inferno* V; Cato's rebuke simultaneously suggests that it too is in need of correction.

The target of the criticism that Dante levels at an earlier self in *Inferno* V, and that he to some extent revokes or palliates in *Purgatorio* II, cannot be simply the *Vita Nuova*; rather, we must remember that the *Vita Nuova* encompasses both the experiments of a poet overly subjected to his models and the moment in which he frees himself from them. "Amor che ne la mente mi ragiona" marks an advance over "Amor, ch'al cor gentil ratto s'apprende" in the same way that submission to Lady Philosophy implies forsaking the physical eros of the tradition ("ch'al cor s'apprende") for the rationally propelled eros of the *Comedy* ("che ne la mente mi ragiona"). Moreover, the textual misuse that characterizes *Inferno* V is no longer present

---

[25] Hollander's position is well represented by his first sentence: "Casella's song is a Siren's song" (*"Purgatorio* II," p. 348). In response, I would point out that the poet deliberately defuses the severity of Cato's charges in the opening of *Purgatorio* III, where he calls Vergil's lapse a "picciol fallo" ("little fault" [9]).

[26] Freccero, "Casella's Song," p. 74.

"Amor che ne la mente" in *Purgatorio* II, where it is deflected not only by Cato but by the pilgrim himself; line 108, "che mi *solea* quetar tutte mie voglie," indicates—both in its use of the past tense and in its echo of another distancing verse, "Le dolci rime d'amor ch'i *solia* / cercar" (italics mine)—that he recognizes the limits of love poetry.

On the other hand, there is no doubt that a correction of "Amor che ne la mente" is implied by Cato's rebuke. On the literal level—Casella's level—the rebuke addresses the episode as a whole, and includes the vain attempt to re-create the ties of friendship in the same form in which they existed on earth (emblematized in the thrice-failed attempt to embrace), as well as the temporary succumbing to the blandishments of love poetry. Appearances by Cato frame the meeting with Casella, offering proleptic as well as retrospective corrections. Indeed, Casella's beautifully nostalgic projection of his love for Dante from the earthly past to the purgatorial present—"Così com' io t'amai / nel mortal corpo, così t'amo sciolta" ("As I loved you in the mortal body, so do I love you freed from it" [88-89])—is undermined by Cato even before it is spoken. In the preceding canto, Cato repudiates Vergil's all too human attempt to win favor by mentioning his wife, "Marzia tua, che 'n vista ancor ti priega, / o santo petto, che per tua la tegni" ("your Marcia, who in her look still prays you, o sainted breast, to hold her for your own" [I, 79-80]). As in his reply to Vergil Cato rejects all earthly ties to his wife, placing her firmly in the past definite ("Marzïa piacque tanto a li occhi miei / mentre ch'i' fu' di là" "Marcia so pleased my eyes while I was over there" [85-86]), so later he reminds Dante and Casella that the earthly ties of friendship are less important than the process of purgation awaiting them.

Although Casella views the canzone he sings as a simple love song, we who have read the *Convivio* are obliged to take its allegorical significance into consideration as well. A textual signpost noticed by critics is the pilgrim's use of the verb *consolare* in his request to Casella: "di ciò ti piaccia consolare alquanto /

l'anima mia . . ." (109-110).[27] Echoing as it does Boethius' title, *consolare* is a verb that figures prominently in the *Convivio* chapter where Dante announces the true identity of the *donna gentile*. Given its connection to Boethius and Lady Philosophy, it may be profitable to briefly consider the history of this word in the *Vita Nuova* and *Convivio*.

Consolare first occurs in the prose of *Vita Nuova* XXXVIII (and in the accompanying sonnet "Gentil pensero") where it refers negatively to the thought of the *donna gentile*: "Deo, che pensero è questo, che in così vile modo vuole consolare me e non mi lascia quasi altro pensare?" ("God, what thought is this, which in so vile a way wants to console me and almost does not let me think of anything else?" [XXXVIII, 2]). If we were to take *consolare* as the sign of Boethius, its presence here would support the notion that the *donna gentile* is Philosophy as far back as the *Vita Nuova*. But the next appearance of *consolare* demonstrates that originally Dante did not always connect the word with Philosophy; he uses it in "Voi che 'ntendendo" to refer not to the thought of the *donna gentile* as one would expect, but to the consoling thought of Beatrice ("questo piatoso che m'ha consolata" of line 32 is the thought that used to go, as in "Oltre la spera," to view Beatrice in heaven). Thus, at a purely textual level *consolare* does not necessarily signify Philosophy and does not necessarily involve Boethius.[28] It is

---

[27] Both Freccero and Hollander make much of Boethius in their articles on Casella's song. Freccero draws attention to a Boethian meter describing the feeding of caged birds, who scorn the food given them in their desire to return home to the woods; this same Boethian passage is noted by Vincent Moleta, " 'Come l'ausello in selva a la verdura,' " *Studi danteschi*, 52 (1979-1980), 1-67, repr. in *Guinizzelli in Dante* (Rome: Edizioni di Storia e Letteratura, 1980). In this book Moleta provides a reading of the *Comedy*'s incipits in a Guinizzellian key, suggesting that Dante "chooses to recall in his last work precisely those canzoni in which the inspirational force of *Al cor gentil*, and above all his transformation of the last two stanzas of that canzone, are most in evidence" (p. 145).

[28] This fact could serve, I believe, as an argument against the original allegorical significance of "Voi che 'ntendendo." If the canzone had been written with the allegory of Lady Philosophy in mind, would Dante not have taken

"Amor che ne la mente"
only in the allegorical gloss to "Voi che 'ntendendo" that Dante for the first time deliberately links the notion of consolation to Philosophy. In *Convivio* II, xii, where *consolare* is repeated in various forms six times ("consolare," "sconsolato," "consolarsi," "consolato," "consolazione," "consolarme"), there is no trace of the negative valence the word bore in *Vita Nuova* XXXVIII. There, in the context of Beatrice's victory, the consoling thought of the *donna gentile* is "vile"; here, in the context of the *donna gentile*'s victory, consolation is ennobled by being presented in Boethian terms.

By the time, then, that we reach "di ciò ti piaccia consolare alquanto / l'anima mia" in *Purgatorio* II, *consolare* has overtly Boethian associations. It also carries with it a history of signifying (with one exception) consolation from an incorrect source, whether the source be labeled the *donna gentile* or Lady Philosophy. As a canzone devoted to the wrong lady, "Amor che ne la mente" is corrected in the *Comedy*: first, in *Purgatorio* II, by Cato's rebuke; then, within the larger context of the autocitations, by being placed below "Donne ch'avete." The canzone from the *Vita Nuova* is located above the canzone from the *Convivio* in order to demonstrate that—chronology notwithstanding—the praise song for Beatrice must be ranked spiritually and poetically above the praise song for Lady Philosophy. In terms of his inner poetic itinerary as reconstructed in the *Comedy*, Dante views the earlier canzone as an advance over the later one.

This point is further conveyed through a consideration of the form and structure of "Amor che ne la mente." It has frequently been noted that "Amor che ne la mente" is closely modeled on

---

pains to attach the key word *consolare* to her in the text of the poem, rather than to Beatrice? The strenuous attachment of *consolare* to the *donna gentile* in the allegorical gloss of *Convivio* II, xii almost seems, from this point of view, like a cover-up. My tendency to believe that the canzoni were initially composed as love poems is strengthened by *Purgatorio* II: Casella's attitude toward "Amor che ne la mente" might be taken as a sign that it too was originally nonallegorical, especially considering that the verses confirming the poem's *dolcezza*—i.e. its status as a love poem—are delivered not by the pilgrim but by the poet.

"Donne ch'avete." It contains the same number of stanzas (five) and is organized on the same principles: in both, an introductory stanza is followed by a graduated series of stanzas dedicated to praising various aspects of the lady (general praise in the second stanza, praise of her soul in the third, and praise of her body in the fourth) followed by a *congedo*. Moreover, the rhyme scheme of the *fronte* of "Amor che ne la mente" repeats that of "Donne ch'avete." Such precise metrical and structural correspondences draw attention to a more basic resemblance; both belong to the *stilo de la loda* or praise-style, in which the poet eschews any self-involvement in order to elaborate an increasingly hyperbolic discourse regarding his lady. The marked similarities between the two canzoni have led critics to suggest that the later poem was conceived as a deliberate attempt to outdo the former.[29] If Dante once intended that his praise of the new lady should surpass his praise of Beatrice, in confirmation of his changed allegiance, then the hierarchy of the *Comedy*'s autocitations serves as a reversal that reinvests "Donne ch'avete" with its original priority.

In *Purgatorio* II we witness a scene in which newly arrived souls are enchanted by a song to a new love, a song that is the textual emblem of their misdirected newcomers' enthusiasm. The *Convivio*'s misdirected enthusiasm for Lady Philosophy is thus replayed on the beach of Purgatory; the singing of "Amor che ne la mente" in *Purgatorio* II signals the re-creation of a moment spiritually akin to the poem's first home, the prose treatise, where indeed Philosophy's sweetness is such as to banish all care from the mind: "cominciai tanto a sentire de la sua dolcezza, che lo suo amore cacciava e distruggeva ogni altro pensiero" ("and I began so to feel her sweetness, that her love drove away and destroyed all other thoughts" [II, xii, 7]). To my knowledge, no one has noted that the drama of *Purgatorio* II exactly reproduces the situation of the first stanza of "Amor

---

[29] This view is expressed by Vincenzo Pernicone in the article "Amor che ne la mente mi ragiona," *Enciclopedia Dantesca*, vol. I, pp. 217-219.

"Amor che ne la mente" che ne la mente," in which the lover is overwhelmed by the sweetness of Love's song:

> Amor che ne la mente mi ragiona
> de la mia donna disïosamente,
> move cose di lei meco sovente,
> che lo 'ntelletto sovr'esse disvia.
>   Lo suo parlar sì dolcemente sona,
> che l'anima ch'ascolta e che lo sente
> dice: 'Oh me lassa, ch'io non son possente
> di dir quel ch'odo de la donna mia!'

Love which in my mind reasons so desiringly about my lady often tells me things about her *which cause my intellect to go astray. His speech sounds so sweetly* that the soul which listens and hears says: "Alas that I am not able to utter what I hear about my lady!"

(1-8; italics mine)

Here too we are faced with a verbal sweetness—"Lo suo parlar sì dolcemente sona," echoed in the *Comedy* by "che la dolcezza ancor dentro mi suona"—whose effect is debilitating; as in the *Comedy* the rapt pilgrims are unable to proceed up the mountain, so in the poem the listening soul—"l'anima ch'ascolta e che lo sente"—loses its powers of expression. In both passages, beauty causes the intellect to go temporarily astray.

Line 4 of "Amor che ne la mente"—"che lo 'ntelletto sovr'esse disvia"—thus provides the paradigm that synthesizes all the facets of this discussion: the souls go off the path (temporarily) as they succumb to the sweetness of the song in *Purgatorio* II; Dante went off the path (temporarily) when he allowed himself to be overly consoled by the sweetness of Philosophy in the *Convivio*. Lady Philosophy was indeed a mistake. On the other hand, the location guarantees salvation; like the serpent which routinely invades the valley of the princes, the distractions of the *Purgatorio* have lost their bite. For all that they are new arrivals, easily led astray by their impulsive attraction to the new delights—erotic or philosophical—which cross their path, the souls of *Purgatorio* II are incapable of erring profoundly. For them, as for their more advanced companions on the terrace of pride, the last verses of the *Pater noster* no longer apply. As in the case of the *donna gentile* episode of the *Vita Nuova*, the Casella episode functions as a lapse, a backward glance whose redemption is implicit in its occurrence.

"Donne ch'avete intelletto d'amore"

The second autocitation takes us to one of the *Comedy*'s most debated moments, the culminating phase of the encounter between the pilgrim and the poet Bonagiunta da Lucca. If we briefly rehearse the dialogue at this stage of *Purgatorio* XXIV, we note that it is tripartite: Bonagiunta asks if Dante is indeed the inventor of a new form of poetry, which begins with the poem "Donne ch'avete intelletto d'amore" (49-51); Dante replies by apparently minimizing his own role in the poetic process, saying that he composes by following Love's dictation (52-54); Bonagiunta then claims to have finally understood why the poetry practiced by himself, his peers, and his predecessors is inferior to the new poetry, which he dubs—in passing—the "sweet new style" (55-63).

Bonagiunta's remarks, which frame the pilgrim's reply, are grounded in historical specificity: his initial query concerns Dante's personal poetic history, invoked through the naming of a precise canzone; his final remarks concern the history of the Italian lyric, invoked through the names of its chief practitioners, " 'l Notaro e Guittone e me" (56). The concreteness of Bonagiunta's statements contrasts with the indeterminate transcendentality of the pilgrim's reply, in which poetic principles are located in an ahistorical vacuum. Not only are the famous *terzina*'s only protagonists the poet and Love ("I' mi son un che, quando / Amor mi spira, noto . . ."), but the absence of any external historical referent is emphasized by an insistent subjectivity, articulated in the stress on the first person ("I' mi son un") at the outset.

"Donne ch'avete"

Structurally, Dante's reply functions as a pivot between Bonagiunta's first question and his later exclamation. The "Amor mi spira" passage thus enables the poet of the *Comedy* to accomplish that shift in subject matter that has so puzzled critics: from the problematic of an individual poet to that of a tradition. Indeed, precisely the neutrality of the pilgrim's reply allows it to serve as a narrative medium conferring significance both on what precedes and what follows; because of its lack of specific content, the pilgrim's statement—"I am one who takes note when Love inspires me"—is able to provide a context first for the composition of "Donne ch'avete," and then for the emergence of the "sweet new style" as a poetic school. Both are defined in terms of a privileged relation to Amor.

By the same token, however, that the central *terzina* confers significance, it also generates ambiguity, by obscuring the terms of the very transition that it facilitates and by deliberately failing to clarify the application of the key phrase "dolce stil novo." Reacting against what they consider the reflex canonization of a school on the basis of a misreading of Bonagiunta's remarks, recent critics have insisted that the expression "dolce stil novo," as used in *Purgatorio* XXIV, is intended to apply only to Dante's own poetry. In other words, they refer Bonagiunta's latter comments back to his initial query. From this point of view (one which seeks to disband, at least within Dante's text, the group of poets known as *stilnovisti*), the "new style" begins with "Donne ch'avete," and it encompasses only Dante's subsequent poetry in the same mode.[30]

---

[30] These verses have given rise to essentially two divergent critical camps: one traditionally sees in Bonagiunta's words an implied reference to a "school" of new poets, and the other maintains that the only *stilnovista* so designated by Bonagiunta is Dante himself. This last position is presented by De Robertis in "Definizione dello stil novo," *L'Approdo*, 3 (1954), 59-64. The matter is complicated by the recent emergence of a third camp which insists not only that there is no school of *stilnovisti* referred to within Dante's text, but further that there is no such school at all. For this point of view, see Guido Favati, *Inchiesta sul Dolce Stil Nuovo* (Florence: Le Monnier, 1975). The historiographical aspects of Bonagiunta's remarks will be discussed in the following chapter, where the critical response will be reviewed as well.

Whereas the historiographical potential of Bonagiunta's concluding statements has sparked controversy, critics have not been similarly divided in their reaction to his earlier remark on "Donne ch'avete." Perhaps one reason for the general consensus regarding the status of "Donne ch'avete" is the unusual consistency in Dante's own attitudes toward this canzone as displayed throughout his career, from the *Vita Nuova* to the *De Vulgari Eloquentia* to the *Comedy*. As the first of the *Vita Nuova*'s three canzoni, it marks a decisive moment in the *libello*: in narrative terms it signals the protagonist's total emancipation from the Provençal guerdon, and in poetic terms it signals his liberation from the so-called tragic, or Cavalcantian, mode. In the *Vita Nuova*, where aesthetic praxis is viewed as a function of ethical commitment, developments in form are strictly coordinated with developments in content; a stylistic triumph can only exist within the context of a conceptual breakthrough. Nowhere is this procedure more observable than in the chapters describing the genesis of "Donne ch'avete."

The account begins with an impasse in the poet's love for Beatrice. In *Vita Nuova* XIV Dante attends a wedding where he sees the *gentilissima*; his resulting collapse is ridiculed by the ladies present. In the aftermath of this event, Dante writes three sonnets: the first is a direct appeal to Beatrice for pity ("Con l'altre donne mia vista gabbate" [chap. XIV]); the second details his physical disintegration upon seeing her ("Ciò che m'incontra, ne la mente more" [chap. XV]); the third further chronicles the state to which he has been reduced by the erotic conflict, "questa battaglia d'Amore," waged within him ("Spesse fiate vegnonmi a la mente" [chap. XVI]). All share an insistence on the self (the three incipits all contain the first-person pronoun), a tendency to self-pity ("e venmene pietà" from "Spesse fiate"), and a preoccupation with death.[31] Moreover, they presume the lover's right to air grievances and ask for redress; the

---

[31] Dante's "e venmene pietà" echoes Cavalcanti's incipit, "A me stesso di me pietate vene." The relation of these sonnets to the Cavalcantian mode will be discussed further in Chapter II.

"Donne ch'avete"

first two sonnets are directly addressed by the lover to the lady, who is implicitly viewed as responsible for his suffering.

The last of these sonnets is followed by a strikingly brief chapter consisting of only two sentences, in which the poet quietly announces a major transition; whereas the preceding poems deal obsessively with his own condition, he shall now undertake to write in a new mode, selflessly:

> Poi che dissi questi tre sonetti, ne li quali parlai a questa donna però che fuoro narratori di tutto quasi lo mio stato, credendomi tacere e non dire più però che mi parea di me assai avere manifestato, avvegna che sempre poi tacesse di dire a lei, a me convenne ripigliare matera nuova e più nobile che la passata.

After I had composed these three sonnets, in which I had spoken to this lady since they were the narrators of nearly all of my condition, deciding that I should be silent and not say more because it seemed that I had revealed enough about myself, although the result would be that from then on I should cease to write to her, it became necessary for me to take up a new and more noble subject matter than the past one.

(XVII, 1)

We notice that the "matera nuova e più nobile che la passata" is predicated on a double-edged verbal renunciation: he may no longer speak about himself ("credendomi tacere e non dire più"), and he may no longer speak to her ("avvegna che sempre poi tacesse di dire a lei"). The result of blocking both traditional outlets and traditional responses will be a new poetry.

The archaic dialogue imposed by the poet on the lady is thus replaced by a monologue whose morphology is based on a poetics of sublimation, a poetics illuminated for the poet by the Florentine Muse of chapter XVIII. Here the topos of the *gabbo* is replayed, but with positive results; both lover and poet are provoked into defining new goals. Rather than locating his supreme desire ("fine di tutti li miei desiderii" [XVIII, 4]) in an event outside of his control (Beatrice's greeting) whose presence is transformational but whose denial induces narrative lapses into self-pity and poetic lapses into regressive modes, the lover learns to use the lady to generate a happiness ("beatitudine") that cannot fail him ("che non mi puote venire meno" [XVIII, 4]) because it is under his own governance. Such total autonomy from referentiality—true beatitude—translates, in poetic terms, into the praise-style; by placing his poetic happiness "in quelle parole che lodano la donna mia" ("in those words that praise my lady" [XVIII, 6]), the poet foregoes the traditionally dualistic mechanics of love poetry and discovers a new mode.

The privileged status of the first poem written in the new style is immediately apparent. Only on this occasion does Dante chronicle the birth of a poem, a birth that is described as a quasi-miraculous event, a creation *ex nihilo*: "la mia lingua parlò quasi come per sé stessa mossa, e disse: *Donne ch'avete intelletto d'amore*" ("my tongue spoke as though moved by itself, and said: 'Donne ch'avete intelletto d'amore' " [XIX, 2]). The inspirational emphasis of this statement from *Vita Nuova* XIX foreshadows the poetic credo of *Purgatorio* XXIV; both texts present "Donne ch'avete" as deriving from a divinely inspired exclusionary relation existing between the poet and a higher authority. The *De Vulgari Eloquentia* also sanctions, albeit in less mystical terms, the special status of "Donne ch'avete": in a text where Dante uses many of his later poems to serve as exempla of excellence in various stylistic and metrical categories, he nonetheless chooses the youthful "Donne ch'avete" as the incipit to follow the formal definition of the canzone, thus establishing this early lyric as emblematic of the entire genre.[32]

---

[32] The canzone is defined and "Donne ch'avete" cited for the first time in *De Vulgari Eloquentia* II, viii, 8. Dante also cites the following later canzoni in the treatise: "Doglia mi reca ne lo core ardire" (II, ii, 8); "Amor, che movi tua vertù da cielo" (II, v, 4 and II, xi, 7); "Amor che ne la mente mi ragiona" (II, vi, 6); "Al poco giorno e al gran cerchio d'ombra" (II, x, 2 and II, xiii, 2); "Traggemi de la mente amor la stiva" (lost) (II, xi, 5); "Donna pietosa e di novella etate" (II, xi, 8); "Poscia ch'Amor del tutto m'ha lasciato" (II, xii, 8); "Amor, tu vedi ben che questa donna" (II, xiii, 13). "Donne ch'avete" is cited a second time in II, xii, 3.

"Donne ch'avete"

The testimony of the *Vita Nuova* and the *De Vulgari Eloquentia* clarifies the appearance of "Donne ch'avete" in *Purgatorio* XXIV, where Bonagiunta invokes the canzone as a badge of poetic identity:

> Ma dì s'i' veggio qui colui che fore
> trasse le nove rime, cominciando
> '*Donne ch'avete intelletto d'amore.*'

> But tell me if I see here him who brought forth the new poems, beginning "Donne ch'avete intelletto d'amore"?
> (*Purg.* XXIV, 49-51)

In fact, Bonagiunta both revives and integrates each of the canzone's previous textual roles: in that "Donne ch'avete" is an inaugural text ("le nove rime") he recapitulates the *Vita Nuova*; in that the canzone sets a standard by which to measure other poetry (" 'l Notaro e Guittone e me") he recapitulates the *De Vulgari Eloquentia*. But Dante does not limit himself to recapitulation; in cantos XXIII and XXIV of the *Purgatorio* he constructs a sustained tribute to "Donne ch'avete" that effectively designates this canzone his supreme lyric achievement.

The episode surrounding the citation of "Donne ch'avete" is complicated by the fact that it involves a double set of characters, issues, and retrospective allusions, for the statements of *Purgatorio* XXIV acquire their full significance only when viewed on the backdrop of *Purgatorio* XXIII. The first sign directing us to a contextual reading of canto XXIV is the apparent absence of the requisite autobiographical marker, an absence rectified by the figure of Forese Donati, the friend Dante meets in canto XXIII. As we shall see, the encounter with Forese provides the necessary prelude to the conversation with Bonagiunta. Structural considerations further support reading canto XXIV in tandem with canto XXIII; we do well to bear in mind that the entire Bonagiunta episode takes place literally within the meeting with Forese.[33]

---

[33] The thematic and structural coherence of these two cantos is noted by Umberto Bosco, who makes a point of treating them as a unit in the commentary

Autocitation and Autobiography

Purgatorio XXIII begins with a description of the pilgrim peering through the green boughs of the tree he and his guides have discovered on the terrace of gluttony, "like one who wastes his life chasing little birds": "come far suole / chi dietro a li uccellin sua vita perde" (2-3). The emphasis on loss in "sua vita perde" sets the canto's tone; as well as initiating the episode, the verb *perdere* will also bring it to a close, in Forese's final words in canto XXIV:

> Tu ti rimani omai; ché 'l tempo è caro
> in questo regno, *sì ch'io perdo troppo*
> venendo teco sì a paro a paro.

> Now you remain behind, for time is dear in this realm, *so that I lose too much* by coming thus with you at equal pace.
> (*Purg.* XXIV, 91-93; italics mine)

The encounter with Forese is precisely about loss, a loss which is recuperated through that redemption of history which is the chief matter of the *Purgatorio*. It is no accident that this of all episodes is used to articulate the fundamental relation of the *Purgatorio* to time. Forese's remark on the importance of time in Purgatory, "ché 'l tempo è caro / in questo regno," echoes the crucial definition of the previous canto, where the pilgrim comments that he had expected to find his friend down below, in Ante-Purgatory, where time is restored for time: "Io ti credea trovar là giù di sotto, / dove tempo per tempo si ristora" (XXIII, 83-84). Although the pilgrim's maxim refers directly to the Ante-Purgatory, with its formulaic insistence on literal time, it in fact glosses the whole of the second realm.

Time is the essential commodity of the *Purgatorio*, the only real eye for an eye that God exacts. The *Purgatorio* exists in

---

of his edition with Giovanni Reggio, *La Divina Commedia*, 3 vols. (Florence: Le Monnier, 1979), *Purgatorio*, pp. 386-394. This same dialectical emphasis pervades the readings of Alberto Del Monte, "Forese," *Cultura e scuola* 4, nos. 13-14 (1965), 572-589; and Vittorio Russo, "*Pg.* XXIII: Forese, o la maschera del discorso," *MLN*, 94 (1979), 113-136.

"Donne ch'avete"

time because the earth exists in time; time spent sinning in one hemisphere is paid back in the other.[34] Because earth is where "vassene 'l tempo e l'uom non se n'avvede" ("time passes and man does not notice" [*Purg.* IV, 9]), Purgatory is where "tempo per tempo si ristora." Climbing Purgatory allows the reel of history to be played backward; the historical fall of the race through time, symbolized by the Arno in Guido del Duca's discourse as it was in Hell by the Old Man of Crete, is reversed.[35] The journey up the mountain is the journey back through time to the place of beginnings, which is in turn the new ending; it is a journey whose goal is the undoing of time through time. The fall that occurred in history can only be redeemed in history; time is restored so that with it we may restore ourselves. This reversal of the fall, most explicitly reenacted in the ritual drama of *Purgatorio* VIII, finds its personal and autobiographical expression in the meeting with Forese Donati.

If Purgatory is the place where we are given the chance, desired in vain on earth, to undo what we have done, the Forese episode is chosen by the poet as the vehicle for articulating these basic principles of the canticle because it is emblematic, more than any other episode, of a fall in Dante's own spiritual biography. The episode's thematics of loss rehearse at a personal level what will later be fully orchestrated in the Earthly Paradise, where Matelda reminds Dante of Proserpina in her moment of loss ("Proserpina nel tempo che perdette / la madre lei, ed ella primavera" "Proserpina in the time when her mother lost her,

---

[34] This underlying notion of debt translates into the economic images that run through the *Purgatorio* to culminate in the startling metaphor of canto XXVIII, 91-96, whereby Eden was God's downpayment on Paradise, but man defaulted while paying back the loan. The economic motifs of the *Comedy* are treated by Joan M. Ferrante, *The Political Vision of the Divine Comedy*, chap. 6, "Exchange and Communication, Commerce and Language" (Princeton: Princeton U. Press, 1984). On time in the *Comedy*, see Franco Masciandaro, *La problematica del tempo nella Commedia* (Ravenna: Longo, 1976).

[35] The Arno's role in personifying the fall of history is succinctly expressed by Guido del Duca's phrase with its emphatic progressive construction: "Vassi caggendo" ("It goes on falling") in *Purg.* XIV, 49. Giuseppe Mazzotta discusses the Old Man of Crete in *Dante, Poet of the Desert*, chap. 1.

Autocitation and Autobiography

and she lost spring" [*Purg.* XXVIII, 50-51]), and where Eve, signifying loss, is continually insinuated into the discourse. Indeed, the opening simile of *Purgatorio* XXIII may be seen as an anticipation of Beatrice's Edenic rebuke; the vain pursuit of little birds finds its metaphorical equivalent in another distracting diminutive, the *pargoletta* of canto XXXI:

Non ti dovea gravar le penne in giuso,
 ad aspettar più colpo, o pargoletta
 o altra novità con sì breve uso.

No young girl or other novelty of such brief use should have weighed your wings downward to await further blows.

(*Purg.* XXXI, 58-60)

The fall that Forese Donati marks in Dante's life is redeemed in cantos XXIII and XXIV of the *Purgatorio*, both biographically and poetically. The moment of failure is placed before the moment of triumph, the encounter with Forese before the dialogue with Bonagiunta. Thus, Dante's so-called *traviamento morale*, as remembered in canto XXIII, is ultimately seen from the perspective of an enduring conquest, as formulated in canto XXIV. The poetic correlative of Dante's spiritual fall is the *tenzone* of scurrilous sonnets exchanged by him and Forese; the *tenzone* stands in contrast to the *stil novo*, celebrated here as the pinnacle of Dante's lyric form in the canzone "Donne ch'avete."[36] There is no further autocitation in the *Purgatorio*

---

[36] Bosco, Del Monte, and Russo all point to the contrast between the *tenzone* and the *stil novo*, referred to by Bosco respectively as the "poison" and the "antidote" (*Purgatorio*, p. 391). Before proceeding, some mention should be made of the doubts that exist regarding the attribution of the *tenzone* to Dante. Domenico Guerri's suggestion that the sonnets are in fact an obscene literary correspondence of the early *Quattrocento* (*La corrente popolare nel Rinascimento* [Florence: Sansoni, 1931], pp. 104-148) went counter to the expressed opinion of Michele Barbi ("La tenzone di Dante con Forese," orig. 1924, repr. in *Problemi di critica dantesca, Seconda serie* [Florence: Sansoni, 1941], pp. 87-188, and in *Rime della Vita Nuova e della giovinezza*, ed. M. Barbi and F. Maggini [Florence: Le Monnier, 1956], pp. 275-373), by whom it was refuted

"Donne ch'avete"

because "Donne ch'avete" is the end-term in the search for the purgatorial mode of pure love poetry; like the Earthly Paradise, the beginning is revealed to be the end.

As a poetic experience, the *tenzone* is present only obliquely, in Dante's encounter with his former verbal antagonist. The lexical gains of the uncompromisingly realistic *tenzone* are registered less in the second canticle than in the first, where we find, for instance, the exchange between Sinon and Maestro Adamo.[37] Far from containing a particularly realistic lexicon,

("Ancora della tenzone di Dante con Forese," orig. 1932, repr. in *Problemi di critica dantesca, Seconda serie*, pp. 189-214). Guerri's thesis was revived forty years later by Antonio Lanza in an Appendix to his *Polemiche e berte letterarie nella Firenze del primo Quattrocento* (Rome: Bulzoni, 1971) entitled "Una volgare lite nella Firenze del primo Quattrocento: la cosidetta tenzone di Dante con Forese Donati—nuovi contributi alla tesi di Domenico Guerri," only to be refuted again by Mario Marti, "Rime realistiche (la tenzone e le petrose dantesche)," *Nuove letture dantesche* (Florence: Le Monnier, 1976), vol. VIII, pp. 209-230, who insists on the evidence of the early commentators (some verses of the *tenzone* are cited by the Anonimo Fiorentino) and of the manuscripts (which are assigned with greater probability to the end of the fourteenth than to the beginning of the fifteenth century). Were Dante's authorship of the *tenzone* to be revoked and my analysis of canto XXIII to lose its textual factor, the biographical/poetic triumph of canto XXIV would still be dialectically preceded by a biographical—if not poetic—fall. On the other hand, precisely the striking parallelism between the two cantos that the existence of the *tenzone* adds to the episode in the *Comedy* seems to constitute further support of its authenticity.

[37] Although Russo points to the presence of "rime realistiche" in *Purgatorio* XXIII ("Forese o la maschera del discorso," p. 126), they seem not extensive enough to constitute a textual echo of the *tenzone* in the canto. Reverse echoes pervade the canto according to Francesco D'Ovidio, who argues that the repetition of Forese's name here makes amends for the use of the nickname "Bicci" in the sonnets, and likewise that the tender insistence on Forese's face (*Purg.* XXIII, 48 and 55) is connected to the "faccia fessa" of the sonnet "Bicci novel, figliuol di non so cui." D'Ovidio's chief claim is that the rhyming of "Cristo" only with itself in the *Comedy* is intended to correct its rhyme with "tristo" and "male acquisto" in the same sonnet; all these points are to be found in "Cristo in rima," *Studii sulla Divina Commedia* (Milan-Palermo: Sandron, 1901), pp. 215-224. More recently, Piero Cudini has returned to the question of the *tenzone* in the *Comedy*, both with respect to its impact on the language of Sinon and Maestro Adamo in *Inferno* XXX, and with respect to the encounter

Purgatorio XXIII is saturated with lyric elements like the antithesis. As the lyric figure par excellence, Dante uses antithesis in canto XXIII to chart the lyric's transcendence of itself. From a traditionally private and rhetorical figure, it stretches to accommodate the deepest moral significance; in narrative terms, we move from the Petrarchism *avant la lettre* that describes the gluttonous souls in the first part of the canto ("piangere e cantar" [10]; "diletto e doglia" [12]; "piangendo canta" [64]) to the passion of Christ, expressed through an antithesis whose rigor is foreign to the lyric experience:

> E non pur una volta, questo spazzo
> girando, si rinfresca nostra pena:
> *io dico pena, e dovria dir sollazzo,*
> ché quella voglia a li alberi ci mena
> che menò Cristo lieto a dire 'Elì,'
> quando ne liberò con la sua vena.
>
> And not just one time as we circle this space is our pain refreshed—*I say pain, and I ought to say pleasure,* for that desire leads us to the trees which led Christ happy to say "Elì" when He freed us with His blood.
> (*Purg.* XXIII, 70-75; italics mine)

That most banal of amatory expedients—pain that is pleasure—thus renders the sublime.[38] The rhetorical achievement of line 72 is concretized in two further antithetical expressions, again radically new: "buon dolor" in "l'ora / del buon dolor ch'a Dio ne rimarita" ("the hour of the sweet grief that rewds us to God" [80-81]), and "dolce assenzo" in "a ber lo dolce assenzo d'i martìri" ("to drink the sweet wormwood of the torments"

---

with Forese (in key moments of the latter he finds the use of rhyme schemes from the sonnets); see "La tenzone tra Dante e Forese e la *Commedia* (*Inf.* XXX; *Purg.* XXIII-XXIV)," *Giornale storico della letteratura italiana*, 159 (1982), 1-25.

[38] À propos of antithesis in canto XXIII and of line 72 in particular, Sapegno cites the anonymous verse "E sto in sollazzo e vivo in gran pena" ("I exist in joy and in great pain"), where "sollazzo" and "pena" are present in their most hackneyed form (*Purgatorio*, pp. 256-257).

[86]). Thus, in the *Purgatorio* "sweet wormwood" describes not the contradictory love of the poet for his lady (as in Petrarch's *Canzoniere*, where his lady's eyes can make honey bitter, or sweeten wormwood: "e 'l mel amaro, et addolcir l'assenzio" [CCXV, 14]), but the soul's paradoxical attachment to the martyrdom of purgation.

Through such textual strategies the poet sets the stage for the elaboration of a new poetic category in *Purgatorio* XXIV, that of the transcendent lyric. Indeed, as though to underscore the importance of canto XXIII for our reading of canto XXIV, Dante introduces the souls of the terrace of gluttony, at the beginning of XXIII, in a *terzina* that proleptically glosses the role of the canzone "Donne ch'avete":

> Ed ecco piangere e cantar s'udìe
> '*Labïa mëa, Domine*' per modo
> tal, che diletto e doglia parturìe.

> And suddenly in tears and song was heard "Labia mea, Domine" in such a way that it gave birth to delight and sorrow.
>
> (*Purg.* XXIII, 10-12)

Embedded within lyric antitheses is a verse with enormous resonance for Dante's conception of the lyric, from the Vulgate's Fiftieth Psalm: "Domine, labia mea aperies; et os meum annuntiabit laudem tuam" ("Lord, open my lips, and my mouth will announce Your praise"). Thus, the gluttons pray to the Lord to open their once closed mouths so that they may sing forth His praises, a fact that illuminates the positioning of Bonagiunta and his poetic discourse on this terrace. As a poet, Bonagiunta also failed to "open his mouth" in praise; he is emblematic of an archaic poetics that stopped short of discovering the praise-style, the "matera nuova e più nobile che la passata" of *Vita Nuova* XVII.[39]

---

[39] In "Dante's Sweet New Style and the *Vita Nuova*," *Italica*, 42 (1965), 98-107, John Scott links these verses of Psalm 50 to the spontaneous speech that generated "Donne ch'avete," so emphasized in the *libello*. For the importance

The gluttons of canto XXIII have turned their mouths from the basest of concerns—"eating," or unrelieved self-involvement—to praising God, in the same way that the discovery of the *stil novo* turns the Italian lyric from the conventional poetics of the "I" to the deflection of the "I" in the poetry of praise. Thus, the gluttons chanting their Psalm are described as souls who are loosening the knot of their obligation, "forse di lor dover solvendo il nodo" (XXIII, 15), in a phrasing that anticipates the loosening of Bonagiunta's "knot" (his uncertainty regarding the reasons for his poetic failure) by the pilgrim. The artifact that symbolizes the conversion that the gluttons have only now achieved—away from the self toward a disinterested focusing on the Other—is "Donne ch'avete," which attains its prominence within the *Comedy* precisely because it marks the moment in which Dante first opens his mouth in a song of praise.

Within the new order imposed by the *Comedy*'s confessional self-reading, in which literal chronology becomes irrelevant, Forese signifies the fall preceding the conversion to Beatrice. Moreover, the pilgrim will specify, in the detailed account of his journey that he offers at the end of canto XXIII, that he proceeded directly from the experience shared with his friend to the meeting with Vergil; thus, we can state that Forese signifies, within the *Comedy*'s ideal scheme, no less than the final fall before the final conversion. That this fall is connected to the displacement of Beatrice is suggested by the fact that Dante's friendship with Forese seems to correspond to the period of depression following Beatrice's death, a period documented by the *Convivio* (and perhaps by Cavalcanti's sonnet rebuking Dante

---

of this Psalm, see Robert Hollander, "Dante's Use of the Fiftieth Psalm," *Dante Studies*, 91 (1973), 145-150, repr. *Studies in Dante*, pp. 107-113. Richard Abrams connects Bonagiunta's gluttony to his inability to achieve the praise-style in "Inspiration and Gluttony: The Moral Context of Dante's Poetics of the 'Sweet New Style,' " *MLN*, 91 (1976), 30-59, as does Mark Musa, "The 'Sweet New Style' That I Hear," in *Advent at the Gates: Dante's Comedy* (Bloomington and London: Indiana U. Press, 1974), pp. 111-128.

for his *vile vita*), in which Beatrice was replaced by other interests to a degree later judged intolerable.[40]

In the absence of precise indices regarding the years after 1290, the decadence of the *tenzone* (dated by internal evidence to 1293-1296) was originally viewed as symptomatic of a literally dissolute period in Dante's life. The illegitimate biographical status once assumed by these texts has been defused by studies insisting that the low style of the *tenzone* is just as conventional as the high style of the courtly lyric. As a result, Dante's straying after the death of Beatrice is now generally interpreted in a more metaphorical light, as a phase of moral and political secularism, involving a philosophical and/or religious deviation from orthodoxy.[41] To the extent that any strictly

---

[40] Cavalcanti's famous and enigmatic sonnet, "I' vegno 'l giorno a te 'nfinite volte," has spawned a variety of interpretations. In answer to D'Ovidio's claim that the sonnet was intended to reprove Dante for his low associations, and in particular for his friendship with Forese ("L'intemerata di Guido," 1896; repr. "La rimenata di Guido," in *Studii sulla Divina Commedia*, pp. 202-214), Barbi asserted that the sonnet enjoins Dante against excessive depression, not decadence ("Una opera sintetica su Dante," 1904; repr. *Problemi di critica dantesca, Prima serie* [Florence: Sansoni, 1934], pp. 40-41). In support of Barbi's thesis is Dante's own use of the expression employed by Cavalcanti in line 9, "la vil tua vita," in the *donna gentile* sequence of the *Vita Nuova*, where "la mia vile vita" refers to the life of tears and suffering he had been leading since Beatrice's death (XXXV, 3). Another current of criticism sees an underlying political motivation; Marti suggests that the resentment of the aristocratic and therefore politically excluded Cavalcanti may have been provoked by Dante's growing political involvement ("Sulla genesi del realismo dantesco," in *Realismo dantesco e altri studi* [Milan: Ricciardi, 1961], pp. 1-32). A convincing reading of the sonnet in a poetic key is that of Marco Santagata, "Lettura cavalcantiana," *Giornale storico della letteratura italiana*, 148 (1971), 295-308, according to whom Guido accuses Dante of leaving the restricted sphere of stilnovist poetics, as in fact he did. The recent contribution of Letterio Cassata, "La paternale di Guido," *Studi danteschi*, 53 (1981), 167-185, is notable mainly for its helpful review of the sonnet's complex hermeneutic history. In conclusion, I would note that there could well be some merit to all the chief interpretations of "I' vegno 'l giorno a te," since all facets of the problematic—depression, Forese, politics, poetic divergence—come together in the critical years following the death of the *gentilissima*.

[41] In "Sulla genesi del realismo dantesco," Marti insists on the stylistically conventional aspect of the *tenzone*, which he says should be viewed in the

Autocitation and Autobiography

personal or erotic failure is involved, it is viewed as part of a larger problematic; the *pargoletta* cited by Beatrice is not only a rival lady (as witnessed by her place in the *Rime*), but is also the central symbolic node of a cluster of transgressions. Among these transgressions are the poems to the *donna gentile*, composed at this time, most likely in 1293-1294. The episode of his life to which Dante later attached the rubric "Forese Donati" is, therefore, a synthesis of the deviations catalogued by Beatrice: the moral ("o pargoletta / o altra novità" [*Purg.* XXXI, 59-60]), and the philosophical ("quella scuola / c'hai seguitata" [*Purg.* XXXIII, 85-86]).[42]

Beatrice forecasts her more specific rebukes with a single compact charge, that of turning away from her to someone else: "questi si tolse a me, e diessi altrui" ("he took himself from

---

context of anti-courtly poetry in general. In the matter of Dante's potentially more serious deviations, Nardi maintains that although Dante never strayed as far from orthodoxy as his friend Cavalcanti, he was not immune from Averroistic influences ("Dante e Guido Cavalcanti," p. 213); his "Dal *Convivio* alla *Commedia*" (in *Dal Convivio alla Commedia: sei saggi danteschi* [Rome: Istituto Storico Italiano per il Medio Evo, 1960], pp. 37-150) delineates Averroistic tendencies in the *Convivio* and even finds residual Averroism in the *Paradiso*. Another critic who stresses the philosophical component of Dante's error is Joseph Anthony Mazzeo, who suggests that the temptations cited by Beatrice, the "serene" of *Purgatorio* XXXI, 45 as well as the "pargoletta" of line 59, should be read in the context of Cicero's passage on Ulysses and the Sirens in the *De Finibus* as representing "simultaneously the sins of the flesh and a misuse of knowledge" ("The 'Sirens' of *Purgatorio* XXXI, 45," in *Medieval Cultural Tradition in Dante's Comedy* [Ithaca: Cornell U. Press, 1960], pp. 205-212). In his commentary to the *Comedy* (which devotes particular attention to the autobiographical aspects of the poem), Bosco stresses the philosophical/religious nature of the *traviamento* (see, for instance, *Purgatorio*, p. 391).

[42] Beatrice refers not only to "that school which you followed" but also to "its doctrine"; as Edward Moore points out, the expression "sua dottrina" (*Purg.* XXXIII, 86) implies a philosophical school of thought (see "The Reproaches of Beatrice," in *Studies in Dante, Third Series: Miscellaneous Essays* [1903; repr. New York: Greenwood Press, 1968], p. 234). Etienne Gilson makes the same point, saying that "Since it is here a question of a *school* and a *doctrine*, Beatrice cannot have been speaking of moral transgressions in this passage" (*Dante and Philosophy*, trans. David Moore [1939; repr. Gloucester, Mass.: Peter Smith, 1968], p. 97). Moore argues against an overly literal interpretation of Dante's fall, concluding that "Religion, as I believe, lost its practical hold on him after the death of Beatrice" (p. 249).

me and gave himself to another" [*Purg.* XXX, 126]). Indeed, the hallmark of Beatrice's personal discourse throughout the Earthly Paradise is negative conversion. She concentrates insistently on the illicit presence of the other; "altrui" is echoed by "altra novità," and finally by "altrove" in the verse "colpa ne la tua voglia altrove attenta" ("the fault of your will elsewhere intent" [*Purg.* XXXIII, 99]). To the thematics of negative conversion is opposed the positive conversion of canto XXIII, where the pilgrim registers the forward turn of *Inferno* I:

> Di quella vita mi volse costui
>   che mi va innanzi, l'altri' ier, quando tonda
>   vi si mostrò la suora di colui
>
> From that life he who goes before me turned me the other day, when the sister of him [the sun] showed herself round to you
>   (*Purg.* XXIII, 118-120)

The full moon over the *selva oscura* marks the poet's tryst with the conversion that will take him, as he explains to his friend, ultimately to Beatrice, "là dove fia Beatrice" (*Purg.* XXIII, 128).

When Dante says to Forese "Di quella vita mi volse costui," he defines the new moment with Vergil ("mi volse") in terms of the old moment with Forese ("quella vita"), the conversion in terms of the preceding fall. The words "quella vita" refer literally to the past life shared by the two friends, a past whose memories are still burdensome (the flip side of Casella's song, which is still sweet):

>   Se tu riduci a mente
>   qual fosti meco, e qual io teco fui,
>   ancor fia grave il memorar presente.
> Di quella vita mi volse costui . . .
>
> If you call to mind what you were with me and I with you, the present memory will still be grievous. From that life he turned me . . .
>   (*Purg.* XXIII, 115-118)

The life-experience shared by Dante and Forese thus assumes a metaphoric value in the *Comedy* that bears little relation to anything we know about the two men. Forese stands in Dante's personal lexicon for his own compromised historical identity, the past—"qual fosti meco, e qual io teco fui"—brought painfully into the present—"il memorar presente." Their life together represents everything the saved soul regrets before being granted forgetfulness: the sum total of personal falls, little deaths, other paths. For Dante, this is everything he left behind when he turned to Beatrice.

In directly linking his friendship with Forese to the encounter with Vergil, in casting the Florentine *traviamento* as the immediate predecessor to the dark wood, Dante far outstrips the literal content of the *tenzone*, which (with its gluttonies, petty thieveries, and untended wives) tells of a more social than spiritual collapse. Nor is he concerned with strict chronology; Forese, who died in 1296, had been dead for four years when the pilgrim wanders into the first canto of the *Inferno*. Such underminings of the factual record, combined with the evasion of textual echoes from the *tenzone*, underscore the metaphorical significance of the Forese episode in the *Comedy*.

The paradigmatic value assigned to the episode necessarily extends to the poetic sphere as well. The conversion from "that life" with Forese to "new life" with Beatrice is also the conversion from the fallen style of the *tenzone* to the new style of "Donne ch'avete." In this ideal chronology, the *tenzone* occupies a position antecedent even to Bonagiunta's old style; it is as complacently rooted in fallen reality as the *stil novo* is free of it. As Dante's personal fall—"quella vita"—is redeemed by the restorative time of Purgatory, so the poetic fall—the *tenzone*—is redeemed by the converted style of the *stil novo*. This poetic conversion takes place in a context of lyric antitheses so overriding that they embrace even the episode's personnel; in the violent contrast between Forese's chaste wife Nella and the "sfacciate donne fiorentine" ("brazen women of Florence" [XXIII, 101]) one could see a continuation of the canto's antithetical mode, carried from the lexical to the figural level. In fact, the

"Voi che 'ntendendo"

terrace of gluttony is played out on a backdrop of contrasting women, good and bad, courtly and anti-courtly: not only Nella and her Florentine opposites, but Beatrice, Piccarda, Gentucca, Mary (from the exempla at the end of canto XXII), and (mentioned in XXIV, 116) Eve.

An episode that deals with lyric themes is thus sustained by the genre's narrative prerequisites, by women. It is not coincidental that in the course of this episode Dante should ask his friend about the location of his sister, or that Bonagiunta should prophesy the aid of a young woman from Lucca; both Piccarda and Gentucca are historical correlatives of the terrace's true heroines, the "ladies who have understanding of love." Most important is the fact that only here does the pilgrim take the opportunity to name Beatrice as the term of his voyage, thus relinquishing his usual practice of indicating her through a periphrasis. He names her because Forese—unlike the majority of the souls he has encountered—knows her, a simple fact with less simple implications. Precisely Forese's historical identity, his connection to a literal past, makes him valuable to a poet whose metaphors require grounding in reality. The fall must have a name, Forese, as salvation has a name, Beatrice, and as conversion occurs under the aegis of Vergil, specifically five days ago, when the moon was full. The irreducible historicity of this poem—the radical newness of its style—retrospectively guarantees all those other poems, and the newness of their style: "le nove rime, cominciando / 'Donne ch'avete intelletto d'amore.'"

"Voi che 'ntendendo il terzo ciel movete"

The last of the *Comedy*'s autocitations, "Voi che 'ntendendo il terzo ciel movete," belongs to *Paradiso* VIII. In the heaven of Venus Dante meets Charles Martel, who declares his whereabouts by citing his friend's canzone, appropriately addressed to the angelic intelligences of this third heaven:

Autocitation and Autobiography

Noi ci volgiam coi principi celesti
d'un giro e d'un girare e d'una sete,
ai quali tu del mondo già dicesti:
'Voi che 'ntendendo il terzo ciel movete'

With one circle, with one circling and with one thirst we revolve with the heavenly Princes, to whom you of the world once did say: "Voi che 'ntendendo il terzo ciel movete"

(Par. VIII, 34-37)

Although readings of Paradiso VIII routinely point to the coincidence between incipit and geographical location, critical inquiry has on the whole done little more than confirm the canzone's superficial suitability.[43] But "Voi che 'ntendendo" is, in fact, far from an obvious choice as the autocitation of the Paradiso, in that it encompasses the defeat and replacement of Beatrice, Dante's paradisiacal guide. Whereas Purgatorio XXIV establishes the Vita Nuova as the bedrock of Dante's poetics, implying that the Convivio is a mistaken detour along the way (an implication confirmed by Purgatorio II), the Comedy's final autocitation—privileged by its position in the Paradiso—seems to return to the Convivio and to Lady Philosophy.[44]

---

[43] In this vein are the readings of Vittorio Vaturi, "Il canto VIII del Paradiso," Lectura Dantis (Florence: Sansoni, 1922); Giovanni Fallani, "Il canto VIII del Paradiso," Lectura Dantis Romana (Turin: Società Editrice Internazionale, 1964); André Pézard, "Charles Martel au Ciel de Venus," in Letture del Paradiso, ed. Vittorio Vettori (Milan: Marzorati, 1970), pp. 71-140; Vincenzo Cioffari, "Interpretazione del canto VIII del Paradiso," Alighieri, 13 (1972), 3-17; Salvatore Accardo, "Il Canto VIII del Paradiso," Nuove letture dantesche (Florence: Le Monnier, 1973), vol. VI, pp. 27-44. Discussions of the heaven of Venus tend to involve comparisons with Francesca, of which Pézard's is the most extreme; the French critic decides that Charles' wife Clemence is in fact present in this heaven, a silent partner for her husband as Paolo is for Francesca. For historical information regarding Dante and the house of Anjou, see Luigi Rocca, "Il canto VIII del Paradiso," Lectura Dantis (Florence: Sansoni, 1903).

[44] In "Purgatorio II: Cato's Rebuke and Dante's scoglio," Hollander states that only "Donne ch'avete" is cited approvingly in the Comedy: "Here is a canzone that is not only true to Beatrice (and that is precisely what the two Convivial odes are not), but, one might argue, true to God (while the

58

"Voi che 'ntendendo"

"Voi che 'ntendendo" appears in the context of an episode that intentionally recalls earlier episodes; the pilgrim's meeting with Charles Martel is modeled on his previous encounters with Casella and Forese. Despite the brevity of Charles' stay in Florence (his visit to the city in 1294 seems to have provided Dante with his only opportunity to meet the Angevin heir), the poet of the *Comedy* views him as a friend, a celestial version of the comrades who populate the slopes of *Purgatory*. A friendship that is prized but somewhat remote, certainly based on a lesser degree of intimacy, is precisely what the poet wants for his last canticle; friendship in the *Paradiso* is intended to contrast with friendship in the *Purgatorio*. Instead of many friends, now there is only one, and this one is a prince whom the poet respected but barely knew. As emblems of the will's attachment to things of this world, friends belong to the dialectic of the second realm, where the soul learns to forego what it most desires for something it desires even more. In *Paradiso* VIII the pilgrim's meeting with a friend underscores, by contrast to earlier meetings, the distanced affectivity of Heaven. Moreover, the meeting is deliberately situated in the sphere of Venus, because the third heaven is dedicated by Dante to dispelling earthly expectations regarding love.

Dante conceives the heaven of Venus as an anticlimax, the textual means by which to disengage the reader (and the pilgrim) from any lingering expectations for earthly (or purgatorial) sen-

---

Convivial odes are not, at least when they are considered as caring more for philosophy than for Revelation)" (p. 353). While I would agree with these remarks in so far as they refer to the status of the canzoni *before* they enter the *Comedy*, I believe that Dante's decision to use them in the *Comedy*, i.e. in a context where positioning implies value, constrains us to look at them from a new perspective. This view is shared by Rachel Jacoff, whose article on Dante's palinodic intent in *Paradiso* VIII provides a complementary analysis of the same episode; see "The Post-Palinodic Smile: *Paradiso* VIII and IX," *Dante Studies*, 98 (1980), 111-122. I do not agree with Carlo Muscetta, "Il canto VIII del *Paradiso*," *Lectura Dantis Scaligera* (Florence: Le Monnier, 1966), who sees "Voi che 'ntendendo" as rising above earthly confusion, nor with Vincent Moleta, who relates the position of the canzone to the fact that it "brings to perfection a notion of spiritual elevation through love" begun by Guinizzelli in "Al cor gentil" (*Guinizzelli in Dante*, p. 129).

timent. He chooses the heaven where both reader and pilgrim most expect to encounter eros—transcendent but still recognizable—as the stage on which to introduce an eros transformed beyond recognition. The poet's intent is to defuse the accumulated conventional significance of "Venus," a significance on which he had capitalized earlier in the poem, and which he preserves in the psychological inclination ascribed to the souls of this heaven. But although the souls of Venus (excluding Charles) avow or are known for their venereal tendencies, these tendencies possess a purely formal value that is countered by the pervasive tone and emphasis of cantos VIII and IX. The denial of the third heaven is the more striking because it is not inviolable; after undercutting affectivity where we expect it, in the heaven of Venus, Dante resurrects it in all its dialectical vigor in the Cacciaguida cantos.

The poet signals his awareness of our expectations in the celebrated opening of the eighth canto, whose twelve verses unfold the intricate Dantesque problematic of "folle amore" (2):

> Solea creder lo mondo in suo periclo
>   che la bella Ciprigna il folle amore
>   raggiasse, volta nel terzo epiciclo;
> per che non pur a lei faceano onore
>   di sacrificio e di votivo grido
>   le genti antiche ne l'antico errore;
> ma Dïone onoravano e Cupido,
>   quella per madre sua, questo per figlio,
>   e dicean ch'el sedette in grembo a Dido;
> e da costei ond' io principio piglio
>   pigliavano il vocabol de la stella
>   che 'l sol vagheggia or da coppa or da ciglio.

Once the world believed, to its peril, that the beautiful Cyprian rayed down mad love, turning in the third epicycle; so that the ancient peoples in their ancient error did honor not only to her, with sacrifice and votive cry, but they honored also Dione and Cupid, the former as her mother, the latter as her son, and they recounted that he had sat in

"Voi che 'ntendendo"

Dido's lap; from her whence I take my beginning they took the name of the star which the sun courts now from behind and now from in front.

(*Par.* VIII, 1-12)

From "the beautiful Cyprian" and her presumed effects, the poet passes, in the next *terzina*, to her cult, practiced by "le genti antiche ne l'antico errore" (6); thence, in lines 7 through 9, to the connection between the "ancient error" and classical culture: line 9, with its reference to Cupid and Dido, implicates no less a text than the *Aeneid*, in whose fourth book the story of Cupid's ruse and Dido's surrender is told. The final *terzina* brings us to the present, and to the issue of the poet's own relation to Venus; whereas the ancients took from this star only a "vocabol," a name or external referent, he—conceiving her differently—takes from her his "principio," his beginning and foundation.[45]

Two key points emerge from this opening passage. First, *folle amore* is recognized, registered, and immediately put into perspective; it is not by chance that the first word of the canto is "Solea." It used to be thus, says the poet, in the time of the "genti antiche ne l'antico errore" (the repetition of the adjective stresses the disjunction from the present), but no longer. The heaven of Venus in this Christian paradise is thus from the start presented in terms of its radical difference: the difference between a *vocabol* and a *principio*, between a superficial and a profound understanding of love. Second, this conceptual difference is immediately related to poetic practice. There is an implied corrective of classical poetry running throughout this heaven: from Vergil whose Dido is compromised at the outset, to Ovid whose volcanic theories are corrected later on. In sharp juxtaposition to these revised ancient poets and texts stand some newer ones; in this heaven we find not only the *Comedy*'s last autocitation but also the *Comedy*'s last lyric poet, the troubadour Folquet de Marselha.

Beginning with the issue of the Cyprian's influence, this heaven

---

[45] The importance of this *terzina* is stressed by Pézard, "Charles Martel au Ciel de Venus," pp. 78-83.

presents us with a graduated series of views regarding Venus: from that of the classical poets, represented by Vergil and Ovid, to that of the courtly lyric, represented by Folquet, to that of Dante's own lyrics, represented by "Voi che 'ntendendo," whose rarified perspective is apparent even in its first verse. Within the context of the third heaven, then, the autocitation serves as part of a general undermining of *folle amore* in all its aspects, both classical and medieval; critics have commented on the canzone's severity, its lack of amorous sweetness, and considered it suitable on these grounds for inclusion into this heaven.[46] In fact, in that "Voi che 'ntendendo" treats love more analytically than passionately, it fits into the general tenor of this heaven's nonerotic treatment of eros. But such a reading, while not incorrect, fails to take into account either the relation of this incipit to the other incipits in the poem, or the actual content of the canzone.

Putting the autocitation of *Paradiso* VIII into diachronic perspective alerts us to the fact that "Voi che 'ntendendo," for all its synchronic aptness, is an apparently inappropriate choice as the canzone to follow and supersede "Donne ch'avete." Such a perspective also encourages us to compare the episode of *Paradiso* VIII with the others that contain quotations from the pilgrim's own poetry. Some commentators have moved in this direction: Bosco establishes a parallel between Charles Martel and Casella, based especially on the reciprocal affection displayed in both episodes and on the presence in both of a canzone; Sapegno, for similar reasons, draws attention to parallels between Charles Martel and Forese.[47] I would carry their observations a step further, suggesting that the meeting with Charles

[46] As a poem dominated by "razionalismo cristiano" (p. 11), Muscetta feels that "Voi che 'ntendendo" is an appropriate choice for this heaven; he is seconded by Accardo and Cioffari.

[47] Accardo comments on the resemblances between the meeting with Charles and the meeting with Casella, while Muscetta points to the meeting with Forese as a term of comparison, explaining that Dante suppresses the earlier dialogue in his later encounter because "Siamo in Paradiso e non più in Purgatorio" (p. 30).

"Voi che 'ntendendo"

Martel is in fact conceived, both structurally and thematically, as a conflation of the two previous meetings.

The moment of encounter between the pilgrim and the prince, in what is the most personalized section of the canto, is modeled on *Purgatorio* II. The inhabitants of Venus are described, immediately before the appearance of Charles Martel, in terms of a beautiful sound; a "Hosanna" heard from within the approaching group of souls is such that the pilgrim will never again cease to desire it:

> e dentro a quei che più innanzi appariro
> sonava '*Osanna*' sì, che unque poi
> di rïudir non fui sanza disiro.
>
> and among those who appeared most in front rang such a "Hosanna" that I have never since been without the desire to hear it again.
>
> (*Par.* VIII, 28-30)

The sound at the beginning of this episode corresponds to the sound at the end of the Casella episode, whose "sweetness still rings inside of me"; both are characterized by the poet's desire to perpetuate their beauty into the present. In the following verses Charles begins to speak; like Casella, he initiates the encounter by revealing that he is Dante's friend. Where Casella attempted to embrace the pilgrim, Charles cites a verse of Dante's poetry as a sign of friendship; he concludes with an offer to interrupt their joyful singing: "e sem sì pien d'amor, che, per piacerti, / non fia men dolce un poco di quïete" ("we are so full of love that, to please you, a little quiet will not be less sweet" [37-39]).

If the language of this last passage is markedly reminiscent of the pilgrim's speech to Casella in *Purgatorio* II (especially the use of "dolce" and "quïete"), line 45 of canto VIII, in which the pilgrim's voice is "di grande affetto impressa" ("stamped with great affection"), surely recalls, as Vaturi noticed, the "grande affetto" with which Casella sought to embrace his friend (*Purg.* II, 77). Most telling are the verses in which Charles presents himself, not by name (his name is not used until the beginning of canto IX, when he is about to disappear), but by evoking the past relation between himself and his visitor:

> Assai m'amasti, e avesti ben onde;
>   che s'io fossi giù stato, io ti mostrava
>   di mio amor più oltre che le fronde.

> Much did you love me, and you had good reason, for had I remained down below, I would have shown you of my love more than the leaves.
>
> (*Par.* VIII, 55-57)

"Assai m'amasti" is a celestial variant of Casella's "Così com' io t'amai / nel mortal corpo, così t'amo sciolta" (*Purg.* II, 88-89), a variant that, by deliberately recalling the purgatorial verses, gives us a measure of the vast difference between the two encounters.

Here the souls converse with the pilgrim not for their own enjoyment, but "per piacerti," for the pilgrim's sake; there they, like the pilgrim, were too ready to sink into the repose generated by Casella's illicit music. Here the pilgrim is entranced by the *Osanna* of the souls, there by a secular song. Here Charles Martel is an oxymoron—a distant friend—who provides the final gloss on Casella's earthbound present tense ("così t'amo") by restricting such affection in heaven to the past absolute ("Assai m'amasti"). Given these facts, we are less surprised by the abrupt transition from the *terzina* quoted above, Charles' most personal and affective statement, to the political discourse which dominates the latter two-thirds of canto VIII, first in relation to Charles' own situation and the house of Anjou, and then in a more theoretical vein, regarding the problem of heredity. As we shall see, politics is used throughout this heaven as the poet's chief means of deflecting the personal, the affective, and the erotic.

The other distancing tool used by the poet in this heaven is rhetoric: the rhetoric of the lengthy geographical periphrases invariably singled out as a feature of these cantos, and employed

"Voi che 'ntendendo" first by Charles in canto VIII, then by Cunizza and Folquet in canto IX. Charles begins his political discourse in line 58 with a series of periphrases encompassing 18 verses (through line 75), by which he indicates the kingdoms that would have been his to rule had he lived: Provence, Naples, Hungary, and Sicily. The periphrasis for Sicily is particularly complex; he begins by situating the island geographically, continues by overturning classical (mythological) volcanic theory and substituting a more naturalistic account, and finishes with a résumé of the island's social history leading to the Sicilian Vespers. The rebellion was caused by bad government, "mala segnoria" (73), in this case that of his grandfather, Charles I of Anjou, who thus provides Charles Martel with a pretext for attacking another member of his family, namely his brother Robert.

While Charles' initial meeting with the pilgrim imitates the Casella episode, this latter part of Charles' discourse (76-84) constitutes the Forese section; it is, I believe, loosely modeled on Forese's invective against his brother, Corso Donati. In both discourses there is a political emphasis, a concern about bad government, a prophetic element, and—strikingly—a brother impugning a brother. Charles' castigation of his brother (the same King Robert so admired by Petrarch and Boccaccio) leads into the didactic sequence on heredity, which corresponds to Forese's didactic diatribe on the lax morals of Florentine women. The most precise parallel between the two episodes is provided by the prophetic element, introduced by the verse "E se mio frate questo antivedesse" ("and were my brother to foresee this" [76]), where the verb *antivedere*, used rarely in the *Comedy*, echoes its appearances in both of Forese's cantos, *Purgatorio* XXIII and XXIV.[48] Although Robert's fate is neither as severe nor as specific as Corso Donati's (who is dragged to Hell on the

---

[48] The verb *antivedere* appears only four times in the *Comedy*: it is used in *Inf.* XXVIII, 78, by the schismatic Pier da Medicina; in *Purg.* XXIII, 109, by Forese in the course of his political invective and prophecy against the Florentine women and their descendants; in *Purg.* XXIV, 46, by Bonagiunta regarding the help to be proffered Dante in his exile by Gentucca; and in *Par.* VIII, 76, by Charles.

tail of a diabolical beast), both fraternal prophecies invoke a coming disaster.

The patterning of this episode on those of Casella and Forese points through sameness to difference; from the intensely familiar use of Forese's name (repeated three times in *Purgatorio* XXIII-XXIV), we have moved to a situation where Charles' name is not even introduced into the episode until after his encounter with the pilgrim has ended. The poet, in what is another example of this heaven's distancing rhetoric, first calls the prince by name in the apostrophe to Clemence, Charles' wife, at the beginning of canto IX: "Da poi che Carlo tuo, bella Clemenza, / m'ebbe chiarito . . ." ("After your Charles, beautiful Clemence, had enlightened me" [1-2]).[49] Eros is evoked—in the possessive "tuo," the adjective "bella"—but simultaneously deflected by two rhetorical strategies: by the apostrophe, which distances itself from the episode at hand through its temporal dislocation into an unspecified future, in which the poet's voice takes the place of the pilgrim's (who had originally asked, in VIII, 44, "Deh, chi siete?"); and by the fact that Carlo and Clemenza both belong to a subordinate clause. The main clause to which they are linked deals with Charles' further remarks ("mi narrò li 'nganni / che ricever dovea la sua semenza" "he narrated the treacheries his seed was to receive" [2-3]), remarks that belong once more to the realm of politics.

The thematic concerns of this heaven are intractably political, indeed such as to compel us to revise the purely autobiographical and retrospective value thus far assigned to Charles Martel, and to reconsider the significance of his identity. In *Purgatorio* II Casella's identity as an enthusiastic but uninformed newcomer is linked to his misdirected singing of "Amor che ne la mente";

---

[49] The commentators have debated as to whether "Clemenza" here refers to Charles' wife or to his homonymous daughter. Those who argue against the wife do so on the grounds that she died in 1295, and that she was therefore dead when Dante apostrophizes her in canto IX. Although the evidence is inconclusive, most modern commentators concur with Del Lungo, cited by Sapegno to the effect that the possessive adjective "tuo" is "essenzialmente coniugale"; in my opinion, the context dictates a wife rather than a daughter.

"Voi che 'ntendendo"

in *Purgatorio* XXIII and XXIV the triumph of the *stil novo* is connected via Forese to a previous fall. In both instances the canzoni are praise songs, one for the wrong lady (Philosophy) and one for the right lady (Beatrice). In *Paradiso* VIII, however, the situation is dramatically different: the pilgrim meets neither a fellow Florentine musician nor versifier, but a prince; and the autocitation is not a praise poem, but a poem of conflict.

"Voi che 'ntendendo," the poem in which the new love for philosophy is privileged over the old love for Beatrice, was written during a period in which Dante experienced these two loves as conflicting; as Foster and Boyde point out, Beatrice's place was "taken by an enormous interest in philosophy and in politics."[50] The incompatibility of these interests is dramatized by the uncompromising stance of the canzone; the exhortation to "resolve to call her your lady henceforth" (48) marks the definitive transfer of allegiance from the first love to the second. Thus, a poem celebrating a lady allegorized as philosophy, written during the decade (following Beatrice's death and the completion of the *Vita Nuova*) in which the poet displays an increasing involvement in philosophy and politics, appears in *Paradiso* VIII in the mouth of a character with a highly political identity—a prince—and in the context of a heaven devoted to political and philosophical concerns.

It is difficult not to see such thematic coincidence as deliberate, especially in the light of the developments of canto IX, where Cunizza and Folquet both inveigh against political corruption, bringing this heaven's quota of politically motivated prophecies to a record high (three in all: Charles predicts disaster for the house of Anjou; Cunizza pits herself against the northern cities of Padova, Treviso, and Feltre; Folquet attacks the Roman curia).

---

[50] *Commentary*, p. 356. Foster and Boyde comment further that if Dante for a time considered philosophy to be implicitly opposed to Beatrice, this is because he then conceived philosophy "in a decidedly 'temporal' light, as though its chief function were to bring man to happiness in this present world" (pp. 356-357). On Dante's Aristotelian rather than Thomistic bias during the period of the *Convivio*, see Gilson, "The Primacy of Ethics," in *Dante and Philosophy*, esp. pp. 105-112.

Autocitation and Autobiography

Like the canzone "Voi che 'ntendendo," in which the literal content strikes an uneasy balance with the *Convivio*'s allegorical interpretation, the characters of this heaven are all dichotomous. Charles is a political figure with no record of venereal excess; as the first soul in Venus' heaven, he serves antiphrastically to underscore the principle of displacement at work here. As eros is deflected by allegory in the canzone, so the remaining characters of this heaven are deflected from their primary personalities: Cunizza's notoriously erotic life is dismissed in 6 lines (31-36), while 27 lines (25-30 and 43-62) are devoted to condemning "la terra prava / italica" ("the depraved land of Italy" [25-26]); likewise Folquet sums up his amatory and poetic career in 12 lines, concentrating instead on his presentation of Raab and his invective against the papal curia. Raab is, of course, symptomatic of this heaven; a Hebrew prostitute who achieves salvation for her aid to Joshua's men, she is presented in canto IX exclusively as a crusader.

The poetics of displacement that governs the heaven of Venus serves to isolate and represent a particular moment in the process of conversion, a moment *in fieri* in which the dialectical elements of the achieved synthesis are still visible in their component parts. The conversion from eros to *caritas* undertaken in cantos VIII and IX is achieved at the outset of canto X, where—in the heaven of the Sun and no longer under the shadow of earth—Love is newly defined in relation to the dynamics of the Trinity: "Guardando nel suo Figlio con l'Amore / che l'uno e l'altro etternalmente spira . . ." ("Looking on his Son with the Love which the one and the other eternally breathe forth" [1-2]). The nonachievement of the previous heaven is not a positive lack, but a symptom of the original conflict, which is still obliquely present, like the shadow of earth that is still felt (a shadow which is, significantly, mentioned for the first and last time in the heaven of Venus [IX, 118]); the fact that Cunizza and Folquet are converts from *folle amore* is registered not positively but negatively, by the duality of their discourses and by the compensation that dictates their political diatribes. The textual status thus assigned by the poet to the third heaven,

"Voi che 'ntendendo"

conceived as the representation of a stage in which the elements of a prior conflict and duality are still visible although no longer conflicting, accounts for the presence and choice of this particular autocitation.

"Voi che 'ntendendo" is a poem about conflict, the conflict experienced by the poet between his love for Beatrice—his mystical, spiritual, and poetical interests—and the other chief interests of his life. Everything about the heaven of Venus speaks to the integration of concerns that on earth were viewed as separate and antagonistic; thus, the pilgrim meets a prince who can quote love poetry, a political lady who loved a poet (a political poet at that), and a poet who became a political figure.[51] The point of the resolutely nonamatory treatment of this heaven is that love can be, and must be, integrated with political and philosophical concerns; in terms of Dante's own career, the point is that the poet must transcend his *Vita Nuova* phase, dominated by an all-consuming if sublimated love, in order to arrive at the *Comedy*, in which eros is welded to a complex of other issues. Although the *Convivio* is the text that effects this transition, the *Convivio*'s error is that it still posits a conflict: either Lady Philosophy or Beatrice. But the conflict that it posits is also a measure of its critical importance as the text that points the poet away from the lyric and parochial sphere of the *Vita Nuova* toward the universality of the *Comedy*.[52] If, in Heaven, Beatrice tolerates the citation of a canzone whose original pur-

---

[51] Cunizza, from a family in political power (she was the sister of the tyrant Ezzelino III da Romano), loved, among others, Sordello, whom this study will show to be—for Dante—a political poet; Folquet became a political figure as Bishop of Toulouse, participating in the Albigensian Crusade. Sordello and Folquet will be discussed in greater detail in Chapter II.

[52] On the transition between the *Vita Nuova* and the *Convivio*, see Salvatore Battaglia, "Il metodo di Dante tra *Vita Nuova* e *Convivio*," in *Esemplarità e antagonismo nel pensiero di Dante* (Naples: Liguori, 1966), pp. 101-120. The importance for the *Comedy* of Dante's political thought as expressed in the last book of the *Convivio* and then in the *Monarchia* is treated by Nardi, "Le rime filosofiche e il *Convivio* nello sviluppo dell'arte e del pensiero di Dante" and "Dal *Convivio* alla *Commedia*," in *Dal Convivio alla Commedia: sei saggi danteschi*, pp. 1-36 and 37-150.

pose was to displace her for "others," she does so to indicate that she and they can now be simultaneously present.

The *Convivio*'s error, then, is in not achieving synthesis, and for this it is in Paradise once more pointedly corrected. When Charles Martel greets the pilgrim, he explains that he is turning with the angelic intelligences of the third heaven, the Principalities, "whom you of the world thus addressed: 'Voi che 'ntendendo il terzo ciel movete' " (36-37). While Dante's canzone is, indeed, addressed to the intelligences of the third heaven, he did not, in the *Convivio*, consider these intelligences to be Principalities. Thus, by way of Charles' polite adjustment, the heaven of Venus becomes the first locus for Dante's self-correction on the matter of angelic hierarchy, an issue resolved finally by Beatrice in canto XXVIII. There she confirms the order laid out by the pseudo-Dionysius in the *De Coelesti Hierarchia*, explaining that Gregory the Great (whom Dante follows in the *Convivio*) had erred.

The most notable difference between the two schemes is the position of the Thrones, whom Gregory lowers from third place (behind the Seraphim and Cherubim) to seventh (above the Angels and Archangels). In *Paradiso* XXVIII the Thrones are the only angelic order to whom Beatrice dedicates a full *terzina*, stating that they belong to the first and highest angelic triad:

> Quelli altri amori che 'ntorno li vonno,
> si chiaman Troni del divino aspetto,
> per che 'l primo ternaro terminonno

> Those other loves who go around them are called Thrones
> of the divine aspect, because they completed the first triad
> (*Par.* XXVIII, 103-105)

Besides this general statement from canto XXVIII, the specific judicial duties of the Thrones are mentioned by Cunizza, who also emphasizes their elevation ("Sù sono specchi, voi dicete Troni, / onde refulge a noi Dio giudicante" "Above are mirrors whom you call Thrones whence God in judgment shines on us" [IX, 61-62]), and much later by the pilgrim ("Ben so io che, se

"Voi che 'ntendendo"

'n cielo altro reame / la divina giustizia fa suo specchio" "I know well that although divine justice makes its mirror in another realm of heaven" [XIX, 28-29]). Not only are the Thrones the most talked about angelic hierarchy in the poem, but a good deal of the interest in them seems to stem from the heaven of Venus, to which they were inappropriately linked in the *Convivio*. Indeed, it seems as though the *terzina* devoted to raising the Thrones at the end of canto XXVIII is matched by the *terzina* devoted to lowering Venus at the canto's beginning; in a context where God is a tiny point, and the heavens nearest to Him are smallest, Venus is singled out for its width, so great that an entire rainbow could not contain it (31-33). The *Comedy* thus redresses the *Convivio*'s imbalance.

In *Paradiso* VIII the emphasis on the Thrones begins indirectly, when Charles Martel locates himself in the third heaven; by specifying that this is the realm of the Principalities, he implies that it is not the realm of the Thrones. The result of his statement is that "Voi che 'ntendendo" is introduced into the text by way of the new order, the Principalities; the sentence structure thus ensures that the canzone is immediately linked to self-correction. In the same way that the third angelic order is made of Principalities, and not of Thrones as the *Convivio* would have it, so the lady now at Dante's side is Beatrice, and not the *donna gentile*. The *Convivio*'s limits are again underscored; as a text it was not able to see with the penetration of the *Comedy*, but rather, like Gregory the Great at the end of canto XXVIII, it must now laugh at its mistakes.

Unlike Gregory, however, the *Convivio*'s mistakes are not restricted to a single issue; its imaginative failures are far more profound. The correction of the *Convivio* in *Paradiso* VIII therefore goes beyond angelology to invest the major thematic concerns of the prose treatise. In the fifth chapter of Book II the *Convivio*'s author, having just outlined the order of the angels, proceeds to apply this doctrine to the first verses of the canzone he is glossing, "Voi che 'ntendendo"; he moves in his discussion from the Thrones, governors of the third heaven, to the incli-

Autocitation and Autobiography

nations and qualities proper to their sphere of influence. As we know, the heaven is Venus, and the disposition is amorous:

> Per che ragionevole è credere che li movitori del cielo de la Luna siano de l'ordine de li Angeli, e quelli di Mercurio siano li Arcangeli, e quelli di Venere siano li Troni; li quali, naturati de l'amore del Santo Spirito, fanno la loro operazione, connaturale ad essi, cioè lo movimento di quello cielo, pieno d'amore, dal quale prende la forma del detto cielo uno ardore virtuoso per lo quale le anime di qua giuso s'accendono ad amore, secondo la loro disposizione.

> So that it is reasonable to believe that the movers of the heaven of the Moon are the order of Angels, and those of Mercury are the Archangels, and those of Venus are Thrones. These last, informed and nourished with the love of the Holy Spirit, effect their operation which is connatural to them, that is the movement of that heaven full of love, from which movement the form of that heaven takes on a virtuous ardor through which the souls down below are kindled to love according to their disposition.
>
> (II, v, 13)

Having established the relation between the Thrones, Venus, and love, and stressing the ability of this heaven to inflame love in souls so disposed, the author passes to the ancients, and to their views on the effects of this heaven: "E perchè li antichi s'accorsero che quello cielo era qua giù cagione d'amore, dissero Amore essere figlio di Venere . . ." ("And because the ancients realized that that heaven was the cause of love down here, they said that Love was the son of Venus" [II, v, 14]).

This set of relations, first established by Dante in the *Convivio*, is resurrected in the opening of *Paradiso* VIII, where the poet once more links the heaven of Venus to classical culture, and where he pursues an identical chain of reasoning: from Venus ("la bella Ciprigna"), to the ancients ("le genti antiche"), to Venus' son Cupid ("ma Dione onoravano e Cupido / quella per madre sua, questo per figlio"), to Vergil ("e dicean ch'el sedette in grembo a Dido"). We now see that this progression is inherited from the *Convivio*, where the links are much more explicit, links between Venus and love and the ancients, and—picking up from where we left off in our quotation of Book II, chapter v—links between Cupid ("Amore" in the *Convivio*) and Vergil: ". . . [li antichi] dissero Amore essere figlio di Venere, sì come testimonia Vergilio nel primo de lo Eneida, ove dice Venere ad Amore: 'Figlio, vertù mia, figlio del sommo padre, che li dardi di Tifeo non curi' " ("the ancients said that Love was the son of Venus, as Vergil testifies in the first book of the *Aeneid*, where Venus says to Love: 'Son, my strength, son of the highest father, you who fear not the bolts of Typhoeus' " [II, v, 14]). Here, as again in the *Comedy*, the poet demonstrates the pagan belief that Cupid was Venus' son by citing the *Aeneid*; whereas in the *Convivio* he cites a passage from *Aeneid* I in which Venus addresses her son, in the *Comedy* he much more powerfully depicts Cupid's role by evoking in one verse the tragedy of Book IV.

Our passage from the *Convivio* concludes by citing not only Vergil on Cupid, but also Ovid ("e Ovidio, nel quinto di Metamorphoseos, quando dice che Venere disse ad Amore: 'Figlio, armi mie, potenzia mia' " "and Ovid, in the fifth book of the *Metamorphoses*, when he says that Venus said to Love: 'Son, my arms, my power' " [II, v, 14]), thus invoking both classical authorities on love. And, as we know, both these authorities are present, and in the same order, in *Paradiso* VIII, where Vergil's indirect presence in line 9 is followed by Ovid's even more indirect presence in Charles Martel's periphrasis for Sicily. The Angevin prince describes Sicily as that island which is darkened by a thick fog between the capes of "Pachino" to the south (Cape Passero) and "Peloro" to the north (Cape Faro), a darkness that is caused not—as the ancients believed—by the ashes spewed forth by the giant Typhoeus imprisoned under Mount Etna, but by sulfurous gases: "non per Tifeo ma per nascente solfo" ("not by Typhoeus but by rising sulfur" [VIII, 70]). The Dantesque periphrasis for Sicily, beginning "E la bella Trinacria" in line 67, is inspired by Ovid throughout, specifically by a passage in

Book V of the *Metamorphoses* in which the Latin poet ascribes the eruptions of Etna to the spouting of the giant Typhoeus, and in which the island (called "Trinacris") is parceled into the same geographical segments picked up by Dante: "He [Typhoeus] struggles hard, and often fights to rise again, but his right hand is held down by Ausonian Pelorus and his left by you, Pachynus."[53]

Dante relies on Ovid in order to revise him, his point being, of course, that Typhoeus is no more to be taken seriously than the beautiful Cyprian of the canto's opening verses; he is not responsible for volcanic eruptions, and she is not responsible for *folle amore*. Both the giant and the goddess are rendered impotent in *Paradiso* VIII. And, if Dante goes out of his way to introduce Ovid into this canto, he does so as part of his overall correction of the passage from the *Convivio*, a passage that contains all the elements later raised in *Paradiso* VIII: the Thrones, the ancients, Vergil, Ovid. Even Typhoeus is present in the *Convivio*, in the citation from *Aeneid* I, where Venus refers to her son as "contemptuous of the Typhoean bolts," i.e. unafraid even of Jupiter, whose thunderbolt had chastened the giant. The *Convivio* passage, in which Dante translates the Vergilian verse with the phrase "che li dardi di Tifeo non curi," constitutes the only occasion, prior to the *Comedy*, in which the giant figures in one of Dante's texts.[54]

These details serve to confirm the relation between *Convivio* II, v and *Paradiso* VIII.[55] In canto VIII Dante systematically

---

[53] The Latin text, taken from the Loeb Classical Library edition, trans. F. J. Miller, 2 vols. (1916; repr. Cambridge: Harvard U. Press and London: William Heinemann, 1971 [vol. I] and 1968 [vol. II]), reads as follows: "nititur ille quidem pugnatque resurgere saepe, / dextra sed Ausonio manus est subiecta Peloro, / laeva, Pachyne, tibi" (*Metamorphoses* V, 349-351).

[54] Typhoeus is among the giants in the pit surrounding Cocytus, and is named in *Inf.* XXXI, 124: "Non ci fare ire a Tizio né a Tifo."

[55] Another corroborative detail of the relation between the two texts is Dante's use of the word *epiciclo* at the outset of *Paradiso* VIII, where Venus is "volta nel terzo epiciclo" (3). This unique occurrence of *epiciclo* in the *Comedy* reflects the *Convivio* passage, which continues, after the section quoted above, with a discussion of the threefold movements of Venus, listed as follows: "uno, secondo che la stella si muove per lo suo epiciclo; l'altro, secondo che lo epiciclo si muove

"Voi che 'ntendendo" presents and discounts point after point from the passage in the *Convivio*: the Thrones have become Principalities; Venus and Cupid alike are an "antico errore"; the poets who believed in them are dupes. But canto VIII goes beyond these particulars to the larger error behind them, to wit, the privileging of classical culture—philosophy over revelation, the *donna gentile* over Beatrice—which is, from the perspective of the later Dante, the *Convivio*'s most serious flaw.[56] The true error of the *Convivio* is the status it accords to ancient beliefs; the critique of canto VIII focuses on one set of ancient beliefs, those regarding Venus. Thus, the *Convivio* passage recounts that, because the ancients realized that the heaven of Venus was the cause of love on earth, they believed that Love or Cupid was her son: "E perchè li antichi s'accorsero che quello cielo era qua giù cagione d'amore, dissero Amore essere figlio di Venere . . ." (II, v, 14). Although the *Convivio*'s author does not accept the classical conclusions, that there is a goddess Venus whose son is Love, he seems not to argue with the basic premise, i.e. that the heaven of Venus causes love on earth. His choice of words, especially his use of the verb *s'accorsero*, seems to indicate his fundamental agreement on this score.

The relation between Venus and causality is precisely what

---

con tutto il cielo igualmente con quello del Sole; lo terzo, secondo che tutto quello cielo si muove seguendo lo movimento de la stellata spera" ("one, according to which the star moves along its epicycle; next, according to which the epicycle moves with the entire heaven and equally with that of the Sun; third, according to which that entire heaven moves following the movement of the starry sphere" [*Convivio* II, v, 16]). Like the other sections from *Convivio* II, v we have discussed, this passage was undoubtedly in Dante's mind when he composed *Paradiso* VIII.

[56] Mazzeo demonstrates that the *Convivio* is excessively dependent on ancient philosophers in its enthusiastic assessment of nature's role in the formation of human beings, and also shows how in the *Paradiso* Dante returns to a position of "greater Christian rigor" (p. 35); see "*Convivio* IV, xxi and *Paradiso* XIII: Another of Dante's Self-Corrections," *Philological Quarterly*, 38 (1959), 30-36. In "*Panis Angelorum*: A Palinode in the *Paradiso*," *Dante Studies*, 95 (1977), 81-94, Daniel J. Ransom contrasts Dante's use of the phrase "pan de li angeli" in *Paradiso* II, 11 with its previous appearance in the *Convivio*, showing how "in the *Paradiso* 'pan de li angeli' reacquires its theological substance" (p. 92).

is at issue in the *Comedy; Paradiso* VIII is at pains to revoke the notion of celestially induced eros. Outright celestial influence is, of course, denied in general terms throughout the *Comedy*, from Marco Lombardo's discourse on free will to Beatrice's attack on the "poison" in Plato's theory of astral return. But, perhaps because the belief in a necessary inclination toward *folle amore* is particularly widespread and pernicious, the poet uses the heaven of Venus specifically to combat the idea that Venus *causes* love on earth;[57] the perils inherent in such beliefs are therefore immediately raised in this heaven's first verse—"Solea creder lo mondo in suo periclo"—with its emphasis on the dangers besetting a misguided world. Nor is the classical position criticized only in these verses; Charles Martel later resumes the topic in his discourse on heredity, explaining that the influences of the heavens, which left to themselves would be disastrously mechanistic, are in fact ordered and regulated by divine providence. This concluding emphasis on astral limitation reinforces the admonition regarding excessive credence with which the canto begins.

The world's peril is perhaps also the peril of the *Convivio's* author; it is interesting that Charles, naming a canzone from the *Convivio*, refers to its author as "del mondo," of the world. At any rate, the correction of the *Convivio* that runs through *Paradiso* VIII ultimately addresses itself to the major issue of the treatise's erroneous trust in classical culture and thought, a trust that is openly condemned by Beatrice in *Purgatorio* XXXIII, where she refers deridingly to the pilgrim's faith in "that school which you have followed" (85-86). This issue is related to the autocitation of *Paradiso* VIII by way of the *donna gentile*, who is allegorized as Lady Philosophy, and whose preeminence in the canzone and in the treatise is part of the *Convivio's* error, and part of what the *Comedy* is correcting. If,

---

[57] Dante's desire to discredit erotic determinism may have autobiographical and palinodic roots; one thinks, for instance, of the sonnet to Cino in which Dante proclaims the subjugation of free will to Love ("Io sono stato con Amore insieme"), a position he dramatizes in the great canzone *montanina* ("Amor, da che convien pur ch'io mi doglia").

"Voi che 'ntendendo"

then, "Voi che 'ntendendo" belongs to a generally corrective framework in *Paradiso* VIII, how do we account for its privileged position among the *Comedy*'s autocitations?

Let us begin by considering the role of "Voi che 'ntendendo" in the context of Dante's lyric poetry. Editions of the *Rime* place the canzone shortly after the poems of the *Vita Nuova*, establishing the priority of "Voi che 'ntendendo" for Dante's post-*Vita Nuova* production.[58] The use of "Voi che 'ntendendo" as a new starting point is, moreover, justified by Dante's own practice; he uses it as lead canzone and point of reference for the sequence of poems devoted to the *donna gentile*, and he places it first in the *Convivio*. The importance attached to this canzone is also signaled by the fact that "Voi che 'ntendendo" is the only one of his lyrics whose incipit Dante cites twice, not only in the *Comedy* but also in the sonnet "Parole mie."

We recall that "Parole mie" explicitly refers to "Voi che 'ntendendo" as a new poetic beginning. Summoning back all the poems previously sent to this lady, the poet addresses his errant words:

Parole mie che per lo mondo siete,
voi che nasceste *poi ch'io cominciai*
a dir per quella donna in cui errai:
'Voi che 'ntendendo il terzo ciel movete'

---

[58] Foster and Boyde place one poem, the sonnet on Lisetta, between "Oltre la spera" (the last sonnet of the *Vita Nuova*) and "Voi che 'ntendendo"; they do this because of Barbi's opinion that the Lisetta sonnet ("Per quella via che la bellezza corre") represents a phase in the conflict between Beatrice and her rival of the *Vita Nuova*. In explaining the order of the poems in their edition, Foster and Boyde comment that they take as a "firm starting-point for Dante's development after the *Vita Nuova* the canzone 'Voi che 'ntendendo'" (Introduction, *The Poems*, p. xxxix). The Barbi-Maggini edition passes from "Rime del tempo della *Vita Nuova*" to "Tenzone con Forese Donati"; Barbi-Pernicone picks up with "Rime allegoriche e dottrinali," of which the first is "Voi che 'ntendendo." Thus the canzone is separated from the poems of the *Vita Nuova* only by the *tenzone* which, not being love poetry, does not affect the priority of "Voi che 'ntendendo." In "Le rime filosofiche e il *Convivio* nello sviluppo dell'arte e del pensiero di Dante," Nardi posits "Voi che 'ntendendo" as the beginning of a new poetic cycle (p. 2).

Words of mine who are throughout the world, you who
were born *when I began* to write for that lady in whom I
erred "Voi che 'ntendendo il terzo ciel movete"
(1-4; italics mine)

"Voi che 'ntendendo" is thus named as the text in which the poet began ("poi ch'io cominciai") to write about "that lady in whom I erred." The judgment expressed by this last phrase, "quella donna in cui errai," is shared by the *Comedy*; indeed, we have thus far concentrated on the *Paradiso*'s correction of "Voi che 'ntendendo" as a poem that subscribes to that misleading lady. But the sonnet "Parole mie" testifies also to a positive significance possessed by the canzone, a significance whose emblem is the expression "poi ch'io cominciai."[59] "Voi che 'ntendendo" is a song of conflict, but also a song of beginning; in the history of Dante's artistic growth, the canzone initiates those fundamental developments that follow Beatrice's death and the writing of the *Vita Nuova*.

The status of "Voi che 'ntendendo" in the *Comedy* hinges on the fact that the canzone marks a turning point, a crucial watershed, in Dante's career. Its position in Dante's canon is in fact analogous to that of the *Convivio*. From the perspective of the *Comedy*, the *Convivio* is both an erring text that has been eclipsed by the return to Beatrice as a primary source of signification, and also—paradoxically—the text that makes the *Comedy* possible. Although in the later Dante's retrospective scheme the *Vita Nuova* is idealized as the repository of the *Comedy*'s fundamental thematics, there is nonetheless an acknowledgment that these themes could not have matured in scope and complexity without the prior intervention of the *Convivio*. "Voi che 'ntendendo," as the *Convivio*'s first canzone and the text in which the poet first adopts a stance that is decisively not that of the *Vita Nuova*, signifies the moment of turning

---

[59] De Robertis notices the authority "Parole mie" confers on "Voi che 'ntendendo," saying that for the sonnet the canzone marks "il vero inizio, il decisivo riconoscimento del *nuovo* fatto" ("Il libro della Vita Nuova e il libro del Convivio," p. 19).

"Voi che 'ntendendo"

from "lyric" to "epic" concerns, a turning that is ultimately responsible for the *Comedy*.

As an autocitation, then, "Voi che 'ntendendo" marks the passage from the restricted world of the *Vita Nuova* to the larger world of the *Convivio*. In one sense the canzone marks this turn negatively, by positing a conflict that was in fact unnecessary, and as the harbinger of a phase that would need to be surpassed. In the *Comedy*, however, the *Convivio*'s conflict is resolved through the simultaneous presence of the two terms that in the treatise could not coexist: "politics" (the prince, and the other figures of this heaven who all bear a political significance) on the one hand, and "Beatrice" on the other. In the *Comedy*, in other words, the conflict of the canzone is reviewed and reread; from this final perspective it is seen as not conflict but poetic growth, forward motion after the stasis of the *Vita Nuova*'s completion.

As the *Convivio* stands in dialectical relation to the *Vita Nuova*, so "Voi che 'ntendendo" stands in dialectical relation to "Donne ch'avete." Whereas the latter text is a *summa*, a fulfillment (and is therefore celebrated in *Purgatorio* XXIV as the pinnacle of Dante's achievement in the lyric mode), the former achieves significance not for what it has done but for what it leaves undone. Whereas "Donne ch'avete" is important for itself, "Voi che 'ntendendo" is important as a sign pointing beyond itself. Whereas "Donne ch'avete" signifies an end (an end that later will be valorized as a repository of all beginnings), "Voi che 'ntendendo" signifies a beginning. Moreover, it draws its value precisely from its relation to its precursor; if "Voi che 'ntendendo" is a new beginning in Dante's career, it is so by virtue of the fact that it is the first of his texts to challenge the assumptions of the *Vita Nuova*.

Not surprisingly, "Voi che 'ntendendo" presents itself as different from its forerunners. The emblem of its difference is the nonlyric word "grandezza," used here in order to praise the new lady, who is "saggia e cortese ne la sua grandezza" (47). Thus, even as a love poem, "Voi che 'ntendendo" bears the signs of its unlikeness; "grandezza" is the lexical representative—along with "transmutata," from line 44, which appears only here in Dante's lyrics—of all the larger and nonlyric themes and concerns that will surface in the *Convivio*. The canzone continues to insist on its special status: its discourse can be proffered only to the angelic intelligences of the third heaven, being too "new" for other ears ("udite il ragionar ch'è nel mio core, / ch'io nol so dire altrui, sì mi par novo" "listen to the speech which is in my heart, for I do not know how to express it to others, it seems so new to me" [2-3]); again in the first stanza the poet draws attention to the novelty of his condition ("Io vi dirò del cor la novitate" "I will tell you of the newness of my heart" [10]). The emphasis on the poem's originality reappears in the *congedo*, where the poet comments that, due to the canzone's difficulty, few will understand it; in the penultimate verse he calls it "diletta mia novella." This sense of literal newness finds its confirmation in the other newness with which this poem is invested; as the first of Dante's love lyrics to carry an allegorical significance, "Voi che 'ntendendo" is a particularly fitting emblem for a turning point.

There is, however, a poem in Dante's canon that might be said to mark a shift more explicitly than "Voi che 'ntendendo," and this is "Le dolci rime," the last poem of the *Convivio*. In the first stanza the poet situates the canzone with respect to its predecessors:

> Le dolci rime d'amor ch'i solia
> cercar ne' miei pensieri,
> convien ch'io lasci; non perch'io non speri
> ad esse ritornare,
>   ma perché li atti disdegnosi e feri,
> che ne la donna mia
> sono appariti, m'han chiusa la via
> de l'usato parlare.
>   E poi che tempo mi par d'aspettare,
> diporrò giù lo mio soave stile,
> ch'i' ho tenuto nel trattar d'amore;
> e dirò del valore,

"Voi che 'ntendendo"

> per lo qual veramente omo è gentile,
> con rima aspr'e sottile

> I must leave the sweet love poems that I was accustomed to seek out in my thoughts; not because I do not hope to return to them, but because the disdainful and harsh acts which have appeared in my lady have closed the way of my usual speech. And since it now seems a time for waiting, I will lay down my sweet style which I have used in treating love, and I will speak of the quality through which man is truly noble, with harsh and subtle rhymes
>
> (1-14)

The exordium explains how the poem came to be written: because his lady's proud behavior has blocked all further discourse with her, the poet is temporarily putting aside "le dolci rime d'amor"; while waiting for her to soften, he proposes to write about nobility, the "valore, / per lo qual veramente omo è gentile," not in his accustomed "soave stile," but with "rima aspr'e sottile."

Like the sonnet "Parole mie," this canzone is introduced as a moment in which the poet is out of his lady's favor. Unlike the sonnet, however, "Le dolci rime" finds a radical solution to the problem. Whereas "Parole mie," in that it is a negative love poem, a renouncing of the beloved, remains within the narrative structure that links the various poems to the *donna gentile*, "Le dolci rime" breaks out from this structure altogether. In the canzone her coldness produces not the lover's quarrel sanctioned by the plot, as in the previous renunciations, but something more significant, namely a change of genre. Rather than continuing to write "sweet love poems," the poet undertakes a new kind of poetry, written in a new register, "with harsh and subtle rhymes." The writing of "Le dolci rime" thus marks the transition to a later stage in Dante's poetic development, the stage characterized by his moral and doctrinal verse; the canzone is in fact, as was noted earlier, the first in a series of moral poems. We see, then, why Foster and Boyde can claim that in "Le dolci rime" Dante "comes about as near to making a fresh start as any mature poet can do," for it is here that Dante first becomes a moral poet.[60] And, because the doctrinal canzoni accommodate a lyric mode to moral themes, they constitute the indispensable link between Dante's early poetry and the *Comedy*.

If the last of the *Comedy*'s autocitations is chosen with a view to marking an internal transition toward the *poema sacro*, we may wonder why "Le dolci rime" is not recited in the *Paradiso* instead of "Voi che 'ntendendo." The fact that the three autocitations are stylistically homogeneous, and that all belong stylistically to the poet's *stil novo* phase, seems not unimportant in this regard. "Le dolci rime" effects a radical discontinuity with respect to the style of its predecessors; as its first stanza declares, it is no longer *soave*. Precisely this characteristic, which on the one hand strengthens its connection to the *Comedy* (where the poet will request, when he needs them, "rime aspre e chiocce"), on the other unsuits it for inclusion among the autocitations. Unlike "Le dolci rime," "Voi che 'ntendendo" can mark the transition to larger themes from *within* the lyric mode, a mode that is essentially amatory and "sweet"; in fact, the canzone's stylistic continuity with "Amor che ne la mente" and "Donne ch'avete" is a major part of its point.

"Voi che 'ntendendo" works both ways: as the initiator of the conflict that would eventually lead Dante to devote himself entirely to philosophy, it points forward to his moral and ethical verse, to "Le dolci rime"; as a love poem to the *donna gentile*, it looks back to the *Vita Nuova*, and to "Donne ch'avete." As compared to the later didactic canzoni, "Voi che 'ntendendo" is part of a continuum that begins in the *Vita Nuova*: Beatrice is still present (although about to be displaced); the *Vita Nuova*'s dictum against nonamatory lyric has not yet been explicitly reversed (although the use of allegory would in itself imply that lyrics can now be composed "sopra altra matera che amorosa").[61] The poem's form links it to the past, and even though

---

[60] *Commentary*, p. 211.

[61] In *Vita Nuova* XXV Dante states that the vernacular lyric should be devoted exclusively to love poetry: "E questo è contra coloro che rimano sopra altra matera che amorosa, con ciò sia cosa che cotale modo di parlare fosse dal principio

"Voi che 'ntendendo"

its meaning may be more difficult to comprehend than that of earlier poems, "tanto la parli faticosa e forte" ("so tiring and hard is your speech" [55]), its last verse exhorts us to remember its beautiful appearance, "Ponete mente almen com'io son bella!" ("Consider at least how beautiful I am!").

If the canzone's exterior beauty connects it to the past, its inner difficulty connects it to the future, to Dante's didactic verse and ultimately to the *Comedy*. And it is, finally, this difficulty that accounts for the presence of "Voi che 'ntendendo" in the heaven of Venus, a "difficult" heaven. As it appears in the second book of the *Convivio*, accompanied by its allegorical gloss, "Voi che 'ntendendo" implies the transition that "Le dolci rime" renders explicit; it implies transition through conflict and ambivalence, the same conflict and ambivalence represented in the heaven of Venus. Precisely because it is about conflict, "Voi che 'ntendendo" can best serve as a marker for the stage beyond conflict, a stage in which both terms have not yet been resolved out of existence, but rather coexist, as Beatrice and the canzone coexist in *Paradiso* VIII. At the same time, in that it is ostensibly a love poem, to which a deeper and more public meaning has been added, "Voi che 'ntendendo" can best dramatize Dante's transition, from within the lyric, to a nonlyric and nonprivate mode.

This last duality, the coexistence of a private mode with a public meaning, is mirrored in the episode of the *Paradiso*. It is appropriate that in the heaven of love we should find the *Comedy*'s last lyric love poem as well as its last lyric love poet; yet, in this heaven, both function less as themselves than as signifiers of what lies beyond them. Both "Voi che 'ntendendo" and Folquet de Marselha (of whom more will be said later) are chosen as emblems of transition from the private to the public, a transition that they themselves do not fully achieve but to which they bear a deictic relation. And perhaps, when all is said

---

trovato per dire d'amore" ("And this is against those who write poetry on a subject other than love, since this method of writing was from the beginning discovered in order to write on love" [XXV, 6]).

and done, all of the *Comedy*'s autocitations are chosen for their ability to point beyond. The three poems share two common features; they all belong to Dante's *stil novo* register, and their incipits all emphasize the intellect. That is, they all point, from within the *stil novo*, to beyond the *stil novo*, to the radically transformed eros of the *Comedy*. "Amor che ne la *mente* mi ragiona," "Donne ch'avete *intelletto* d'amore," "Voi che 'ntendendo il terzo ciel movete"—the intellective stress of these verses unite all these canzoni as redeemed poetry.

The aim of this chapter has been to clarify some of the autobiographical impulses at work in the *Comedy*. If autobiography is a mode in which the urge for order is particularly acute, an urge that is translated into a teleological imperative, the autobiography of the *Comedy* is governed by a dual pressure: the one exerted by the mode, and the other by the providential framework. In the *Comedy*, all characters, all themes, all texts and their makers are inserted into a providential structure that guarantees the nature of the ending. In the autobiographical instance (and all of Dante's texts are profoundly autobiographical), the pressure imposed by providence is supplemented by the pressure implicit in the discourse, a narrative exigency that accounts for the self-consuming revisionism of these texts. This pressure, always present as the deep meaning of Dante's narrative structure, appears on the surface in some more "superficial" forms: the prose and the *divisioni* of the *Vita Nuova*, the gloss of the *Convivio*, the autocitations of the *Comedy*. From this point of view it was a foregone conclusion that the final autocitation would signify not itself but the guaranteed ending; "Voi che 'ntendendo" is yet one more new beginning to be transformed—"transmutata"—into a sign for the *Comedy* itself. And finally, in passing from Dante's treatment of himself to his treatment of his peers, we should note that the teleological imperative structured into his own "life" is, naturally, imposed onto the lives of others.

II

Lyric Quests

Historiography Revisited:
" 'l Notaro e Guittone e me"

The historiographical knot of the *Comedy* centers, appropriately enough, around the knot of *Purgatorio* XXIV: "il nodo / che 'l Notaro e Guittone e me ritenne / di qua dal dolce stil novo ch'i' odo!" (55-57). Whereas the first part of the pilgrim's conversation with Bonagiunta deals solely with Dante's internal poetic biography, implicitly situating "Donne ch'avete" with respect to his total oeuvre, Bonagiunta's reply raises external questions of poetic genealogy and historical precedence. Whereas the pilgrim articulates poetic principles in a vacuum, the older poet draws the historical implications of those principles, discovering in the pilgrim's poetic credo a criterion of measurement by which he judges earlier Italian poetry—" 'l Notaro e Guittone e me"—and finds it lacking. There are, in fact, two distinct moments accommodated by the dialogue's triadic structure; the personal and the historical are both present. We cannot, given the identity of the pilgrim's interlocutor and the nature of his comments, combined with the additional poetic references of *Purgatorio* XXVI, avoid the historiographical intentions of this passage. On the other hand, its historiographical weight does not detract from its impact at the level of autobiography.[1]

[1] In my opinion, Dante wishes to make both the following points in this

Lyric Quests

Dante intends us to draw a line between old and new; to this end, he provides us with names, both in canto XXIV and again in canto XXVI, that we can sketch in on either side of the imagined boundary, thus obtaining a rough chronology. Canto XXIV extends the scope of the investigation backwards to the beginning of the Italian tradition by mentioning the Notary, Giacomo da Lentini; we notice that the passage refers only to poetic masters, *capiscuola*, who implicate not only themselves but also their followers in an arc that spans each phase of the early Italian lyric: from the Notary, head of the Sicilian school, to Guittone, head of the Tuscan school, to Bonagiunta, a mediator, or Siculo-Tuscan.[2] We notice, also, the binary oppositions—we/you, one/other—that structure Bonagiunta's rejoinder, emanating from the original polarity at the heart of his

---

passage: (1) there is a new style that pertains to a group of new poets; this is the *stil novo* in the generic sense, defined historically as that style or manner to which the older poets named here cannot aspire; (2) within this new style, there is a truly new style, characterized by the *nove rime*, and this is Dante's own *stil novo*. A similar conclusion is reached by Franco Suitner, " 'Colui che fore trasse le nove rime,' " *Lettere italiane*, 28 (1976), 339-345. A balanced case for the existence of the school, based in particular on the perceptions of other poets, as documented by the various poetic challenges of contemporaries like Guido Orlandi and Onesto degli Onesti, is made by Mario Marti, *Storia dello Stil nuovo*, 2 vols. (Lecce: Milella, 1973); volume I also provides a useful summary of earlier criticism on the *stil novo*. For a résumé of more recent critical opinion, see Marti's "Sullo Stil nuovo e sugli stilnovisti: linee della problematica recente," *Cultura e scuola* 16, nos. 63-64 (1977), 19-28. Another moderate interpretation is that of Antonio Enzo Quaglio, *Gli stilnovisti*, in *Lo Stilnovo e la poesia religiosa*, vol. I of *Il Duecento: Dalle origini a Dante* (Bari: Laterza, 1970).

[2] The priority of the Sicilian school for Dante is established by *De Vulgari Eloquentia* I, xii, 2. Contini considers Bonagiunta "l'autentico trapiantatore dei modi siciliani in Toscana" (*Poeti del Duecento*, vol. I, p. 258). On Bonagiunta in the *Comedy*, see: James E. Shaw, "Dante and Bonagiunta," *The Annual Report of the Dante Society*, 52-54 (1936), 1-18; Maria Simonelli, "Bonagiunta e la problematica dello stil novo," *Dante Studies*, 86 (1968), 65-83; Marcello Ciccuto, "Dante e Bonagiunta: reperti allusivi nel canto XXIV del *Purgatorio*," *Lettere italiane*, 34 (1982), 386-395; R. L. Martinez, "The Pilgrim's Answer to Bonagiunta and the Poetics of the Spirit," *Stanford Italian Review*, 3 (1983), 37-63.

Historiography Revisited

discourse, the prepositional phrase "di qua dal," that effectively divides all poets into "here" or "there," "us or them":

> "O frate, *issa vegg' io*," diss' elli, "il nodo
> che 'l Notaro e Guittone e me ritenne
> *di qua dal* dolce stil novo ch'i' odo!
> *Io veggio* ben come *le vostre* penne
> di retro al dittator sen vanno strette,
> che de *le nostre* certo non avvenne;
> e qual più a gradire oltre si mette,
> non vede più da *l'uno a l'altro* stilo";
> e, quasi contentato, si tacette.

"O brother, *now I see*," he said, "the knot which held the Notary and Guittone and me *on this side of* the sweet new style which I hear! *I see* well how *your* pens follow closely after the dictator, which with *ours* certainly did not happen; and he who sets himself to proceed further sees no more *from one to the other* style." And, as if satisfied, he was silent.

(55-63; italics mine)

The dichotomy is temporal, extending from the stressed "now" of understanding ("issa vegg' io," "io veggio") to the "then" of ignorance, from "our" nonperforming pens to "your" capable ones, from "one to the other" style. The fact that on one side we find carefully chosen names and on the other the amorphous category "dolce stil novo" only strengthens the disparity, the sense of an unbridged gap.

Purgatorio XXVI adds to the general picture provided by canto XXIV: the historical framework is enlarged to incorporate the Provençal tradition; more names are forthcoming. An Italian poet, Guinizzelli, is singled out from the unprivileged past as a precursor to the privileged present; his poetry is carefully connected to Dante's and to the "dolce stil novo" invoked by Bonagiunta by a double use of the key word "dolce": "Li dolci detti vostri" of XXVI, 112 echoes "rime d'amor . . . dolci e leggiadre" from XXVI, 99. If the plural of canto XXIV, "vostre penne," is dismissed by some critics as a sudden shift to the honorific (permissible in early Italian syntax), the plural of canto XXVI is not so easily bypassed.³ Here Dante calls Guinizzelli a poetic father, who has engendered not only Dante himself, but also other love poets; presumably, as Guinizzelli's metaphoric "sons," these others are contemporaries of Dante: "il padre / mio e de li altri miei miglior che mai / rime d'amor usar dolci e leggiadre" ("the father of me and of the others my betters who ever used sweet and graceful rhymes of love" [97-99]). In the light of this passage a plural connotation to "dolce stil novo" is, I believe, inescapable. *Purgatorio* XXVI thus serves to confirm and buttress canto XXIV: the later canto not only strengthens our sense of a dichotomized poetic history (even picking up Guittone again as an example of the old style), but also continues to wrap a deliberate anonymity around the practitioners of the new; where before they were hidden by the phrase "vostre penne," they are now identified cryptically as "miei miglior" in line 98.

The anonymity that afflicts Dante's "betters" is suggestive. The sense of a plural is required in order to create the historical framework Dante desires in this context; tradition, continuity, genealogy, paternity—the concepts he is here invoking—all require groupings, pluralities, for their enactments. Moreover, the plurals of cantos XXIV and XXVI are consonant with earlier groupings from a historically minded text Dante certainly has

---

³ Much of the discussion of *Purgatorio* XXIV has centered on the value of "vostre penne"; while accepting the theoretical possibility of a shift in Bonagiunta's speech from *tu* to *voi*, Marti points out that "vostre penne" in line 58 is answered by "de le nostre," where the reference to a group is certain, in line 60 (*Storia dello Stil nuovo*, vol. I, p. 48). And Vittorio Russo, who denies that there is an implicit reference to a school of *stilnovisti* in this passage, nonetheless does not consider the argument that "vostre" is an honorific to be persuasive; he prefers to break the impasse created by "vostre penne" by substituting the textual variant "nove penne" ("Il 'nodo' del Dolce Stil Novo," *Medioevo romanzo*, 3 [1976], 236-264). Mark Musa, "The 'Sweet New Style' That I Hear," does away with the group of *stilnovisti* by taking "vostre" as the honorific and "penne" as "wings," so that the passage refers to the poet's "wingèd flight behind Love" (p. 128).

in mind in these sections of the *Purgatorio*, namely the *De Vulgari Eloquentia*. There he was more explicit regarding those of his contemporaries he considered his poetic comrades, on one occasion using an expression that seems (as has frequently been noted) like an anticipation of the formula "dolce stil novo," referring to Cino da Pistoia and himself as the vernacular poets who have composed "dulcius subtiliusque" ("more sweetly and subtly" [I, x, 2]). On another occasion he specifies that those Tuscan poets who have achieved vernacular excellence are Cavalcanti, Lapo, himself, and Cino (I, xiii, 4). Faced with these passages, we realize that in the *Comedy* Dante does indeed, while creating an undifferentiated poetic chorality as a backdrop for his efforts, accord a special status to his own—named— "nove rime." We notice, for instance, that whereas *dolce* is ostentatiously used in canto XXVI, *novo* is not. Instead, Guinizzelli's poetry pertains to the "uso moderno": "Li dolci detti vostri, / che, quanto durerà l'uso moderno, / faranno cari ancora i loro incostri" ("Your sweet verses, which, as long as the modern use will last, will make their ink still dear" [112-114]). The twice-used *novo* of canto XXIV ("nove rime," "stil novo") is avoided in canto XXVI; its burden of epistemological newness is replaced by the mere chronological inventiveness of "moderno."[4] Within the "new style," Dante thus reserves radical newness for himself.

If Dante is deliberately vague with reference to his peers, he is never less accountable than in his poetic credo. Perhaps the most striking feature of the "I' mi son un" *terzina* is its programmatic lack of specificity. In *Purgatorio* XXIV Dante claims that he is a poet who takes note when Love in-spires him and

[4] The variant "nove penne" would result in a suggestive triple use of *novo* in canto XXIV. À propos of "moderno uso" and the slightly downgraded status it implies in comparison with "nove rime" and "stil novo," it seems not insignificant that, on the only other occasion in which "uso" and "moderno" are paired in the poem, Dante should carefully dissociate himself from "the modern use"; thus he tells Marco Lombardo that he has been graced to see God's court "per modo tutto fuor del moderno uso" ("in a manner wholly outside modern use" [*Purg.* XVI, 42]).

who signifies according to Love's dictation; herein, he has Bonagiunta categorically state, lies the only difference between his method of composition and that of his immediate precursors. He has learned to bypass the traditional line of authority—the "saggio" of his earlier sonnet—in order to draw his inspiration directly from the source: Amor. In this *terzina*, and within the context of love poetry, the relation between the dictator (Love) and the transcriber (Dante) is exactly analogous to the relation between God and the poet within the larger context of the *Comedy*: as Dante specifies in *Paradiso* X, speaking of "quella materia ond' io son fatto scriba" ("that matter of which I am made the scribe" [27]), he is God's secretary, taking down reality as dictation. The "dittator" of *Purgatorio* XXIV, 59—Amor—is therefore an analogue, within the lyric and amatory sphere, of the other *dittator*—God, also Amor—within the poem's overall structure. Because the only external referent in this process is an outside, indeed transcendent, authority, and because none of us can check with God as to what Dante saw, or with Love as to the fidelity of Dante's transcription, the apparently humble role of scribe results in a license to write the world, in fact to play God unchecked.

Without denying that Dante subscribes wholeheartedly to the notion that his poem is the instrument of a divine message, I would suggest that as a poetic strategy granting the poet absolute freedom and authority, the fiction of the *Comedy* is unparalleled. If, in Singleton's formula, the fiction of the *Comedy* is that it is no fiction, then it follows that the strategy of the *Comedy* is that there is no strategy.[5] Precisely such a conceptual exercise is at the core of the formulation of *Purgatorio* XXIV, whose content has been painstakingly examined for its troubadour components, its trinitarian resonances, but whose method of brilliant evasiveness has been less generally acknowledged.[6] The effect of the celebrated *terzina* is to create for Dante

[5] *Commedia: Elements of Structure* (1954; repr. Baltimore: Johns Hopkins U. Press, 1977), p. 62.

[6] On troubadour resonances in the formulation of *Purgatorio* XXIV, see: Cesare De Lollis, "Dolce stil novo e 'noel dig de nova maestria,' " *Studi me-*

a vantage from which to assess the history of the love lyric—
as within the poem as a whole, the scribal function permits an
assessment of universal history—and to reassign value and priority
as he chooses. The arbitrariness, or at least discontinuity, of
some of these assessments is evident if we look at Dante's prior
opinions as expressed particularly in the *De Vulgari Eloquentia*,
a text that bears the burden of historical truth (i.e. one that is
verifiable in human terms) much less lightly than the *Comedy*.
The *Comedy* (which predictably employs many more forms of
vero, verità, etc. than less subjective texts like the *Convivio*)
respects no truth but its own, least of all that composite and
approximate truth men know as history; in the words of one
critic "Dante in his *Comedy* never serves history; he uses it."[7]
To use history is to revise it, a pattern amply documented by
Dante's treatment of that slice of history represented by his
immediate peers—other poets.

The view of the vernacular lyric past that informs the *Comedy*
is inherited from the *De Vulgari Eloquentia*, where Dante at-
tempts a history of the lyric beginning with Peire d'Alvernhe
(whom he mistakenly believes to be among the "antiquiores
doctores" [I, x, 2]) and ending with himself.[8] Although the
treatise is explicit regarding the superiority of Dante and his
group, a sense of historical continuity prevails, not yet dispelled

---

dievali, 1 (1904), 5-23; Alberto Del Monte, " 'Dolce stil novo,' " *Filologia romanza*, 3 (1956), 254-264; Silvio Pellegrini, " 'Quando Amor mi spira,' " *Studi mediolatini e volgari*, 6-7 (1959), 157-167. Giuseppe Mazzotta stresses the *terzina*'s trinitarian echoes in *Dante, Poet of the Desert*, pp. 204-206, as does Martinez, "The Pilgrim's Answer to Bonagiunta and the Poetics of the Spirit." Pellegrini recognizes the *terzina*'s evasiveness, saying that "una certa indeterminatezza è connaturata al linguaggio dell'incontro fra Dante e Bona-giunta" (p. 160).

[7] Irma Brandeis, *The Ladder of Vision: A Study of Dante's Comedy* (New York: Doubleday, 1960), p. 61. The expression "Vero è" is frequently used as a verse opening by Dante in the *Comedy*.

[8] Cesare De Lollis bases Dante's erroneous belief in Peire's antiquity on information received from the Provençal biographies and on Peire's position in the manuscripts; see "Intorno a Pietro d'Alvernia," *Giornale storico della letteratura italiana*, 43 (1904), 28-38.

by the absolute polarity of the *Comedy*. The historicity of the treatise is revealed by the author's care to move chronologically from school to school, devoting separate chapters to each one in order to establish their discrete historical identities. Thus, he passes from a discussion of the Sicilians in chapter xii of Book I to the Tuscans in chapter xiii and the Bolognese in chapter xv; moreover, all poetic catalogues observe the sequence Provençal-Old French-Italian.[9] Most telling in this regard are the catalogues of incipits in Book II, chapters v and vi, which present the reader with nothing less than miniature histories of the lyric. The most complete catalogue, that of II, vi, lists incipits from the following poets, in the following order:

Giraut de Bornelh
Folquet de Marselha
Arnaut Daniel
Aimeric de Belenoi
Aimeric de Pegulhan
King of Navarre [Thibaut de Champagne]
Judge of Messina [Guido delle Colonne]
Guido Guinizzelli

[9] In his treatment of each poetic school, Dante collects a group of poets around a key figure, much as he collects the *stilnovisti* around himself. The poets of the Sicilian and Apulian contingent are Guido delle Colonne, Cielo d'Alcamo, Giacomo da Lentini, and Rinaldo d'Aquino. At this period Dante seems to regard Guido delle Colonne as the most notable figure in this group (perhaps because of his influence on Guinizzelli), citing him first in the chapter and choosing him for the lists of II, v and vi; see Marti, "Dante e i poeti della scuola siciliana" and "Il giudizio di Dante su Guido delle Colonne," in *Con Dante fra i poeti del suo tempo*, 2d ed. rev. (Lecce: Milella, 1971), pp. 9-28 and 29-42. The Tuscans Bonagiunta of Lucca, Gallo of Pisa, Mino Mocato of Siena, and Brunetto of Florence take their places around Guittone, while the Bolognese Guido Ghislieri, Fabruzzo de' Lambertazzi, and Onesto degli Onesti are grouped around their leader, "maximus" Guido Guinizzelli. The sequence of Provençal-Old French-Italian is followed in all the lists, beginning with the short one of I, ix, 3, which presents Giraut de Bornelh, Thibaut of Navarre, and Guido Guinizzelli in that order as the three representatives of their languages; Dante seems to be indicating that the lyric developed in Provence before northern France and in northern France before Italy.

Historiography Revisited

Guido Cavalcanti
Cino da Pistoia
"amicus eius"[Dante]

Not only is the correct progression maintained, but the nationalities are represented according to Dante's estimation of their importance: five Provençals, one Old French, and five Italians. The same procedure obtains within the Italian group, who follow the order Sicilian-Bolognese-stilnovist (or, in Dante's terminology of the time, "new Tuscan"), and who are represented by one Sicilian, one Bolognese, and three *stilnovisti*.[10]

Where these lists deviate from the facts, they may be seen to posit an ideal ranking that begins to approximate the type of subjective judgment found in the *Comedy*. The positions at the catalogue's beginning and end are significant in this regard. At the top we find Giraut de Bornelh, whom Dante had earlier

[10] It should be noted that I follow the order of the list as given by Mengaldo in his 1979 Ricciardi edition of the *De Vulgari Eloquentia*, which is also that given by Aristide Marigo (*De Vulgari Eloquentia*, 3d ed. with appendix by Pier Giorgio Ricci [Florence: Le Monnier, 1968]); however, the editions of Ludovicus Bertalot (*Dantis Alagherii De Vulgari Eloquentia* [Geneva: Olschki, 1920]) and Bruno Panvini (*De Vulgari Eloquentia* [Palermo: Andò, 1968]) place the "Iudex de Messana" (Guido delle Colonne) after Guinizzelli and Cavalcanti, thus destroying perfect historical order among the Italians while preserving the larger sequence from Provençal to French to Italian. For a refutation, see Mengaldo's comments in the Introduction to his 1968 edition of the *De Vulgari Eloquentia* (Padova: Antenore, 1968), where he discusses the order of the lists and the manuscript tradition, stressing the deliberate chronology of the catalogues and their significance in attesting to the revolutionary historicity of the treatise (pp. LXXXV-LXXXVI). (All further references to Mengaldo's Introduction to the *De Vulgari Eloquentia* will be to this edition of 1968.) In the Introduction to his anthology of Dante's troubadours, *Vulgares eloquentes: Vite e poesie dei trovatori di Dante* (Padova: Liviana, 1961), Gianfranco Folena also remarks on the historiographical intent demonstrated by the catalogue of II, vi, which he sees as a progression from the classical troubadours at its head (Giraut, Folquet, Arnaut) to the later troubadours who mark the turn to Italy in their lives and poetic production, Aimeric de Belenoi and Aimeric de Pegulhan (p. VIII). Another useful annotated anthology, with translations, is that provided by Bruno Panvini, *Le poesie del De Vulgari Eloquentia: Testi e note* (Catania: Giannotta, 1968).

labeled the Provençal poet of rectitude and as such his own Occitanic equivalent. Although Giraut in fact belongs in first place chronologically, the inexactness of Dante's information regarding the troubadours would suggest that Giraut is in first place because Dante wanted him there as the ideal initiator of the series. Giraut at the beginning balances Dante at the end; the list moves from the Provençal poet of rectitude to his Italian counterpart. In Dante's own case, the manipulation of chronology is evident; although he was born before Cino, Dante places himself after the Pistoian as the ideal culmination of the tradition that began with Giraut. Such privileging of himself and his comrades is a constant in the treatise and is responsible also for other idiosyncratic deviations from the historical record. For instance, we would expect the discussion of the Italian schools to include a final chapter on the newest group, Dante's own, following the chapter dealing with Guinizzelli, their precursor. There is no such chapter because Dante has already referred to his own group in the chapter dealing with Guittone and the other Tuscans; immediately after the scathing denunciation of those old Tuscans in chapter xiii, the author breaks into a panegyric, whose opening is significantly marked by the adversative "Sed": "But although almost all the Tuscans are rendered insensitive by their low language, we feel that some know what excellence of the vernacular is, and these are Guido, Lapo, and one other, Florentines, as well as Cino of Pistoia, whom I unfairly name last, constrained by worthy reasons" (I, xiii, 4).

This abrupt departure from the almost pedantic regularity that governs most of the treatise takes us definitively into the realm of Dante the "militant critic," as he has been labeled in some recent studies.[11] The departure itself is caused, one sus-

---

[11] The two most significant investigations of Dante as critic both refer to his "militancy" in their titles: Marti, "Gli umori del critico militante," in *Con Dante fra i poeti del suo tempo*, pp. 69-121; Mengaldo, "Critica militante e storiografia letteraria," in the Introduction, *De Vulgari Eloquentia*, pp. LXXVII-CII. Folena, in the Introduction to *Vulgares eloquentes* and Quaglio, *Gli stilnovisti*, also discuss Dante's relations with his peers and predecessors, as do: Edmund G. Gardner, "Dante as Literary Critic," in *Dante: Essays in Com-*

pects, by the presence of Guittone d'Arezzo, the poet toward whom Dante is consistently most militant; the need for chronological progression is waived by the need to introduce Guittone's successors immediately, as an opposition force that will effectively cancel the Tuscan and his satellites from the record. Indeed, it is precisely in its attitude toward the poet from Arezzo that the *De Vulgari Eloquentia* most anticipates the *Comedy*, shedding the historicized restraint that is its trademark. Thus, the chapter on the Tuscans is unique in not containing citations from the work of the poets mentioned. Although it is Dante's practice, in treating the Sicilians and Bolognese, and indeed throughout the treatise, to follow each poet's name with an incipit, in chapter xiii this procedure is not respected; here, rather than include quotations from the Tuscan poets he has named (Guittone of Arezzo, Bonagiunta of Lucca, Mino Mocato of Siena, Brunetto of Florence), Dante presents as his examples anonymous doggerel taken from the municipal dialects of each of these cities, which are thus represented by folk art rather than by their poets. Even more striking is the deletion of Guittone from the catalogue of II, vi, especially since his absence cannot be explained as an oversight; the exhortation that follows the list names—and denounces—precisely him: "Let the followers of ignorance who extol Guittone d'Arezzo and certain others therefore cease, for in their vocabulary and construction these poets never lost their plebeian habits" (II, vi, 8).

Because the *De Vulgari Eloquentia* has gone so far in denigrating Guittone, and because Dante does not reverse his earlier opinion, the *Comedy* can confine itself to confirming Dante's original judgment of the Tuscan poet. Hence, *Purgatorio* XXVI repeats the tone and even the language of the treatise; the *Comedy*'s "stolti" (as Dante refers to believers in the primacy

---

memoration (1921; repr. Freeport, N.Y.: Books for Libraries Press, 1968), pp. 83-104; Silvio Pellegrini, "Dante e la tradizione poetica volgare dai provenzali ai guittoniani," *Cultura e scuola* 4, nos. 13-14 (1965), 27-35; Ignazio Baldelli, "Dante e i poeti fiorentini del Duecento," *Lectura Dantis Scaligera* (Florence: Le Monnier, 1968); Enzo Noè Girardi, "Dante critico, saggio e postille," *Italianistica*, 6 (1977), 203-224.

Lyric Quests

of Giraut, in a passage that by implication considers followers of Guittone equally benighted) echo the *De Vulgari Eloquentia's* "followers of ignorance." There is, however, a notable difference between the treatise and the poem. In the treatise, the weight of history is such that Dante feels obliged to present supporting evidence for his claims against Guittone, and hence insists on the Aretine's "plebeian" qualities of diction and construction: first in the chapter dedicated to the Tuscans, where he says that Guittone "nunquam se ad curiale vulgare direxit" ("never addressed himself to the courtly vernacular" [I, xiii, 1]) and goes on to specify that the writings of these poets are strictly municipal in character; and again in the passage cited above, following the catalogue of II, vi, where the use of the verb *plebescere* picks up the former distinction between *dicta municipalia* and *dicta curialia*. These statements, for all their highhandedness, are in marked contrast to the *Comedy*, where Guittone is declassed on mystical rather than linguistic grounds, where the only reason, if it can be called that, offered for his poetic inferiority is the blanket explanation of *Purgatorio* XXIV, which attributes his pedestrian verse (along with that of the other earlier poets) to a lack of inspiration, an inability to follow Love. Thus it is Guittone's lack, and not Dante's desire to discredit him, that accounts for the treatment he receives in the sacred poem.

Guittone is the only poet from canto XXIV to be mentioned a second time, a recurrence that signals the transition from the cool and apparently objective indictment of " 'l Notaro e Guittone e me" to the more heated and overtly autobiographical controversies of canto XXVI.[12] In order to bring Guittone back into the discourse, Dante has Guinizzelli first praise Arnaut Daniel, calling him the "miglior fabbro del parlar materno,"

[12] In "Il canto XXVI del *Purgatorio*," *Nuova Lectura Dantis* (Rome: Signorelli, 1951), Aurelio Roncaglia discusses the canto's two poles of critical objectivity and autobiographical subjectivity (p. 18). Also on this canto, see Angelo Monteverdi, "Il canto XXVI del *Purgatorio*," *Lectura Dantis Scaligera* (Florence: Le Monnier, 1965) and Gianfranco Folena, "Il canto di Guido Guinizzelli," *Giornale storico della letteratura italiana*, 154 (1977), 481-508.

and then add that this newly affirmed primacy of Arnaut's is incontestable, despite those fools who think Giraut de Bornelh ("quel di Lemosì") the greater poet; Guinizzelli concludes by pointing out, rather gratuitously, that an analogous situation used to exist in Italy, where similar fools considered Guittone d'Arezzo the supreme poet, until finally the truth prevailed (we notice, in this moment of extreme subjectivity, Dante's insistence on "il ver," repeated twice in the course of six lines):

> "O frate," disse, "questi ch'io ti cerno
>   col dito," e additò un spirto innanzi,
> "fu miglior fabbro del parlar materno.
> Versi d'amore e prose di romanzi
>   soverchiò tutti; e lascia dir li stolti
>   che quel di Lemosì credon ch'avanzi.
> A voce più ch'al ver drizzan li volti,
>   e così ferman sua oppinïone
>   prima ch'arte o ragion per lor s'ascolti.
> Così fer molti antichi di Guittone,
>   di grido in grido pur lui dando pregio,
>   fin che l'ha vinto il ver con più persone. . . . "

"O brother," he said, "the one there whom I indicate with my finger," and he pointed to a spirit ahead, "was a better craftsman of the mother tongue. Verses of love and proses of romances he surpassed all—and let the fools talk who think that he of Limoges is superior. They turn their faces toward rumor rather than the truth, and so they form their opinion before listening to art or reason. So did many of the oldtimers with Guittone, from cry to cry giving praise to him only, until with most people the truth conquered. . . . "

(*Purg.* XXVI, 115-126)

Guittone is thus embedded in a dialectical structure that encompasses old and new, false and true, on a historiographical grid whose Provençal components are the key to his undoing;[13]

---

[13] The historiographical grid of canto XXVI also comprises, as scholars have

by coupling Guittone with Giraut, the most renowned troubadour of his day, Dante makes the denunciation all the more telling. Rather than denying the fame of these poets, he simply denies that their fame was justified.

Although undoubtedly effective, this method of attacking Guittone has serious repercussions of a revisionist nature. One result is to raise Arnaut definitively above Giraut, in sharp contrast to the situation in the *De Vulgari Eloquentia*, where if anything Giraut is the privileged poet. Although I do not agree with those critics who, like Santangelo, argue for the exclusive primacy of Giraut during the period of the *De Vulgari Eloquentia*, the special status accorded the poet from Limoges in the treatise is indisputable.[14] Giraut is the troubadour whose

---

noticed, interesting intertextual components: Dante's reference to Guinizzelli as ''il padre / mio'' echoes Guinizzelli's reference to Guittone, in the incipit of his sonnet to the Aretine, as ''[O] caro padre meo''; Dante's use of the rare verb *imbarcare* in line 75 echoes Guinizzelli's use of it, again in the sonnet to Guittone; Dante's stress on ''il ver'' (lines 121 and 126) recalls Guinizzelli's reply to Bonagiunta, ''Omo ch'è saggio non corre leggero,'' where the Bolognese poet appeals twice to the ''truth.'' See Ernest Hatch Wilkins, ''Guinizelli Praised and Corrected,'' in *The Invention of the Sonnet and Other Studies in Italian Literature* (Rome: Edizioni di Storia e Letteratura, 1959), pp. 111-113, and most recently, Franco Suitner, '' 'Colui che fore trasse le nove rime.' ''

[14] Salvatore Santangelo's book, *Dante e i trovatori provenzali* (Catania: Giannotta, 1921), suffers from the schematic rigidity with which the author, insisting that Dante had access to only one troubadour *canzoniere*, assigns certain poets to discrete stages of Dante's development with no possibility of contamination; a recent critique is provided by Maurizio Perugi in his exhaustive study of Arnaldian echoes in Dante's texts, ''Arnaut Daniel in Dante,'' *Studi danteschi*, 51 (1978), 59-152 (see esp. pp. 103-108). Some of the numerous articles devoted to Dante and the troubadours begin as reviews of Santangelo's book; among these are E. Hoepffner, ''Dante et les Troubadours,'' *Études Italiennes*, 4 (1922), 193-210, and Luigi Pastine, ''Dante e i trovatori,'' *Il Giornale dantesco*, 26 (1923), 15-26 and 128-141. Other contributions on this topic are: A. Jeanroy, ''Dante et les Troubadours,'' in *Dante: Mélanges de Critique et d'Érudition françaises publiés à l'Occasion du VIe Centenaire de la Mort du Poète* (Paris: Union Intellectuelle Franco-Italienne, 1921), pp. 11-21; J. Véran, ''Dante et les Troubadours,'' *La Revue Hebdomadaire* 30, fasc. 27 (1921), 93-103; A. G. Ferrers Howell, ''Dante and the Troubadours,'' in *Dante: Essays in Commemoration*, pp. 191-223; Henri Hauvette, ''Dante et la Poésie provençale,'' in *La France et la Provence dans l'Oeuvre de Dante* (Paris: Boivin, 1929), pp. 107-146; A. Parducci, ''Dante e i trovatori,'' in *Provenza e Italia* (Florence: Bem-

incipit represents the *langue d'oc* in the discussion of the common origin of Romance languages in I, ix; he is the Provençal poet of rectitude, paired with Dante among the Italians, in II, ii; and he heads the lists of II, v and II, vi, devoted respectively to canzoni that begin with hendecasyllables, and canzoni that are examples of the "gradum constructionis excellentissimum." In two of these categories he is without an Occitanic rival since he is the only troubadour cited (I, ix and II, v). Where other troubadours are also present, Giraut is invariably above the others (II, ii and II, vi). Arnaut overlaps with Giraut twice, and on both occasions he is "beneath" him: in one case he is the Provençal poet of love, paired with Cino among the Italians, while Giraut is the poet of rectitude (II, ii), and in the other he is two places below Giraut in the list of composers in the high style (II, vi). On the other hand, Arnaut is mentioned in two places where no other troubadour, including Giraut, is present; in both instances he serves as a representative of technical excellence, first for the use of the indivisible stanza (II, x) and secondly for the use of the stanza containing no rhymes in itself (II, xiii).

Thus, although Giraut and Arnaut share the honor of being the only troubadours in the *De Vulgari Eloquentia* who are each mentioned four times in all, they emerge from the treatise with markedly distinct poetic physiognomies. The divergence between the two poets is borne out by their placement; Giraut appears earlier in the treatise, even once in the philosophically oriented first book, whereas Arnaut begins to appear with more frequency in the technical sections at the end of Book II. Giraut is in the loftier position, but Arnaut is perhaps the more studied. Indeed, it is debatable which is in fact the higher tribute—Giraut's classification with Dante in the category of poet of rectitude, or the frank avowal of imitation that is accorded Ar-

---

porad, 1930), pp. 81-95; Luigi Peirone, *Lingua e stile nella poesia di Dante* (Genova: Edizioni Universitarie, 1967). Also useful are the anthology of H. J. Chaytor, *The Troubadours of Dante* (1902; repr. Geneva: Slatkine Reprints, 1974) and the bibliographical study of F. Pirot, "Dante et les Troubadours," *Marche romane*, 15 (1965), 213-219.

naut. For, despite his typical chariness in admitting influence, Dante explicitly says that he copied Arnaut in the composition of his *sestina*; his exact words are "nos eum secuti sumus cum diximus 'Al poco giorno e al gran cerchio d'ombra' " ("we followed him when we composed . . ." [II, x, 2]). The gap between Arnaut's position in the treatise and his position in the poem is therefore not so great as has been supposed; rather, the *Comedy* preserves and renders explicit, in its delineation of a "fabbro," the *De Vulgari Eloquentia*'s implicit tribute to a master stylist. With respect to the *De Vulgari Eloquentia*, then, Dante's opinion of Arnaut has not so much changed as intensified. What has changed, apparently, is his opinion of the poet who had been at the head of the lists, Giraut de Bornelh.

The status of "quel di Lemosì" is structurally connected—through the ratio of *Purgatorio* XXVI, which equates Giraut and Guittone, Arnaut and Guinizzelli—to the status of the poet from Arezzo. Although Guittone's oppressive presence as the cultural dictator of his day has been duly observed, it would be well to remind ourselves of the extent of Dante's own indebtedness to his Tuscan precursor, an indebtedness that spans his career, from the early *tenzoni* with the older Guittonian poet Dante da Maiano to the passages in the *Comedy* (particularly the invectives) that bear the imprint of the Aretine's oratorical style.[15] The young Dante starts as an imitator, exchanging son-

---

[15] For the influence of Guittone on the so-called *tenzone del duol d'amore* between Dante Alighieri and Dante da Maiano, see Marti, "Gli umori del critico militante," esp. pp. 71-77; for the pervasive Guittonianism of Dante's early lyrics, see Foster and Boyde, *Commentary*, pp. 1-71. Contini concludes his review of Francesco Egidi's edition of Guittone, *Giornale storico della letteratura italiana*, 117 (1941), 55-82, with a brief discussion of Guittone in Dante, in which he speaks of "un Guittone quasi dantesco" (p. 82).

Guittone's influence on the *Comedy* falls into two main categories. Most apparent is the influence of his political poetry on the political invectives, where Dante appropriates not only the Aretine's impassioned tone but also some of his specific trademarks. Like Guittone, Dante punctuates his invectives with apostrophes and rhetorical questions. Taking as a basis for comparison the canzone "Ahi lasso, or è stagion de doler tanto" and the invective of *Purgatorio* VI, we find the following borrowed techniques in the *Comedy*: the standard

Historiography Revisited

nets that recapitulate the worst of Guittone's rhetorical excesses and virtuosic obscurantism. As in the first *tenzone* Dante da Maiano begins with the exposition of a "vision" that needs decoding, so later Dante himself will request similar assistance from his peers in the sonnet that becomes the first lyric of the *Vita Nuova*, "A ciascun'alma presa e gentil core." Cavalcanti's reply to that sonnet may be used to effectively mark the end of Dante's first Guittonian stage; Dante had found a new poetic master. On the other hand, we must specify that the Guittonianism from which Dante is freed by Cavalcanti is but the first such stage in his poetic career; after his *stil novo* phase, which is best defined in negative terms as a rejection of the prevailing norm determined by Guittone, Dante develops the less restricted poetic language evidenced by the *petrose* and the moral canzoni.[16] It is at this point that Guittone makes his reappearance

---

Guittonian opening in "Ahi" (which characterizes numerous Dantesque invectives and apostrophes); the use of apostrophes and rhetorical questions for denunciation and accusation (indeed, both poets go so far as to direct such a question to God: compare Guittone's "Deo, com'hailo sofrito, / deritto pèra e torto entri 'n altezza?" ["God, how have you suffered it, that justice perish and injustice be raised on high?" 14-15] with Dante's "E se licito m'è, o sommo Giove . . . son li giusti occhi tuoi rivolti altrove?" ["And if it be allowed me, O supreme Jove . . . are your just eyes turned elsewhere?" 118-120]); the use of heavy sarcasm, of repetition and anaphora (anaphora in particular is cultivated by Dante in his invectives), of aphorisms; and intense rhetorical play in the form of etymological puns and the like. To a lesser degree, one can spot the impact of Guittone's religious poetry on the *Comedy*; compare, for instance, his *lauda* for Saint Dominic, "Meraviglioso beato," with the tribute to the saint in *Paradiso* XII. In fact, since Guittone wrote lauds for both Dominic and Francis, it would seem that he provided the paradigm for the double tribute of *Paradiso* XI and XII. Another suggestive connection between Guittone's *canzoniere* and the *Comedy* regards Cavalcante de' Cavalcanti, Guido's father; the possible allusions to heterodoxy in Guittone's exhortation to "messer Cavalcante" (XXVI; see esp. 43-44) seem to anticipate *Inferno* X.

[16] On the first page of their *Commentary*, Foster and Boyde define the *stil novo* as a purist movement and comment that "to appreciate the *stilnovo* one must know what those poets reacted against, what they rejected"; at the end of the Guittonian section, they state that "when the reaction, or rather revolution, is complete, one can indeed speak of a *new* style, determined antithetically in polemic against the prevailing taste" (p. 71). In *Dante's Style in*

in Dante's lexicon and style, contributing most notably to the great lyrical sermons like "Doglia mi reca ne lo core ardire."

Despite Guittone's manifest importance as the first Italian poet to open up the vernacular to moral and political themes, criticism on Guittone has tended to reflect Dante's verdict of his Tuscan precursor.[17] But Dante's denunciation is too strong to be taken at face value; his very insistence on Guittone serves to set the Tuscan apart from other contemporaries he does not

---

His Lyric Poetry (Cambridge: Cambridge U. Press, 1971), Patrick Boyde claims that, from the rhetorician's point of view, Dante's development as a lyric poet occurs in two distinct phases; the first phase (corresponding to the *stil novo*) is one in which "all the developments take the form of a contraction or restriction in the range of expressive means," whereas in the second phase (corresponding to the moral canzoni and the *petrose*) "the developments all represent an expansion" (p. 317).

[17] The traditional view of Guittone is stated by De Sanctis, who accords him moral value but no poetic artistry or inspiration. Scholars aware of Dante's debt to Guittone long sought excuses for Dante's refusal to acknowledge the Aretine, rather than face his essential arbitrariness in this matter; thus De Lollis, in "Arnaldo e Guittone," *Idealistiche Neuphilologie: Festschrift für Karl Vossler* (Heidelberg: Carl Winter, 1922), pp. 159-173, argues that Dante rejects Guittone because his ideal lyric canon admits only love poetry, not political poetry. The basic comprehensive work on Guittone is Claude Margueron, *Recherches sur Guittone d'Arezzo* (Paris: Presses Universitaires de France, 1966); other studies on Guittone include: Achille Pellizzari, *La vita e le opere di Guittone d'Arezzo* (Pisa: Nistri, 1906); Francesco Torraca, "Fra Guittone," in *Studi di storia letteraria* (Florence: Sansoni, 1923), pp. 108-152; Alberto Del Monte, "Guittone dell'aridità," in *Studi sulla poesia ermetica medievale* (Naples: Giannini, 1953), pp. 113-186; Maria Teresa Cattaneo, "Note sulla poesia di Guittone," *Giornale storico della letteratura italiana*, 137 (1960), 165-203 and 325-367; Achille Tartaro, *Il manifesto di Guittone e altri studi fra Due e Quattrocento* (Rome: Bulzoni, 1974), pp. 13-75; Agnello Baldi, *Guittone d'Arezzo fra impegno e poesia* (Cercola: Società Editrice Salernitana, 1975); Vincent Moleta, *The Early Poetry of Guittone d'Arezzo* (London: The Modern Humanities Research Association, 1976). Specifically on Dante's unfairness in dealing with Guittone is the article by Giuseppe Bolognese, "Dante and Guittone Revisited," *Romanic Review*, 70 (1979), 172-184. Contini speaks of the "assidua denigrazione compiuta da Dante" vis-à-vis Guittone, which is nonetheless "un omaggio reso alla sua attualità" (*Poeti del Duecento*, vol. I, p. 191), while Quaglio stresses Dante's need to rid himself of Guittone, "un pericoloso rivale" (*Gli stilnovisti*, p. 20).

consider important enough to mention, like Chiaro Davanzati or Monte Andrea. The impassioned cry at the end of *De Vulgari Eloquentia* II, vi—"Subsistant igitur ignorantie sectatores Guictonem Aretinum"—and the contrived reinsertion of Guittone into the dialogue of *Purgatorio* XXVI point not away from the Aretine but toward him: to his continuing significance, rather than to his lack thereof. We might note those features of Guittone's career that are particularly suggestive. First, there is the fact that the manuscript tradition presents him as essentially two different poets, "Guittone" before his conversion and "Frate Guittone" after his joining a new religious order, the Milites Beatae Virginis Mariae, in 1265.[18] While "Guittone" wrote love poetry whose incessant hammering on the *senhal* "gioia" with its rhyming counterpart "noia" is undeniably tedious, "Frate Guittone" wrote moral verse whose vigor and energy are undeniably effective. Second, Guittone was forced to leave Arezzo for political reasons. Although his poetry never achieves the grandeur of Dante's "l'essilio che m'è dato, onor mi tegno" ("the exile which is given me I hold an honor" ["Tre donne," 76]), his self-defense in "Gente noiosa e villana" forecasts the tone of moral superiority that characterizes analogous passages in Dante's verse. Guittone was also a political poet, whose attack on Florence in "Ahi lasso, or è stagion de doler tanto," written after the defeat of the Guelphs at Montaperti, anticipates the bitter sarcasm of the *Comedy*'s Florentine invectives; like Dante in his political tirade of *Purgatorio* VI, Guittone has mastered a style that is grounded in the specific but not limited thereby, whose historicity is capable of generating a universal reproof.

---

[18] On Guittone's conversion and the probable date for his joining the "Knights of the Blessed Virgin Mary," popularly dubbed Frati Gaudenti, see Margueron, p. 22 and pp. 36-40. On the manuscript division into love poetry and moral poetry, see Francesco Egidi, ed., *Le rime di Guittone d'Arezzo* (Bari: Laterza, 1940), pp. 285-286. Guittone's poems are cited and numbered according to Egidi's edition, except for the following canzoni, taken from *Poeti del Duecento*, vol. I: "Tuttor, s'eo veglio o dormo"; "Ahi lasso, or è stagion de doler tanto"; "Ora parrà s'eo saverò cantare"; "Comune perta fa comun dolore"; "Magni baroni certo e regi quasi."

We should add that Guittone, through his letters, is the only Italian poet before Dante to contribute significantly to the development of vernacular prose style.[19] Finally, all of this literary activity takes place in a language whose composite quality has caused one linguist to speak not—with Dante—of "dicta municipalia," but rather of "cosmopolitismo guittoniano," an expression that more accurately reflects the scope of Guittone's aspirations, and of his prestige.[20]

Of all his Italian predecessors, Guittone alone attempted what Dante would later accomplish—a fact that Dante, unaided by hindsight, was less inclined to discount than we. The central event in this problematic is Guittone's conversion, a conversion that led not only to a different kind of life, as in the case of Folquet de Marselha (it is interesting that both poets left behind a wife and children), but also to a different kind of writing. Although Dante never acknowledges Guittone's religious experience, one suspects that he did not view it favorably. Members of the order to which Guittone belonged were called Frati Gaudenti, because of their alleged laxity; Dante's mockery of the Frati Gaudenti through the characters of Catalano and Lode-

---

[19] Cesare Segre writes on Guittone's prose in *Lingua, stile e società: Studi sulla storia della prosa italiana* (Milan: Feltrinelli, 1963), pp. 95-175. Santangelo discusses Guittone's prose with reference to the prose of the *Convivio* in " 'Sole nuovo' e 'sole usato': Dante e Guittone," in *Saggi danteschi* (1926-27; repr. Padova: Cedam, 1959), pp. 93-129; he believes that the famous passage at the end of the first book of the *Convivio* on the coming of a "new sun" refers not to the vernacular's rise to preeminence over Latin, as is generally supposed, but to the fact that the prose of the *Convivio* will surpass the prose of Guittone's *Lettere*. Pellizzari points out that Guittone's verse letters are responsible for introducing *prosimetrum* into Italian literature (p. 216).

[20] The expression "cosmopolitismo guittoniano" is used by Giacomo Devoto, *Profilo di storia linguistica italiana* (Florence: La Nuova Italia, 1953), p. 56. Silvio Pellegrini rejects Dante's definition of Guittone's language as "municipal" in *"De vulgari eloquentia*, Libro I, capp. 10-19," *Studi mediolatini e volgari*, 8 (1960), 155-163, where he claims that the judgments of the *De Vulgari Eloquentia* are biased because the treatise privileges poetry written in an immaterial and abstract lexicon. Carlo Salinari, in the Introduction to his anthology, *La poesia lirica del Duecento*, 2d ed. rev. (Turin: Unione Tipografico-Editrice Torinese, 1968), refers to Guittone's "linguaggio aulico" (p. 24).

ringo in the *bolgia* of the hypocrites, and his implied connection between their previous state as "Jovial Brothers" ("Frati godenti fummo" [*Inf.* XXIII, 103]) and their present state as members of the "brotherhood of sad hypocrites" ("collegio / de l'ipocriti tristi" [*Inf.* XXIII, 91-92]), is undoubtedly linked to his anti-Guittonianism. Guittone seems to have been well-acquainted with Loderingo, one of the order's principal founders: the two were companions in the monastery of Ronzano, and Guittone commiserated with him on his undeserved tribulations in a canzone reverentially addressed to "Padre dei padri miei e mio messere" ("Father of my fathers and my lord"). On the other hand, for all Dante's derision of Guittone's religious affiliations, he can hardly have overlooked verses like the following:

Vergognar troppo e doler, lasso, deggio,
poi fui dal mio principio *a mezza etate*
in loco laido, desorrato e brutto,
ove m'involsi tutto,
e venni ingrotto, infermo, pover, nuto,
cieco, sordo e muto,
desviato, vanito, morto e peggio

Too much must I shame and sorrow, alas, since from my beginning *to middle age* I was in a filthy, dishonorable, and ugly place, in which I was completely caught up, and I came [from it] sick, infirm, poor, nude, blind, deaf, and dumb, *off course, out of my senses, dead and worse*
("Ahi, quant'ho che vergogni e che doglia aggio,"
5-11; italics mine)

Here we have Guittone's *selva oscura*, complete with the coincidence between his "a mezza etate" and Dante's "mezzo del cammin." Most arresting is the phrase "desviato, vanito, morto e peggio," which contains the voyage metaphor used repeatedly by Guittone: "desviai, tu me renvii" ("I went off the path, you put me back on") he says to God in another strikingly "Dantesque" composition ("Vergogna ho, lasso, ed ho me stesso ad ira," 95).

Guittone adumbrates not only the condition of the *Comedy*'s pilgrim, but also the beliefs of its poet; he too is a *scriba Dei*. In one canzone he undertakes to speak out against atheism, buttressed not by his own wisdom but by God's:

> Ma non del mio saver dico giá farlo,
> ma del suo, per cui parlo;
> ché la sua gran mercé sper mi proveggia
> ed amaestri e reggia
> la lingua mia in assennando stolti.
>
> But not with my own learning do I say that I will do it,
> but with His, for Whom I speak; since His great mercy
> provides me with hope, and teaches me, and guides my
> tongue in making fools wise.
>
> ("Poi male tutto è nulla inver peccato," 16-20)

Similarly, in his famous conversion poem, "Ora parrà s'eo saverò cantare," Guittone rejects the troubadour equation between poetry and Love; he claims that God is the only true source of inspiration and, using the metaphor of the poem as a ship so familiar to readers of the *Comedy*, he advises the poet to "make God his star" (19). Most significant with respect to Guittone's poetics is the statement with which he defends himself in the canzone "Altra fiata aggio giá, donne, parlato" for his arduous verse; the nominal subject of his poem, chastity, has generated a larger discourse that he knows will displease some of his readers:

> Ditt'aggio manto e non troppo, se bono:
> non gran matera cape in picciol loco.
> Di gran cosa dir poco
> non dicese al mestieri o dice scuro.
> E dice alcun ch'è duro
> e aspro mio trovato a savorare;
> e pote esser vero. Und'è cagione?
> che m'abonda ragione,
> perch'eo gran canzon faccio e serro motti,
> e nulla fiata tutti

locar loco li posso; und'eo rancuro,
ch'un picciol motto pote un gran ben fare.

I have said much and not too much, if good; a great subject is not contained by a small space. To say little about a great thing does not befit the task or is obscure. And some say that my poetry is hard and harsh to savor; and this may be true. What is the reason? That my discourse abounds, because I make a great canzone and I bind the words, and never can I find a place for all of them; which I regret, because a little word can accomplish a great good.

(159-170)

Here Guittone justifies the length and "harshness" of his poem (using the same adjective, *aspro*, that Dante will use in the exordium of his first moral composition, "Le dolci rime") by invoking the greatness of his subject. Indeed, the weightiness of the theme is such that Guittone's thoughts—his "ragione"—must still exceed the boundaries of the container. Thus, for the poet who has a truly "gran matera," even a "gran canzon" remains a "picciol loco."[21]

At 170 lines "Altra fiata aggio giá" is 10 lines longer than the *Comedy*'s longest canto, but, as Guittone himself seems to realize, merely lengthening the genre that he has is not the

---

[21] This issue of length has some interesting ramifications; the contiguous elevation of Arnaut and disparagement of Guittone in *Purgatorio* XXVI is perhaps not unrelated. Whereas Guittone feels that the lyric is not long enough to accommodate his discourse, Arnaut is a declared devotee of compression; at Love's command, he says, he will make a "breu chansson de razon loigna" ("brief song with a long theme" [XVI, 4]). Brevity is thus the hallmark of the love poet, and Guittone's lack of it is one more sign of his aspiration to a different—and forbidden—status. The relative lengths of love poems and moral poems in his *canzoniere* support this hypothesis. Whereas Guittone's longest love canzone is 115 lines, and the average length of his love canzoni is 68 lines, his longest moral canzone is 219 lines, and the average length of his moral/political canzoni is 102 lines. Dante, although less extreme, follows the same pattern: the average length of his love canzoni is 71 lines and the average length of his moral canzoni is 136 lines. Dante's longest canzone is the moral poem deeply indebted to Guittone, "Doglia mi reca," which has 158 lines.

solution to his problem. What he needs to hold his "gran matera" is something altogether new, a really "gran canzon," perhaps—like the *Comedy*—the equivalent of many canzoni stitched together. Although Guittone is not capable of the Dantesque leap required for such an invention, he is capable of a sense of mission much like Dante's, as articulated for instance in the last verse of "Altra fiata aggio giá," where he states that "a little word can accomplish a great good," or, more succinctly, in his claim that his God-given task is to "make fools wise." It is not surprising, therefore, that Dante returns to Guittone precisely as he embarks upon his own mission to make fools wise. In a famous passage of the *De Vulgari Eloquentia* Dante establishes that the *magnalia*, the greatest and most worthy topics on which to write poetry, belong to the three categories of "armorum probitas" ("prowess of arms"), "amoris accensio" ("kindling of love"), and "directio voluntatis" ("directing of the will"), and assigns representative Provençal and Italian poets to each of these categories: "About these [topics] alone, if we recall rightly, we have found illustrious men to have written poetry in the vernacular, that is Bertran de Born on arms, Arnaut Daniel on love, Giraut de Bornelh on rectitude; Cino of Pistoia on love, his friend on rectitude" (II, ii, 8). Cino's friend is, of course, Dante, who thus claims for himself the title of poet of rectitude, whose purpose is to direct the wills of others. In claiming such a title, and in citing his poem on avarice, "Doglia mi reca," as the example of his poetry in this mode, Dante cannot fail to be aware of the other major Italian lyric poet to have written on such matters. This is Guittone, who wrote not only about avarice but about all the seven deadly sins (most overtly in his sonnet sequence on the vices and virtues), and whose canzoni deal explicitly with the social manifestations of good and evil.

In this passage of the *De Vulgari Eloquentia* Dante's Provençal equivalent is Giraut de Bornelh, whose cited poem is the *sirventes* "Per solatz revelhar," in which Giraut deplores the passing of the chivalric virtues *solatz* and *pretz*; as the opening lines state, he writes in order to reawaken these slumbering and exiled virtues:[22]

Per solatz revelhar,
Que s'es trop endormitz,
E per pretz, qu'es faiditz,
Acolhir e tornar,
Me cudei trebalhar

To reawaken pleasure which has been too long asleep and to bring back and welcome true worth, which is exiled, I have decided to put myself to work

(1-5)

The chief enemy of the old values is the avarice of the present nobility, a group that no longer practices the generosity of their ancestors. In his contrastive analysis of "Per solatz revelhar" and "Doglia mi reca," Michelangelo Picone demonstrates Dante's enlargement of Giraut's themes from the socially circumscribed world of troubadour ethics to a universally formulated moral indictment.[23] Mediating between these two texts are the moral canzoni of Guittone d'Arezzo, an Italian poet who had already assimilated the lessons of Giraut de Bornelh and adapted his Occitanic morality to Tuscany, his Provençal *sirventes* to Italian, thus becoming the initiator of the Italian tradition of the *directio voluntatis*. If "Doglia mi reca" hearkens back to the troubadour moralist Giraut de Bornelh, and to his moral *sirventes*, it hearkens back equally to the moral poetry of Guittone d'Arezzo. In fact, in his discussion of "Doglia mi reca" as an example of Dante's mature lyric style, Patrick Boyde stresses the poem's Guittonian elements and suggests as a general structural model "Altra fiata aggio giá," Guittone's exhortation to chastity;[24] both poems

---

[22] Giraut's texts are from Adolf Kolsen, ed., *Sämtliche Lieder des Trobadors Giraut de Bornelh* (1910; repr. Geneva: Slatkine Reprints, 1976).

[23] "Giraut de Bornelh nella prospettiva di Dante," *Vox Romanica*, 39 (1980), 22-43.

[24] "Style and Structure in 'Doglia mi reca,' " in *Dante's Style in His Lyric Poetry*, pp. 317-331; on Dante's debt to Guittone and the structural similarities between "Doglia mi reca" and "Altra fiata aggio giá," see esp. pp. 321-324.

begin as direct appeals to an audience of "ladies" who eventually make room for the authors' wider concerns. It is interesting, moreover, that in "Doglia mi reca" Dante should declare his intention to write clearly and openly: "ché rado sotto benda / parola oscura giugne ad intelletto" ("for rarely under a veil does the obscure word reach the intellect" [57-58]). Considering that "Altra fiata aggio giá" contains Guittone's most celebrated defense of his obscurity, it is not impossible that Dante, aware of his debt to that poem, intends thus to inscribe an implicit disclaimer into his own composition.

One might go further, and speculate that Dante's insistence on clarity is also an implicit attempt to establish Giraut, rather than Guittone, as the poetic forebear of his text; a major part of the troubadour's legend centers in fact around his formulation of a *trobar leu*, or plain style, as the appropriate vehicle for moral verse.[25] Dante's choice of Giraut as his ideal precursor in the moral mode is borne out by the *De Vulgari Eloquentia*, where two of Giraut's four incipits are from *sirventes*. "Si per mo Sobre-Totz no fos," cited in the list of II, vi, deals with themes similar to those treated in "Per solatz revelhar"; again

---

[25] On Giraut's *trobar leu* and the relation of his style to his moral concerns, see Linda M. Paterson, *Troubadours and Eloquence* (Oxford: Clarendon Press, 1975), chap. 3. The fact that Giraut says he prefers the plain style does not mean, however, that he consistently employs it; in fact, the concision of his verse often renders it obscure, as J.-J. Salverda de Grave points out in *Observations sur l'Art lyrique de Giraut de Borneil*, Mededeelingen der koninklijke nederlandsche Akademie van Wetenschappen, afd. letterkunde, Nieuwe reeks, deel 1, no. 1 (Amsterdam: Noord-Hollandsche, 1938): "La caractéristique la plus frappante du style de Giraut est son extrême concision, qui est une des causes principales de la difficulté qu'on éprouve à interpréter son oeuvre" (p. 47). Giraut's tendency toward gnomic verse greatly influenced Guittone's style as well as Dante's in such poems as "Doglia mi reca"; it is all the more interesting, therefore, that the key Giraldian term *leu* should appear in "Doglia mi reca," where Dante says that he will now use a "costrutto / più lieve" (55-56). This and other echoes of Giraut's poetry in Dante's lyrics are noted by De Lollis in "Quel di Lemosì," *Scritti vari di filologia per Ernesto Monaci* (Rome: Forzani, 1901), pp. 353-375. Ferrers Howell considers that the canzone "Poscia ch'Amor," which is particularly replete with Provençalisms, is "an attempt to write in Giraut's manner" ("Dante and the Troubadours," p. 215).

Historiography Revisited

the troubadour world is in grave disarray. Particularly significant is the eschatological departure from the usual themes that begins in the sixth stanza, where the poet deduces from the general decadence that all men, including the most powerful, should concern themselves with the afterlife, when their power will be gone and they will be in the hands of the true king; Giraut offers as his "wise counsel" that it is preferable to correct one's faults here than to find them a burden later on. This theme intensifies in the next stanza, becoming an overt prayer to the "One and Triune God" at the poem's end. Indeed, Giraut's commitment to morality is such that even in a love poem like "Si·m sentis fizels amics," cited in I, ix, he is capable of announcing that "Oimais semblara prezics / Mos chans" ("from now on my song will seem a sermon" [46-47]).[26] This insistence on his poetry as a "prezics," which served Giraut so well in the *De Vulgari Eloquentia*, is ultimately responsible, I believe, for his demotion in the *Comedy*. Whereas in the treatise Giraut's moral themes are an asset, allowing him to be a forecaster of Dante, his figural adumbration as poet of rectitude, in the *Comedy* these same moral themes are a liability, because they inevitably link Giraut to the rejected Italian practitioner of the *directio voluntatis*, Guittone d'Arezzo.[27] Moreover, in the *Comedy*

---

[26] Paterson points out that Giraut's "didactic approach affects his love songs as well as his *sirventes*" (p. 142), and quotes Salverda de Grave, according to whom for Giraut "l'amour a été en grande partie matière à moralisation" (*Observations sur l'Art lyrique de Giraut de Borneil*, p. 16).

[27] Contini suggests that Dante rejects Giraut because the troubadour's commitment to *rectitudo* "lo avvicinava piuttosto a Guittone che al Dante morale" ("Dante come personaggio-poeta della *Commedia*," p. 58); I would amend that Giraut's *rectitudo* links him *both* to Guittone *and* to "Dante morale," since the three are inseparably linked. Picone argues that Dante condemns Giraut because he is identified with the *canzoni morali*, hence with the *Convivio* and the *donna gentile*; thus the *Comedy* replaces Giraut, "poeta della *virtus* mondana," with Folquet, "poeta della *Virtus* divina" ("Giraut de Bornelh nella prospettiva di Dante," p. 43). However, since the canzone "Voi che 'ntendendo" is much more associated with the *Convivio* and the *donna gentile* than is Giraut de Bornelh, and is nonetheless rehabilitated within the *Comedy*, the *Comedy*'s failure to accommodate Giraut is more likely due, in my opinion, to his connection via *rectitudo* to Guittone. Antonio Stäuble, "Le *Rime* della 'rettitudine'

Dante no longer seems inclined to acknowledge any vernacular poet of rectitude before himself, whether this be the immediate precursor Guittone or the more removed Giraut; he prefers to intimate, as in *Inferno* I where he designates Vergil the sole source of "lo bello stilo che m'ha fatto onore" ("the beautiful style that has brought me honor" [87]), that he draws his poetic nourishment from a more distant past.

Neither Guinizzelli nor Arnaut, the poets praised in *Purgatorio* XXVI, wrote moral verse. This factor seems paramount in their positioning; both poets are almost exclusively love poets, supreme within this context, who here purge their metaphoric and textual passions in the refining fire.[28] Arnaut Daniel was canonized in the *De Vulgari Eloquentia* as the Provençal love poet par excellence; nonetheless Dante's purgatorial celebration of the troubadour has elicited some mixed critical reaction, which still surfaces in the tendency to limit Arnaut's impact on Dante to his importance as a technical model, primarily in the *rime petrose*, and to claim that aesthetic criteria are alone responsible for his presence in *Purgatorio* XXVI.[29] Stylistic considerations

---

nella coscienza poetica di Dante," *Studi e problemi di critica testuale*, 8 (1974), 82-97, argues that Dante suppresses those poets who are his models in the area of moral poetry, namely Giraut and Guittone. De Lollis was working in this direction in "Arnaldo e Guittone," where he notes Dante's preference for love poetry, i.e. Arnaut, over moral/political poetry, i.e. Guittone.

[28] The nonamatory poetry of Arnaut and Guinizzelli is minimal: Arnaut wrote one *sirventes*, "Pois Raimons e·n Trucs Malecs"; Guinizzelli wrote a few sonnets on literary and moral themes. In accord with Roncaglia, "Il canto XXVI del *Purgatorio*," followed by Perugi, "Arnaut Daniel in Dante," and Folena, "Il canto di Guido Guinizzelli," I discount the biographical status of their lust; the point is that they are love poets.

[29] A number of critics, including Hoepffner, Hauvette, and Véran, articulate their surprise at Dante's admiration for Arnaut; Hoepffner endorses the position taken by W. P. Ker in "Dante, Guido Guinicelli and Arnaut Daniel," *Modern Language Review*, 4 (1909), 145-152 (repr. in *Form and Style in Poetry* [London: Macmillan, 1928], pp. 319-328), when he claims that Dante's admiration for Arnaut rests "essentiellement sur la forme, et non sur le fond" ("Dante et les Troubadours," p. 200). Maurice Bowra, on the other hand, defends the notion of a thematic as well as formal convergence between Dante and Arnaut, arguing that Arnaut too possesses an idealized conception of love; see "Dante

are indeed an integral part of Arnaut's fascination, but precisely because he goes further than any previous troubadour in fusing formal values with his deepest identity, deriving style from an internalized erotic mysticism that is uniquely his. Dante is not so much interested in literal similarities, such as those critics insisted on positing between Guilhem de Montanhagol's chaste love and the *stil novo*, as he is in an ideal consonance;[30] he finds in Arnaut an intensity of amorous commitment that prefigures his own, a poet who displays throughout his verse an overt link between eros and praxis, eros and knowledge. Not only is Arnaut objectively the greatest of the *Comedy*'s troubadours, from the poetic standpoint, but his understanding of the poet's métier is much like that articulated in *Purgatorio* XXIV; in Arnaut's poetry we find a total identification of the lover and the poet, as well as an insistence on Love as the exclusive source of poetic inspiration. Thus, in verses that proleptically combine the "fabbro" metaphor of *Purgatorio* XXVI with the poetic credo of *Purgatorio* XXIV, Arnaut claims to "forge and file words of worth with art of Love" (II, 12-14); he, like Dante, is initiated into a school where Love is the teacher:[31]

---

and Arnaut Daniel," *Speculum*, 27 (1952), 459-474, and the review by Marco Boni, in *Studi danteschi*, 33 (1955-56), 167-174. Both Elio Melli, "Dante e Arnaut Daniel," *Filologia romanza*, 6 (1959), 423-448, and Gianluigi Toja, in the Introduction to his edition, *Arnaut Daniel: Canzoni* (Florence: Sansoni, 1960), provide excellent bibliographical surveys of the criticism on Arnaut Daniel and Dante. Mauro Braccini, "Paralipomeni al 'Personaggio-Poeta' (*Purgatorio* XXVI 140-7)," in *Testi e interpretazioni: Studi del Seminario di filologia romanza dell'Università di Firenze* (Milan-Naples: Ricciardi, 1978), pp. 169-256, examines Arnaut's Provençal discourse within the larger phenomenon of the *Comedy*'s plurilingualism.

[30] The case for Guilhem de Montanhagol's *prestilnovismo* is made by De Lollis, in "Dolce stil novo e 'noel dig de nova maestria.' " As Aurelio Roncaglia points out, the entire movement to find stilnovist precedents is a misguided one; see "Precedenti e significato dello 'stil novo' dantesco," in *Dante e Bologna nei tempi di Dante* (Bologna: Commissione per i testi di lingua, 1967), pp. 13-34.

[31] Paterson, *Troubadours and Eloquence*, chap. 5, stresses the "unity of love and art" in Arnaut's poetry, giving more examples of this theme on pages 187-188. Michelangelo Picone, *Vita Nuova e tradizione romanza* (Padova: Liviana,

farai, c'Amors m'o comanda,
breu chansson de razon loigna,
que gen m'a duoich de las artz de s'escola

I will make, because Love commands me, a brief song with a long theme, for well has he trained me in the arts of his school

(XVI, 3-5)

If Love commands, then a poet can truly write "new" poetry. Of all the troubadour claims for newness, only Arnaut's is—for Dante—invested with the epistemological guarantee required to legitimize his "chantar tot nou" ("wholly new song" [XIV, 44]); only Arnaut's poetry, therefore, can be considered a true precursor of the "nove rime."

Arnaut Daniel, the last lyric poet in Purgatory, is the *Comedy*'s quintessential love poet, in the same way that "Donne ch'avete," the canticle's last autocitation, is its quintessential love poem. In his first spoken verse Arnaut points forward to another poet, the only lyric poet in Paradise, Folquet de Marselha. As has frequently been remarked, this line from the *Comedy*, "Tan m'abellis vostre cortes deman" ("So much does your courteous request please me" [*Purg*. XXVI, 140]), echoes an incipit of Folquet's, indeed precisely the one cited in the *De Vulgari Eloquentia* (II, vi, 6), namely "Tant m'abellis l'amoros

---

1979), comments similarly: "È Arnaldo il primo poeta in volgare che formula con grande chiarezza il tema dell'identificazione di amore e poesia" (p. 39). Although one could assert the primacy of Bernart de Ventadorn for this tradition—one thinks of the well-known verses pointed to in this context by Silvio Pellegrini, " 'Quando Amor mi spira,' " p. 165: "Chantars no pot gaire valer, / si d'ins dal cor no mou lo chans; / ni chans no pot dal cor mover, / si no es fin' amor coraus" "Singing cannot be worth anything if the song does not come from within the heart; and the song cannot come from within the heart, if within it there is not true love" (Moshé Lazar, ed., *Bernard de Ventadour, Troubadour du XIIe Siècle: Chansons d'Amour* [Paris: Klincksieck, 1966], p. 64)—Arnaut is the first, as Braccini notes, to associate Love "non con il generico *trobar* ma con il suo aspetto espressamente tecnico" ("Paralipomeni al 'Personaggio-Poeta,' " p. 252). All quotations of Arnaut are from Toja's edition.

pessamens."³² Thus Arnaut indicates the identity of his successor; by echoing Folquet's love poem he implies that the troubadour from Marseilles will be the next (and last) of the *Comedy*'s love poets. Like Arnaut, Folquet is placed among those with lustful tendencies; moreover, the "folle amore" of *Paradiso* VIII, 2 recalls Arnaut's "passada folor" of *Purgatorio* XXVI, 143.³³ In the episode of *Paradiso* IX Folquet briefly addresses himself to his past history as a "mad lover," stressing the intimate bond between himself and the heaven of Venus: "e questo cielo / di me s'imprenta, com' io fe' di lui" ("and this heaven is imprinted by me, as I was by it" [95-96]); to clarify the nature of the bond, he offers three classical parallels, saying that neither Dido nor Phyllis nor Hercules burned with greater love than he (97-102).³⁴ Interestingly, the poem echoed by Arnaut and cited in the *De Vulgari Eloquentia* testifies to just such an excessive love as Folquet describes in the *Paradiso*: "no·us am saviamens" ("I do not love you wisely") says the poet to his lady at the beginning of stanza V, and later he adds

[32] The echo of Folquet's "Tant m'abellis l'amoros pessamens" in the *Purgatorio*'s "Tan m'abellis vostre cortes deman" was noted by Nicola Zingarelli in his seminal study on Folquet in the *Comedy*, *La personalità storica di Folchetto di Marsiglia nella Commedia di Dante*, 2d ed. rev. (1897; repr. Bologna: Zanichelli, 1899), p. 25. See also the various reviews of Zingarelli's book: Cesare De Lollis, *Rassegna bibliografica della letteratura italiana*, 5 (1897), 127-132; Michele Scherillo, *Bullettino della Società Dantesca Italiana*, 4 (1897), 65-76; Francesco Torraca, *Nuova antologia*, 153 (1897), 152-165. Scherillo's "Dante et Folquet de Marseille," *Nouvelle Revue d'Italie*, 18 (Sept.-Oct. 1921), 59-75, is essentially the same article as his 1897 review. Folquet's poetry is quoted and numbered according to the edition of Stanisław Stroński, *Le Troubadour Folquet de Marseille* (Cracow: Librairie "Spółka Wydawnicza Polska," 1910).

[33] These parallels between the treatment of Arnaut and Folquet are noted by Franco Suitner, "Due trovatori nella *Commedia* (Bertran de Born e Folchetto di Marsiglia)," *Atti della Accademia Nazionale dei Lincei*, Memorie, Classe di Scienze morali, storiche e filologiche, Serie VIII, vol. XXIV, 5 (1980), 579-643.

[34] Zingarelli theorizes that the three classical parallels are an oblique reference to Folquet's three loves, and to the fact that the *canso* "Tant m'abellis" is sent, in its last line, to "tres donnas" (*La personalità storica di Folchetto di Marsiglia nella Commedia di Dante*, p. 40).

"Trop vos am mais, dona, qu'ieu no sai dire" ("I love you too much more, lady, than I know how to say" [41]). Such sentiments may be found throughout Folquet's love poetry; in XIII he tells us that "amiei follamen" ("I loved madly" [29]), using a variant of the key term *folle*, and twice he refers to the lady he adores (I, 31; VI, 25).

Folquet is suited for the heaven he inhabits not only as a lover in Venus but also as an extremely rhetorical and contrived poet in the heaven of Rhetoric.[35] As a lover he exemplifies the sublimation of erotic love into divine love—something he accomplishes while still on earth by choosing to give up his life as court poet and successful merchant for the monastery. The sublimation of eros that Folquet emblematizes is reproduced dramatically, by placing him in this heaven, and stylistically, by placing in this heaven some of the *Paradiso*'s most daring examples of a transcendent linguistic eroticism. We have seen that in the heaven of Venus personal intimacy is deflected, as in the case of Dante's meeting with Charles Martel, by a dominant political discourse and a strategic use of rhetoric. In his meeting with the troubadour, the pilgrim requires nine lines just to ask Folquet his name: because God sees all, and Folquet sees in God, Folquet can see and satisfy Dante's desire to know who he is, as indeed Dante himself would do for him, were he in Folquet as Folquet is in him. The first and last lines in this passage are hallmarks of a rhetorical copulation that now takes the place of any more direct affectivity: the union between God and Folquet, "Dio vede tutto, e tuo veder s'inluia" ("God sees all, and your sight in-Hims itself" [*Par.* IX, 73]), leads to the union of Folquet and Dante, "s'io m'intuassi, come tu t'inmii" ("if I were to in-you myself, as you in-me yourself" [81]).[36]

---

[35] According to the correspondences Dante sets up in *Convivio* II, xiii between the heavens and the branches of learning, the heaven of Venus is also the heaven of Rhetoric. Stroński comments on the artificial and contrived nature of Folquet's poetry, saying that the troubadour was considered "le maitre du style subtil" (p. 86*).

[36] Enzo Esposito, "Il canto IX del *Paradiso*," in *Letture del Paradiso*, ed. Vittorio Vettori, pp. 141-166, refers to the three neologisms, "s'inluia," "m'intuassi," "t'inmii," as "i segni eroici d'un tentativo di approssimazione semantica all'inesprimibile" (pp. 158-159).

This passage is preceded by a description of Folquet, "L'altra letizia, che m'era già nota / per cara cosa" ("The other joy, who was already known to me as a precious thing" [67-68]), who comes to the pilgrim's attention "qual fin balasso in che lo sol percuota" ("like a fine ruby on which the sun is striking" [69]). Here the phrase "cara cosa" and the reference to Folquet as a precious gem echo Cunizza's original introduction of the troubadour, in which she calls him "questa luculenta e cara gioia" ("this resplendent and precious jewel" [37]); surely the repetition of "cara" and the insistence on Folquet as a precious jewel reflect his reputation as a poet of precious verse and *caras rimas*. The love poet who was so concerned to delineate the rhetorical and covert aspects of his passion, asking in one poem "s'ieu no·m sai cobrir, qui m'er cubrire?" ("if I cannot conceal myself, who will conceal me?" [IX, 32]), and whose biographers dwell on his use of "screen ladies" to hide the true object of his affections, now partakes of a love whose rhetoric is disengaged from the games of eros and from the service of concealment.[37]

The strategies of concealment were already, less complicatedly, dismantled by Arnaut, who tells the pilgrim that he cannot and will not hide himself: "qu'ieu no me puesc ni voill a vos cobrire" (*Purg.* XXVI, 141). His use of the verb *cobrir*, which figures so prominently in Folquet's lexicon, may be seen as another anticipation of Folquet, especially in that it immediately follows the recall of "Tant m'abellis."[38] *Cobrir* runs through

[37] Folquet's use of "screen ladies" causes a misunderstanding that leads to the loss of his true love; see Stroński, *Razo* 1, pp. 4-6. On the relation of the use of "screen ladies" by Folquet to the *donne dello schermo* of the *Vita Nuova*, see Zingarelli, pp. 45-46.

[38] This is not to deny the usual interpretation of line 141, namely that it is a palinode of Arnaut's *trobar clus*, as suggested by Sapegno, *Purgatorio*, p. 292. Regarding antecedents for *Purgatorio* XXVI, 143, "consiros vei la passada folor," for which Perugi suggests the incipit of a *canso* by Guillem de Berguedà, "Consiros cant e planc e plor," I would like to point also to the opening of Folquet's XXVII (a crusade song and the only one of the poems doubtfully attributed to Folquet which Stroński tends to accept as authentic); here we find, along with the initial "Consiros," a song that is antithetically composed both of joy and tears, as in the *Purgatorio*'s "Ieu sui Arnaut, que plor e vau cantan": "Consiros, cum partitz d'amor, / chant mesclatz de joy e de plor" (XXVII, 1-2). A reconstruction of Arnaut's purgatorial speech is provided by Perugi,

Folquet's *canzoniere*, in thematic contrast to its opposite, *des-cobrir*, which stands at the other pole as the poet's unobtainable desire: "Chantan volgra mon fin cor descobrir" ("In singing I would like to disclose my true heart" [VI, 1]).[39] The necessity for concealment generates a painful tension; the lover wants to reveal himself to his beloved, "To you I would like to reveal the pain that I feel" (IX, 29), but he may not, precisely because "If I cannot conceal myself, who then will conceal me"? (IX, 32). To disclose is to dis-cover (*des-cobrir*), and discovery—either of the self or of the beloved—is not possible in the world of "courtly love," where masks and games are essential; in heaven, where they are not needed, the pilgrim's thoughts are spontaneously revealed to the troubadour through the divinely open medium of Paradise. It is worth noting that in his poetry Folquet did on one occasion suggest a turning to an unconcealed love; this anomalous use of *cobrir* occurs in his last poem, significantly not a love song, but a crusade song: "Hueimais no·y conosc razo / *ab que nos puscam cobrir,* / si ja Dieu volem servir" ("Henceforth I know no reason *with which we can cover ourselves,* if indeed we want to serve God" [XIX, 1-3; italics mine]). In other words, to serve God we must put aside the

---

"Arnaut Daniel in Dante," pp. 116-139; Folena, "Il canto di Guido Guinizzelli," pp. 504-507; and Mauro Braccini, "Paralipomeni al 'Personaggio-Poeta,' " Appendix I, "Sul testo dei vv. 140-7," pp. 224-229. For a linguistic analysis of these verses, see Nathaniel B. Smith, "Arnaut Daniel in the *Purgatorio*: Dante's Ambivalence toward Provençal," *Dante Studies,* 98 (1980), 99-109.

[39] *Cobrir* and related words appear in Folquet's poems as follows: *cobrir* in III, 27; VI, 22; IX, 32; XIV, 15; XV, 57; XIX, 2; *celar* in IX, 30, 34; *celadamen* in IX, 31; *cobertamen* in XIV, 23. *Descobrir* appears only once, in VI, 1. Interestingly, the *tenso* with "Tostemps" also centers around concealment; the poets debate the pros and cons of loving a promiscuous lady who openly displays her love versus those of loving a loyal lady who keeps her love hidden. Folquet argues for the former, surprising his partner, who had considered him too refined a lover to make such a choice ("mas vos qi es fis amayre" [XV, 55]); are the courtly games of concealment so trying that they drive the lover to prefer openness even to fidelity? Regarding the verb *cobrir* in Arnaut's purgatorial speech, Braccini notes that " 'parlar . . . ab cubertz entresens' è per Bernart de Ventadorn requisito dell'amore e il *celar* compare fin da Guglielmo IX" ("Paralipomeni al 'Personaggio-Poeta,' " p. 208).

strategies of closure that govern human love; we must uncover—or discover—ourselves, and stand revealed.

Folquet is the love poet of Paradise precisely because of the disclosed nature of his service to God, well-known to his contemporaries and demonstrated by the Provençal biography; after withdrawing to a Cistercian monastery, he became, eventually, Bishop of Toulouse, avid participant in the Albigensian Crusade, and loyal supporter of Saint Dominic:[40]

> abandonet lo mon; e si se rendet a l'orde de Cistel ab sa muiller et ab dos fillz qu'el avia. E si fo faichs abas d'una rica abadia, qu'es en Proensa, que a nom lo Torondet. E pois el fo faichs evesques de Tolosa; e lai el muric.

> he left the world. And he gave himself to the Cistercian order with his wife and the two sons that he had. And he was made abbot of a rich abbey which is in Provence which is called *lo Torondet*. And then he was made Bishop of Toulouse. And there he died.

The upheaval in Folquet's life chronicled by the *vida* is reflected in his last poems, the *planh* for his dead lord, Barral, and the two crusade songs. A tone of melancholic withdrawal runs through all three poems, but is particularly apparent in the lament, where the traditional complaints are compounded by an unusually defined sense of the futility of earthly life and earthly love:

> Et er, qan foz plus poiatz,
> faillitz a guisa de flor
> que, qand hom la ve genssor,
> adoncs ill chai plus viatz;
> mas Dieus nos mostr' ab semblans
> que sol lui devem amar

---

[40] See Stroński for the details of Folquet's religious career, and for his positive assessment of Folquet's character, pp. 87*-99*. On Folquet's negative image and the *Chanson de la Croisade*, see also Suitner, "Due trovatori nella *Commedia*," pp. 633-636. The text of the *vida* is from Jean Boutière and A.-H. Schutz, eds., *Biographies des Troubadours*, 2d ed. rev. (Paris: Nizet, 1964), p. 471; all of the Provençal biographies will be quoted from this edition.

e·l chaitiu segl' azirar
on pass' om com vianans,
qu'autre pretz torn' en desonor
e totz autre sens en folor
mas de cels que fan sos comans.

And now, when you have most risen up, you fall down like a flower which, when one sees it at its most beautiful, then it falls the soonest; but God shows us with [such] examples that we must love only Him and despise the miserable world where man passes through as a voyager, for other worth turns into dishonor and all other understanding into madness, except [the understanding] of those who carry out his commands.

(XVII, 45-55)

In a genre that normally goes no further than to forecast secular desolation as a result of one man's death, this troubadour suggests that the death of his lord be read in an overtly religious key, as a lesson in *contemptus mundi*; the fall of this "flower" must be seen to signify not just the demise of a particular state or system but rather the eventual demise and consequent unworthiness of all mortal things.

It is a short step from Folquet's *planh* to his conversion; after the recognition that we are but "voyagers" in a transitory world ("on pass' om com vianans" [52]) comes the sure knowledge that "we must love only Him" ("que sol lui devem amar" [50]). If the *planh* for Barral illuminates the spiritual condition required for conversion from human to divine love, thus adumbrating one aspect of Dante's troubadour, Folquet's crusade songs prefigure the militant stance adopted by the poet in Paradise. The language used by Folquet in heaven to present Raab, and later in his denunciation of the Roman Curia, is the language of a crusader; both Christ's "triumph" (*Par.* IX, 120) and Joshua's "glory" (124) are viewed as victories in which Raab provided critical assistance to the heroic conquerors. Such a metaphoric construct comes easily to a poet who wrote at least two crusade songs, reminding us in one that "such death [death in a crusade] is good" (XIX, 22). Indeed, the *razo* refers to this poem twice as a "prezicansa," or sermon, precisely because of its hortatory mission, and the critical tradition as far back as Zingarelli derives the apostolic tone of the last section of *Paradiso* IX from the tone of Folquet's crusade songs.[41] In this context, we can readily admit Folquet's suitability as the poet to take Giraut's place in the *Comedy*'s version of the lists of the *De Vulgari Eloquentia*; he moves from second place, immediately below Giraut in the catalogue of II, vi, to first place, his privileged position in Paradise, on the basis of his converted love and his divinely militaristic mission. On the other hand, although Folquet usurps the supreme position held by Giraut in the earlier text, his role in the *Comedy* is not the equivalent of Giraut's in the *De Vulgari Eloquentia*. Mirroring the heaven in which he is situated, Folquet is dichotomous, as is apparent from the two distinct linguistic registers adopted by his discourse: one reflects the preciosity of his love poems and the other the fervor of his crusade songs.[42]

Folquet is not a poet of rectitude. His *canzoniere* presents us with fourteen love poems (of which I-IX give a hopeful view of love and X-XIV are negative), one *tenso* on an erotic theme (XV), one *cobla* of an unfinished *canso* (XVI), the lament for Barral (XVII), and the two crusade songs (XVIII and XIX). In other words, we find here two distinct kinds of love poetry, one motivated by a secular love and one by a divine love.[43] What

---

[41] The reference to a *prezicansa* is in Stroński's *Razo* IV, p. 8. The connection between Folquet's crusade songs and the invective at the end of *Paradiso* IX is made by Zingarelli, pp. 62-72; Folena, in the Introduction to *Vulgares eloquentes*, refers to the invective of canto IX as "la perorazione finale in chiave di sirventese morale e di canzone di crociata" (p. X).

[42] Toja elaborates on Zingarelli's idea that the linguistic registers of *Paradiso* IX are intended to reflect both Folquet the poet/lover and Folquet the apostle; see "Il canto di Folchetto da Marsiglia," *Convivium*, 34 (1966), 234-256.

[43] The poems of doubtful attribution do not in any way alter my argument. Besides love poems, there is one crusade song (XXVII) and two religious songs dealing with repentance (XXVIII and XXIX); of these, Stroński does not think any but the crusade song is even possibly authentic. Stäuble too refutes Mengaldo's argument that Folquet is the *Comedy*'s poet of rectitude, saying "pre-

we do not find is a concerted attempt to direct people in the living of their everyday lives, or to provide an anatomy of morals, as Giraut does within the limits of the chivalric code and Guittone does within a much larger Christian and civic scheme. The category of poet of rectitude is in fact not available to the lyric poets of the *Comedy*; rather, they may aspire to a poetics of erotic conversion, like Folquet. The two lyric poets in Dante's lexicon who require such a category, Giraut and Guittone, are rejected out of hand, their authority as precursors denied, their presence in the *Comedy* entirely negative. Within this general picture, however, we find one possible textual echo with some suggestive implications. The *Comedy*'s first invocation to the Muses—"O Muse, o alto ingegno, or m'aiutate; / o mente che scrivesti ciò ch'io vidi, / qui si parrà la tua nobilitate" ("O Muses, o high genius, help me now; o memory that wrote down what I saw, here will your nobility appear" [*Inf.* II, 7-9])—recalls the incipit of Guittone's great conversion poem, "Ora parrà s'eo saverò cantare" ("Now it will appear if I know how to sing"). Dante's verses pick up and recombine two specific textual elements: Guittone's first word, "Ora," reappears in the injunction to the Muses, "or m'aiutate," with the same purpose of marking a new poetic beginning; Guittone's second word, the striking verb "parrà," reappears in "qui si parrà la tua nobilitate" (the only time this form of the verb *parere* appears in the *Inferno*), bearing the same semantic weight of a newly achieved poetic destiny articulated in the moment of its first manifestation.[44] Both passages are the markers of a moment of textual revelation; both are concerned with letting it be known that "I know how to sing." Thus, at the *Comedy*'s beginning, as he effects the most sensational of transitions, Dante echoes

---

feriremmo vedere in Folchetto e nella sua conversione una 'figura' dell'evoluzione dall' 'Amor' alla 'Charitas,' dall'amore profano all'amore sacro, cioè un'ulteriore espressione del 'superamento' della poesia amorosa" ("Le *Rime* della 'rettitudine' nella coscienza poetica di Dante," p. 93).

[44] *Parrà* appears in the *Comedy* only five times: *Inf.* II, 9; *Purg.* II, 66; *Purg.* IV, 91; *Par.* V, 25; *Par.* XVI, 77. Interestingly, in *Paradiso* V Dante comes very close to imitating Guittone: "Or ti parrà, se tu quinci argomenti."

the verse of a lesser forebear, as he effects his own lesser transition.[45] The passage from love poetry to moral poetry is a crucial one, with a direct bearing on the *Comedy*; as the initiator of that passage, the launcher of that transition, Guittone is here implicitly recognized—as the only one of Dante's lyric precursors who could actively imagine, if not the *Comedy* itself, at least the space that the *Comedy* would later fill.

Fathers and Sons: Guinizzelli and Cavalcanti

If, in the *Comedy*, Guittone is a presence, repeatedly vilified, Cavalcanti is an absence, just as systematically denied his due. We have already touched on Cavalcanti's pivotal role as Dante's early mentor, his first freely chosen vernacular poetic *auctoritas*. Cavalcanti's importance is overtly acknowledged in a poem like the *plazer* "Guido, i' vorrei che tu e Lapo ed io," where his privileged position as head of the group of young poets is reflected by his emphatic initial position in the verse. Guido is the fourth character to be introduced into the *Vita Nuova*, after Dante, Beatrice, and Amor; he makes his first appearance in chapter III, where Dante is discussing the response to the *libello*'s first sonnet:

> A questo sonetto fue risposto da molti e di diverse sentenzie; tra li quali fue risponditore quelli cui io chiamo primo de li miei amici, e disse allora uno sonetto, lo quale comincia: *Vedeste, al mio parere, onne valore.* E questo fue quasi lo principio de l'amistà tra lui e me, quando elli seppe che io era quelli che li avea ciò mandato.

> To this sonnet many replied with differing points of view; among these respondents was the one I call the first of my

---

[45] Another Guittonian echo at the beginning of the *Comedy* is posited by Aino Anna-Maria Paasonen, "Dante's 'Firm Foot' and Guittone d'Arezzo," *Romance Philology*, 33 (1979), 312-317, who believes that the famous crux of *Inferno* I, 30, "sì che 'l piè fermo sempre era 'l più basso," echoes a passage from Guittone's letters.

friends, and at the time he composed a sonnet, which begins: "Vedeste, al mio parere, onne valore." And this may be said to mark the beginning of the friendship between him and me, when he learned that I was the one who had sent him this.

(*Vita Nuova*, III, 14)

The seemingly casual citation of Guido's sonnet in this passage is noteworthy; the incipit is in fact the only fragment of vernacular poetry to be incorporated into the text of the *Vita Nuova*, and is thus implicitly placed on a par with the classical Latin verses that are cited in chapter XXV. Also, in chapter III Guido is named with the periphrasis, "primo de li miei amici," which will mark all his subsequent entrances into the *libello*: in chapter XXIV he is "questo primo mio amico," as again in chapters XXV and XXX. In XXV Guido and Dante are united in a common poetic front against those modern poets who "compose foolishly" (the expression "rimano stoltamente" would seem to anticipate the "stolti" of *Purgatorio* XXVI); in XXX, where Guido is mentioned for the penultimate time, Dante considers his friend an indispensable supporter of his project to write in the vernacular, and dedicates the book to him: "questo mio primo amico a cui io ciò scrivo" ("this my first friend, to whom I write this" [XXX, 3]).

Cavalcanti is thus the only contemporary vernacular poet to be overtly cited in the *Vita Nuova* and to have an active role in the narrative. The text to which we next turn in charting the developing attitude of Dante toward his first friend is the *De Vulgari Eloquentia*. Here we find Guido in his accustomed place as the leader of the *stilnovisti*; the group referred to earlier in the incipit of "Guido, i' vorrei che tu e Lapo ed io" is transposed, in the same order, into the treatise's "Guido, Lapo and one other [Dante], Florentines, and Cino of Pistoia" (I, xiii, 4).[46]

---

[46] On the status of the sonnet "Guido, i' vorrei che tu e Lapo ed io," its reflection of the *stil novo* as a group and its relation to the *De Vulgari Eloquentia*, see Guglielmo Gorni, " 'Guido, i' vorrei che tu e Lippo ed io' (sul canone del Dolce Stil Novo)," *Studi di filologia italiana*, 36 (1978), 21-37, and also the

Guinizzelli and Cavalcanti

In the long list of II, vi, Cavalcanti is in his correct position, after Guinizzelli and before Cino and Dante. "Donna me prega," Guido's most famous canzone, is cited twice in the treatise; considering how few canzoni Guido wrote (two full ones and an isolated stanza), he would therefore seem to be well represented. We note, however, that "Donna me prega" is not cited among the "illustres cantiones" of II, vi; Dante prefers to cite instead the incomplete canzone, "Poi che di doglia cor conven ch'i' porti," saving "Donna me prega" for the technical sections at the end of Book II. Most notably, the addition of a fourth name to the list of names inherited from "Guido, i' vorrei," the name of Cino da Pistoia, signals the radical shift in perspective wrought by the treatise, whereby Cavalcanti's place as "first friend" is taken over by Cino.[47] Throughout the treatise, Cino's name is coupled with Dante's, most frequently in the formula through which Dante avoids using his own name by referring to himself as Cino's friend. Thus, the expression "amicus eius" takes the place of "primo amico." When Dante announces that the Italian vernacular is supreme in the lyric mode, "Cino and his friend" are introduced as those poets who have composed most sweetly and subtly in it (I, x, 2). Only Cino and Dante are specifically named as poets who have demonstrated the *vulgare illustre* in their poetry (I, xvii, 3). Cino—not Cavalcanti—is the Italian poet of love, the companion to Dante, Italian poet of rectitude. Cino is included in the shorter list of II, v, devoted to canzoni that begin with hendecasyllables, whereas Cavalcanti is not. Thus, although Guido's nominal position as the oldest and hence leading member of *stilnovisti* is

---

reply of Domenico De Robertis, "Amore e Guido ed io . . . (relazioni poetiche e associazioni di testi)," *Studi di filologia italiana*, 36 (1978), 39-65. Gorni's article is reprinted in his *Il nodo della lingua e il verbo d'amore: Studi su Dante e altri duecentisti* (Florence: Olschki, 1981), pp. 99-124.

[47] Mengaldo and Marti both discuss the fact that Cino takes Guido's place as part of the subtle anti-Cavalcantian polemic of the *De Vulgari Eloquentia*; see Mengaldo, Introduction, *De Vulgari Eloquentia*, p. XCIII; Marti, "Con Dante fra i poeti del suo tempo," pp. 106-112.

respected, he is never singled out in the *De Vulgari Eloquentia* as he is in the *Vita Nuova*.

Dante's attitude in the treatise forecasts the severer silence of the *Comedy*, where Guido is the great nonpresence among the poets. First of all, Guido is the only love poet in the *Comedy* to be named and discussed in Hell, a negative privilege whose repercussions still affect our critical stance. What has perhaps gone unappreciated is the intentionality of Dante's decisions with respect to his first friend. In the same way that there is no love poetry in the *Inferno*, a canticle that accommodates only misquotations, so there can be no love poets; by definition any love poet, no matter how plebeian, belongs to the *Purgatorio*. In keeping with this implicit structural principle, no love poet ever appears in the first canticle: Francesca is a reader, not a practitioner; Pier della Vigna is the textual representative of the prose style of the Federician chancellery, not of the *scuola siciliana*; Bertran de Born functions according to the *De Vulgari Eloquentia*, as a poet of arms.[48] In this context, Guido's solitary status as the only love poet even to be discussed in the *Inferno* is the more noteworthy. The discussion belongs, of course, to *Inferno* X, where Dante meets the heretical bedfellows Farinata degli Uberti and Cavalcante de' Cavalcanti, Guido's father. We remember the celebrated exchange between father and friend, in which Cavalcante senior insists divisively—or, in the canto's terms, "heretically"—on poetry as a form of competition, a way of determining "altezza d'ingegno." Assuming that the

---

[48] Contini says of Francesca that she is "un'usufruttuaria delle lettere, quel che si dice una lettrice, non una produttrice in proprio" ("Dante come personaggio-poeta della *Commedia*," p. 42). Leo Spitzer, "Speech and Language in *Inferno* XIII," *Italica*, 19 (1942), 81-104 (repr. in *Dante: A Collection of Critical Essays*, ed. John Freccero, pp. 78-101), and Ettore Paratore, "Analisi 'retorica' del canto di Pier della Vigna," *Studi danteschi*, 42 (1965), 281-336, discuss Piero's prose writings as the antecedents for the style of *Inferno* XIII. An analysis of *Inferno* XIII as an intertextual parody of Piero's *Eulogy*, an encomiastic piece written for Frederick II, is provided by William A. Stephany, "Pier della Vigna's Self-Fulfilling Prophecies: The *Eulogy* of Frederick II and *Inferno* 13," *Traditio*, 38 (1982), 193-212. Bertran de Born will be discussed in the next section of this chapter.

journey through Hell is undertaken on the basis of intellectual superiority, he wants to know where Guido is; piqued that his son has been denied a privilege accorded to Dante (the irony being that Guido is assigned through this very conversation the negative privilege of a position in Hell), he asks "Why isn't he with you?" with its implication that "you are no better than he." The relationship between Dante and his first friend is thus cast in a competitive light, which recurs in the only other episode in which Guido is mentioned, that of *Purgatorio* XI.

The dialectical tribute of *Inferno* X—Guido is, after all, unique in being accorded even an implied intellectual parity with Dante—is more fully articulated in *Purgatorio* XI. Here the original complimentary expression, "altezza d'ingegno," is replaced by a more specific poetic accolade, regarding "la gloria de la lingua," as Guido is inserted into a progressive continuum of cultural history:

> Credette Cimabue ne la pittura
>   tener lo campo, e ora ha Giotto il grido,
> sì che la fama di colui è scura.
> Così ha tolto l'uno a l'altro Guido
>   la gloria de la lingua; e forse è nato
> chi l'uno e l'altro caccerà del nido.
>
> Cimabue thought to hold the field in painting, and now Giotto has the cry, so that his [Cimabue's] fame is dark. Thus one Guido has taken from the other the glory of our tongue, and perhaps he is born who will chase the one and the other from the nest.
>
> (94-99)

In the poetic hierarchy established here, Guido Cavalcanti takes the linguistic palm from the first Guido, Guinizzelli, to lose it in his turn to a third poet, who can only be Dante himself.[49]

---

[49] The commentary tradition as recorded by Guido Biagi (including the early commentators Jacopo della Lana, the Ottimo, Pietro di Dante, Benvenuto, Francesco da Buti, and the Anonimo Fiorentino) is unanimously in favor of Guinizzelli and Cavalcanti as the two Guidos of *Purgatorio* XI (see *La Divina Com-*

The tribute to Cavalcanti is real, for the sentence structure associates "la gloria de la lingua" with him, but it is also immediately undercut, by the menacing presence of the unnamed third. It is thus a mistake to concentrate on the presumed humility inherent in Dante's not naming himself, or on the rhythmic and impersonal passing of fame from one artistic peak to the next, which is the final burden of Oderisi's speech: "La vostra nominanza è color d'erba, / che viene e va" ("Your renown is

---

media nella figurazione artistica e nel secolare commento, vol. II, pp. 202-204); the tradition is somewhat less firm in the identification of the unnamed third. Although the consensus is for Dante (Jacopo, the Ottimo, Benvenuto, Francesco), there are early murmurings on the implications of such a statement; thus the Anonimo Fiorentino is uncertain as to whether the third poet is Dante, because although Dante is in fact the greatest poet of his day, for him to say so would be an act of pride, "e ragionevolmente non può esser ripreso l'A[utore] di superbia" (p. 204). An amusing solution is provided by Alessandro Vellutello (1544), who suggests that "mosso da profetico spirito," Dante is here referring to Petrarch (p. 205). More to the point is Antonio Cesari (1824-1826), who comments: "Addio D[ante], a bel rivederci qua col sasso in collo, con gli altri superbi . . . !" (p. 205). In fact, the articulation of Dante's own pride on the terrace of pride is surely intentional, a key to the dialectical workings of this *cornice*, as the pilgrim himself confirms when shortly thereafter, in an unusually explicit moment, he confesses his penchant for *superbia* (*Purg.* XIII, 136-138). Returning to the question of the two Guidos, in "L'uno e l'altro Guido," *Ausonia* 23, nos. 2-3 (1968), 9-13, Guido Di Pino argues that they are Guittone and Guinizzelli, rather than Cavalcanti and Guinizzelli; his suggestion, although rejected by Marti on linguistic grounds (*Storia dello Stil nuovo*, vol. I, p. 57), has found some supporters (e.g. Picone, *Vita Nuova e tradizione romanza*, p. 32; Ciccuto, "Dante e Bonagiunta," p. 390). In my opinion, Dante's attitude toward Guittone is such as to preclude the possibility that he would ever associate the Aretine—however briefly—with "la gloria de la lingua." But Guittone is not therefore entirely absent from this terrace, which deals so exhaustively with art and poetry; as Sapegno has noticed, Provenzan Salvani's words, "Più non dirò, e scuro so che parlo" ("I will speak no more, and I know that I speak obscurely" [*Purg.* XI, 139]), echo Guittone's "Scuro saccio che par lo / mio detto, ma' che parlo / a chi s'entend' ed ame" ("I know that my discourse seems obscure, but I speak to those who understand and love" [Tuttor, s'eo veglio o dormo," 61-63]). Far from viewing this Guittonian allusion as "proof" that the first Guido is Guittone (see Ciccuto, p. 390), I would read it as an oblique statement on Guittonian poetics: by means of this textual echo Dante locates Guittone's poetic pride in his willful obscurity.

the color of grass, which comes and goes" [*Purg.* XI, 115-116]). In the *terzina* devoted to the poets, Dante does not speak of an impersonal coming and going, but of a highly personal wresting away; the verbs he chooses are active, and even violent: one Guido "has taken" from the other, the third "will chase" both from the nest. Particularly suggestive is this last verse, "chi l'uno e l'altro caccerà del nido," especially when we consider that Cavalcanti is *in fact* driven from the nest, by being denied his rightful place in the *Comedy* as an acknowledged major shaper of Dante's poetic growth.

One possible rightful place for Cavalcanti would be *Purgatorio* XXVI, where instead he is present, if at all, only among the anonymous poetic "betters" invoked by Dante while paying tribute to his "father," Guinizzelli. As Cino takes Cavalcanti's place in the *De Vulgari Eloquentia*, so Guinizzelli takes his place in the *Comedy*; one might say that the order of usurpation established in *Purgatorio* XI, where Cavalcanti "takes" from Guinizzelli, is reversed in *Purgatorio* XXVI. The tribute of canto XXVI culminates a long history in Dante's texts for the Bolognese poet, who is first referred to as the "saggio" of the sonnet in *Vita Nuova* XX: "Amore e 'l cor gentil sono una cosa, / sì come il saggio in suo dittare pone" ("Love and the noble heart are one thing, as the wise man claims in his verse"). The reference to Guinizzelli and his canzone at this point in the *Vita Nuova*'s narrative is, of course, far from casual. As first the *Vita Nuova* depicts the transition from Dante's early Guittonianism to his Cavalcantian stage, it then depicts the transition from his Cavalcantianism to the moment when, in "Donne ch'avete," he finds his own voice.[50] We might restate this by saying that, just as Cavalcanti first frees Dante from subjection to a Guittonian mode, so Guinizzelli later frees him from sub-

---

[50] The *Vita Nuova* reflects the transitions of Dante's lyric production as a whole. Thus, referring to their edition, Foster and Boyde assign poems 1-6 to the Tuscan manner, whereas number 7, "Tutti li miei penser parlan d'Amore," they consider a transitional poem, "indebted almost equally to the old models and the new" (*Commentary*, p. 77); poems 8-10 they place squarely in the Cavalcantian mode.

jection to a Cavalcantian mode. However, since this second transition occurs at a more advanced stage of Dante's development, and since Dante never takes on Guinizzelli's voice to the extent that he had earlier taken on Cavalcanti's (both because Dante is now too mature to be so influenced, and because he is deliberately engaging a poet, Guinizzelli, whose voice is less pronounced), it would be more accurate to say that at this juncture Dante uses Guinizzelli—in order to break Cavalcanti's hold and thus move in a direction more compatible with his own ultimate goals. Such use of Guinizzelli is apparent in "Donne ch'avete," whose radically hyperbolic discourse is built on the optimistic foundation of love as an ennobling force put forth by Guinizzelli in "Al cor gentil," and is therefore punctually acknowledged in the poem immediately following "Donne ch'avete," namely the sonnet of *Vita Nuova* XX, with its tribute to the new *auctoritas*: the "saggio," Guinizzelli.

Guinizzelli is treated in the *Vita Nuova* as an important but distant precursor; he is referred to deferentially but with none of the enthusiasm, the respect at close quarters, accorded Cavalcanti. Cavalcanti, however, pays the price for his prominence in the *libello* by suffering a demotion in the *De Vulgari Eloquentia*, where he is replaced by Cino as Dante's poetic ally and confidant. Guinizzelli reaps the benefits of being only a remote *saggio* in the *Vita Nuova*, continuing unscathed into the *De Vulgari Eloquentia*, where his status is enhanced. He is the first Italian poet to be named in the treatise, accompanying Giraut de Bornelh and Thibaut de Champagne as the representative poets in their respective languages and poetic cultures in I, ix. "Al cor gentil" is cited in the list of II, v, and another canzone, "Tegno de folle 'mpres', a lo ver dire," in the list of II, vi. As the leader of the Bolognese school of poets, Guinizzelli is called "maximus Guido" in I, xv, 6. He is mentioned for the last time in II, xii, where "Di fermo sofferire" is given as an example of a poem in the high style beginning with a *settenario*. All in all, Guinizzelli makes five appearances in the *De Vulgari Eloquentia*, one less than Cino and one more than Cavalcanti; even more interesting, however, is that he appears where neither Cino nor

Cavalcanti does, namely in the *Convivio,* one of only three contemporary poets to be mentioned in that predominantly classical text. Thus, Guinizzelli can be seen to move through Dante's texts in a crescendo of increasing importance. In the *Convivio,* "Al cor gentil" is again responsible for his prominence, as it was in *Vita Nuova* XX; the context is a discussion on the nature of true nobility, where Dante buttresses his argument by referring to "quel nobile Guido Guinizzelli" and his canzone (IV, xx, 7). The epithets that adorn Guinizzelli's name bear witness to the status quo he manages to preserve in Dante's esteem over the years; if he is not "saggio" he is "maximus," and if he is not "maximus" he is "quel nobile Guido Guinizzelli." And, although being in the *Convivio* does not guarantee success in the *Comedy* (it does not benefit Bertran de Born nor Giraut, the other contemporary poets so honored), in the case of Guinizzelli there is no backsliding.[51] Only in the *Comedy* is his position finally altered, and for the better: from an adjective he becomes a substantive; from a wise man he becomes a father.

Dante's purgatorial recognition of Guinizzelli does not in itself violate the truth. Guinizzelli's insistence that nobility is derived from internal worth rather than external status is of capital importance, as we have seen, not only in the lyric Dante but also in the social and political discourses of the *Convivio's* last book; and, although the idea had been succinctly stated by Guittone ("Non ver lignaggio fa sangue, ma core, / ni vero pregio poder, ma vertute" "Blood does not make true nobility, but heart, nor does power make true worth, but virtue" ["Comune perta fa comun dolore," 49-50]), who in this respect as in so many others is the first articulator of the "bourgeois" perspective, it was associated with Guinizzelli. Guinizzelli's most notable stylistic feature, his analogies, were highly successful in entrenching an abstract social concept as a lyric tenet; later, when Dante in the *Convivio* wants to argue that the imperfectly

---

[51] Mengaldo comments that Guinizzelli's eminent position is an unusual constant in Dante's texts (Introduction, *De Vulgari Eloquentia,* p. XCIV). See also Raffaele Spongano, "La gloria del primo Guido," *Dante e Bologna nei tempi di Dante,* pp. 3-12.

disposed soul is not capable of receiving the divine infusion of nobility, he has recourse to paraphrasing one of the analogies from "Al cor gentil": "sì come se una pietra margarita è male disposta, o vero imperfetta, la vertù celestiale ricever non può" ("as when if a precious stone is badly disposed, or indeed imperfect, it cannot receive celestial influence" [IV, xx, 7]). Guinizzelli supplies the program of praise adopted in the *Vita Nuova* as a means of breaking with the reflexivity of the traditional lyric format; the paradigm for a poetics based on "quelle parole che lodano la donna mia" is Guinizzelli's sonnet "Io voglio del ver la mia donna laudare," whose basic principle is reelaborated immediately in the first stanza of "Donne ch'avete" (2-3), and later in the sonnet presented as a consummate example of "lo stilo de la sua loda" (XXVI, 4), namely "Tanto gentile e tanto onesta pare." Finally, as the last stanza of "Al cor gentil" brilliantly testifies (a stanza whose self-consciousness is the key to Guinizzelli's newness), Guinizzelli's similes prepare the way for Dante's metaphors. By placing the blame for his analogies on the original Writer, God, Who in His book of the universe makes ladies so like angels ("Tenne d'angel sembianza" "She had the semblance of an angel" [58]), Guinizzelli seems to forecast a new kind of writing, in which ladies are literally angelic, conductors to the divine.[52]

The use of Guinizzelli to inaugurate the praise-style in the *Vita Nuova* has the double-edged result of breaking not only with the tradition but specifically with Cavalcanti, a poet whose lexicon does not admit *laudare*.[53] However, such a break, which occurs at the level of content—to praise or not to praise—should not be exaggerated; Cavalcanti remains, throughout the *Vita*

---

[52] In the face of Dante's accolade, scholars have assiduously debated the true extent of Guinizzelli's innovations. For a résumé of the *querelle*, see Marti, *Storia dello Stil nuovo*, vol. I, pp. 60-62 and vol. II, pp. 351-376; see also the recent contribution of Guglielmo Gorni, "Guido Guinizzelli e la nuova 'mainera,' " in the centennial volume *Per Guido Guinizzelli* (Padova: Antenore, 1980), pp. 37-52, repr. in *Il nodo della lingua e il verbo d'amore*, pp. 23-45.

[53] This point is made by Contini, "Cavalcanti in Dante," orig. 1968, repr. in *Un'idea di Dante*, p. 147.

Nuova, the indisputable source of Dante's style. It is Cavalcanti who initiates the Florentine mode in which Dante follows, and who is responsible for the anti-Guittonian program of linguistic simplification that Dante will adopt.[54] Thus, whereas Guinizzelli sent Guittone a reverential sonnet addressing him as "[O] caro padre meo," Cavalcanti was always resolute in distinguishing himself from the old school as represented by the Aretine (the yoking of a Guittonian exterior to the Aristotelian content of "Donna me prega" is intended to be, and is, subversive). He attacks Guittone in the sonnet "Da più a uno face un sollegismo," accusing him of being both philosophically and poeti-

[54] Contini states that "se l'esperimento stilnovistico deve ridursi a un' iniziativa e a un nome, questo non può essere che quello del Cavalcanti," and that "lo Stil Novo nel senso proprio, cioè fiorentino, . . . legittimamente potrebbe chiamarsi la scuola del Cavalcanti" (*Poeti del Duecento*, vol. II, pp. 445, 488). Another critic who emphasizes Cavalcanti's critical importance for Dante is De Robertis, especially in *Il libro della Vita Nuova*. Most associated with Cavalcanti's cause is Guido Favati, who points out that Dante is not the sole articulator of stilnovist poetics, but rather that he is preceded in this by Guido; see his "Contributo alla determinazione del problema dello Stil Nuovo," *Studi mediolatini e volgari*, 4 (1956), 57-70. In fact, Favati's book, *Inchiesta sul Dolce Stil Nuovo*, which is known for its rejection of the *stil novo* as a group phenomenon, could be seen less as an attack on the group than as a manifesto for Cavalcanti: "Dunque, non una 'scuola,' ma un singolo maestro, il Cavalcanti, e, per un tempo più o meno lungo, uno scolaro, l'Alighieri . . ." (p. 90). Even more peremptorily, Favati insists that there exists neither a common poetic project, nor a group of friends, but only "una isolata e prepotente personalità: quella di Guido Cavalcanti, che nessuno ritiene di poter accomunare ad altri" (p. 105). Although I sympathize with Favati's position, I fear that he reckons without Dante: the notion of a school, as presented in the *De Vulgari Eloquentia* and the *Comedy*, is a vehicle that Dante develops precisely in order to cancel any earlier overriding personality, such as Cavalcanti's; by concentrating on the fraternity, Dante ultimately highlights the member of the fraternity who baptizes it and brings it into being, namely himself. For, no matter how many caveats we may utter, as long as we use the expression *dolce stil novo*—Dante's expression—we mentally place Dante at the center of the poetic configuration. It is to this determinism that I believe Favati is reacting, his solution being to deny that Dante testifies to the existence of a group of poets. In my opinion, however, there is little doubt that Dante wants to create the image of a group; the questions (to the extent that this image exceeds the reality) are why, and to what end.

cally deficient; in the first quatrain he concentrates on Guittone's logical ineptitude, his inability to construct syllogisms, moving in the second quatrain to his rhetorical and expressive faults:

> Nel profferer, che cade 'n barbarismo,
> difetto di saver ti dà cagione;
> e come far poteresti un sofismo
> per silabate carte, fra Guittone?
>
> Regarding your expression, which is often incorrect, your lack of knowledge accuses you; and how could you compose—in verse—even a sophism, fra Guittone?
> (5-8)

In the sextet Cavalcanti continues to disparage his Tuscan precursor, drawing careful attention to his specific weaknesses: his inability to create a "figura," a word most likely to be interpreted not as a rhetorical figure but in the larger Cavalcantian sense as a fully objectified psychological reality ("Per te non fu giammai una figura" "No figure ever came to life through you" [9]); the harshness of his speech ("induri quanto più disci" "you grow harder the more you learn" [11]); and his didacticism ("e pon' cura, / ché 'ntes' ho che compon' d'insegnamento / volume" "and be careful, for I've heard that you are composing a volume of teachings" [11-13]).[55] Cavalcanti, like Dante after him, finds particularly infuriating Guittone's pretensions to moral authority, his audacious claim to "insegnamento," and he ends his sonnet by categorically dismissing Guittone's ability to discharge such a function: "Fa' ch'om non rida il tuo proponimento!" ("Make sure that your proposal is not ridiculed!" [14]).

Dante inherits from Cavalcanti a language of refined eroticism which, by virtue of being stripped of the burdensome ornamentation of the preceding schools, is now capable of probing

---

[55] For a reading of this sonnet that concentrates on Cavalcanti's accusations as expressions of his poetic principles, see Marcello Ciccuto, "Il sonetto cavalcantiano: Da più a uno face un sollegismo," *Critica letteraria*, 6 (1978), 305-330.

and articulating even the intricacies of the *figura*; as Cavalcanti says to Guido Orlandi in the sonnet "Di vil matera mi conven parlare," his language is "sottile e piano" (10), subtle and at the same time clear. It is hardly surprising therefore that Dante should inherit from Cavalcanti also his contempt for Guittone, considering that the new Cavalcantian style articulates its basic ideological premises precisely by means of an anti-Guittonian polemic. Dante's indictment of Guittone is derived, in this respect, from Cavalcanti, and is one more eloquent testimony to the profound impact of his Florentine mentor. Indeed, from this perspective we could view the anti-Guittonian outburst of *Purgatorio* XXVI as an indicator of Cavalcanti's stubbornly subterranean presence, even in the moment of his most manifest absence. Nonetheless, whatever we may want to read between the lines of canto XXVI, the fact remains that Cavalcanti is not present, that he is denied any overt recognition. And, whereas Dante's tribute to the first Guido does not in itself fly in the face of available evidence, his essential exclusion of the second Guido does.[56] Cavalcanti cannot be excluded from any group of contemporary lyric poets who have influenced Dante if that group is to reflect reality. Taking together the fact of the *Comedy*'s great glowing tribute to Guinizzelli and the fact of its almost total silence on Cavalcanti, it is difficult not to come to the conclusion that Dante deliberately suppresses Cavalcanti and tries to redress the imbalance by paying disproportionate attention to Guinizzelli. Cino's disappearance is less problematic: because in the *De Vulgari Eloquentia* he is essentially a stopgap used to fill the space left by Cavalcanti, his presence in the treatise does not foreshadow his presence in the poem. He is not significant enough to be included in the *Comedy*'s poetic itinerary, precisely because he is too good a friend; poetically, Cino is Dante's mirror image, an elegiac version of Dante in

---

[56] Although technically Cavalcanti could not be made to appear in the *Comedy*, since he was still alive in the spring of 1300, Dante could certainly have manipulated the *Comedy*'s textual reality to pay him a greater tribute, if he chose, as he manipulates it to condemn Boniface for instance.

his sweetest mode.⁵⁷ Rather than exerting influence, Cino absorbed it, thereby guaranteeing his exclusion from the *Comedy*.

But Cavalcanti is in fact present, precisely where we would expect him to be—at the level of language, the arena in which he could not be suppressed. His importance for Dante is finally reflected by his intertextual prominence in the *Comedy*, greater than that of any other lyric poet, including Guinizzelli.⁵⁸ There is, I submit, a Cavalcantian "story" encoded into the *Comedy*; but to tell this story correctly, we should first return to the Cavalcantian moments of the *Vita Nuova*. Cavalcanti's most overt textual presence in the *Vita Nuova* is generally said to extend from chapter XIV through XVI, concentrated in the three sonnets that belong to the sequence of the *gabbo* and its aftermath, sonnets that are replete with anxious *spiriti*, trembling souls, and internal earthquakes, and in which death is a constant presence, most fully articulated in the spectral crying of the stones in the middle sonnet: "le pietre par che gridin: 'Moia, moia' " ("the stones seem to cry out: 'Die! Die!' " [8]). We could extend his presence back to the ninth chapter, which contains the sonnet "Cavalcando l'altr'ier per un cammino," arguing that the poems of chapters IX and XII (X and XI contain

---

⁵⁷ Referring to the *De Vulgari Eloquentia*, Mengaldo comments that "Cino sta principalmente come metafora dello stilnovismo dantesco" (Introduction, *De Vulgari Eloquentia*, p. XCIV). On Cino, see: Maria Corti, "Il linguaggio poetico di Cino da Pistoia," *Cultura neolatina*, 12 (1952), 185-223; the various studies by De Robertis: "Cino e le 'imitazioni' dalle rime di Dante," *Studi danteschi*, 19 (1950), 103-177, "Cino e i poeti bolognesi," *Giornale storico della letteratura italiana*, 128 (1951), 273-312, "Cino e Cavalcanti o le due rive della poesia," *Studi medievali*, 18 (1952), 55-107, "Cino da Pistoia e la crisi del linguaggio poetico," *Convivium*, raccolta nuova, 1 (1952), 1-35; and Guglielmo Gorni, "Cino 'vil ladro': parola data e parola rubata," *Il nodo della lingua e il verbo d'amore*, pp. 125-139.

⁵⁸ With respect to the Cavalcantian echoes in the *Comedy*, Contini comments as follows: "Simili rilievi ricevono senso pieno solo dalla parchezza con cui risuonano nella *Commedia* testi volgari non danteschi" ("Cavalcanti in Dante," p. 156). I do not find convincing Vincent Moleta's arguments for a strong Guinizzellian presence in the *Comedy*; see his " 'Come l'ausello in selva a la verdura,' " in *Guinizzelli in Dante*, in which he traces many of the *Comedy*'s bird similes to the second verse of "Al cor gentil."

no poetry) also betray a Cavalcantian presence, indeed in their first words.[59] In chapter IX the poet meets Love while he is, according to the incipit, "riding along a road," and learns that his love-service is being reassigned to a "novo piacere," that is to the second screen lady. Because of his overly zealous attention to this lady, Beatrice withdraws her greeting in chapter X, and the narrator sends her, again at Love's bidding, the poem of chapter XII in which he declares his steadfast love and pleads for forgiveness. The poem entrusted with this mission is "Ballata, i' vòi che tu ritrovi Amore." In my opinion, the first words of each composition—"Cavalcando" and "Ballata"—are intended to refer to Cavalcanti, one directly to his name ("Cavalcando" is a *hapax* in the Vita Nuova and Dante's lyric production in general, and is especially striking in its initial capitalized position), and the other to his favorite genre, the *ballata*.[60]

On the basis of this episode, we could say that the disfavor

---

[59] The poem in chapter XIII, immediately preceding the *gabbo* sequence, is "Tutti li miei penser parlan d'Amore," labeled transitional by Foster and Boyde since it combines traditional elements like "amorosa erranza" (11) with Cavalcantian ones like "tremando di paura" (8). However, in that the thoughts of the sonnet's incipit fail to achieve the harmony ("accordanza" [12]) desired by the poet, the sonnet in fact prefigures the radical fragmentation that dominates its three successors in chapters XIV-XVI and that is typical of the Cavalcantian mode.

[60] Ignazio Baldelli, in the article "ballata" of the *Enciclopedia Dantesca*, vol. I, pp. 502-503, compares the frequency with which Cavalcanti uses this form (eleven poems, amounting to one-fifth of his *canzoniere*, are *ballate*) to its marginal status in Dante's lyric production (six *ballate* in all, and only one, the one of the Vita Nuova, is written for Beatrice). Dante's exclusion of the *ballata* from his *stil novo* is noted by De Robertis, who comments that "La grande ballata lirica muore con Guido" ("Le rime di Dante," p. 307, n. 1). The significance of "Ballata, i' vòi che tu ritrovi Amore" within the economy of the Vita Nuova is noted by Vincent Moleta, "The Vita Nuova as a Lyric Narrative," *Forum Italicum*, 12 (1978), 369-390, who not only considers the *ballata* to be an indicator of Cavalcanti's presence, but demonstrates that the three poetic phases of Vita Nuova I-XIX are organized in a crescendo by genre: (1) the Guittonian phase is marked by the use of the double sonnet, a form generally eschewed by the *stilnovisti*, in chapters VII and VIII; (2) the Cavalcantian phase is marked by the *ballata* of chapter XII; and (3) the Dantesque phase is marked by the canzone in chapter XIX, "Donne ch'avete."

into which Cavalcanti falls in the *Comedy* is already apparent in the *Vita Nuova*. Cavalcanti's radical negativity, which he expounds in its theoretical dress in "Donna me prega," manifests itself in his apparently lighter pieces through his insistent recourse to mediation; the lady, whom he elsewhere proclaims to be unknowable, is in the sonnets and *ballate* simply rendered unknowable by the use of various other creatures, the "giovane donna di Tolosa" and the "foresette nove," who displace her. Although these presences are in themselves beneficent, their effect is to further distance the possibility of *canoscenza*; indeed, the *ballata* "Era in penser d'amor quand' i' trovai" presents us with "due foresette nove" who mediate "la Mandetta," who in turn mediates (according to the preceding sonnet, "Una giovane donna di Tolosa") the original lady, thus putting the poet at two removes from the original catalyst of desire. In the sonnet of *Vita Nuova* IX, whose first word "Cavalcando" declares its relation not only to Cavalcanti but also to the *pastorela*, the genre invoked by Cavalcanti in his *ballate*, Love instructs the poet to turn to a "novo piacere," much as to the "foresette nove."[61] The result is the loss of Beatrice's greeting. Cavalcantian mediation fails again in chapter XII, where the narrator sends his lady a poem that identifies itself as a *ballata* in its first word, the only *ballata* of the *Vita Nuova*, and receives no reply. The response to proceeding along this Cavalcantian path is thus a negative one, an analysis with which Guido himself would doubtless agree; more problematic, from his point of view, would be the fact that the *Vita Nuova* then supplies another path. That Cavalcanti is put into perspective in the *Vita Nuova* is evidenced finally by the episode of chapter XXIV, whose ambiguous resonance anticipates the episodes of *Inferno* X and *Purgatorio* XI. In chapter XXIV we learn that the *senhal* belonging to Guido's lady Giovanna, "Primavera," may be interpreted as "prima verrà" ("she will come first"), to indicate

---

[61] On the relation of Dante's sonnet to the troubadour *pastorela* and to Cavalcanti's version thereof, especially with respect to "Era in penser d'amor," see Picone, *Vita Nuova e tradizione romanza*, chap. III, "Dalla *Pastorella* alle donne dello schermo."

that she precedes Dante's lady, Beatrice, as John the Baptist precedes Christ. We must infer that Guido precedes Dante in the same way; as John the Baptist prepares the way for Christ, so Guido prepares the way for the one who will surpass him, the one who will chase him from the nest.

Turning to the *Comedy*, we find that its Cavalcantian echoes embrace the three lyric forms in which the poet worked: the sonnet, the *ballata*, and the canzone. The sonnet represented is the praise poem, "Biltà di donna e di saccente core," Cavalcanti's variant of Guinizzelli's "Io voglio del ver la mia donna laudare"; the sonnet's octave consists of a catalogue of natural wonders, beginning with the incipit's "Beauty of woman and of a knowing heart," while the sextet informs us that none of the above can equal the beauty of the poet's lady: "ciò passa la beltate e la valenza / de la mia donna" ("the beauty and worth of my lady surpass all this" [9-10]). Both of the verses that find their way into the *Comedy* belong to the second quatrain:

aria serena quand' apar l'albore
e bianca neve scender senza venti;
rivera d'acqua e prato d'ogni fiore;
oro, argento, azzuro 'n ornamenti

serene air when the dawn appears and white snow falling without wind, water's bank and field of every flower, gold, silver, azure in ornaments

(5-8)

Line 6, "e bianca neve scender senza venti," reappears in *Inferno* XIV, 30, "come di neve in alpe sanza vento" ("as snow in the mountains without wind"); line 8, "oro, argento, azzuro 'n ornamenti," resurfaces in *Purgatorio* VII, 73, "Oro e argento fine, cocco e biacca" ("Gold and fine silver, cochineal and white lead").[62] As we shall see, both verses are placed in contexts that

---

[62] Both echoes from "Biltà di donna" are noted by Contini, "Cavalcanti in Dante," p. 145. A further textual analogue between "Biltà di donna" and the passage in *Purgatorio* VII may be found in the comparisons with which both conclude: Cavalcanti's "e tanto più d'ogn' altr' ha canoscenza, / *quanto lo*

ultimately address themselves to Cavalcanti's rationalist philosophy. The first belongs to the description of the burning sand in the third ring of Hell's seventh circle, housing the violent against God; this image of a desert whose ardor is continually reinforced by falling flakes of fire exemplifies Dante's technique of using violently natural or "anti-natural" images in the circle of violence (as compared to the circle of fraud, where the surroundings are described in terms of man-made, rather than natural, correlatives):

> Sovra tutto 'l sabbion, d'un cader lento,
>   piovean di foco dilatate falde,
>   come di neve in alpe sanza vento.

> Over all the sand swollen flakes of fire were slowly raining down, like snow in the mountains without wind.
> <div align="right">(<i>Inf.</i> XIV, 28-30)</div>

The hushed and timeless quality of Cavalcanti's windless snow is thus used to evoke the horror of a truly timeless downpour that is not snow, but its opposite, not raining water but raining fire.

If the perfect earthly beauty of "Biltà di donna" gives way to the violated transvestite beauty of *Inferno* XIV on the one hand, on the other it is transformed into the super-natural beauty of the valley of the princes in *Purgatorio* VII:

> Oro e argento fine, cocco e biacca,
>   indaco, legno lucido e sereno,
>   fresco smeraldo in l'ora che si fiacca,
> da l'erba e da li fior, dentr' a quel seno
>   posti, ciascun saria di color vinto,
>   come dal suo maggiore è vinto il meno.

> Gold and fine silver, cochineal [scarlet] and white lead, indigo, wood polished and bright, fresh emerald in the mo-

---

ciel de la terra è maggio" (12-13; italics mine) makes its way into Dante's "*ciascun saria di color vinto, / come dal suo maggiore è vinto il meno*" (77-78; italics mine).

ment it is split; each one would be surpassed in color by the grass and by the flowers placed in that valley, as the lesser is surpassed by the greater.

(*Purg.* VII, 73-78)

We note that the sentence structure duplicates that of "Biltà di donna": a series of substantives is first accumulated and then declared unequal to the wondrous thing named last. Dante presents us with a list of exquisite natural objects of great brilliance, all overshadowed by the flowers and grasses of the valley; the unsurpassable beauty that was once associated with Cavalcanti's lady belongs now to the valley of the princes. Dante has again taken one of the nature tableaux from "Biltà di donna" and placed it in a setting that is an implicit commentary; indeed, both *Inferno* XIV and *Purgatorio* VII provide paradigmatic contexts exemplifying two alternative outcomes for the rationalist point of view. In one case, the anti-natural oxymoronic image of the raining flakes of fire reflects the negative outcome of a rationalist philosophy that, by reifying nature as the highest referent for worth and beauty, becomes—like the sodomites in the same circle—sterile and self-immolating; an exaggerated estimation of nature's importance is by definition anti-natural, because it fails to recognize nature's Maker.[63] In the second case, we have the other possibility: nature can be accommodated within a super-natural setting as long as its subordinate status is acknowledged. Thus, the rationalist perspective is legitimate insofar as it is not radical, that is, as long as it will bow to a

---

[63] That nature is dependent on God is spelled out in the outline of Hell found in *Inferno* XI, precisely in the description of the circle of violence; here we learn that "natura lo suo corso prende / dal divino 'ntelletto e da sua arte" ("nature takes her course from divine intellect and from its art" [*Inf.* XI, 99-100]). Eugene Vance points to the raining flakes of fire in *Inferno* XIV as "anti-natural" in "Désir, rhétorique et texte (Semences de différence: Brunet Latin chez Dante)," *Poétique*, 42 (1980), 137-155. Vance's views on Dante's use of Cavalcanti in this passage are marred by his apparent belief that Dante draws his comparison of fire to snow from "Biltà di donna," although the sonnet contains no such comparison ("cette comparaison-ci ne découle pas de l'Écriture, mais plutôt d'un *canzo* [sic] amoureux de Guido Cavalcanti" [p. 148]).

higher reality "come dal suo maggiore è vinto il meno": a reality as superior to it as the colors of the purgatorial valley are superior to the colors provided by nature on earth.

Dante's discourse is predicated on the notion that the lady of Cavalcanti's texts, for all her superlative worth and beauty, does not finally serve to connect the poet to ultimate worth and beauty, i.e. to God; thus even a relatively "optimistic" and Guinizzellian composition like "Biltà di donna" is a worthy target (here too, in fact, we note that the "canoscenza" of line 12 is exclusively hers, not his), because it draws its potential negativity from the theoretical repository of "Donna me prega." The canzone itself is invoked in *Inferno* X, by way of the rhyme words in the passage immediately following the naming of Guido in line 63:

> Le sue parole e 'l modo de la pena
> m'avean di costui già letto il *nome*;
> però fu la risposta così piena.
> Di sùbito drizzato gridò: "*Come*?
> dicesti 'elli ebbe'? non viv' elli ancora?
> non fiere li occhi suoi lo dolce *lume*?"

> His words and the nature of the punishment had already revealed his name to me; hence was my answer so full. Suddenly rising up, he cried: "What? Did you say 'he had'? Does he not still live? Does the sweet light not strike his eyes?"
>
> (64-69; italics mine)

The use of *nome*, *come*, and *lume* recalls a celebrated section of the second stanza of "Donna me prega," where the same three words are used in rhyme, with *lume* as the *rimalmezzo*:[64]

> In quella parte — dove sta memora
> prende suo stato, — sì formato, — *come*
> diaffan da *lume*, — d'una scuritate

[64] Singleton notes the occurrence of *come, nome,* and *lume* in both texts; see *Commentary* to the *Inferno*, p. 154, where he also discusses the question of *lome* versus *lume* ("lume," as adopted by Petrocchi, is an acceptable Sicilian rhyme).

> la qual da Marte — vène, e fa demora;
> elli è creato — ed ha sensato — *nome*,
> d'alma costume — e di cor volontate.

It [love] takes its being in the part where memory resides; just as a transparent being receives its form from light, so love is formed by a darkness which comes from Mars, and it dwells there [i.e. where it takes its form]. It is a created thing, and has a name denoting its sensory nature; it is a habit of the soul, and a desire of the heart.

(15-20; italics mine)

The second stanza of "Donna me prega" offers a definition of love that begins by saying that love resides "dove sta memora," that is, in the sensitive rather than intellective soul, and then proceeds to assign the origin of love to Mars, the planet of anger and violent irrational feelings. In the following stanza, the poet again stresses love's connection with that faculty of the soul that is "non razionale, — ma che sente" ("not rational, but which feels" [31]); once more, then, love is assigned to the seat of the passions, the sensitive soul, which corresponds to the body rather than to the intellect. The effects of such an association are apparent in the next verses:

> for di salute — giudicar mantene,
> ché la 'ntenzione — per ragione — vale:
> discerne male — in cui è vizio amico.
> Di sua potenza segue spesso morte

Love deprives reason of health [salvation], since appetite takes the place of reason: he to whom vice is a friend judges badly. From love's power death often follows . . .

(32-35)

Thus love infects reason and judgment and, in the strikingly simple verse that falls at the poem's mathematical center (not including the *congedo*), love is explicitly aligned with death: "Di sua potenza segue spesso morte . . ." Since love cancels the light of reason, it inevitably leads to spiritual death; the association between love and darkness is made not only in the second stanza, where love is said to originate in a darkness ("scuritate") that comes from Mars, but again in the closing verses of the last stanza, where the earlier "scuritate" is echoed by the phrase " 'n mezzo scuro": "For di colore, d'essere diviso, / assiso — 'n mezzo scuro, luce rade" ("Without color, cut off from being, love dwells in a dark place, and puts out the light" [67-68]). Love's alignment with death and the dark powers is thus complete; it not only comes from darkness, but it dwells in darkness, and destroys the light.

Whatever our position on the question of Cavalcanti's alleged Averroism, so hotly debated by Nardi and Favati, there can be no doubt that the love Guido professes in "Donna me prega" is diametrically opposed to the love Dante professes in the *Comedy*.[65] Cavalcanti aligns love and death, Dante love and life; the

---

[65] Nardi is, of course, the champion of the Averroist thesis, while Favati maintains that Cavalcanti belongs within the context of orthodox neo-Aristotelian scholasticism. A mediating current is represented by the position of Fernando Figurelli, who accepts Nardi's thesis in attenuated form; see "Guido Cavalcanti," in *Orientamenti culturali. Letteratura italiana: I Minori* (Milan: Marzorati, 1961), pp. 217-240. Although all of Nardi's writings on the lyric reflect his point of view, his position is most clearly articulated in "L'averroismo del 'primo amico' di Dante" and "Di un nuovo commento alla canzone del Cavalcanti sull'amore" (this last essay also contains a summary of earlier critical opinion; both are in *Dante e la cultura medievale*, pp. 93-129 and 130-152); "Noterella polemica sull'averroismo di Guido Cavalcanti," *Rassegna di filosofia*, 3 (1954), 47-71; "Dante e Guido Cavalcanti" and "L'amore e i medici medievali" (both in *Saggi e note di critica dantesca*, pp. 190-219 and 238-267). Support for Nardi is provided by Paul Oskar Kristeller, "A Philosophical Treatise from Bologna Dedicated to Guido Cavalcanti: Magister Jacobus de Pistorio and his 'Questio de Felicitate,' " in *Medioevo e Rinascimento: Studi in onore di Bruno Nardi*, 2 vols. (Florence: Sansoni, 1955), vol. I, pp. 425-463; the existence of the treatise with its affectionate dedication does in fact show "that there was a direct personal connection between at least one 'Averroist' philosopher at Bologna and Guido Cavalcanti" (p. 441). Favati's writings on this subject include: "La canzone d'amore del Cavalcanti," *Letterature moderne*, 3 (1952), 422-453; "Guido Cavalcanti, Dino del Garbo e l'averroismo di Bruno Nardi," *Filologia romanza*, 2 (1955), 67-83; and, most recently, the chapter on Cavalcanti in his book, *Inchiesta sul Dolce Stil Nuovo*. Other prominent "non-Averroists" are J. E. Shaw, *Guido Cavalcanti's Theory of Love: The Canzone d'Amore and Other Related Problems* (Toronto: U. of Toronto Press, 1949), who puts Cavalcanti in the context of the Christian Neoplatonism of Albertus

ending of "Donna me prega" reads like the antithesis of the *Paradiso*, or rather the *Paradiso* reads like a sustained contradiction of "Donna me prega." Returning to *Inferno* X, one can hardly doubt the significance of evoking the crucial second stanza of "Donna me prega" immediately after the pilgrim has uttered his notorious riposte to Cavalcanti senior:

> E io a lui: "Da me stesso non vegno:
>   colui ch'attende là per qui mi mena,
>   forse cui Guido vostro ebbe a disdegno."
>
> And I to him: "I come not on my own; the one who waits there leads me through here, to the one whom your Guido perhaps held in disdain."
>
> (61-63)

The thesis that Guido's disdain is directed at Beatrice, that is at the possibility that an earthly lady may be a divine signifier

---

Magnus, and Mario Casella, "La canzone d'amore di Guido Cavalcanti," *Studi di filologia italiana*, 7 (1942), 97-160; Casella claims that Cavalcanti is simply the poetic expositor of the "dottrina aristotelico-tomista" (p. 153). Interestingly, a recent contribution by Ferdinando Pappalardo corrects both Nardi and Favati, while demonstrating Cavalcanti's strict Aristotelianism (and pointing out that Guido does not agree with Magister Jacobus); see "Per una rilettura della canzone d'amore del Cavalcanti," *Studi e problemi di critica testuale*, 13 (1976), 47-76. For all that he does not see any specific Averroism in "Donna me prega," Pappalardo underlines the canzone's radical overturning of the traditional equations between love and virtue and love and happiness, stressing that—unlike Guinizzelli or Dante—Cavalcanti recognizes in love "la forza animatrice della natura, della realtà tutta, ma non più la potenza che dal profondo suscita il cammino della civiltà, e che guida i destini dell'umanità verso la felicità e il progresso" (p. 74), and that Dante's path, therefore, is one that "Guido non volle e non seppe seguire" (p. 76). A likely textual indicator regarding Dante's view is his use of the phrase "possibile intelletto" in *Purgatorio* XXV, 65, with reference to Averroes' mistaken doctrine on the disjunction of the possible intellect from the soul. Dante, who here characterizes Averroes as a "savio . . . errante" (63), was surely aware of the prominent position of the phrase *possibile intelletto* in line 22 of Cavalcanti's poem (see Contini, "Cavalcanti in Dante," p. 155); perhaps his point is not specifically that Guido is an Averroist, but rather that he too is an erring sage. On Guido and radical Aristotelianism in *Inferno* X, see Maria Corti, *Dante a un nuovo crocevia* (Florence: Libreria commissionaria Sansoni, 1981), pp. 77-85.

and hence a carrier of beatitude, is further supported by the subsequent evocation of "Donna me prega," the text in which Guido categorically denies that ladies can transmit significance to their lovers.[66] As the pilgrim surely fails to convince Guido's father that his journey could not have been undertaken as a solitary enterprise, so the poet failed to convince his friend that his intellectual/poetic journey need not have been solitary, that *canoscenza* was indeed accessible. In *Inferno* X, then, the canzone "Donna me prega" is condemned as the chief exponent of Cavalcanti's rationalistic view, whereby love is a natural passion incapable of accommodating significance, metaphor, or beatitude.

[66] My interpretation of line 63 is, of course, apparent from my translation, in which I have rendered "cui" not as "quem" (i.e. Vergil), but as "ad eum quem," or, if we follow Dante in historicizing the Signifier as a woman, "ad eam quam" (the argument as to whether Beatrice or God is intended is a spurious one, since they amount to the same thing; however, in that Dante and Guido share a past as love poets, and Beatrice is that localized version of the divine that Dante chose and Guido refused to discover within love poetry, she would seem the more appropriate choice). Although the commentary tradition was univocal in reading line 63 as a reference to Vergil until the late nineteenth century, critical opinion has of late tended to opt for Beatrice; see, among others, Antonino Pagliaro, "Farinata e Cavalcante," in *Ulisse: Ricerche semantiche sulla Divina Commedia*, vol. I, pp. 185-224 (this essay is the elaboration of "Il disdegno di Guido," orig. in *Letterature moderne*, 1 [1950], 447-459); Contini, who comments that "pare accertato che grammaticalmente l'oggetto del 'disdegno' sia Beatrice (non Virgilio e non Dio); e che dunque Guido sia presentato come avverso alla sublimazione di Beatrice, al suo trasferimento sul piano trascendente" (*Poeti del Duecento*, vol. II, p. 489); and Marti, "Cavalcanti, Guido," *Enciclopedia Dantesca*, vol. I, esp. p. 895. Grammar aside, it would seem that the point of the *terzina*'s last line is not to further qualify "colui ch'attende là," but to elaborate the notion of "per qui mi mena." Also suggestive is the fact that on the only other occasion in which Dante uses a formula like "Da me stesso non vegno," i.e. in *Purgatorio* I where Vergil says "Da me non venni" (52), he immediately backs it up with a reference to Beatrice: "donna scese del ciel" (53). For further information, see Pier Luigi Cerisola, who exhaustively details the hermeneutic history of this famous crux in "Il 'disdegno' di Guido Cavalcanti (*Inf.* X, 61-63)," *Aevum*, 52 (1978), 195-217, while also attempting to restore Vergil (interpreted metaphorically as the instigator of Dante's transition to a politically motivated and nonrestricted poetics) as the object of Guido's disdain.

Guinizzelli and Cavalcanti

Inferno X is about closure, a concept whose emotional paradigm is the "dispitto" or "disdegno" that characterizes the canto's two major episodes: the aggressive closure of Farinata's arrogant disdain; the paranoid closure of Cavalcante's premature certainties; the closure of heresy, entombment, death, and Hell. The Last Judgment is ultimate closure; for when the present merges with the future, the damned, whose "mala luce" ("bad light" [100]) allows them to see only distant events, will be cut off from the light of knowledge altogether. Guido fits into this context precisely as a theoretician of closure. It is not surprising, therefore, that Farinata's didactic discourse regarding the present and the future should contain phrases that are strikingly reminiscent of Cavalcanti's poetry. As events draw near, Farinata explains, "tutto è vano / nostro intelletto" ("our intellect is entirely vain" [103-104]); unless others bring them information, "nulla sapem di vostro stato umano" ("we know nothing of your human state" [105]). These verses are noteworthy for their persistent stress on the incapacity of our intellect, a theme that runs through Cavalcanti's lyrics; even more pronounced, however, is the Cavalcantian tone of the following *terzina*, in which one of Guido's key words, *canoscenza*, is modified by another, *morta*:

> Però comprender puoi che tutta morta
> fia nostra conoscenza da quel punto
> che del futuro fia chiusa la porta.
>
> Therefore you can comprehend that all our knowledge shall be dead from that moment when the door of the future shall be closed.
>
> (106-108)

While proclaiming the death of knowledge, the irredeemable loss of *conoscenza*, this *terzina* simultaneously literalizes, in the image of the closing door, the spiritual closure that is the hallmark of both this canto and its chief protagonists.

Nonetheless, it should be noted that Dante does not choose to close Guido within the limits of *Inferno* X, a fact that is stressed immediately in the pilgrim's last words to Farinata, containing his final message for Cavalcanti senior: "Or direte dunque a quel caduto / che 'l suo nato è co' vivi ancor congiunto" ("Now tell therefore that fallen one that his son is still among the living" [110-111]). These verses, with their emphatic "ancor congiunto," refer not only to Guido's literal life, in the spring of 1300, but also to his metaphoric life, a matter on which Dante is deliberately ambivalent, i.e. open.[67] Indeed, as the echo from "Biltà di donna" in *Inferno* XIV is counterbalanced by the echoes from the same sonnet in *Purgatorio* VII, so the infernal evocation of the condemned canzone is also countered by a sequence of purgatorial reminiscences. This time Dante draws on the *ballata* "In un boschetto trova' pasturella," a poem which is undoubtedly the intertext for the meeting with Matelda in *Purgatorio* XXVIII. Once again, as in the valley of the princes, the locale chosen for the Cavalcantian echoes is an "earthly paradise," a place of extraordinary natural beauty; into this springtime world of singing birds and many-colored flowers walks a lady who, as the most beautiful natural object of all, is identified with the setting and with spring itself. Textually, such a tableau is associated with Cavalcanti, whose lady's *senhal* is "Primavera" according to the *Vita Nuova*, and who describes just such a lady in another *ballata*: "Fresca rosa novella, / piacente primavera, / per prata e per rivera / gaiamente cantando" ("Fresh new rose, beautiful spring, through the fields and on the banks gaily singing"). Therefore, when Dante enters the eternal spring of his Earthly Paradise ("qui primavera sempre e ogne frutto" "here is always spring and every fruit" [*Purg.* XXVIII, 143]), and meets a lady singing and picking flowers, we know we are on Cavalcantian territory. We are dealing here, however, not simply with an oblique reference to a typically Cavalcantian scene, but with a precise series of allusions to a specific poem.[68]

---

[67] I agree with Contini that Dante's silence on Cavalcanti reflects a deliberate strategy adopted in order to avoid explicitly judging him ("Cavalcanti in Dante," p. 143).

[68] The most developed discussion I have seen of the textual relation between

Guinizzelli and Cavalcanti

Cavalcanti's *ballata* begins: "In un boschetto trova' pasturella / più che la stella — bella, al mi' parere" ("In a little wood I found a shepherdess, more beautiful than the stars, in my opinion"). The privileged position Dante accords this *ballata* may be inferred from his previous use of it in *Inferno* II, where the expression "più che la stella" refers to Beatrice's eyes in a passage whose lyric resonance has already been discussed. As regards *Purgatorio* XXVIII, we note that this *ballata* is the only one of Cavalcanti's compositions to situate its narrative within a *boschetto*, a fact that was no doubt instrumental in making it Dante's choice as a textual backdrop for this episode, located in "la divina foresta spessa e viva" ("the divine forest dense and alive" [*Purg.* XXVIII, 2]) of the Earthly Paradise. Since Dante intentionally makes use of verses from each stanza of the *ballata*, in order to evoke the poem as a whole, we give it in its entirety (the italicized verses are the ones Dante draws on most explicitly):

In un boschetto trova' pasturella
più che la stella — bella, al mi' parere.

    Cavelli avea biondetti e ricciutelli,
e gli occhi pien' d'amor, cera rosata;
    con sua verghetta pasturav' agnelli;
[di]scalza, di rugiada era bagnata;
    cantava come fosse 'namorata:
er' adornata — di tutto piacere.

    D'amor la saluta' imantenente
e domandai s'avesse compagnia;
    ed ella mi rispose dolzemente
che sola sola per lo bosco gia,

Dante and Guido in these cantos is provided by Bosco in his recent edition; see *Purgatorio*, esp. pp. 472-473. Singleton, in *Journey to Beatrice* (1958; repr. Baltimore: Johns Hopkins U. Press, 1977), comments on the importance of Cavalcanti's "In un boschetto" as a backdrop for the meeting of canto XXVIII; he argues that Dante deliberately evokes the earlier poem in order to emphasize the difference between it and the *Comedy*, where the pilgrim's "love" for Matelda is not physically gratified (pp. 214-216).

e disse: "Sacci, quando l'augel pia,
allor disïa — 'l me' cor drudo avere."

Po' che mi disse di sua condizione
e per lo bosco augelli audìo cantare,
   fra me stesso diss' i': "Or è stagione
di questa pasturella gio' pigliare."
Merzé le chiesi sol che di basciare
ed abracciar, — se le fosse 'n volere.

Per man mi prese, d'amorosa voglia,
e disse che donato m'avea 'l core;
   menòmmi sott' una freschetta foglia,
là dov'i' vidi fior' d'ogni colore;
   e tanto vi sentìo gioia e dolzore,
che 'l die d'amore — mi parea vedere.

In a little wood I found a shepherdess, more beautiful than the stars in my opinion. / Her hair was blond and in curls, her eyes full of love, her face like a rose. With her little staff she was pasturing the lambs; barefoot, she was bathed with dew. *She was singing as though she were in love*; she was adorned with everything beautiful. / I greeted her amorously right off, and asked her if she had company; she answered me sweetly *that she was going through the wood completely alone*, and said: "Know that when the bird chirps, then my heart desires to have a lover." / When she told me of her condition, and *throughout the wood I heard the birds sing*, I said to myself: "Now is the time to take joy from this shepherdess." Grace I asked of her only to kiss and embrace, if this was her desire. / She took me by the hand, with amorous desire, and said that she had given me her heart; she led me under the fresh leaves, *there where I saw flowers of every color*, and so much joy and sweetness did I feel there that I seemed to see the god of love.

Purgatorio XXVIII opens with a musical symphony whose chief contributors are the singing birds and the rustling leaves;

the words "augelletti" (14), "cantando" (17), and "foglie" (17) are all bits of the Cavalcantian mosaic being created. Twice in the prelude to Matelda's arrival Dante uses the unusual double adjective intensifier that marks the progress of Cavalcanti's shepherdess, "che sola sola per lo bosco gia" (the pilgrim heads into the countryside "lento lento" in line 5, and the water is moving "bruna bruna" in line 31), only to switch to Cavalcanti's characteristic diminutive in the verses that bring Matelda into view: "una donna soletta che si gia / e cantando e scegliendo fior da fiore" ("a lady all alone who went along singing and choosing flower from flower" [40-41]). The pilgrim addresses Matelda as the lyric poet addresses his lady, saying "Deh, bella donna" (43);[69] his love for her is figured in the three similes of profane classical love that are rehearsed in the scene following their encounter: she reminds him of Proserpina in the moment when she is ravished by Pluto and loses "spring," i.e. the beautiful world in which she lived before her abduction (49-51; the word *primavera*, with its Cavalcantian echoes, is here used for the first time in the poem); the splendor of her eyes (of which she gives him a "gift," as the shepherdess gives a gift of her heart) is like that of Venus' eyes, in the moment that she falls in love with Adonis (64-66); the width of the stream between them seems like that of the Hellespont separating Hero and Leander (70-75). The flowers Matelda picks are, like those of the *ballata*, "d'ogni colore"; they "paint" the way on which she walks (42), and are referred to metonymically as "colors": "trattando più color con le sue mani" ("arranging many colors with her hands" [68]). Finally—were the singing birds, the colored flowers, the solitary damsel, the atmosphere of profane and lyric love, and the evocation of "primavera" not enough—

---

[69] Dante refers to Matelda as "la bella donna" throughout, for the last time in *Purgatorio* XXXIII, 134. By so doing, he signals his departure from Cavalcanti, whose heroine is a *pasturella*; Matelda, although a *pasturella* vis-à-vis Beatrice, is a *donna* in her own right, a fact that contributes to the irrelevance of physical gratification. Matelda's role as a lyric lady is further evoked by the withholding of her name until XXXIII, 119, in the same way that the lady's *senhal* is reserved for the end of the *canso*.

Lyric Quests

Dante adds a last overt quote from the *ballata*. The first verse of canto XXIX, "Cantando come donna innamorata," is a replay of Guido's "cantava come fosse 'namorata," and thus serves to cast the lyric episode of canto XXVIII into final relief before passing into the new mode signaled by the allegorical procession.

It would seem, therefore, that a measure of textual redemption is indeed accorded Cavalcanti in the *Comedy*, and that this occurs in *Purgatorio* XXVIII (having been forecasted in *Inferno* II) vis-à-vis the *ballata*, a form that Cavalcanti makes particularly his and that Dante, conversely, uses infrequently.[70] Even so, it should be noted that the most Guido can recuperate in *Purgatorio* XXVIII is what he had in *Vita Nuova* XXIV, i.e. the position of a great but transcended precursor. In the episode of the Earthly Paradise we find the ratios of the *Vita Nuova* writ large: as the *boschetto* to the *divina foresta*; as the *ballata* to the canzone; as Matelda/Primavera to Beatrice, who will arrive in *Purgatorio* XXX; as the early Cavalcantian *stil novo* to the "true" *stil novo* of the *Vita Nuova*—a text insistently invoked in these cantos and obliquely named in XXX, 115—so is Guido to Dante. Cavalcanti is the only love poet, or indeed lyric poet, to have his poetic history traced so extensively in the *Comedy*; his path takes in *Inferno* II, X, XIV, *Purgatorio* VII, XI, XXIV, XXVI, and XXVIII-XXIX. On the other hand, he is the only love poet to be discussed in Hell, and to be exposed to insinuations regarding heresy and atheism that have become a permanent part of the legend surrounding his name. In the light of all the above, we might go so far as to suggest that the *Comedy* offers Cavalcanti a choice, and that this is the reason that the allusions to him are so carefully balanced between the *Inferno* and the *Purgatorio*, and that Dante takes such precautions not to judge him absolutely, to leave the door of the future

---

[70] It seems not insignificant that Dante should single out a *ballata* for such an important role in the *Purgatorio*, since it is not only a form that he himself rejected, but it is Guido's great contribution to the new style, his *stil novo* par excellence. Thus, even at a formal level the lines between the two poets are sharply drawn; what pertains to the one does not pertain to the other, and vice versa.

(as Farinata calls it) open; in this sense, Cavalcanti's option is *Inferno* X or *Purgatorio* XXVIII. In the first case he is "dead," but he retains a peculiar stature by virtue of the fact that he has detoured himself from the direct line of Dante's precursors, represented by Guinizzelli; he is damned, but not quite surpassed. In the second case he is redeemed, but must pay the price by becoming *the* precursor par excellence, most valued but also most surpassed: like John the Baptist, an eternal forerunner of the greatness to come.

Finally, Guido's naturalistic paradise is associated with that of the classical poets, who are the other chief textual contributors to canto XXVIII. Their Golden Age informs Dante's Earthly Paradise, along with the Cavalcantian love lyric; their stories of profane love—embodied in the similes of Proserpina and Pluto, Venus and Adonis, Hero and Leander—stand behind the eroticism of the pilgrim's encounter with Matelda, along with the Provençal *pastorela*. Like their paradise, then, Guido's is shadowed by an attendant *forse*. Indeed, the charged ambivalence surrounding Guido throughout the *Comedy* finds its best emblem in three verses, all containing *forse*, all belonging to the sphere of poetic influence: the first two—"forse cui Guido vostro ebbe a disdegno" and "forse è nato / chi l'uno e l'altro caccerà del nido"—are answered by an even more tellingly elliptical verse at the end of canto XXVIII: "forse in Parnaso esto loco sognaro" ("maybe, in dreaming of Parnassus, they dreamed of this place" [141]). Are we to imagine Guido smiling, like Vergil and Statius when they learn that their pagan dreams adumbrated a Christian truth? Their dreams had validity, but they are nonetheless just dreams; as Dante leaves Guido's lady to meet his own, the dreams of classical and vernacular precursors alike recede into the distance.

The Poetry of Politics: Bertran and Sordello

The analogy, which I intend to propose, between the *Comedy*'s two remaining lyric poets—Bertran de Born and Sordello—is by no means self-evident.[71] Thomas Bergin, for instance, sets up a structural pattern whereby there is a trio of Provençal poets in the *Comedy*, composed of Bertran in the *Inferno*, Arnaut Daniel in the *Purgatorio*, and Folquet in the *Paradiso*. Faced with a fourth poet who wrote in the *langue d'oc*, Bergin concludes that Dante does not mean Sordello to " 'count' as a Provençal figure," that "Dante sees in Sordello not the Provençal poet but the Italian-born patriot and judge of princes."[72] However, this interpretation violates one sense of the episode, for Sordello's tribute to Vergil at the beginning of *Purgatorio* VII is undoubtedly the tribute of one poet to another. It would seem that we are dealing with Dante's tendency to favor contradictory or counterbalancing structures over neat straightforward ones. In the same way that the odd asymmetrical canticle of thirty-four cantos creates a new order by bringing the total number of cantos to one hundred, so the presence of a fourth troubadour who mars the neat symmetrical triad of Provençal poets may point to two overlapping structures: the trio posited by Bergin and the duo suggested here, which, significantly, includes as its pivotal figure precisely the poet excluded by the first arrangement. The claim that Sordello should be juxtaposed with Bertran de Born, as Cacciaguida with Brunetto or Piccarda with Francesca, is based on a simple but, I believe, telling observation: of all the lyric poets in the *Comedy* only Bertran and Sordello are not primarily love poets. In other words, if we look not at the restricted group of Provençal poets, but at the larger group of all the lyric poets who appear in the *Comedy*—Bertran de Born, Sordello, Bonagiunta da Lucca, Guido Guinizzelli, Arnaut Daniel, and Folquet de Marselha—the first two stand out as poets whose primary poetic missions are different from those of the others. Indeed, Bertran and Sordello are revealed as the *Comedy*'s two "political" poets.[73]

[71] An earlier form of this section appeared in *PMLA*, 94 (1979), 395-405.

[72] "Dante's Provençal Gallery," *Speculum*, 40 (1965), 25. The idea of three troubadours in the *Comedy*, one for each canticle, was anticipated by E. Hoepffner in "Dante et les Troubadours," pp. 196-197.

[73] Bosco, *Purgatorio*, p. 94, refers to Sordello as "un poeta politico"; Folena

Bertran and Sordello

The reading proposed here has the further merit of throwing light on a longstanding crux of Dante criticism. The stature Dante grants Sordello in the *Comedy* has long perplexed scholars, since it seems far out of proportion to his actual achievements. Not only does the meeting with Sordello, in the sixth canto of the *Purgatorio*, serve as the catalyst for the stirring invective against Italy that concludes the canto, but Sordello is assigned the important task of guiding Vergil and Dante to the valley of the princes and identifying its various royal inhabitants. This seems a large role for a minor poet who was, and is, chiefly known as the author of a satirical lament with political overtones, the lament for Blacatz. Thus, although there is a definite consonance between the tone of the lament and the hortatory attitude of the character in the *Comedy*, Sordello's poetic oeuvre does not by itself convincingly account for his function in the poem; nonetheless, in the absence of other explanations, critics have traditionally agreed that we must turn to Sordello's *planh* for an understanding of his position in the *Comedy*.[74] In this so-called lament Sordello violently satirizes the princes of Europe, whom he criticizes for their cowardice;

---

comments that Sordello is present to Dante "soprattutto per la sua ispirazione etico-politica" (Introduction, *Vulgares eloquentes*, p. VIII).

[74] The *planh* is proposed as the source of Dante's inspiration by D'Ovidio in "Sordello," *Studii sulla Divina Commedia*, pp. 1-13 (although this book was published in 1901, the study on Sordello was originally printed in the *Corriere di Napoli* in 1892, as the author explains on p. 10). De Lollis develops this insight in *Vita e poesie di Sordello di Goito* (Halle: Max Niemeyer, 1896), esp. "Il Sordello dantesco," pp. 90-116. In *Sul "Sordello" di Cesare De Lollis* (Venice: Olschki, 1896), Torraca disagrees with De Lollis' position (pp. 41-43), but fails to suggest a concrete alternative to the *planh*, thus becoming the initiator of the tradition which maintains that Dante must have known more about Sordello than we do. See also E. G. Parodi, "Rassegna di studi sordelliani," *Bullettino della Società Dantesca Italiana*, 4 (1897), 185-197, and, more recently, Guido Favati, "Sordello," *Cultura e scuola* 4, nos. 13-14 (1965), 551-565. In "Dante and Sordello," *Comparative Literature*, 5 (1953), 1-15, C. M. Bowra makes a case for the importance of Sordello's narrative poem, "Ensenhamens d'onor," as does Ruggero M. Ruggieri, "Tradizione e originalità nel lessico cavalleresco di Dante: Dante e i trovatori," in *L'umanesimo cavalleresco italiano: Da Dante a Pulci* (Rome: Edizioni dell'Ateneo, 1962), esp. pp. 67-71.

in fact, the work is more a *sirventes* than a *planh*, more a diatribe against the living than a lament for the dead. The poem begins conventionally enough, bewailing the death of Blacatz and complaining, in the usual manner, that all virtue and bravery have died with him; it soon becomes apparent, however, that his death is more a pretext than a theme. Consequently, Blacatz is not mentioned again after the first verse:[75]

> Planher vuelh en Blacatz en aquest leugier so,
> ab cor trist e marrit; et ai en be razo,
> qu'en luy ai mescabat senhor et amic bo,
> e quar tug l'ayp valent en sa mort perdut so;
> tant es mortals lo dans qu'ieu non ai sospeisso
> que jamais si revenha, s'en aital guiza no;
> qu'om li traga lo cor e que·n manio·l baro
> que vivon descorat, pueys auran de cor pro.
>
> Premiers manje del cor, per so que grans ops l'es
> l'emperaire de Roma, s'elh vol los Milanes
> per forsa conquistar . . .
>
> I want to lament Sir Blacatz in this light melody, with a sad and afflicted heart; and I have good reason, for in him I have lost a lord and a good friend, and because all that is virtuous is lost in his death. This damage is so fatal that I have no hope that it can ever be remedied, if not in this way: let his heart be taken out and the barons eat of it who live without heart—then they will have heart enough. / Let the first to eat of the heart, because he has great need of it, be the Emperor of Rome, if he wants to conquer the Milanese by force . . .
>
> (1-11)

Using throughout the poem the alimentary motif of Blacatz' heart as a source of courage for the cowardly kings, Sordello pillories a different prince in each stanza, all for being too weak and spineless to fight for their rightful territories.

[75] Quotations are from *Sordello: Le Poesie*, ed. Marco Boni (Bologna: Libreria Antiquaria Palmaverde, 1954).

Bertran and Sordello

The Sordello of *Purgatorio* VII is also given to judging the behavior of rulers; here, too, he rebukes the princes for negligence and for failing to govern properly. His indictment includes many of the same families, and although in most cases Dante's Sordello is dealing with the next generation, there is one overlapping king.[76] The lofty Dantesque concept of the sovereign's moral obligation to his subjects has taken the place of the simple feudal attitude of the *planh*, in which loss of land is considered a stain on the personal honor of the prince, but once this inevitable shift has been taken into account the correspondences between the historical Sordello and the Sordello of the *Comedy* are clear enough. And yet they are inadequate, for neither Sordello's poetry nor his Lombard origins, which permit him to greet Vergil with the famous verse "O Mantoano, io son Sordello / de la tua terra!" ("O Mantuan, I am Sordello of your land!" [*Purg.* VI, 74-75]), justify his prominence in the *Comedy* in a more than mechanical way. It is this gap between the real and the fictional that has made Sordello the subject of so much critical debate, to the point of being labeled "l'enigma dantesco" by one scholar who believed that only the discovery of new biographical material would resolve Dante's problematic esteem for this minor poet.[77] It is my purpose to show that there are internal reasons for Sordello's role and stature, beyond those already adduced, and that Dante's underlying logic and intentions in the Sordello episode may best be clarified by means of a comparison with the *Comedy*'s other political poet, Bertran de Born.

Bertran too was celebrated for laments; those traditionally attributed to him are both for Prince Henry of England, also

---

[76] The only ruler to appear in both lists is Henry III of England. In Sordello's *planh* we find: the Emperor Frederick II, Louis IX of France, Henry III of England, Ferdinand III of Castile and León, James I of Aragon, Thibaut I of Navarre, Raimon VII of Toulouse, Raimon Bérenger IV of Provence. Dante's negligent princes are: Emperor Rudolf I, Ottokar II of Bohemia, Philip III of France, Henry of Navarre, Peter III of Aragon, Charles I of Anjou, Henry III of England, and William Montferrat.

[77] Vincenzo De Bartholomaeis, *Primordi della lirica d'arte in Italia* (Turin: Società Editrice Internazionale, 1943), p. 208.

called the Young King, with whom the poet was presumably on intimate terms.[78] They are the famous "Si tuit li dol e·lh plor e·lh marrimen" and the less well-known "Mon chan fenisc ab dol et ab maltraire."[79] Unlike Sordello's *planh* for Blacatz, these are true laments, following the customary format of both praising the dead man and mourning his loss:

Si tuit li dol e·lh plor e·lh *marrimen*
E las dolors e·lh dan e·lh chaitivier
Qu'om anc auzis en est segle dolen
Fossen ensems, sembleran tot leugier
Contra la mort del *jove rei engles*,
Don rema pretz e jovens doloros
E·l mons oscurs e teintz e tenebros,
Sems de tot joi, ples de tristor e d'*ira*.

(1-8; italics mine)

[78] For the legend of Bertran de Born and the Young King, see Olin H. Moore, *The Young King: Henry Plantagenet 1155-1183*, in *History, Literature and Tradition* (Columbus: Ohio State U., 1925), and William D. Paden, Jr., "Bertran de Born in Italy," in *Italian Literature: Roots and Branches* (Essays in Honor of Thomas Goddard Bergin), ed. Giose Rimanelli and Kenneth John Atchity (New Haven: Yale U. Press, 1976), pp. 39-66. Although Moore suggests that Bertran may not have been as intimate with Prince Henry as the poet claims (pp. 38-47), Dante and his contemporaries certainly believed in this intimacy.

[79] Modern scholarship has raised the question of the authenticity of "Si tuit li dol." Carl Appel, in his edition of Bertran, *Die Lieder Bertrans von Born* (Halle: Max Niemeyer, 1932), places "Si tuit li dol" among the poems of doubtful attribution, as does L. E. Kastner, in "Notes on the Poems of Bertran de Born," *Modern Language Review*, 32 (1937), 219. For a résumé of the critical opinion on this matter, see D'Arco Silvio Avalle, in his edition of the poet to whom some scholars assign the *planh*, *Peire Vidal: Poesie* (Milan-Naples: Ricciardi, 1960), vol. I, p. cxvi, n. 1. The traditional attribution of "Si tuit li dol" to Bertran is so firmly ingrained that the poem has been included in anthologies under his name even by scholars who acknowledge that the authorship is questionable; see, e.g. *Anthology of the Provençal Troubadours*, ed. R. T. Hill and T. G. Bergin, 2d ed. rev. (New Haven: Yale U. Press, 1973), vol. II, p. 37, and *Medieval Song: An Anthology of Hymns and Lyrics*, trans. and ed. James J. Wilhelm (New York: Dutton, 1971), p. 164. The only recent compiler to omit "Si tuit li dol" from a selection of Bertran's poems is Frederick Goldin, *Lyrics of the Troubadours and Trouvères* (New York: Anchor-Doubleday, 1973). Bertran is cited according to Appel's edition.

Bertran and Sordello

> If all the sorrow, tears, anguish, pain, loss, and misery which man has heard of in this sorrowful life were heaped together, they would all seem light compared to the death of the young English king; for him worth and youth grieve, and the world is dark, covered over, and in shade, lacking all joy, full of sadness and spite.

Bertran is capable not only of the obsessive grief of "Si tuit li dol" ("marrimen," "jove rei engles," and "ira" are all repeated in the same position in each stanza), but also of the vivid delight in battle found in his *sirventes*. In these poems, Bertran constantly urges the barons on to battle, as does Sordello in his lament for Blacatz. Sordello, however, recommends war as an antidote for reprehensible cowardliness and as a means of securing lost territory, whereas Bertran's reasons for warmongering are unabashedly mercenary and self-serving, and his chief concern is loot. Thus, even when Bertran and Sordello share similar social themes and a similar polemical bent, Bertran's verse lacks the didactic element that distinguishes the poetry of Sordello. In the lament for Blacatz and in the longer narrative poem, "Ensenhamens d'onor," Sordello dispenses instruction on the chivalric code, as the title of the latter work ("The Teachings of Honor") makes explicit. It is this aspect of Sordello's poetry and personality that must have initially appealed to Dante and provided him with the starting point for the figure of the *Comedy*.

The canto in which the travelers first meet Sordello, *Purgatorio* VI, belongs, as is well known, to the *Comedy*'s triad of political cantos, along with the sixth cantos of the *Inferno* and the *Paradiso*. Although the political thematics of *Purgatorio* VI become most overt in the invective beginning "Ahi serva Italia, di dolore ostello" ("Ah enslaved Italy, hostel of grief" [76]), it is signaled from the line in which Dante apostrophizes a soul, as yet unidentified, by referring to the part of Italy from which it came: "o anima lombarda" (61). This soul turns out to be Sordello, whose Lombard origins draw him to Vergil. The invective is therefore fueled by the ironic contrast between Sordello's loving response to Vergil as a fellow Mantuan ("e l'un l'altro abbracciava" "and one embraced the other" [75]) and the discord characteristic of Italy, where fellow citizens "gnaw" rather than embrace each other ("e l'un l'altro si rode / di quei ch'un muro e una fossa serra" "and one gnaws at the other, of those whom one wall and one moat enclose" [83-84]). The appellation "anima lombarda" also serves to bring to mind another episode—again political—where an Italian place-name is used as a form of address, namely the one in which Farinata calls out: "O Tosco che per la città del foco / vivo ten vai" ("O Tuscan, who through the city of fire go alive" [*Inf.* X, 22]). There are numerous correspondences, heightened by verbal echoes, in the presentations of Farinata and Sordello, who both appear in episodes dealing with love of one's native land: both souls are isolated and disdainful; both are first noticed by Vergil, using the same expression.[80] The necessary password on each occasion is a sound evoking the *patria*: Farinata hears Dante's Tuscan accent, and Sordello reacts to Vergil's first word, "Mantüa."

Perhaps most striking is the structural correspondence between the two episodes; in both a conversation is suddenly interrupted, suspended without a word of explanation, and just as suddenly resumed. Farinata and Dante are interrupted by Cavalcante de' Cavalcanti; they stop conversing until he disappears and then begin again as though he had not existed. Similarly, the conversation between Sordello and Vergil is interrupted by the narrator's apostrophe to Italy, which cuts in and continues to the end of the sixth canto. So abrupt is the break that when the conversation resumes at the beginning of the seventh canto, Sordello does not yet know who Vergil is. These devices serve rhetorically to underscore Sordello as a

---

[80] Benedetto Croce calls Sordello the "Farinata del Purgatorio" (*La poesia di Dante* [Bari: Laterza, 1921], p. 112). In "Il canto VI del *Purgatorio*" (1940; repr. in *Letture scelte sulla Divina Commedia,* ed. Giovanni Getto [Florence: Sansoni, 1970], pp. 577-593), Giovanni Gentile points to Vergil's use of the expression "Vedi là" in both episodes; most of the similarities between these two episodes have been previously noted in one commentary or another.

purgatorial corrective to Farinata. In Hell, love of one's native land is put into a context of "heresy" or divisiveness, so that Farinata is able to turn common Tuscan origins into barriers of family allegiance and party affiliation. In Purgatory, common Lombard origins become the reason for an embrace; Sordello's immediate reaction to the word "Mantüa" is part of a context that stresses unity, here the unity resulting from a shared birthplace. Sordello, then, is related in three ways to the theme of politics in the *Comedy*. First, he is intrinsically connected by virtue of his historical identity as a poet concerned about the behavior of rulers in his day. Second, he is connected by his situation in the sixth, political, canto of the *Purgatorio*, where his embrace of Vergil, exemplifying political unity, gives rise to the invective in which Dante deplores the lack of unity in Italy. Third, Sordello is the poetic refocusing of Farinata, the lens through which the theme of love of one's native land reappears on the slopes of Mount Purgatory.

The common denominator in these various aspects of the Dantesque Sordello is the concept of political unity, played against its contrary, discord and fragmentation. Within this context, but in a linguistic sphere, there is a particular feature of Sordello's career that may well have determined Dante's development of his role. Sordello was that anomaly among poets— one who wrote in a language not his own. Although an Italian from Goito near Mantua, he wrote in Provençal. That Dante was intrigued by this is clear from what he has to say about Sordello in the *De Vulgari Eloquentia*: "[Sordello], being a man of great eloquence, abandoned his native vernacular not only in writing poetry, but in all forms of expression" (I, xv, 2). Thus, Dante finds it a particular sign of Sordello's eloquence that he should have abandoned his native tongue not just "in poetando," but "quomodocunque loquendo," in any form of discourse whatsoever.[81] Significantly, Dante does not cite any of Sordello's poetry in the *De Vulgari Eloquentia*; all that seems

---

[81] Mengaldo discusses the various interpretations of Dante's remark in his commentary to the Ricciardi *De Vulgari Eloquentia*, p. 120.

to interest him is the concept of linguistic internationalism that Sordello here embodies. The Latin treatise is, in part, a polemic against linguistic provincialism; the *vulgare illustre* as practiced by Dante and his friend Cino da Pistoia is conceived as the Italian that would be in common use if Italy were not divided into many warring city-states but were one united nation, an Italian strained of provincial and municipal impurities.[82] Dante singles out Sordello for praise because Sordello too reacted against the limitations of his regional dialect and, although it was not for him to discover the Italian *vulgare illustre*, he did the next best thing: he turned to a *vulgare* that was already *illustre*, namely Provençal.

The *De Vulgari Eloquentia* posits an identity between political and linguistic unity; thus, the story of the Tower of Babel as recounted at the beginning of the treatise shows how the fragmentation of the original shared language into many new ones made it impossible for the builders to work together and led ultimately to their political differentiation: they came to the work "with one same language," but they left it "estranged from one another by a multiplicity of tongues" (I, vii, 6). In the *Comedy* Sordello stands for the reversal of this linguistic fall, for the initiative that would ideally lead back to the same language for all, which in turn would spell political harmony. Viewed in this context, the words with which Sordello honors Vergil in *Purgatorio* VII become singularly appropriate:

---

[82] Dante explains his position on the *vulgare* as a national language as follows: "But to say that [the vernacular] has been deliberated in the most excellent court of the Italians seems a jest, since we lack a court. To which it is easy to respond. For even though a court, in the sense of a unified court, like the court of the King of Germany, does not exist in Italy, nevertheless its parts are not absent; and as the parts of that court [the German court] are unified by one Prince, so the parts of this court [the Italian] are unified by the grace-given light of reason. Therefore, although we lack a Prince, it would be false to say that the Italians lack a court, since we have a court, even if it is physically dispersed" (*De Vulgari Eloquentia*, I, xviii, 5). Mengaldo links Dante's convictions on political and linguistic unity to his exile, aptly referring to him as "sprovincializzato dall'esilio" (Introduction, *De Vulgari Eloquentia*, p. LXXII).

Bertran and Sordello

"O gloria di Latin," disse, "per cui
   mostrò ciò che potea la lingua nostra,
   o pregio etterno del loco ond' io fui,
qual merito o qual grazia mi ti mostra?"

"O glory of the Latins," he said, "through whom our tongue showed what it could do, o eternal honor of the place that I was from, what merit or what grace reveals you to me?"

                                                              (16-19)

No one has a better right than Sordello to speak of "Latins" or of "our" tongue; in his crossing of linguistic boundaries he showed himself to be a true cosmopolitan, or "Latin," aware of the common heritage that underlies all the languages of Romania and makes them interchangeable, "ours" as it were.[83] It is not because he is as great a poet as Vergil that Sordello is chosen to eulogize him but because he demonstrates in his own person the unity of a linguistic tradition that is rooted in Latin language and literature and that cannot be divorced from a political tradition rooted in the Roman Empire. As there is in fact one language, shared by a Roman poet and a Lombard troubadour, so should there be one Empire. And thus we come back, by a slightly different route, to Sordello as an emblem of political unity in the *Comedy*. Because he thought nothing of crossing both the linguistic and political boundaries of his day, Sordello stands in opposition to the emperor, who in the invective of canto VI is accused of *not* crossing boundaries: by remaining in Germany, the emperor allowed Italy to disintegrate into a swarm of warring factions and the inherent unity of the Holy Roman Empire to be destroyed.

---

[83] Ettore Paratore convincingly demonstrates that Dante did indeed recognize a Latin vernacular (from which the literary Latin of the classical poets was abstracted in the same way that the Italian *vulgare illustre* is abstracted from the spoken Italian language) as the root of the Romance vernaculars; see "Il latino di Dante," in *Tradizione e struttura in Dante* (Florence: Sansoni, 1968), esp. pp. 136-153.

Bertran de Born is also present in the *De Vulgari Eloquentia* where, as we have seen, he is the prototype of the poet of arms in a Romance language, a martial poet for whom Dante can find no equivalent in Italian letters. His poetic credentials in the treatise are excellent: he is in the company of Arnaut Daniel, the Provençal representative of love poetry, and Giraut de Bornelh, the Provençal poet of rectitude; in the same passage Dante quotes the incipit of one of his *sirventes*, in which he rejoices in a forthcoming battle (II, ii, 8). Moreover, unlike Sordello, Bertran is one of the select group of contemporary poets (comprising also Guinizzelli and Giraut) to appear in the *Convivio*, where he is the only poet in a group of nobles being praised for their generosity (IV, xi, 14). In accomplishing the startling revision of the *Comedy*, where Bertran is instead located in the ninth *bolgia* of the eighth circle of Hell among the "seminator di scandalo e di scisma" ("sowers of discord and schism" [*Inf.* XXVIII, 35]), Dante's starting point must have been the sanguinary and bloodthirsty qualities of Bertran's verse, reproduced in the carnage of the ninth *bolgia*. But Dante's elaboration of Bertran does not rest primarily on his poetry. The key to the Dantesque character lies in the reports about Bertran that circulated in the Provençal *vidas* and *razos*. These accounts exaggerate Bertran's already inflated notion of himself as Prince Henry's counselor; we learn from them that Bertran was Henry's chief advisor, personally responsible for fanning the hostilities between the prince and his father, Henry II. Moreover, and most important, one *vida* specifies that Bertran did this "ab sos sirventes," with his poetry:[84]

---

[84] This passage is from the first of the two biographies of Bertran de Born (*Biographies des Troubadours*, p. 65). The case for Dante's knowledge both of Bertran's poetry and of the Provençal biographies is stated by Moore, pp. 74-78. Michele Scherillo, "Dante e Bertram dal Bornio," *Nuova antologia*, 155 (1897), 82-97, considers that the excessive importance Dante assigns to Bertran's role in the Young King's rebellion is based on his belief in the "leggenda provenzale" (p. 90).

Bertran and Sordello

Seingner era totas ves quan se volia del rei Enric e del fill de lui, mas totz temps volia que ill aguessen guerra ensems, lo paire e·l fils e·l fraire, l'uns ab l'autre. E toz temps volc que lo reis de Fransa e·l reis d'Engleterra aguessen guerra ensems. E s'il aguen patz ni treva, ades se penet *ab sos sirventes* de desfar la patz e de mostrar com cascuns era desonratz en aquella patz.

He was lord whenever he wished of King Henry and of his son, but he always wanted them to wage war against each other, the father and the son and the brother, the one against the other. And he always wanted the King of France and the King of England to wage war. And if they made peace or a truce, he immediately strove *with his sirventes* to undo the peace and to show how each one was dishonored by that peace.

(italics mine)

The sinners of the ninth *bolgia* display wounds on their bodies that correspond to the wounds they inflicted on the social fabric during their lifetimes. Hence Bertran arrives carrying his head before him like a lantern; it is severed from his body to indicate that he severed the son from the father. His account of his sin conforms closely to the *vida*:[85]

"E perché tu di me novella porti,
   sappi ch'i' son Bertram dal Bornio, quelli
che diedi al re giovane i ma' conforti.
Io feci il padre e 'l figlio in sé ribelli;
   Achitofèl non fé più d'Absalone
e di Davìd coi malvagi punzelli.
Perch'io parti' così giunte persone,
   partito porto il mio cerebro, lasso!,

[85] There are also verbal similarities between the *vida* and the *Comedy*: "lo paire e·l fils e·l fraire, l'uns ab l'autre" is echoed in Hell by "il padre e 'l figlio in sé" (*Inf.* XXVIII, 136); "l'uns ab l'autre" may be further echoed in *Purgatorio* VI, where Dante contrasts "l'un l'altro abbracciava" with "l'un l'altro si rode."

dal suo principio ch'è in questo troncone.
Così s'osserva in me lo contrapasso."

"And so that you may carry news of me, know that I am Bertran de Born, the one who gave the evil counsels to the Young King. I made the father and the son into rebels against each other; Achithophel did no more for Absalom and David with his wicked barbs. Because I disjoined persons thus united, I carry my brain, alas!, disjoined from its root in this trunk. So in me the *contrapasso* is observed."
(*Inf.* XXVIII, 133-142)

In a canto whose theme, the sowing of discord, is fundamentally political, Bertran's sin is distinctly so; although the social unit he affected is technically the family, the family in question is a royal one, so that his actions are necessarily viewed as having social and political consequences. In fact, not only Bertran's but all the sins of *Inferno* XXVIII can be classified as social and political: Mohammed and Alì (and Fra Dolcino, mentioned by Mohammed) brought schism into the church; Pier da Medicina was a troublemaker in the courts of Romagna; Gaius Scribonius Curio indirectly started the civil wars by inciting Caesar to cross the Rubicon; Mosca de' Lamberti authorized the killing of Buondelmonte, thus giving rise to the Florentine factions and internecine fighting of Dante's own day. In that these souls are political exempla, they are not developed as characters in any way, but are permitted only depersonalized existences under the label "seminator di scandalo e di scisma." This is especially glaring in Bertran's case since such treatment is unexpected; both the *De Vulgari Eloquentia* and the *Convivio* attest to Dante's interest in him as poet and personality. Yet here Bertran too is kept at a distance, expounding the nature of his sin and its exact repercussions with mathematical clarity and enunciating the law of the *contrapasso*. The clinical tone of his speech is heightened by the pathetic interpolations "Oh me!" and "lasso!" so at variance with his discourse as a whole. In a canto where all the sinners are exemplary, Bertran is served up as the last and

Bertran and Sordello

supreme exemplum: his sin is the worst, his punishment the most gruesome.[86]

All of Dante's efforts in *Inferno* XXVIII are directed toward making a political statement. The tone of the canto is set by the opening rhetorical question, which simultaneously names the material at hand and distances it:

> Chi poria mai pur con parole sciolte
> dicer del sangue e de le piaghe a pieno
> ch'i' ora vidi, per narrar più volte?
>
> Who could ever fully tell of the blood and wounds that I now saw, even if in loosened words and after numerous attempts?
>
> (1-3)

Subsequently Dante mentions Livy, who as historian of Rome attempted many such descriptions "pur con parole sciolte," i.e. in prose. This unique reference to the august political chronicler belongs to the fifteen-line comparison of lines 7 through 21, which describes five battles encompassing the political history of southern Italy from Roman times to the takeover of Charles of Anjou, and whose bewildering array of proper names has the

[86] On a textual level as well, the entire canto is a preparation for its pièce de résistance, Bertran de Born. There are echoes of Bertran's poetry throughout *Inferno* XXVIII, beginning with the structural imitation of the opening of "Si tuit li dol" in lines 7-21; see Singleton, *Commentary* to the *Inferno*, pp. 496, 502, 506, and Michelangelo Picone, "I trovatori di Dante: Bertran de Born," *Studi e problemi di critica testuale*, 19 (1979), 71-94. The classic studies of this episode are Michele Scherillo, "Bertram dal Bornio e il Re giovane," *Nuova antologia*, 154 (1897), 452-478, and "Dante e Bertram dal Bornio"; De Lollis' review of Scherillo in *Bullettino della Società Dantesca Italiana*, 1, nuova serie 5 (1897-1898), 69-73; and Vincenzo Crescini, "Il canto XXVIII dell'*Inferno*," *Lectura Dantis* (Florence: Sansoni, 1907), repr. in *Letture scelte sulla Divina Commedia*, ed. Giovanni Getto, pp. 383-398. Mario Fubini discusses the deliberate depersonalizing of the sinners of this canto through the use of a distancing rhetoric in "Il canto XXVIII dell'*Inferno*," *Lectura Dantis Scaligera* (Florence: Le Monnier, 1967), pp. 999-1021. Other recent studies include Marianne Shapiro, "The Fictionalization of Bertran de Born," *Dante Studies*, 92 (1974), 107-116, and Franco Suitner, "Due trovatori nella *Commedia* (Bertran de Born e Folchetto di Marsiglia)."

Lyric Quests

effect of battering the reader with historical and political data. Furthermore, *Inferno* XXVIII contains reminiscences of other cantos in the *Inferno* where Dante airs his political beliefs, namely *Inferno* VI, where he discusses Florence with Ciacco, and *Inferno* X, where he meets Farinata. In canto VI Dante questions Ciacco as to the whereabouts of five well-known Florentines; one of these men, Mosca de' Lamberti, turns up in canto XXVIII among the sowers of discord. The dialogue between Dante and Mosca recalls an earlier dialogue between the pilgrim and Farinata; in both cases Dante retorts acrimoniously, saying something that—theological imprecision notwithstanding—causes the sinner even greater suffering. A last link between these cantos is the prophesying that occurs in all of them (politics being in some respects the art of successfully foretelling the future): in *Inferno* VI Ciacco hints at Dante's exile by predicting the overthrow of his party; Farinata, in *Inferno* X, also alludes to Dante's exile, before going on to discuss the nature of foresight in Hell. It hardly seems coincidental that in *Inferno* XXVIII "l'antiveder" ("foresight" [78]) should once more be practiced, this time by Mohammed and Pier da Medicina; rather, these correspondences are signposts marking the similar thematic concerns that underlie all three cantos.

As a canto that deals with a political theme—specifically, *desfar la patz*, the "unmaking of peace," to borrow a phrase from the Provençal *vida*—*Inferno* XXVIII stands in opposition to that canto of unity and peacemaking, *Purgatorio* VI. Stylistic points of comparison support this conclusion. In his reading of *Purgatorio* VI, Aurelio Roncaglia draws attention to the recurrence of formulas denoting separation ("nave sanza nocchiere" "ship without a helmsman," "sella vòta" "empty saddle," "vedova Roma" "widowed Rome") in the invective against Italy.[87] *Inferno* XXVIII also ties a motif of separation to a discourse on politics; however, the metaphoric rending of the *Pur-*

---

[87] See "Il canto VI del *Purgatorio*," *Rassegna della letteratura italiana*, 60 (1956), 409-426, where Roncaglia comments that "La frequenza di questa sigla avulsiva rappresenta la tormentosa fissità d'uno stato sentimentale di lacerazione" (p. 419).

gatorio is literalized in the *Inferno*, where political bereavement is expressed through physical wounds. Hence we find, to mention only two of the *bolgia*'s inhabitants, Alì "fesso nel volto dal mento al ciuffetto" ("with his face cleft from his chin to his forelock" [33]) and Pier da Medicina "che forata avea la gola / e tronco 'l naso infin sotto le ciglia, / e non avea mai ch'una orecchia sola" ("who had his throat pierced and his nose cut off up to his eyebrows, and who never had more than one ear at a time" [64-66]). Another similarity between the cantos is the massive use in each of proper names, which serve to stress the historical, specific, and ephemeral nature of politics. In *Inferno* XXVIII, for instance, we find between lines 14 and 18 the names Ruberto Guiscardo, Ceperan, Pugliese, Tagliacozzo, and Alardo; in *Purgatorio* VI, in only two lines, we find Montecchi, Cappelletti, Monaldi, and Filippeschi (106-107).

Inferno XXVIII, then, stands in opposition to *Purgatorio* VI, in much the same way as does *Inferno* X. In the episodes of Farinata and Sordello the theme "division versus unity" is treated under the rubric, so to speak, of "love of one's native land." In the episodes of Bertran and Sordello, the same theme is treated under the rubric "poets who in their poetry fostered either divisiveness or unity." The Provençal *vida* specifically declares that Bertran strove to stir up trouble between father and son "with his *sirventes*"; there is perhaps an allusion to this in Dante's verse "quelli / che diedi al re giovane i ma' conforti" ("the one who gave the evil counsels to the young king" [134-135]), where the nature of the "conforti" is not specified but certainly implied. Bertran is Sordello's poetic counterpart, a fact that is confirmed and thrown into relief by their being the only lyric poets in the *Comedy* to concentrate on political concerns. Bertran's political poetry fostered disunity and schism by encouraging the Young King to disobey his father, while Sordello's, by criticizing the princes in a way that prefigures Dante's own critical stance of *Purgatorio* VI and VII, served the final goal of political unity. Bertran and Sordello are exempla of the uses to which a poet can put his poetry in the service of the state. As political poets, who address a wider audience than do love poets, they have a proportionately greater responsibility: Bertran misused his position and mishandled his responsibility; Sordello, the counterexemplum, behaved responsibly by putting his poetry to good use. Their poetry thus becomes emblematic of everything that each comes to stand for in the *Comedy*: one for separating, disjoining, undoing, taking apart what ought to be united; the other for crossing over, bringing together, reuniting what has been torn asunder. The relationship between the two political poets is one more strand in the web of overlapping political themes that converge in the sixth and seventh cantos of the *Purgatorio* and that could be diagramed as follows:

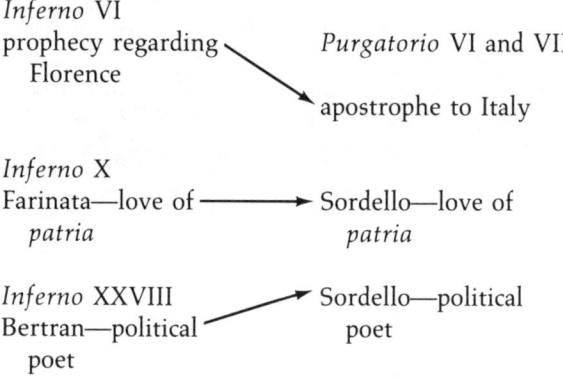

We can now see why Sordello is treated far more sympathetically in the *Comedy* than his poetic stature or position in life would lead us to expect. The historical Sordello has been absorbed by a Sordello whose function confers on him some signal honors and privileges not granted to any other lyric poet. For instance, although as a rule only epic poets move in the *Comedy*, Sordello moves. Since he cannot leave Ante-Purgatory, he does not move significantly upwards in the way that Vergil and Statius do; he is nonetheless the only lyric poet to move at all. (I am not referring to static motion that is part of punishment or purgation, like Guinizzelli's movement through the flames.) In that Sordello's presence spans three cantos, from

Purgatorio VI to VIII (he is last mentioned in *Purgatorio* IX, 58: "Sordel rimase e l'altre genti forme" "Sordello remained and the other noble souls"), he holds the stage longer than any of his peers, who suffer narrative as well as geographical confinements and are thus limited to one canto appearances. Sordello greets Vergil in a manner that foreshadows Statius' greeting of Vergil later on, and—most important—he serves as guide to the travelers, even saying "a guida mi t'accosto" ("I will take your side as guide" [*Purg*. VII, 42]), thus implicitly aligning himself with the other two poet-guides, Vergil and Statius. All in all, Sordello's preeminence among the lyric poets in the *Comedy* is such as to suggest that he enjoys quasi-epic status, a status underscored by the similarity between the valley of the princes and Limbo, the home of the classical poets. Moreover, the word *onesto*, etymologically related to *onore*, which with its various derivatives occurs eight times in *Inferno* IV and is Limbo's verbal talisman, is twice used in connection with Sordello, both times strategically: first in the initial presentation of canto VI ("e nel mover de li occhi onesta e tarda" "and in the slow dignified movement of your eyes" [63]), and then in the re-presentation at the beginning of canto VII ("Poscia che l'accoglienze oneste e liete" "After the dignified and joyful greetings" [1]). These efforts to link Sordello to the *Comedy*'s epic and classical poets also serve to separate and distinguish him from the *Comedy*'s lyric love poets.

By the time Dante came to write the sacred poem, he was incapable of—or uninterested in—unalloyed aesthetic judgments; hence Sordello, owing to his role as a moral and political poet in the service of political unity, is given marks of distinction not accorded to other lyric poets, even though this group includes some whom we would consider poetically greater than he. For that matter, Bertran is a greater poet than Sordello, objectively speaking, and we have seen how little this fact counts in the final judgment. Sordello's position depends entirely on the importance Dante attaches to political unity and peace as the basis, the *sine qua non*, of mankind's temporal well-being. Sordello's poetry does not aspire to the educational value of epic poetry, nor does it speak to all humanity; Dante's point, however, is that it comes closer to embodying these ideals than does any other form of lyric poetry. Consequently, Dante deliberately links Sordello to the epic poets. He also takes care to show that, in this respect as well, Bertran is the exact opposite of Sordello. The description of Bertran in *Inferno* XXVIII as a trunk who carries its head like a lantern ("'e 'l capo tronco tenea per le chiome, / pesol con mano a guisa di lanterna" "and it held the truncated head by the hair, dangling in its hand like a lantern" [121-122]), and lights the way for itself by itself ("Di sé facea a sé stesso lucerna" "Of itself it made for itself a lamp" [124]), cannot but call to mind Statius' tribute to Vergil in *Purgatorio* XXII:

Facesti come quei che va di notte,
    che porta il lume dietro e sé non giova,
    ma dopo sé fa le persone dotte

You did as one who goes by night, who carries the light behind him and helps not himself, but makes those who come after him wise

(67-69)

Bertran is a grotesque inversion of Vergil: in one there is total severance, a self-sufficiency that is not strength but meaninglessness, whereas in the other there is a sharing, a passing on, and an illumination of others at the expense of oneself.

In his presentation of Bertran and Sordello as polar opposites, Dante definitively alters the historical record, and in such a way as to affect the poetic record as well: Bertran's poetic reputation was not enhanced by the *Comedy*, and Sordello's certainly was. Sordello, who wrote a biting and savage poem (which, had it been acted on, would have resulted in fighting in every corner of Europe), is reincarnated as an emblem of unity; whereas Bertran, whose poems in fact had little political impact, becomes an emblem of schism. The point is that neither of these recreations, although justifiable, is without its arbitrary features. Dante was not interested in finding for each character in his poem a niche to correspond exactly to the merits of that person as a historical figure; rather, he begins with ideal categories that will illuminate the structure of reality as he sees it, and into these he fits his characters. So it is for souls in general, and so it is for poets. If Dante has two political poets, they must perforce have more than gossip value; they must illustrate more than the fate that each found on dying. The ideal categories would naturally have to do with the use or misuse of their poetry, and Dante would look for figures whose biographies and poetic output worked well within these categories, even if not slavishly corresponding in all details. Accordingly, Dante's treatment of Bertran de Born and Sordello presents us with a deliberate revision of history for didactic purposes; in this instance the objective is to impart a moral lesson concerning the ways the poet uses his gifts vis-à-vis society, and specifically to illustrate—within the relation of the poet to the body politic—his indivisible responsibility to the state.

The Lyric Picture: Patterns of Revision

In concluding this chapter on Dante's treatment of his lyric peers, I would like to turn briefly to the historiographical perspective of his contemporaries, as embodied in the anonymous sonnet "Infra gli altri difetti del libello."[88] As the first line

[88] The attribution of this sonnet to Cino is based on the identification of the lady in the sextet as Selvaggia, Cino's lady; I think it more probable that the poem was written by someone else annoyed at Cino's exclusion from the *Comedy*. Although Gerolamo Biscaro, "Cino da Pistoia e Dante," *Studi medievali*, nuova serie, 1 (1928), 492-499, supports Cino's paternity of this sonnet and two others that attack Dante, Cino's authorship is denied by Zingarelli in his review of Biscaro, *Studi danteschi*, 14 (1930), 184-185, as well as by Sapegno, *Il Trecento* (Milan: Vallardi, 1934), p. 45. Marti places this sonnet among Cino's "Rime dubbie" in his edition *Poeti del Dolce stil nuovo* (Florence: Le Monnier, 1969); this is the edition I have used. The sonnet also rebukes Dante for failing to give Onesto degli Onesti his due; for a general discussion of Onesto's position vis-à-vis the *stilnovisti*, see Marti, "Onesto da Bologna, lo Stil nuovo e Dante," in *Con Dante fra i poeti del suo tempo*, pp. 45-68.

indicates, the poem is a critique of the *Comedy*, here pejoratively referred to as the "libello" (a term Dante uses for the *Vita Nuova*, but never for the *Comedy*); the sonneteer claims that, "among the other defects of the little book," composed by Dante "lord of all rhymes," there are two so great as to justify the belief that Dante's soul has not gone to Paradise. Both of these defects are of a poetic nature. First, Dante is accused of not having mentioned Onesto degli Onesti, the Bolognese follower of Guittone and Guinizzelli and poetic correspondent with Cino whom Dante places in the Bolognese school in the *De Vulgari Eloquentia*; cleverly imitating the *Comedy*'s own technique of appropriating reality, the poet accuses Dante not of failing to include Onesto in his *Purgatorio*, but of failing to speak with Onesto, when he appeared in Purgatory next to Arnaut Daniel:

> L'un è che ragionando con Sordello
> e con molt'altri della dotta lima,
> non fe' motto ad Onesto, di ben cima,
> ch'era presso ad Arnaldo Daniello.

> The first [defect] is that, while speaking with Sordello and with many others of learned polished verse, he did not speak to Onesto, of much renown, who was next to Arnaut Daniel.

(5-8)

In the sextet the poet accuses Dante of a second omission, this time in the *Paradiso*, where he failed to recognize a lady who stood with Beatrice "nel bel coro divino" (10). Since this lady is described as the "only phoenix" to have reached "Sion" (heaven) by way of the Apennines, she has been identified with Selvaggia, Cino's lady, who traditionally died in the Apennines near Pistoia; we may take the alleged omission of Selvaggia from the *Comedy* to stand for the omission of Cino, which would doubtless have startled those contemporary readers who took the testimony of the *De Vulgari Eloquentia* at face value, and who knew of the long friendship between the two men.

What is interesting about this sonnet is that a contemporary, perhaps sensing the enormous prestige that would later be accorded the "libello's" opinions, should record his indignation

The Lyric Picture

at two of its literary exclusions. More important than the specific poets involved is the sonnet's general indictment, for it essentially accuses Dante of arbitrary behavior in his treatment of other poets. This treatment may perhaps be best summarized by noting those poets whose reputations suffer at the hands of the Comedy, and those whose reputations are enhanced. We might set up two categories, one for those whom the Comedy revises negatively, and another for those whose metamorphosis is positive:[89]

NEGATIVE REVISION

1. Guittone d'Arezzo: the negative treatment of the De Vulgari Eloquentia continues into the Comedy, where it is intensified.
2. Guido Cavalcanti: the ambivalence of the Comedy diminishes the stature that was his in the Vita Nuova and, to a lesser degree, in the De Vulgari Eloquentia.
3. Giraut de Bornelh: no longer the De Vulgari Eloquentia's Provençal poet of rectitude, he is diminished in stature by being paired with Guittone in the Comedy.
4. Bertran de Born: rather than being the De Vulgari Eloquentia's only poet of arms, he is an emblem of schism in the Comedy.

POSITIVE REVISION

1. Guido Guinizzelli: the remote "saggio" of the Vita Nuova and "maximus" of the De Vulgari Eloquentia becomes the "padre" of the Comedy.

---

[89] Harold Bloom's theory of literary revisionism comes to mind here. Bloom posits an age of generous influence, lasting from Homer to Shakespeare, and says of Dante: "At the heart of this matrix of generous influence is Dante and his relation to his precursor Virgil, who moved his ephebe only to love and emulation and not to anxiety" (The Anxiety of Influence: A Theory of Poetry [1973; repr. paperback ed. New York: Oxford U. Press, 1975], p. 122). Whatever Dante's relation to Vergil, which we will discuss in the next chapter, there is no doubt that in dealing with contemporaries—whose poetic identities, unlike Vergil's, were still in the making, and whose reputations are to this day greatly shaped by the Comedy—Dante was less loving. In fact, his treatment of these poets suggests a degree of anxiety that is remarkable if one considers that it is experienced by a poet of enormous stature vis-à-vis poets who are, in the larger picture, only literary curiosities with respect to him.

2. Arnaut Daniel: the *De Vulgari Eloquentia*'s Provençal poet of love becomes the "miglior fabbro" of the *Comedy*.
3. Folquet de Marselha: from a poet of little importance in the *De Vulgari Eloquentia* he is raised to the love poet of Paradise.
4. Sordello: mentioned in passing in the *De Vulgari Eloquentia* as a linguistic curiosity, he becomes an emblem of political and linguistic unity in the *Comedy*.

Of the eight figures listed above, four are of primary importance as Dante's vernacular masters; these are Guido Cavalcanti, Guido Guinizzelli, Guittone d'Arezzo, and Arnaut Daniel. Guinizzelli and Cavalcanti were most important in the first phase of Dante's lyric development, what Boyde calls the "restrictive" phase, whereas Guittone and Arnaut belong to the second or "expansive" phase. In each of these phases, one poet exerts more influence over content or direction, the other over form or style. In the first phase, Guinizzelli provides the new *materia*, the concept of disinterested love, while Cavalcanti provides the new style; in the second phase, Guittone occupies a position analogous to Guinizzelli's, in that he is responsible for a shift in content, toward the poetry of the *directio voluntatis*, whereas Arnaut's role is analogous to Cavalcanti's. Indeed, the similarities between Arnaut and Cavalcanti are marked enough to suggest a further reason for Arnaut's prominence in the *Comedy*: Dante uses him to displace Guido, allowing his second stylistic master to absorb some of the recognition owed to the first. We note that both poets are praised on linguistic grounds—Cavalcanti for "la gloria de la lingua" and Arnaut as the "miglior fabbro"—and that they have a history of overlapping in Dante's texts; they are both mentioned in the technical chapters at the end of the *De Vulgari Eloquentia*: Arnaut in II, x and xiii, Cavalcanti twice in II, xii. Moreover, as with Cavalcanti, there is a competitive streak in Dante's relation with Arnaut. Thus, he sets up a stylistic contest between himself and Arnaut in the matter of the *sestina*: although in general excessive use of the same rhyme sound is to be avoided, Dante says, the rule may be relaxed in the event that the poet is undertaking a new and never before attempted technical feat; in this case his excess is permitted, as on the day of his investiture special privileges are accorded the new knight (II, xiii, 13). As an example of a technical feat that is "novum aliquid atque intentatum," Dante offers precisely the canzone in which he seeks to outdo Arnaut Daniel, the so-called double *sestina* "Amor, tu vedi ben che questa donna."

But the competitive streak that surfaces in Dante vis-à-vis Arnaut remains harmless, never taking the turn of *Purgatorio* XI, and again we may speculate that Dante found Arnaut's insistence on certain themes less threatening than Cavalcanti's similar preoccupations. Specifically, in both poets we find a stress on the poet as artificer, coupled with the emphatic claim that the source of his art is only and exclusively Love; thus Cavalcanti, displaying an affection for the verb *limare* ("to file" or "polish") shared by if not inherited from Arnaut, writes to Guido Orlandi that "Amore ha fabricato ciò ch'io limo" ("Love has made that which I polish"). In the same sonnet, "Di vil matera mi conven parlare," Cavalcanti not only echoes Arnaut's "obre e lim / motz de valor / ab art d'Amor" ("I forge and file words of worth with art of Love" [II, 12-14]), but by the same token he anticipates a good deal of Dante's poetic credo of *Purgatorio* XXIV;[90] he reminds Orlandi, a poet in the Guittonian

---

[90] In the Introduction to his edition of Arnaut, Toja observes that there are more images of craftsmanship in Arnaut's poetry than in that of any earlier troubadour (p. 74, n. 1). Paterson, *Troubadours and Eloquence*, lists examples of the poet-artisan topos in Arnaut (p. 189) and in other troubadours (p. 189, n. 1); Braccini comments that Arnaut and Cavalcanti have this set of images in common ("Paralipomeni al 'Personaggio-Poeta,' " p. 251). Besides the use of *limar* in II, 12, Arnaut also uses the noun *lima* ("file") in X, 4, while Cavalcanti's association with this image is so strong that Guido Orlandi plays on it in his reply *per le rime* to Cavalcanti's "Di vil matera." Orlandi's sonnet begins "Amico, i' saccio ben che sa' limare," and ends with the word "limo," in imitation of Cavalcanti's last verse "Amore ha fabricato ciò ch'io limo"; however, whereas Cavalcanti uses "limo" to mean "I polish," in the elevated context of Love's inspiration, Orlandi uses it to mean "mud," and accuses his friend precisely of a nonelevated carnal passion: "Io per lung' uso disusai lo primo / amor carnale: non tangio nel limo" ("I have long given up the first carnal love: I do not touch the mud" [15-16]).

manner, that his knowledge of Ovid and his use of equivocal rhyme do not qualify him to speak of love, or to consider himself a poet in Cavalcanti's league:

> non pò venire per la vostra mente
> là dove insegna Amor, sottile e piano,
> di sua manera dire e di su' stato.
>
> Into your mind cannot come the place where Love teaches, subtly and softly, to speak of his manner and of his state.
>
> (9-11)

In these verses Love instructs the poet as to content, "di sua manera dire e di su' stato," whereas the striking last verse, "Amore ha fabricato ciò ch'io limo," brings up the question of style, saying explicitly that Love is the true maker of this poetry. It is hardly surprising that, faced with a poet who formulates the relation of the poet to Love in terms almost identical to those of canto XXIV, Dante should displace him by conjuring up a similar but more distant precursor, one who wrote in Provençal rather than Italian. To do justice to Cavalcanti would require Dante to acknowledge that the linguistic program called the *stil novo* was in fact first formulated not by him but by his first friend.[91]

Returning to Dante's four vernacular masters, we note the following pattern of revision: of the first two—Guinizzelli and Cavalcanti—he acknowledges the one who influenced his poetic direction, and rejects the one who influenced his poetic form, whereas with the second two—Guittone and Arnaut—the reverse is true. In both phases, however, we note that Dante acknowledges the safer poet, the older poet, the one who is

---

[91] This is the point made by Favati in "Contributo alla determinazione del problema dello Stil Nuovo," where he stresses the connection between the formulations of "Di vil matera" and those of *Purgatorio* XXIV. In the canzone "Io non pensava che lo cor giammai" Cavalcanti articulates the relation between the poet and Love in similar terms, even anticipating the image of the book used in the *Vita Nuova*: "Canzon, tu sai che de' libri d'Amore / io t'asempli quando madonna vidi" ("Song, you know that I transcribed you from the books of Love when I saw my lady" [43-44]).

further away. Moreover, Guido Cavalcanti and Guittone d'Arezzo, the poets whom Dante rejects, have one extremely significant characteristic in common. Both are poets Dante suspects of having been new before him: Guittone because he opened the Italian lyric to new issues, Cavalcanti because he invented the new style. Putting it differently, we could say that if Cavalcanti's mistake lies in claiming Amor as his source, Guittone's lies in claiming God. Furthermore, although they are the most explicit victims of Dante's urge to rewrite poetic history, the pattern operates throughout: few of the contemporary lyric poets who actually appear in the *Comedy* are strong; indeed, three of them—Sordello, Bonagiunta, and Folquet—could be categorized as weak. The strongest lyric poet in the *Comedy* is Dante himself; after him, along with Guinizzelli and Arnaut, one could place Bertran de Born, who is canceled by being in Hell. Like Cavalcanti, whose nonpresence is masked both by Guinizzelli and by Arnaut, Guittone too suffers a double displacement, not only in *Purgatorio* XXIV and XXVI but also earlier, at the hands of Sordello. In fact, the arbitrary features inherent in Dante's use of Sordello are magnified if we consider that a poem of Guittone's, who is a more significant political poet than Sordello as well as being one who wrote in Italian, is in fact the vernacular force behind *Purgatorio* VI through VIII, cantos that derive at most a pallid and mechanical inspiration from the lament for Blacatz.

The poem in question, whose pervasive influence in cantos VI-VIII has, to my knowledge, gone unremarked, is the canzone "Magni baroni certo e regi quasi";[92] in it Guittone exhorts two great lords and rulers of Pisa, Count Ugolino della Gherardesca and Nino Visconti, Ugolino's grandson and lord of Gallura in northern Sardinia, to come to the aid of their city: "Magni baroni certo e regi quasi, / conte Ugulin, giùdici di Gallore" ("Great barons certainly and almost kings, Count Ugolino [and]

---

[92] Although Contini records Dante's use of line 71, "donna de la provincia e regin' anco," for *Purgatorio* VI, 78, "non donna di provincie, ma bordello!" (*Poeti del Duecento*, vol. I, p. 238), no one seems to have noticed Dante's intensive use of this canzone as a backdrop for these cantos.

Judge of Gallura" [1-2]). The poem combines a moral theme on the identity of goodness and greatness ("Tutti rei parvi son, tutti bon' magni" "All evil men are small, and all good men great" [15]) with a political commentary on the need for Pisa's rulers to bring their power to bear constructively. Pisa's plight is rendered dramatically; the city is personified as a once beautiful lady now stripped of her beauty, status, sons, and friends:

> Infermat'è, signor mii, la sorbella
> madre vostra e dei vostri, e la migliore
> donna de la provincia e regin' anco,
> specchio nel mondo, ornamento e bellore.
> Oh, come in pia[n]ger mai suo figlio è stanco,
> vederla quasi adoventata ancella,
>   di bellor tutto e d'onor dinudata,
> di valor dimembrata
> soi cari figli in morte e in pregione,
> d'onne consolazione
> quasi in disperazione,
> e d'onni amico nuda e d'onni aiuto?

She is sick, my lords, the beautiful lady, mother of you and yours, the greatest lady of the province, indeed a queen, mirror of the world, ornament and beauty. Oh, how her son never tires of weeping, to see her become almost a serving-girl, denuded of all beauty and honor, of valor dismembered, her dear sons dead and in prison, without consolation, almost in desperation, naked of all friends and all aid.

(69-80)

Reminding Ugolino and Nino that the power to save their city is in their hands (86-96), and that the eyes of the whole world are upon them (97-99), the poet tells them that the choice is between dishonor and honor (100-102); they are to model themselves not on the many tyrants and kings who destroy their lands, but on the "good Romans," repositories of true valor:

De tiranni e di regi assai trovate:
merzé, non v'assemprate
a tiranni di lor terra struttori,
ma a Roman boni, in cui ver valor foe

Of tyrants and kings you will find many; please, do not be like the tyrants destroyers of their lands, but like good Romans, in whom there was true valor

(103-106)

Finally, the poet warns the two potentates that there are two paths by which to proceed in life: "son este due malizia e bonitate" ("these two are malice and goodness" [121]); the path of malice leads to ruin and the path of goodness to peace and honor in perpetuity.

The gist of this canzone is repeated with surprising fidelity in *Purgatorio* VI through VIII, where Dante first signals his use of it by echoing and reversing Guittone's description of Pisa, "donna de la provincia e regin' anco" (71), in his opening fusillade against Italy, "non donna di provincie, ma bordello!" (*Purg.* VI, 78), and then goes on to reproduce the basic structure of the canzone in his invective: again a poet urges the powerful to awaken to their civic responsibilities, and again the organs of statehood—the Empire, the country, the cities—are pictured as abandoned, desolate, and infirm. As in the canzone, so here a long series of lacks is rehearsed, in the course of which Rome is personified as an abandoned woman, "vedova e sola" (113), who day and night calls out to her lord; the list culminates in the description of Florence as "quella inferma" (149), thus ending on the image of sickness with which Guittone's catalogue of woes begins. Guittone's lesson regarding the difference between "tiranni" and "Roman boni" is also punctually echoed by Dante, who essentially repeats Guittone's belief that Italy is populated by tyrants ("De tiranni e di regi assai trovate") in his comment "Ché le città d'Italia tutte piene / son di tiranni" ("For the cities of Italy are all full of tyrants" [124-125]). Indeed, Dante's subsequent thought, that every ignoble leader of a political faction who comes along immediately dares to become a "Marcellus," i.e. an adversary to the Empire ("e un Marcel diventa" in line 125 seems to refer to one Marcellus characterized by Lucan as a strenuous opponent to Caesar), further echoes Guittone; as the "tiranni" of the canzone are followed by a reference to "Roman boni," so in the more critical and less trusting world of the purgatorial invective the "tiranni" are followed by "Roman cattivi." Dante's point is that his contemporaries have modeled themselves not on good Romans, but on the bad ones like Marcellus.

However, the *Comedy*'s most suggestive use of Guittone's canzone is to be found in its treatment of the two figures to whom "Magni baroni" is addressed; in the *Comedy* Count Ugolino and Nino Visconti become conspicuous examples of political careers that fail or succeed according to Guittone's maxim: one, Ugolino's, fails because it is based on "malizia"; the other, Nino's, succeeds because it is based on "bonitate." Both figures play key roles in the development of cantos VI through VIII as political cantos. Although Ugolino does not appear in person, as does Nino, he is indirectly present in the expression "l'un l'altro si rode" (*Purg.* VI, 83), which is intended not only to contrast the mutual gnawing of Italian citizens with the mutual embrace of Vergil and Sordello, but also to echo the only other passage in the poem in which humans gnaw each other: that most despairing testimony to the destitution wrought by Italy's political factionalism, the episode of Ugolino. There too we find the syntax of mutuality, tied not to love but to hate: "ch'io vidi due ghiacciati in una buca, / sì che *l'un capo a l'altro* era cappello" ("I saw two frozen in one hole, such that the head of one was a hat to the other" [*Inf.* XXXII, 125-126; italics mine]). There too we find the verb *rodere* linked to human beings:[93]

---

[93] *Rodere* is used in reference to human relations only in the context of these episodes, i.e. twice regarding Ugolino and once in *Purgatorio* VI. Its two other occurrences in the poem do not refer to people: in *Inferno* XXXIV, 131, it modifies the stone which has been "gnawed" by the stream passing through it; in *Paradiso* V, 134, it describes the heat of the sun, which "gnaws" or consumes the vapors of the atmosphere.

"non altrimenti Tidëo si rose / le tempie a Menalippo per disdegno" ("not otherwise did Tydeus gnaw the temples of Menalippus in his rage" [*Inf.* XXXII, 130-131]), says the narrator of Ugolino and his grisly repast, and Ugolino himself later speaks of the "traditor ch'i' rodo" ("the traitor whom I gnaw" [*Inf.* XXXIII, 8]). Finally, the fratricidal strife between citizens that Ugolino embodies is represented in *Purgatorio* VI even prior to the great invective, in the scene at the beginning of the canto that sets the stage for the later narrative outburst by showing us the victims of Italy's political crimes, the souls who died violent deaths.

Although the *Purgatorio*'s chief victims of violent death—Iacopo del Cassero, Bonconte da Montefeltro, Pia de' Tolomei—are presented in canto V, the opening of canto VI shows the pilgrim surrounded by a "thick crowd" of souls whose very numbers and anonymity serve as eloquent indices of Italy's precarious political condition. Among these is one named by periphrasis as "quel da Pisa / che fé parer lo buon Marzucco forte" ("the one from Pisa who made the good Marzucco show his strength" [17-18]). This is most likely Gano Scornigiani, the son of the Pisan nobleman Marzucco Scornigiani, whom Dante had occasion to meet at Santa Croce, where Marzucco lived as a priest after his retirement from the world; it was Gano's death that gave Marzucco the opportunity to display his fortitude. Interestingly, Gano was embroiled in the feuding between Ugolino and Nino over control of Pisa, which was the outcome of Ugolino's bringing Nino into power as *capitano del popolo* in 1285; Gano, whose family had long ties with the Visconti, took Nino's side and was killed in 1287 by Ugolino's men.[94] Thus, Dante places here a soul whose personal situation is an emblem of Italy's problems: this man, deliberately named

---

[94] Ugolino, a Ghibelline, most likely took his grandson, a Guelph, into power in order to appease the Pisan Guelphs; on Ugolino's dealings as head of Pisa, a position he occupied from 1284-1288, when he was imprisoned, see Simonetta Saffiotti Bernardi, *Enciclopedia Dantesca*, vol. V, pp. 795-797. On Gano and Marzucco Scornigiani, see the articles by Renato Piattoli, *Enciclopedia Dantesca*, vol. V, pp. 87-88.

only by city and family connections, is a Pisan killed at the behest of another Pisan, Ugolino, on account of his loyalty to yet a third Pisan, Nino Visconti. Nino himself will appear only two cantos later, in the valley of the princes, in an episode redolent not only with nostalgia but with family pride; he does not believe that the viper of the Milanese Visconti will make his remarried wife as honorable a sepulchre as his own coat of arms, the cock of Gallura. Although Nino is treated lovingly, as an old friend, Dante always refers to him with the title of his office, the same title used by Guittone; he is "giudice Nin gentil" in VIII, 53, and "giudice" again in line 109 (this double use of "giudice" is the more noteworthy because the word occurs only one other time, in *Purgatorio* XXXI, 39, for God). A final suggestive correlation is provided by the fact that Guittone too had personal contacts with Nino, to whom he addresses the affectionate sonnet "Giudice de Gallura, en vostro amore," and with the Scornigiani; Marzucco had incurred a debt to Guittone's father, and Guittone wrote him once to request repayment and a second time to congratulate him on joining holy orders.[95]

Dante's extensive use of Guittone's canzone as a textual backdrop for these political cantos has gone unrecognized, as he intended; Sordello is the poet the pilgrim meets in *Purgatorio* VI. Dante uses Sordello to point to the importance of political commitment in poetry, and he therefore connects Sordello to Folquet, who is intended to suggest—not embody—the fusion between love poetry and political poetry that alone can make a poet truly great. Indeed, such a fusion seems to be the *sine qua non* for surpassing what Dante sees as the lyric stage of poetic development. Most poets never go beyond this stage and Folquet is no exception, for although his commitment changes the course of his life, it did not deeply affect his poetry. But the very

---

[95] Guittone's letters to Marzucco are numbers XVIII (regarding the debt) and XXX (regarding holy orders); the second is a verse letter in the form of a canzone beginning "Messer Marzuccho Scornigian, sovente." See the edition of Francesco Meriano, *Le lettere di frate Guittone d'Arezzo* (Bologna: R. Commissione pei testi di lingua, 1922).

dichotomy between eros and politics that Dante sees in Folquet and reflects in the heaven of Venus serves to suggest an ideal state beyond dualism and dichotomy. This ideal fusion is further evoked through the oblique presence of Sordello, who was the protégé and "dilectus familiaris" of Charles I of Anjou, grandfather of the Charles Martel who dominates *Paradiso* VIII, as well as the notorious abductor and lover of Cunizza, who introduces Folquet in *Paradiso* IX.[96] Perhaps Cunizza's humility in presenting Folquet, reminiscent of Guinizzelli's introduction of Arnaut, stands for Sordello's humility in front of a poet who actually put his beliefs into action. At any rate, Folquet serves as a kind of summary of all the *Comedy*'s Provençal poets: not only is his political *engagement* forecast by Sordello and his love poetry by Arnaut, but he was in life a good friend of Bertran de Born's, who should have emulated him in directing his energies toward holy rather than secular wars.[97]

The episode of the last lyric poet is thus used to suggest an eventual necessary synthesis between love poetry and political poetry, a synthesis that Dante may have had in mind as early as the *De Vulgari Eloquentia*. Indeed, I would suggest that the treatise's three *magnalia*—"armorum probitas," "amoris accensio," and "directio voluntatis"—adumbrate the *Comedy*'s three types of poets: political poets, love poets, and epic poets. Turning to the well-known passage of *De Vulgari Eloquentia* II, ii, 6-8, we note that Dante arrives at his three poetic topics by way of a discourse that begins with the tripartite division of man's soul; man's vegetative soul pursues the useful ("utile"), his animal soul pursues pleasure ("delectabile"), and his rational

---

[96] In the Introduction to his edition of Sordello, Boni discusses the troubadour's life and his relations with Charles I; Charles refers to Sordello as "dilectus familiaris et fidelis noster" in the document granting him certain feudal castles in the Abruzzi (Boni, p. XCVIII). Regarding Sordello's abduction of Cunizza, which was arranged by Cunizza's brother Ezzelino da Romano, see Boni, pp. XXIXff.

[97] Stroński recounts that Bertran de Born was Folquet's dearest friend (p. 39*); ironically, the two poets retired from secular life at the same time and even entered "deux abbayes-soeurs de l'ordre cistercien" (p. 58*).

soul pursues the honest ("honestum"). These three paths may be further defined: the goal of those who seek the useful is in fact "salus," salvation in a material sense, as pertaining to the preservation of one's self, one's family, one's homeland, and so on; those who seek pleasure desire "venus," physical love; and those who seek the honest desire "virtus" or virtue.[98] To each of these new categories—"salus," "venus," and "virtus"—there corresponds a poetic subject matter most suited to it; and for each of these poetic *magnalia* there are poets: poets of arms, of love, and of rectitude. We therefore end up with the following three sets, all stemming from the original Aristotelian division of the soul:

vegetative soul	sensitive soul	rational soul
utile	delectabile	honestum
salus	venus	virtus
armorum probitas	amoris accensio	directio voluntatis
poet of arms:	poets of love:	poets of rectitude:
Bertran de Born	Arnaut Daniel & Cino da Pistoia	Giraut de Bornelh & Dante

Political poets are precisely those who deal with the issue of salvation in a secular and social context; although the meaning of "armorum probitas" is dictated by context and medieval usage as "prowess of arms," we should not forget the original moral impact of the word *probitas*. With this expression Dante seeks to indicate not simply martial poetry, but poetry charged with the moral and political militancy required to preserve ethical life for society as a whole. From this perspective, we can understand the *Convivio*'s association of a political poet, Bertran, with a social virtue, liberality; as for Dante's subsequent treatment of this troubadour, it seems he decided that Bertran was not in fact motivated by *probitas*, that his search for *salus* had become a search for schism instead. Love poets do, of course, pursue *venus*, at least at first, but they, like their political com-

[98] For the further glossing of these terms see Mengaldo's commentary, pp. 151-153.

The Lyric Picture

rades, may aspire to the last category, created by fusing the previous two: the love lyric, with its itinerary preserved but expanded in that it is now directed to God rather than to the lady, is infused with a new social morality. The *Comedy*'s highest exponents of the first two categories are therefore difficult to classify, because they are markers of the transition to the third: thus, Sordello is "quasi-epic," and Folquet is a love poet presented in an aura of politics. We see, moreover, why Folquet cannot be considered a true poet of rectitude; in the same way that the word *honestum* is associated in the *Comedy* with classical or "epic" poetry, so the last category, that of the *directio voluntatis*, becomes the category of epic poets. Although originally formulated to accommodate the moral lyrics that point to the *Comedy*, like "Doglia mi reca," the poetry of the *directio voluntatis* ultimately exceeds all lyric classifications, serving instead to define the poet's last step; only epic poets, in Dante's sense of the term, combine eros with commitment, fusing the search for *salus* and *venus* into the search for *virtus*, and thereby becoming poets of rectitude.

III
Epic Resolution

Prelude: the *Opere minori*

Dante's basic canon of classical poets is formed as early as the *Vita Nuova*, where he has already assembled the group that forms the nucleus of his training in Latin letters, a group that continues to appear together throughout his oeuvre until it comes, virtually unaltered, into the *Comedy*. In *Vita Nuova* XXV the five poets of this original group are presented in characteristic poses:

> Che li poete abbiano così parlato come detto è, appare per VIRGILIO; lo quale dice che Iuno, cioè una dea nemica de li Troiani, parloe ad Eolo, segnore de li venti, quivi nel primo de lo Eneida: *Eole, nanque tibi,* e che questo segnore le rispuose, quivi: *Tuus, o regina, quid optes explorare labor; michi iussa capessere fas est.* Per questo medesimo poeta parla la cosa che non è animata a le cose animate, nel terzo de lo Eneida, quivi: *Dardanide duri.* Per LUCANO parla la cosa animata a la cosa inanimata, quivi: *Multum, Roma, tamen debes civilibus armis.* Per ORAZIO parla l'uomo a la scienzia medesima sì come ad altra persona; e non solamente sono parole d'Orazio, ma dicele quasi recitando lo modo del buono OMERO, quivi ne la sua Poetria: *Dic michi, Musa, virum.* Per OVIDIO parla Amore, sì come se fosse persona umana, ne lo principio de lo libro

Prelude: the *Opere minori*

c'ha nome Libro di Remedio d'Amore, quivi: *Bella michi, video, bella parantur, ait.*

That the poets have written as is said appears through VERGIL; who says that Juno, a goddess unfriendly to the Trojans, spoke to Aeolus, lord of the winds, in the first book of the *Aeneid: Eole, nanque tibi,* and that this lord answered her: *Tuus, o regina, quid optes explorare labor; michi iussa capessere fas est.* According to this same poet an inanimate thing speaks to animate beings, in the third book of the *Aeneid: Dardanide duri.* According to LUCAN the animate being speaks to the inanimate thing: *Multum, Roma, tamen debes civilibus armis.* According to HORACE a man speaks to knowledge itself as if to another person; and not only are these the words of Horace, but he gives them as though reciting in the manner of HOMER, in his *Ars Poetica: Dic michi, Musa, virum.* According to OVID Love speaks, as though it were a human person, in the beginning of the book called *Remedia Amoris: Bella michi, video, bella parantur, ait.*

(XXV, 9; capitals mine)

Vergil is in the place of honor and is the only poet to be quoted twice. He is represented by the *Aeneid,* his epic, as is Lucan by the *De Bello Civili* or *Pharsalia,* in any case his only extant work. Horace is, if not quite the "Orazio satiro" of *Inferno* IV, nonetheless the nonlyric poet of the *Ars Poetica.* Homer, quoted by way of the *Ars Poetica,* receives his requisite nod; in fact, Dante's attentiveness to his Latin authors and to their reverence for the Greek poet is such that he has anticipated the appearance of Homer, referring to him in chapter II as well. The least known of these poets is thus the only one to appear outside of chapter XXV. Ovid, for whom Dante cites the *Remedia Amoris,* is presented as the authority on Love.[1]

---

[1] For a general presentation regarding Dante's use of and attitudes toward his most frequently mentioned classical poets, as well as further bibliography, see the various articles in the *Enciclopedia Dantesca*: Ettore Paratore, "Giovenale," vol. III, pp. 197-202; Ettore Paratore, "Lucano," vol. III, pp. 697-702;

The poet absent from the roster of the *Vita Nuova* is Statius, whose omission is rectified in the *De Vulgari Eloquentia*. In the treatise Dante mentions Vergil three times, Ovid twice, Statius once, Lucan once, and Horace once.[2] Vergil is again preeminent in being the most quoted of the poets and the first one to be presented when they appear as a group. Horace is once more the preceptor of the *Ars Poetica*, giving advice to fledgling poets: "This is what our master Horace teaches us, when in the beginning of the *Ars Poetica* he says 'Take your subject' " (II, iv, 4). Indeed, in the context of the *De Vulgari Eloquentia* all the classical poets are to be seen as teachers, models to be imitated. The replacement of Homer by Statius is therefore to be expected, since one cannot imitate what one cannot read. In the only passage in the treatise where the Latin poets are presented en masse, as a canon, Dante plainly says that they are to be studied: "And it would perhaps be most useful, in order to acquire the habit [of composing in the high style], to have studied the standard poets, that is Vergil, the Ovid of the *Metamorphoses*, Statius, and Lucan" (II, vi, 7). The expression Dante uses in this passage, "regulatos . . . poetas," may well serve as a summation of what Dante thought of these poets in this period: not only are they regularized according to established literary standards, but they are themselves *regulae* for those who come later, providing rules to be learned and followed.

In the *Convivio* the group of classical poets cited is larger, an indication of Dante's widening cultural horizons and a reflection of the work's philosophical rather than technical concerns. Whereas the *Convivio* contains many fewer vernacular poets than does the *De Vulgari Eloquentia*, its tally of classical poets has lengthened to include Juvenal and to reinclude Homer. Nor does this number of seven classical poets—Vergil, Ovid, Lucan, Statius, Juvenal, Homer, Horace—do justice to the full wealth

---

Guido Martellotti, "Omero," vol. IV, pp. 145-148; Giorgio Brugnoli and Roberto Mercuri, "Orazio," vol. IV, pp. 173-180; Ettore Paratore, "Ovidio," vol. IV, pp. 225-236; Ettore Paratore, "Stazio," vol. V, pp. 419-425; Domenico Consoli and Alessandro Ronconi, "Virgilio," vol. V, pp. 1030-1049.

[2] See the Appendix for the precise locations.

of the *Convivio*'s classical erudition, which can be accurately gauged only by taking into consideration the philosophers and prose writers who also crowd its pages: especially Aristotle and Boethius (the first two authors to be mentioned), Cicero and Seneca.³ The *Convivio*'s heightened awareness of antiquity seems related to a change in Dante's treatment of the classical poets, the scope of whose authority has been significantly enlarged. Whereas in the *Vita Nuova* and the *De Vulgari Eloquentia* they were brought forward as embodiments of proper rhetorical procedure, in the *Convivio* their works are pressed into service as illustrations of correct human—rather than poetic—behavior; Dante now sees these poets are providers of ethical insights as well as rhetorical precepts. This important development is most visible in the chapters of the fourth book in which the references to classical poets are particularly concentrated. Indeed, the crescendo of references to classical poets in the treatise's last book is marked enough to threaten the supremacy of Aristotle and the philosophers; in a text dominated by "il Filosofo," the prevalence of poets over philosophers in Book IV points ahead to the *Comedy*, where Vergil and not Aristotle is the pilgrim's guide, representing the most that natural man and reason can attain.⁴

The discussion of true nobility that dominates the *Convivio*'s

---

³ The *Convivio*, a philosophical work, is especially rich in classical and nonclassical philosophers. Roughly in order of appearance, the following philosophers and writers appear: Aristotle, Boethius, St. Augustine, Hippocrates, Galen, Seneca, Taddeo Alderotti, Cicero, Ptolemy, Plato, Alfraganus, Socrates, Dionysius, Pythagoras, Euclid, Anaxagoras, Democritus, Algazel, Avicenna, Alpetragus, Albertus Magnus, Orosius, Livy, Zeno, St. Jerome, Uguccione da Pisa, Epicurus, Zenocrates, St. Thomas, Egidio Romano, Aesop. To add to the classical congestion, there are also figures like Cato, Marcia, and Aeneas.

⁴ In *Significato del Virgilio dantesco* (Florence: Le Monnier, 1967), Domenico Consoli discusses what Vergil represents in the *Comedy* and the question of why the Latin poet was chosen as Dante's guide over Aristotle; a similar treatment, whose exhaustive footnotes are essentially a history of critical attitudes toward these issues, is that of Aldo Vallone, "Interpretazione del Virgilio dantesco," *Alighieri*, 10 (1969), 14-40. Another summary of critical opinions on Vergil may be found in Mario Santoro, "Virgilio personaggio della *Divina Commedia*," *Cultura e scuola* 4, nos. 13-14 (1965), 343-355.

fourth book requires a description of the spiritual attributes most suited to each of the four ages of man's life, these being *adolescenza, gioventute, senettute,* and *senio.* In order to illustrate these attributes, Dante draws on the works of four classical poets, one for each of the four ages: Statius for *adolescenza,* Vergil for *gioventute,* Ovid for *senettute,* and Lucan for *senio.* Each age receives a separate chapter devoted to it and is illustrated exclusively from the works of the poet assigned to it, so that in effect each poet has a chapter of the *Convivio* dedicated to him. Dante uses these chapters to highlight the poets and their work in an altogether new way; one has the impression that, having decided on Book IV as the *Convivio*'s "literary" book (the treatise's three vernacular poets all make their appearances here as well), Dante then earmarks four of its chapters for an in-depth treatment of his favorite classical poets. Particularly suggestive is his use of epithets; whereas in the *Convivio*'s earlier books Dante is content to call a poet by name, or with a simple periphrasis like "Stazio poeta del tebano Edipo" ("Statius poet of Oedipus the Theban" [III, viii, 10]), in these special chapters of Book IV he uses compact but highly charged phrases to articulate his feelings about a given poet.[5] In some cases these expressions are strikingly similar to the periphrases Dante will later use in the *Comedy,* thus showing that his sense of these poets is beginning to crystallize. Statius is called "lo dolce poeta" ("the sweet poet" [IV, xxv, 6]), a

[5] From these epithets, as well as from the detailed summaries of the classical texts found in these chapters, Ulrich Leo, in "The Unfinished *Convivio* and Dante's Rereading of the *Aeneid,*" *Mediaeval Studies,* 13 (1951), 41-64, concludes that "before the composition of ch. XXV of Book IV of the *Convivio,* Dante has reread his Latin classics, and that with a completely new and personal reaction" (p. 59). Although I concur with Leo's general findings, I am not sure the evidence justifies his specific conclusion that Dante reread the *Aeneid* between the writing of chapters xxiv and xxv of Book IV. I prefer to think that Dante's rediscovery of the classics runs concurrently with the composition of the *Convivio* as a whole, and that he chooses these chapters to celebrate the Latin poets in particular; in support of this interpretation, I would note that although the *Convivio*'s vernacular poets are also confined to Book IV, no one has concluded that Dante had just reread "Al cor gentil."

Prelude: the *Opere minori*

characterization Dante echoes in *Purgatorio* XXI when Statius describes the sweetness of his voice: "Tanto fu dolce mio vocale spirto" ("So sweet was my vocal spirit" [88]). Similarly, Vergil is called "lo maggiore nostro poeta" ("our greatest poet" [IV, xxvi, 8]), an expression that brings to mind the *Comedy*'s reference to the Latin poet as "nostra maggior musa" ("our greatest Muse" [*Par.* XV, 26]).

Chapter xxv is given over to Statius; in order to give examples of *stupore, pudore,* and *verecundia* (the three constituents of *vergogna,* named as the appropriate state of mind for *adolescenza*), Dante retells much of the first book of the *Thebaid,* where Adrastus king of Argus marries his daughters Argia and Deipyle to the Thebans Polyneices and Tydeus. The narrative is interrupted only to present the next virtue and to reintroduce Statius as the chapter's resident *auctoritas*: thus, after defining *stupore,* Dante begins "E però dice Stazio, lo dolce poeta, nel primo de la Tebana Istoria, che quando Adrasto . . ." ("And therefore Statius, the sweet poet, says in the first book of the *Thebaid* that when Adrastus . . ." [IV, xxv, 6]), and then tells of the king's astonishment at seeing Polyneices in a lion skin and Tydeus in a covering made of wild boar, twin fulfillments of the prophecy which foretold that he would marry his daughters to a lion and a boar.[6] Proceeding to *pudore,* Dante cites the modesty of Argia and Deipyle on meeting their future mates: "Onde dice lo sopra notato poeta ne lo allegato libro primo di Tebe . . . le vergini palide e rubicunde si fecero" ("Whence the above mentioned poet in the already cited first book of Thebes says . . . the vergins became pale and blushing" [IV, xxv, 8]).

---

[6] It is not clear why Adrastus, who is described in the *Thebaid* as passing from middle age to the threshold of old age, should be the example of the adolescent virtue of *stupore.* Did Dante get so carried away with his story that he lost track of whom he was pairing with what emotion? P. Mustard, in "Dante and Statius," *MLN,* 39 (1924), 120, proposes the lines describing Adrastus' age, "medio de limite vitae / in senium vergens" ("verging toward old age from the middle part of life" [*Thebaid* I, 390-391]), as a possible source for the first line of the *Comedy.* The text is from *P. Papini Stati Thebais et Achilleis,* ed. H. W. Garrod (Oxford: Clarendon, 1906).

Finally, *verecundia* is illustrated by the suitor Polyneices' shame at revealing his tainted ancestry: "Onde dice questo medesimo poeta, in quella medesima parte, che quando Polinice . . ." ("Whence the same poet, in that same part of his book, says that when Polyneices . . ." [IV, xxv, 10]). A visual tableau from the *Thebaid* is thus enacted in the pages of the *Convivio*, each new image connected to the previous one by the insertion of the reference to the author, which is repeated three times to correspond to the three *passioni* requiring illustration.

Chapter xxvi belongs to Vergil; in it events in the life of Aeneas are used as examples of temperance, fortitude, love, courtesy, and loyalty, all virtues appropriate to *gioventute*. Dante draws his examples from the fourth, fifth, and sixth books of the *Aeneid*: Aeneas' temperance is shown when he leaves Dido; his fortitude when he goes alone with the Sibyl into the underworld; his love in his kindness toward the old Trojans and in his instruction of Ascanius; his courtesy in the part he played in the funeral rites of Misenus; and his loyalty in giving the prizes he had promised to the victors of the games. Because the examples are not all drawn from one episode, the story-line is less unified than in the Statius recital, but in compensation the narrative is infused, as Ulrich Leo points out, with greater passion and personal involvement:[7]

> E quanto raffrenare fu quello, quando, avendo ricevuto da Dido tanto di piacere quanto di sotto nel settimo trattato si dicerà, e usando con essa tanto di dilettazione, elli si partio, per seguire onesta e laudabile via e fruttuosa, come nel quarto de l'Eneida scritto è! Quanto spronare fu quello, quando esso Enea sostenette solo con Sibilla a intrare ne lo Inferno a cercare de l'anima di suo padre Anchise, contra tanti pericoli, come nel sesto de la detta istoria si dimostra!
>
> And how much holding back was that, when, having received from Dido as much pleasure as we will describe below in the seventh treatise, and finding with her such de-

[7] "The Unfinished *Convivio* and Dante's Rereading of the *Aeneid*," p. 59.

Prelude: the *Opere minori*

light, he departed, in order to follow an honorable and praiseworthy path and a fruitful one, as is written in the fourth book of the *Aeneid*! And how much spurring forward was that, when Aeneas dared to enter Hell alone with Sibyl to find the soul of his father Anchises, facing many dangers, as is shown in the sixth book of the afore-mentioned history!

(*Convivio* IV, xxvi, 8-9)

It is, moreover, a tribute to Vergil that his hero should be chosen to exemplify *gioventute*, the age which Dante considers "colmo de la nostra vita" ("the peak of our life" [IV, xxvi, 3]). Vergil himself is mentioned four times in chapter xxvi; while two of these references ("lo nomato poeta" [11] and "lo predetto poeta" [14]) are simple recalls, two describe Vergil in terms that point directly to the *Comedy*: besides being called "lo maggior nostro poeta" (8), echoed in *Paradiso* XV, he is also "questo altissimo poeta" (13), a phrase that later recurs in *Inferno* IV.

Ovid and Lucan receive less attention than Statius and Vergil, in the *Convivio* as in the *Comedy*.[8] The next chapter of *Convivio* IV, that of *senettute*, is assigned to Ovid; after many references to Cicero's *De Senectute*, Dante ends the chapter with a story from the *Metamorphoses* about King Aeacus, in whom all the virtues appropriate to this age (prudence, justice, generosity, and affability) are gathered. Although the practice of inserting a story from the works of the assigned poet into the *Convivio* is thus continued, no handsome epithet adorns Ovid's name, to whom Dante refers twice simply as "Ovidio" (IV, xxvii, 17 and 19). Lucan fares better. The *Pharsalia*'s story of Cato and Marcia, told as an allegory of the noble soul returning to God, is a

[8] Paul Renucci, in *Dante, Disciple et Juge du Monde Gréco-Latin* (Clermont-Ferrand: G. de Bussac, 1954), points out that in the *Comedy* Ovid and Lucan are treated with less veneration than the others: "Présentés aux Limbes sans l'ornement d'une épithète, et derniers nommés de la 'belle école' d'Homère, ils son environnés d'un moindre respect que les *maximi*" (p. 330). In fact, Dante does not hesitate to compare himself favorably to Ovid and Lucan in *Inferno* XXV, where he tells both poets to be silent, whereas he never explicitly calls himself the superior of Vergil.

Epic Resolution

long and elaborate one which takes up much of chapter xxviii, whereas the story of King Aeacus is told rather hurriedly at the end of chapter xxvii. Moreover, although Lucan is only named once, he receives one of the epithets typical of these chapters; he is "quello grande poeta Lucano" (IV, xxviii, 13). While Lucan's position is doubtless enhanced by the importance Dante attaches to Cato, the treatment of Ovid is not atypical, for Ovid is one of the poets Dante most uses, but—with respect to other major poets—least acknowledges. Thus, although one might deduce from these chapters of the *Convivio* that the relative importance of the classical poets for Dante in this period would be reflected by the order Vergil-Statius-Lucan-Ovid, in actual practice Ovid follows Vergil as the poet who is most in evidence: in the *Convivio* Vergil is mentioned ten times, Ovid eight times, Lucan five times, Statius five times, Juvenal four times, Homer twice, and Horace twice. Interestingly, Moore verifies that this same pattern—in which Vergil is first, followed by Ovid, Lucan, and Statius in that order—operates through Dante's work as a whole.[9]

---

[9] Edward Moore, *Studies in Dante, First Series: Scripture and Classical Authors in Dante* (1896; repr. New York: Greenwood Press, 1968), calculates that Vergil is quoted or referred to in Dante's work about 200 times, Ovid about 100, Lucan about 50, and Statius between 30 and 40 (p. 4). Enrico Proto, who follows in Moore's footsteps looking for points of contact between Dante's text and those of his Latin authors, confirms Ovid's standing as the *Comedy*'s principal classical source after Vergil; see "Dante e i poeti latini," *Atene e Roma*, 11 (1908), 23-48, 221-236; *Atene e Roma*, 12 (1909), 7-24, 277-290; *Atene e Roma*, 13 (1910), 79-103, 149-162. Renucci, *Dante, Disciple et Juge du Monde Gréco-Latin*, and Augustin Renaudet, *Dante Humaniste* (Paris: Les Belles Lettres, 1952), further explore Dante's relation to the classical poets, especially with respect to his borrowings from them, as does Ettore Paratore, *Tradizione e struttura in Dante* (for a general overview, see esp. "Dante e il mondo classico" [pp. 25-54] and "L'eredità classica in Dante" [pp. 55-121]). On this subject, see also: P. H. Wicksteed, "Dante and the Latin Poets," in *Dante: Essays in Commemoration*, pp. 159-187; Vito Sirago, "Dante e gli autori latini," *Lettere italiane*, 3 (1951), 99-134; Hermann Gmelin, "Dante und die römischen Dichter," *Deutsches Dante Jahrbuch*, 31-33 (1953), 42-65; Alessandro Ronconi, "Per Dante interprete dei poeti latini," *Studi danteschi*, 41 (1964), 5-44; Guido Martellotti, "Dante e i classici," *Cultura e scuola* 4,

Prelude: the *Opere minori*

The prose text in which we can observe the transition from the rhetorical and figurative Vergil of the *opere minori* to the prophetic and imperial Vergil of the *Comedy* is the second book of the *Monarchia*, which, because it seeks to legitimize Roman sovereignty, draws heavily on Latin literature. The arguments of Book II are buttressed primarily by poets and historians, including Livy, Cicero, Lucan, and Orosius.[10] But by far the most visible classical authority in the *Monarchia* is Vergil, who is quoted or referred to seventeen times in all. Vergil's dominant presence in Book II, where Dante quotes only from the *Aeneid*, the poem of Empire, is heralded in Book I, where—as though to set the stage—Dante quotes from the fourth Eclogue, indeed from the same passage announcing the return of Astraea that he will later use in *Purgatorio* XXII.[11] Thus, in *Monarchia* I, xi, 1, Vergil enters the text as "Virgilius," author of the *Eclogues*, while in Book II he takes on the qualities that characterize him throughout the work: here Dante outdoes any of his earlier statements about Vergil, calling him first "divinus poeta noster" (II, iii, 6), and, shortly thereafter, "noster Vates" (II, iii, 12). Both these expressions—"our divine poet" and "our seer"—confer upon the Latin poet a new and unique status; in comparison with the *Convivio*, where the terms of praise have technical poetic overtones pointing to the Mantuan as the greatest member of a poetic fraternity ("questo altissimo poeta," for instance, reminds us of Vergil's status as a poet in the high style), the *Monarchia* adopts a terminology that sets Vergil apart from other poets, taking him out of the fraternity altogether. In this treatise's more political than poetic universe,

---

nos. 13-14 (1965), 125-137; Alan Robson, "Dante's Reading of the Latin Poets and the Structure of the *Commedia*," in *The World of Dante: Essays on Dante and his Times*, ed. Cecil Grayson (Oxford: Clarendon Press, 1980), pp. 81-121.

[10] Livy is quoted or referred to 13 times, Cicero 8, Lucan 6, and Orosius 4. Ovid, Homer, and Boethius are referred to twice each; Seneca and Juvenal once. It goes without saying that there are no vernacular poets in the *Monarchia*.

[11] The importance of this passage for Dante is evidenced by the fact that he also uses it in *Epistola* VII, 6, so that it appears in his work three times in all. For Dante's sense of Vergil as the poet of Empire, see Charles Till Davis, *Dante and the Idea of Rome* (Oxford: Clarendon Press, 1957), esp. pp. 100-138.

Epic Resolution

Vergil stands out for his prophetic capacities, his divine gifts of divination. His "sight" has political implications; it can hardly be accidental that on the occasion in which Dante calls Vergil "noster Vates," he quotes a passage from *Aeneid* III detailing the Italian origins of Dardanus, the founder of Troy. Aeneas thus returns to the land of his fathers, a fact that constitutes one more sign of the providential nature of his mission. In each of the fifteen other instances in which Vergil is mentioned in the *Monarchia*, he is "Poeta noster," a periphrasis as eloquent in its simplicity and ubiquity as the more majestic "divinus" and "Vates." Thus, already in the second book of the *Monarchia*, Vergil is so familiar a figure that he is denoted with a periphrasis that the reader is expected to identify exclusively with him; as here he is *Poeta noster*, so in the *Comedy* he will be *duca* and *maestro*.

The Vergil who emerges from the *Monarchia* is an imperial and Augustan figure; he belongs in the general category of illustrious thinkers, poets and historians—"ystoriographi . . . poete illustres" (I, xvi, 2)—whom Dante calls upon to witness the general happiness of the human race during the reign of Augustus, "sub divo Augusto monarcha" (I, xvi, 1). This call is issued at the end of Book I, initiating the spate of references to Vergil that runs through Book II, and culminating in the indirect final reference to the Latin poet found in this book's last paragraph, where Dante refers to Italy by one of its Vergilian names, "Ausonia": "O felicem populum, o Ausoniam te gloriosam" ("O happy people, O glorious Ausonia" [II, xi, 8]). The *Monarchia*'s last Vergilian moment thus anticipates the *Comedy*'s first canto, where the prophecy of the *veltro* echoes Jupiter's prophecy in the first book of the *Aeneid*, where Vergil speaks of God as an Emperor, and where "umile Italia" is a Christian variant of "Ausoniam te gloriosam."[12] If the imperial Vergil of the *Monarchia* finds his immediate expression in *In-*

---

[12] In accordance with Ronconi, *Enciclopedia Dantesca*, vol. V, p. 1045, I take "umile Italia" as bearing a positive moral significance, in contrast with the other Vergilian phrase from *Inferno* I, "'l superbo Ilión" (75). "Humble Italy" will be saved, whereas "proud Ilium" fell.

Prelude: the *Opere minori*

ferno I, *Inferno* IV articulates the epic Vergil; it is here that Vergil is again called "l'altissimo poeta," as he was in the *Convivio*. The fact that *altissimo* is used twice in *Inferno* IV (in line 95 Homer is "quel segnor de l'altissimo canto") stresses the canto's role within the text: *Inferno* IV constitutes the *Comedy*'s first direct statement on the poetry of classical antiquity, i.e. poetry written in the high style.[13] Vergil is the *altissimo poeta*, the ultimate exponent of that style, as he was in the *Vita Nuova*. Indeed, *Inferno* IV presents a remarkably similar picture to that of the *libello*: again the salute to Homer is upstaged by Dante's patent admiration for the known quantity, Vergil. The distribution of the key word *onore* and its derivatives furnishes a clue in this regard. It is used eight times in all: three times for the poets of Limbo as a group; once for Dante himself, who receives "more honor" when he is allowed to join the charmed circle of poets as its sixth member; and once for Aristotle. The remaining three uses are all references to Vergil, the only individual to be so treated; thus, were we to take *Inferno* IV out of context, as a set piece to compare with the earlier works, we would find that Vergil is still supreme, as he was throughout the *opere minori*.

[13] E. G. Parodi, in his review of the seventh Scartazzini edition of the *Comedy*, *Bullettino della Società Dantesca Italiana*, 23 (1916), points out that Dante repeats *altissimo* in *Inferno* IV because the word has a technical significance which precludes its substitution by another (p. 13). On Vergil's return to Limbo and *Inferno* IV in general, see: Francesco D'Ovidio, "Il saluto dei poeti del Limbo al reduce Virgilio," in *Studii sulla Divina Commedia*, pp. 520-531; G. Troccoli, "Onorate l'altissimo poeta," in *Saggi danteschi*, new ed. rev. (Florence: Le Monnier, 1948), pp. 11-32; Augustin Renaudet and Siro A. Chimenz, "Il canto IV dell'*Inferno*," *Nuova 'Lectura Dantis'* (Rome: Signorelli, 1954); Francesco Mazzoni, "Saggio di un nuovo commento alla *Commedia*: il canto IV dell'*Inferno*," *Studi danteschi*, 42 (1965), 29-204; Giorgio Brugnoli, "Omero sire," *Cultura neolatina*, 27 (1967), 120-136; Giorgio Padoan, "Il Limbo dantesco," orig. 1969, repr. in *Il pio Enea, l'empio Ulisse* (Ravenna: Longo, 1977), pp. 103-124; Gioacchino Paparelli, "Virgilio e le anime del Limbo," orig. 1951, repr. in *Ideologia e poesia in Dante*, pp. 139-169; Fiorenzo Forti, "Il limbo e i megalopsicoi della Nicomachea," orig. 1961, repr. in *Magnanimitade: studi su un tema dantesco* (Bologna: Pàtron, 1977), pp. 9-48; Amilcare A. Iannucci, "Limbo: The Emptiness of Time," *Studi danteschi*, 52 (1979-1980), 69-128.

Epic Resolution

Putting *Inferno* IV back into context, we find that Vergil is indeed supreme—in the first circle of Hell. This is to state baldly the problematic that will now engage us, namely the paradox of Vergil's situation. In terms of *Inferno* IV, we remember that *onore* bears not only positive but also negative connotations, since it functions as both the sign of Limbo's difference from the rest of Hell, and the sign of its difference from Heaven, whose currency is not "honor" but "joy" and "ineffable gladness" (*Par.* XXVII, 7). Vergil resides within this limbo of perpetual tension, of simultaneously positive and negative significance; to emphasize either one of these two poles of meaning is to distort Dante's creation, which depends on the simultaneous conjunction of opposites, of being and nonbeing. It is therefore not so much theologically vain as poetically unrealistic to speculate about Vergil's possible salvation, since it is an essential condition of his existence in the poem that he shall also cease to exist: his presence is predicated on his talent for absence. Because of his function as a paradox at the heart of the poem, there is a potential adversative at the end of any statement about Vergil, an insistent *tamen* that this eschatological world has imposed on the Latin poet's own, more humanly scaled, *forsan*.[14] Vergil embodies the most that natural man can attain, yet he is not saved; he is the greatest of poets, yet the lesser Statius can replace him. In the following pages, I will attempt to show how the Vergilian paradox operates at the level of narrative, resulting in two distinct but tightly coordinated storylines: as one maps the progressive undermining of Vergil's

---

[14] In his Introduction to *Virgil: A Collection of Critical Essays* (Englewood Cliffs, N.J.: Prentice-Hall, 1966), Steele Commager discusses the *Aeneid*'s deep ambivalence, remarking that "A perpetual *forsan*, 'perhaps,' hovers over the *Aeneid*," and reminding us that "Virgil added the word [*forsan*] to Homer in his famous imitation: *forsan et haec olim meminisse iuvabit*, 'perhaps, some day, it will be a pleasure to remember these things' " (p. 13). Dorothy Sayers' remark on paradox in the *Comedy*, that because of it "problems and ambiguities in the interpretation of [its] allegorical symbolism can seldom be settled by an 'either-or,' but on the contrary usually demand an answer involving 'both-and' (from "The Paradoxes of the *Comedy*," in *Introductory Papers on Dante* [London: Methuen, 1954], p. 182), is a critical principle that applies eminently to Vergil, himself one of the *Comedy*'s chief paradoxes.

Vergil: "Poeta fui"

authority, i.e. of his appeal to the intellect, the other records the simultaneous growth in the pilgrim's love for him, i.e. in his appeal to the will. Given these complementary and contradictory lines of development, it will be apparent that Dante has used the figure of Vergil to structure an inescapable dialectic into his text.

Vergil: "Poeta fui"

It is no secret that Dante's imitation of the *Aeneid* decreases as the *Comedy* progresses. Whitfield points out that of the two hundred uses of Vergil claimed by Moore, "90 of these passages concern the *Inferno*, 34 the *Purgatorio*, and 13 the *Paradiso*, while the rest are scattered in Dante's other writings."[15] Petrocchi establishes a pattern of inverse relation between Dante's use of translations from the *Aeneid* and his use of translations from the Bible: while translations from the Roman text occur seven times in the *Inferno*, five times in the *Purgatorio*, and only once in the *Paradiso*, translations from the Christian text occur twelve times in the *Paradiso*, eight times in the *Purgatorio*, and only twice in the *Inferno*.[16] The *Inferno* is thus Ver-

[15] J. H. Whitfield, *Dante and Virgil* (Oxford: Blackwell, 1949), pp. 73-74.

[16] Giorgio Petrocchi, "Itinerari nella *Commedia*," *Studi danteschi*, 41 (1964), 68. As we would expect, Vergil is by far the most translated poet in the *Comedy*; indeed, his only rival is not another poet, but the Bible. According to the statistics compiled by Felicina Groppi, *Dante traduttore*, 2d ed. rev. (Rome: Tipografia Poliglotta Vaticana, 1962), Vergil's verse is translated in the *Comedy* thirteen times (this figure does not include Vergilian reminiscences, like Casella's attempt to embrace the pilgrim, or the episodes of Vergilian inspiration, like that of Pier della Vigna), while the text contains only three other translations of classical authors: one from Cicero's *De Amicitia* (the probable source for Thaïs' dialogue in *Inferno* XVIII, 133-135), and two from Lucan's *Pharsalia* (neither of the passages adduced by Groppi strike me as direct translations, however). There are twenty-two translations from the Bible. On this subject, see also: Alessandro Ronconi, "Parole di Dante: per una semantica dei virgilianismi," *Lingua nostra*, 11 (1950), 81-85; Enzo Esposito, "Dante traduttore di Virgilio," *L'Italia che scrive*, 48 (1965), 335-336; and, on Dante as translator in the *Convivio*, Mario Marti, "Aspetti stilistici di Dante traduttore," in *Realismo dantesco e altri studi*, pp. 108-125.

gil's canticle, dominated by his presence and saturated with his text. Nonetheless, despite Vergil's very real preeminence in the first canticle, he is not immune from an implicit critique even within its bounds; in other words, he does not lose his authority all at once, at the beginning of the *Purgatorio* when Cato rebukes him, but in a more subtle fashion, step by step from the moment he enters the poem.[17] When Vergil arrives an hourglass is set, and the grains of sand fall one by one until, in *Purgatorio* XXX, the glass is empty.

The stature that the text will work to diminish must first be established, at the poem's outset: in canto I, where Vergil's authority is unassailable, even in his evident exclusion; in canto II, where Beatrice initiates, with reference to the Latin poet, the use of the *captatio benevolentiae* tied to the theme of earthly fame; in canto III, which openly adopts the mechanisms of the Vergilian afterlife for the *Comedy*; and in canto IV, where Vergil is hailed by his august comrades. If *Inferno* III contains more crude Vergilian echoes than any other canto in the poem, *Inferno* IV less blatantly evokes the *Aeneid*; the description of Limbo's "nobile castello," surrounded by its seven walls and dry riverbed, is reminiscent of the symbolic architecture and topography found in *Aeneid* VI.[18] Dante seems to be deliberately imitating a mode whose trappings he will gradually shed as the

---

[17] In his definitive study on *Inferno* I, 63, the crux in which Vergil is described as "chi per lungo silenzio parea fioco," Robert Hollander concludes that Vergil is silent because he did not bear witness to the Truth, an interpretation that lends support to the notion that the *Comedy*'s undermining of Vergil begins with its first presentation of him. See the first chapter of *Il Virgilio dantesco: Tragedia nella Commedia* (Florence: Olschki, 1983). Vergil's lack of faith is discussed from a theological point of view by Kenelm Foster, "The Two Dantes," in *The Two Dantes and Other Studies* (Berkeley and Los Angeles: U. of California Press, 1977), pp. 156-253.

[18] D'Ovidio mentions the influence of Vergil's Elysian fields on Dante's conception of the *nobile castello* in "Non soltanto lo bello stile tolse da lui," *Studii sulla Divina Commedia*, p. 226. The "simbolismo figurativo" of the characterizations in *Inferno* IV is discussed by Forti, "Il limbo e i megalopsicoi della Nicomachea," p. 31, and the "allegorical focus" of the topography of Limbo is treated by John Guzzardo, "The Noble Castle and the Eighth Gate," *MLN*, 94 (1979), 137-145.

Vergil: "Poeta fui"

exigencies of his own art take over, as though to underscore the point that after joining the classical poets and becoming one of their fraternity, he will keep on going, leaving them behind. Dramatically, the relation between Vergil and his charge in these first cantos is a formal one: if we consider the use of the emblematic nouns assigned to Vergil at the end of canto II, in the verse "tu duca, tu segnore e tu maestro" ("You the leader, you the lord, and you the master" [140]), we note that Vergil is regularly called *buon maestro* and *duca mio*, without any additional affective terminology; he is also referred to simply as *poeta*. The tenor of the rapport between the pilgrim and his guide during the first stage of their journey is best summed up by the recurrent expressions denoting absolute confidence in Vergil's judgment and understanding: he is all-knowing ("quel savio gentil, che tutto seppe" "that gentle sage, who knew all" [*Inf.* VII, 3]), and the sea of all wisdom ("E io mi volsi al mar di tutto 'l senno" "And I turned to the sea of all wisdom" [*Inf.* VIII, 7]).[19]

Interestingly, both these hyperbolic tributes to Vergil's wisdom precede the encounter with the devils at the gates of Dis, the first episode to seriously call into question Vergil's abilities as guide. When Dante turns to Vergil, "al mar di tutto 'l senno," he does so in order to ask his guide the meaning of the signals being exchanged by the Stygian watchtowers, signals that effectively mark the beginning of a series of events whose culmination will be the advent of the heavenly intercessor toward

---

[19] Perhaps Dante's phrase, "mar di tutto 'l senno," is related to the following etymology of Vergil's last name reported by Domenico Comparetti: "Marone ei fu detto dal mare, perchè siccome il mare abbonda di acque, così abbondava in lui la sapienza, più che in ogni altro" (*Virgilio nel medio evo*, new ed. rev. by Giorgio Pasquali, 2 vols. [1872; repr. Florence: La Nuova Italia, 1943-1946], vol. I, p. 179). Another word used to denote Vergil in the early cantos of the *Inferno* is *magnanimo*, used only twice in the poem, for Vergil in *Inferno* II and Farinata in *Inferno* X. The term seems particularly appropriate for Vergil in that it reached the Middle Ages, as John Scott shows, already burdened with a contradictory semantic value, i.e. both positive and negative connotations; see "Dante magnanimo," in *Dante magnanimo: studi sulla Commedia* (Florence: Olschki, 1977), pp. 239-345.

the end of canto IX. The pilgrim's query is followed by the arrival of the boatman Phlegyas, who eventually deposits the travelers at the entrance to Dis; it is preceded by a unique instance of flashback in the *Comedy*'s narration: although Dante and Vergil arrive at the foot of a tower in the last verse of canto VII, canto VIII begins by explaining that long before they had arrived at the tower they saw the exchange of signals between it and a more distant companion. Rather than minimize this narrative occurrence, the poet does everything in his power to emphasize it, opening canto VIII with a self-conscious insistence on both the new beginning and the use of flashback: "Io dico, seguitando, ch'assai prima / che noi fossimo al piè de l'alta torre" ("I say, continuing, that long before we had arrived at the foot of the high tower" [*Inf.* VIII, 1-2]). In fact, canto VIII's exordium is so pronounced that in order to account for it the early commentators came up with a biographical explanation, according to which Dante composed the first seven cantos of the *Inferno* before his exile and returned to canto VIII after a long interruption.[20] Even more unusual than the exposed narrative link, "Io dico, seguitando," is the retrograde narration, which causes Benvenuto to comment that the author here "turns back in an artificial order."[21] I would suggest that these narrative jolts are deliberately employed by Dante in order to mark an ideological jolt, indeed a crucial ideological turning point: namely, the moment in which we begin to realize that Vergil is not infallible, nor, as he has been viewed up to now, the fount of all wisdom.

Rehearsing certain features of Vergil's behavior in canto IX, we recall that the intransigence of the devils causes his mo-

[20] Benvenuto relates with great relish the story of the seven cantos left behind by Dante when he was exiled, how (because divine providence did not wish so excellent a work to be lost) they were found among his papers and taken to a citizen famous for his eloquence, who recognized their perfection and sent them to Marchese Malaspina, with whom Dante was staying; he concludes "and he began to proceed anew and to join together the unformed material, saying: *Io dico seguitando*, i.e. continuing with the material interrupted by exile" (vol. I, p. 274).

[21] "Et hic nota quod autor retrocedit ordine artificiali" (vol. I, p. 275).

Vergil: "Poeta fui"

mentary lack of faith in Beatrice, rendered by his use of doubting expressions, as in "Pur a noi converrà vincer la punga" ("Yet we must be the ones to win this fight" [*Inf.* IX, 7]), followed by the uncompleted "se non . . ." ("unless . . ." [8]); his doubts and confusion lead to his inability to bypass the devils who block the way. Vergil's failure is carefully linked to his classical identity;[22] the episode is stocked with classical characters, whose names reverberate throughout the canto ("quella Eritón cruda," "le feroci Erine," "Megera," "Aletto," "Tesifón," "Medusa," "Tesëo," "Gorgón," "Cerbero vostro"), and who are thematically connected to the canto's key revelation regarding the Latin poet. In order to reassure his charge, Vergil now reveals that he has made this trip before, at the behest of a sorceress from the *Pharsalia*, Erichtho: "congiurato da quella Eritón cruda / che richiamava l'ombre a' corpi sui" ("conjured by that cruel Erichtho who called back the shades to their bodies" [*Inf.* IX, 23-24]). Thus, under the pretext of allaying the pilgrim's fears, Dante raises far greater fears regarding his guide; the astonishing invention here related, whereby the Thessalian witch from Lucan's poem once deployed Vergil for one of her nefarious missions, casts a long and intentional shadow over the Roman poet.[23] We note, moreover, that Vergil is portrayed as

---

[22] Mark Musa links Vergil's "defeatist attitude" and his paganism in "At the Gates of Dis," *Advent at the Gates*, pp. 65-84. The classical literary ambience of *Inferno* IX is discussed by David Quint, "Epic Tradition and *Inferno* IX," *Dante Studies*, 93 (1975), 201-207.

[23] In this I disagree with D'Ovidio, who argues that Dante invents Erichtho precisely to emphasize Vergil's innocence of magic arts, since if he were a true magician he would hardly be at her beck and call: "[Dante vuole] insinuare come il preteso mago fosse stato lui all'occorrenza zimbello d'una vera maga" ("Dante e la magìa," in *Studii sulla Divina Commedia*, pp. 100-101). À propos of D'Ovidio's interpretation, I would like to draw attention to a curious exchange from the pages of the *Classical Journal* that dramatically, if unwittingly, illuminates the problems inherent in Dante's treatment of Vergil. The debate was sparked by one Anna P. MacVay who, totally innocent of Dante scholarship, points to the episodes in the *Comedy* she considers most damning to her favorite author's reputation; she mentions Beatrice's "fake promise" to Vergil in *Inferno* II, the invention of a link between Vergil and the hateful Erichtho, the revision of the *Aeneid*'s account of the founding of Mantova, the presence of saved

taking his lack of free will and Erichtho's power over him entirely for granted, a fact Dante emphasizes by having him say "ella *mi fece* intrar dentr' a quel muro" ("she *made me* enter within that wall" [26; italics mine]), and that he now displays the same flaccid attitude in dealing with Medusa; he never doubts her ability to deaden the pilgrim's will—in literal terms, to petrify him—as Erichtho had once deadened his: "ché se 'l Gorgón si mostra e tu 'l vedessi, / nulla sarebbe di tornar mai suso" ("for if the Gorgon shows herself and you were to see her, there would be no more returning above" [56-57]).[24] Erich-

---

pagans, especially "the minor poet Statius"—in short, she hits the crucial passages for the Vergilian problematic throughout the *Comedy*, in defense of her thesis that Dante's love for Vergil is mere lip service, and that he selfishly mistreats his *auctor* in order to enhance himself ("Dante's Strange Treatment of Vergil," *Classical Journal*, 43 [1948], 233-235). MacVay's arguments are countered in the following volume by R. V. Schoder, S.J., who is well acquainted with scholarship on the *Comedy* and whose rebuttals frequently take the form of reading the various episodes allegorically; in the case of Erichtho he follows D'Ovidio, pointing out that Vergil is merely a helpless victim ("Vergil in the *Divine Comedy*," *Classical Journal*, 44 [1949], 413-422). The exchange is instructive because, although Schoder's defense of Dante is fundamentally sound—Dante does love Vergil—he is forced to justify episodes in which, as MacVay rightly perceived, Vergil is being undermined.

[24] D'Ovidio's thesis that Vergil was Erichtho's stooge, that he sees himself as her victim and speaks of her with resentment ("verso la quale insomma si atteggia a vittima" [99]), is precisely to the point; he was her victim, but he should not have been. D'Ovidio's further observation that the spirits summoned by Erichtho in the *Pharsalia* come unwillingly, a fact that he brings to Vergil's defense, serves only to highlight the difference between Lucan's text and Dante's, where there is finally no such thing as constraint to do evil: "ché volontà, se non vuol, non s'ammorza" ("for will, if it does not will, is not put out" [*Par.* IV, 76]). Similarly, Lucan's depiction of Erichtho as one who is outside the law, to whom the gods concede all that is normally forbidden—"omne nefas superi prima iam voce precantis / concedunt carmenque timent audire secundum" ("Already at the first sound of her prayer the gods grant every evil, and fear to hear a second spell" [*Pharsalia* VI, 527-528])—would strengthen Dante's belief that a Christian, serving the Christian God, would never succumb to her. On the Erichtho episode in the *Pharsalia*, and the *Pharsalia* as an anti-*Aeneid*, see Lao Paoletti, "Lucano magico e Virgilio," *Atene e Roma*, 8 (1963), 11-26. Lucan's text is from *M. Annaei Lucani, Belli Civilis Libri X*, ed. A. E. Housman (1926; repr. Oxford: Blackwell, 1958).

Vergil: "Poeta fui"

tho derived her power over Vergil from his passive participation; had he not in some way subscribed to the imaginative constructs that sustained her, lending them his credence and his will, she would have been as powerless over him as the devils are now in the face of the heavenly intercessor. It seems not accidental that the angel opens the gates with a *verghetta*, thus accomplishing with a diminutive Vergil (a not improbable *double-entendre*, given the association of Vergil's name with the Latin *virga*) what the full-sized Vergil cannot do for himself.[25]

In the interpolated episode of Filippo Argenti, which takes place immediately before this series of events at the city's gates, while the travelers are crossing the Styx, Vergil not only behaves "correctly" in his harsh treatment of the wrathful Florentine, but even echoes the Gospel in his approbation of the pilgrim's equally harsh behavior: "Alma sdegnosa, / benedetta colei che 'n te s'incinse!" ("Disdainful soul, blessed is she who bore you!" [*Inf.* VIII, 44-45]).[26] The inflated evangelical language adopted by Vergil in this scene and the almost excessive

[25] In *The Classical Tradition* (1949; repr. New York: Oxford U. Press, 1957), Gilbert Highet comments as follows on the spelling "Virgilius": "This misspelling began at a very early date, perhaps because of Vergil's nickname Parthenias, 'Miss Purity.' . . . In the Middle Ages the name was taken to refer to Vergil's powers as a magician, because *virga* means *wand*" (p. 584). Perhaps the later tradition was influenced by Suetonius' account, found in Donatus' commentary, of the poplar branch—"virga populea"—which was planted according to custom in Vergil's place of birth and quickly equalled in size trees planted long before; it became known as Vergil's tree—"arbor Vergilii"—and was an object of veneration for pregnant women (this story and the Latin quotations are from the *Vita Vergili* in the Loeb Classical Library edition of Suetonius, trans. J. C. Rolfe, 2 vols. [London: William Heinemann and New York: The Macmillan Co., 1913-1914], vol. II, pp. 464-465). Regarding Dante's own usage, R. Sabbadini concludes that he used the learned form of his day, namely "Virgilio" ("Dante scriveva 'Virgilio' o 'Vergilio'?," *Giornale storico della letteratura italiana*, 35 [1900], 456). In "The Tragedy of Divination in Inferno XX," *Studies in Dante*, pp. 131-218, Robert Hollander traces the various *virgae* of Dante's classical poets and the *verghe* of the *Comedy* (pp. 175-184), noting that "*virga* may have seemed to Dante to have its close ties with the very orthography of the name of his greatest *auctor*" (p. 182).

[26] Vergil echoes Luke 11:27: "Beatus venter qui te portavit" ("Blessed is the womb that bore you").

approval he extends to the pilgrim are designed to align him with Christian principles, showing his distance from the sinners and his endorsement of divine judgment; however, by the same token, they are also designed to highlight his subsequent pagan failure in canto IX. The events of *Inferno* IX are doubtless intended as a decisive first fall from grace; nonetheless, since Dante's strategy toward Vergil is to create a sense of intimate contradiction in the character by approaching him through a lens of dialectically shifting perspectives, it should not surprise us to find him hard at work attenuating the damage of canto IX in a subsequent canto. Thus, canto XII is, in its treatment of Vergil, an inverse replay of canto IX; it contains many of the same elements found in the earlier canto, but they have been rearranged to cast Vergil in a positive rather than negative light. The first sign of the upcoming Vergilian thematic in canto XII is the simile of the alpine rockslide beginning in the canto's fourth line, where the use of the word *ruina* prefaces a discussion of the infernal *ruine* in lines 31 through 45. Because the *ruine* were caused by Christ's harrowing of Hell, they are the physical sign of Hell's defeat and can be counted on to bring out the worst in its denizens: the "ira bestial" of the Minotaur here in canto XII; the fraud of Malacoda and his band of devils later in canto XXI. Because Vergil made his first trip through Hell before its harrowing, the *ruine* function as pointers to his ignorance, and hence are signs of his defeat as well: Malacoda exploits Vergil's ignorance regarding the bridges and the *ruine* in order to deceive him. Vergil's problem is that he doesn't really exist in A.D. time, Christological time (as witnessed by his B.C. deference to Medusa), with the result that the *ruine*—A.D. referents in a B.C. world—will work against rather than for him.

In canto XII, however, Vergil successfully diverts the Minotaur's attention, so that he and the pilgrim can descend the ravine into the seventh circle. In answer to Dante's unspoken question regarding the *ruina* whose slope they are negotiating, Vergil offers an explanation, prefaced with the explicit reminder that this matter is ultimately out of his ken, since it is not part of his previous experience of lower Hell:

Vergil: "Poeta fui"

Or vo' che sappi che l'altra fiata
ch'i' discesi qua giù nel basso inferno,
questa roccia non era ancor cascata.

I want you to know that the other time I came down here
to lower Hell, this rock had not yet fallen.

(*Inf.* XII, 34-36)

Proceeding cautiously on this unfamiliar terrain ("se ben discerno" in line 37), Vergil notes that shortly before the arrival of "the one who took the great booty of the uppermost circle" (i.e. Christ) the earth quaked; he explains the quake in terms of the Empedoclean doctrine whereby order depends on the discord of the elements, and chaos would result from their concord: "da tutte parti l'alta valle feda / tremò sì, ch'i' pensai che l'universo / sentisse amor . . ." ("on all sides the deep foul valley trembled so, that I thought the universe felt love" [40-42]). Although Vergil is technically wrong in ascribing the earth's tremor to the concord of the elements, in saying that the universe "felt love" he has in fact intuited the correct cause of the quake: the universe felt love in that it felt the arrival of Christ. This intuitive triumph on Vergil's part is complemented by his competent handling of the classical creatures who stand in his way, first the Minotaur and then the centaur Nessus. The difference between his handling of these classical guardians and those who perched on the ramparts of Dis (whom we were told Vergil knew so well [*Inf.* IX, 43]—too well perhaps?) is underlined by the invocation of two classical heroes who also figured in canto IX: in dealing with the Minotaur, Vergil taunts him by reminding him of Theseus, " 'l duca d'Atene, / che sù nel mondo la morte ti porse" ("the duke of Athens, who gave you death up in the world" [17-18]); later, in castigating Nessus for the evil brought about by his impulsive will, he rehearses for the pilgrim the centaur's relation to Deianira, the wife of Hercules, who killed Nessus for attempting to rape her (66-69). Both Theseus and Hercules are *figurae Christi*, heroes who descended to the underworld to rob it of its booty, and as such both are mentioned in *Inferno* IX: Theseus by the Furies, who still clamor for revenge ("mal non vengiammo in Teseo l'assalto" "badly did we not avenge ourselves on Theseus" [*Inf.* IX, 54]);[27] and Hercules implicitly by the angel, who reminds the devils of Cerberus' ill-fated attempt to withstand the hero:

> Che giova ne le fata dar di cozzo?
> Cerbero vostro, se ben vi ricorda,
> ne porta ancor pelato il mento e 'l gozzo.
>
> What profits it to butt against the fates? Your Cerberus, if you remember well, still bears his chin and throat peeled for this.
>
> (*Inf.* IX, 97-99)

Theseus and Hercules are classical forerunners of Christ, early harrowers of Hell whose actions symbolize infernal defeat. By invoking them in canto XII, Vergil shows how well he has absorbed the lesson of the *messo celeste* from canto IX. Vergil is nothing if not a quick study: he now knows how to deal with the Minotaur and the centaur, showing contempt for his classical counterparts; he even is able to explain the *ruine*. However, just as his explanation of the *ruine* is only in part correct, so too is his newly recovered authority severely limited.[28] Vergil can be taught how to deal with classical monsters, but not how to deal with devils, as the pilgrim reminds him, referring to his

---

[27] Giorgio Padoan discusses the Furies' line, "mal non vengiammo in Teseo l'assalto," with relation to Theseus as a *figura Christi* in "Teseo 'figura Redemptoris' e il cristianesimo di Stazio," orig. 1959, repr. in *Il pio Enea, l'empio Ulisse*, pp. 125-150.

[28] Vergil's previous shows of authority with the classical monsters Charon (*Inf.* III, 94-96), Minos (*Inf.* V, 21-24), Cerberus (*Inf.* VI, 25-27), and Plutus (*Inf.* VII, 7-12) all precede his debilitating encounter with the devils at the gates of Dis. These earlier exchanges, with their ritualistic repetition of the formula "vuolsi così colà dove si puote / ciò che si vuole, e più non dimandare" (III, 95-96; V, 23-24), have a curiously stylized "learned" quality about them, as if Vergil were carefully executing previously memorized instructions without being quite sure of the results. Judging from the fact that Vergil's warnings become longer and more original (in the last encounter, with Plutus, he dispenses with the old formula altogether, substituting a new version perhaps of his own invention), there seems to be a gradual increase in his confidence, which makes his subsequent failure all the more glaring.

Vergil: "Poeta fui"

teacher less than tactfully as one who can overcome all but the devils at the gate: "Maestro, tu che vinci / tutte le cose, fuor che ' demon duri / ch'a l'intrar de la porta incontra uscinci" ("Master, you who conquer all things, except for the tough demons who came out against us at the entrance of the gate" [*Inf.* XIV, 43-45]). This seemingly unnecessary periphrasis in canto XIV testifies to Dante's unwillingness to let his character off the hook for very long, and in fact, canto XIV's undermining of Vergil and classical culture does not cease with the pilgrim's remark about the devils. Here we find the shabby figure of Capaneus (whom Vergil treats with a vehemence perhaps intensified by the pilgrim's stinging words), reduced from the heroic if blasphemous proportions that were his in the *Thebaid*, as well as the Old Man of Crete, a textual construct that revises classical sources, primarily the *Aeneid* and the *Metamorphoses*, by conflating them with the Biblical account of Nebuchadnezzar's dream. Most interestingly, from our point of view, is the revision of the *Aeneid* that Dante puts into Vergil's mouth with respect to the rivers of Hell.[29] After Vergil has explained that Acheron, Styx, Phlegethon, and Cocytus all derive from the statue's tears, the pilgrim remains confused regarding the whereabouts of Phlegethon and Lethe, in the case of Phlegethon because he does not realize he has already seen it as the river of blood surrounding the seventh circle, and in the case of Lethe because Vergil has not mentioned it. As a result, Vergil must explain that Lethe, which in the *Aeneid* he placed in the Elysian fields, in fact does not belong to the underworld at all—"Letè vedrai, ma fuor di questa fossa" ("Lethe you shall see, but outside of this ditch" [*Inf.* XIV, 136])—thus reversing his own earlier statement.

Such corrections, not of Vergil's poetic persona, but of his text, the *Aeneid*, occur with increasing frequency as the travelers proceed through Hell. These corrections raise fundamental

---

[29] In his reading of *Inferno* XIV, now in *Tradizione e struttura in Dante*, pp. 221-249, Ettore Paratore discusses Capaneus, the Old Man of Crete, and the rivers of Hell; vis-à-vis the latter, he remarks that Dante's silence regarding Phlegethon when it first appears seems designed to provoke a later conversation with Vergil on the subject (pp. 237-239).

Epic Resolution

questions regarding the status of Vergil's poem, and indeed, since the *Aeneid* is the chief text to have appeared before the *Comedy*, regarding textuality in general: questions of belief and disbelief, falsity and truth. Paradigmatic in this respect is the reference to the *Aeneid* in *Inferno* XIII, where Vergil responds to Pier della Vigna's rebuke by explaining that it was necessary for the pilgrim to break one of his branches in order to believe him possible; for although a similar marvel is recounted in the *Aeneid*, the pilgrim's belief in so remarkable a transformation could not have been secured simply by a reading of that text:

> "S'elli avesse potuto creder prima,"
> rispuose 'l savio mio, "anima lesa,
> ciò c'ha veduto pur con la mia rima,
> non averebbe in te la man distesa;
> ma la cosa incredibile mi fece
> indurlo ad ovra ch'a me stesso pesa. . . . "

My sage replied: "If he had been able to believe before, O wounded soul, that which he has seen only with my verses, he would not have stretched out his hand against you; but the unbelievable thing made me lead him to a deed that weighs upon me. . . . "

(*Inf.* XIII, 46-51)

The fact that a man has become a tree is termed a "cosa incredibile," something that by its nature cannot be accepted on the basis of a prior account, no matter how authoritative, but which, if it is to be believed, must be verified through one's own actions and experience. Therefore, because Vergil's book is in-credible, Dante must break the branch. But, the question arises: if Dante cannot believe Vergil's text, why should we believe Dante's? Why is Pier della Vigna less in-credible than his prototype, Polydorus? Any answer to such questions involves the basic poetic strategies of the *Comedy*, and, foremost among them, its choice of an allegorical mode in which the literal level is perceived as true, i.e. as that which, by definition, must be believed.

Vergil: "Poeta fui"

Although the truth is not always immediately believable, it will always ultimately command belief, simply because it is true. It is not coincidence that Dante first defines his poem, calling it a *comedìa*, in the context of an episode that raises these same issues of truth and falsehood, belief and disbelief. When the monster Geryon swims up through the murky air at the end of canto XVI, the poet tells us that he is in the position of a man who must recount an unbelievable truth and for whom it would be easier to keep silent, since his story will only bring him the reproaches of his listeners, but who must speak:

> Sempre a quel ver c'ha faccia di menzogna
> de' l'uom chiuder le labbra fin ch'el puote,
> però che sanza colpa fa vergogna;
> ma qui tacer nol posso . . .
>
> To that truth which has the face of a lie a man should always close his lips as long as he can, since without fault it brings him shame, but here I cannot be silent . . .
> (*Inf.* XVI, 124-127)

Dante here lets us know that he doesn't expect us to believe his account of what he saw, but that nonetheless we must, for his story is "quel ver c'ha faccia di menzogna"—a truth which has the appearance of a lie. Because we are not likely to believe this lying truth, he resorts to an oath, swearing by the notes of his poem, "questa comedìa," that he in fact saw what he says he saw: "e per le note / di questa comedìa, lettor, ti giuro . . . ch'i' vidi" ("and by the notes of this comedy, reader, I swear to you . . . that I saw" [*Inf.* XVI, 127-130]).[30] What has not

---

[30] The use of "vidi" here reflects one of Dante's simplest but most effective strategies for enlisting our belief, i.e. the use of the verb *vedere*, one of the most common verbs in the poem. We have already mentioned a similar technique, the use of the sentence opening "Vero è . . ." It seems not coincidental that in this same canto Dante is praised for his ability to speak the truth clearly and succinctly (*Inf.* XVI, 76-81). When *ver* is used at the end of the canto, in "quel ver c'ha faccia di menzogna," it cannot fail to recall this previous use, in which three souls, on hearing the pilgrim's words about Florence, look at each other "com' al ver si guata" ("as one stares at the truth" [78]).

been sufficiently recognized is that the poem is here defined, not only as a *comedìa*, but also as "quel ver c'ha faccia di menzogna," and that this last phrase is nothing but a gloss for the first: a *comedìa* is that truth which has the appearance of a lie but which is nonetheless always a truth.[31] If the *Aeneid* is a *tragedìa* instead, according to the definition offered in *Inferno* XX, this is because it is the opposite of the *Comedy*: a truthful lie, rather than a lying truth.

Although the *Aeneid* tells a truth, its truth was not intended by its author, but was revealed retrospectively through the unfolding of divine providence. By the same token, although the *Aeneid* partakes of historical verities, it is ignorant of the greatest of historical verities, namely the birth of Christ. Because it is, in this sense, a truthful lie, the *Aeneid* can and must be corrected.[32] The *Comedy*'s most sustained correction of the *Aeneid*

---

[31] I do not mean to deny that *comedìa* may also encompass the typical rhetorical components of the genre as described in the Epistle to Cangrande, namely a style that is not consistently sublime and a happy ending, but I do mean to suggest that Dante intends much more by these terms in the *Comedy* than he indicates in the Epistle. For a similar reading of Geryon's arrival, which stresses the parallelism between Geryon's "faccia d'uom giusto" (*Inf.* XVII, 10) and the "ver c'ha faccia di menzogna," as well as noting the connections between *Inferno* XVI and *Inferno* XX, see Franco Ferrucci, "Comedìa," *Yearbook of Italian Studies*, 1 (1971), 29-52, repr. as "The Meeting with Geryon," in *The Poetics of Disguise: The Autobiography of the Work in Homer, Dante, and Shakespeare*, trans. Ann Dunnigan (Ithaca: Cornell U. Press, 1980), pp. 66-102. The results of our similar readings are, however, divergent, since Ferrucci takes the episode as Dante's indication to us that his poem is merely metaphoric, made of "lies," while I take it as his claim that the poem, which may at times appear to be lying, is always telling the "truth." In this I agree with Hollander, who responds to Ferrucci's arguments by writing that "If he [Geryon] is a poetic *menzogna*, in Dante's treatment he becomes a *menzogna vera* ("Dante Theologus-Poeta," *Studies in Dante*, p. 76). Indeed, the parallelism, mentioned above, between Geryon's "faccia d'uom giusto" and the "ver c'ha faccia di menzogna" is instructive in this regard, since it constitutes an inversion: on the one hand is Geryon's "honest face," which masks a deceitful core; on the other is the poem's "lying face," which masks the truth. Thus Geryon and the *comedìa* are opposites; it follows that, since Geryon is falsehood (Dante goes out of his way to label him "quella sozza imagine di froda" [*Inf.* XVII, 7]), the *comedìa* must be truth.

[32] Hollander's suggestion that Dante viewed the *Aeneid* as "quasi-historical"

Vergil: "Poeta fui"

occurs in *Inferno* XX, in the *bolgia* of the diviners and false prophets, where Dante systematically invokes each of his Latin *auctores*: Statius, Ovid, Lucan, and Vergil. The canto is dominated by Vergil, who begins to speak in line 27 and, but for a six-line break in which Dante asks a question, does not give up the floor until the canto's penultimate verse, line 129. After harshly reprimanding the pilgrim for his tears, elicited by the grotesque and twisted shapes of this *bolgia*'s inhabitants, Vergil presents the various soothsayers and, concomitantly, the texts of his *auctores*: Amphiaraus from the *Thebaid*, Tiresias from the *Metamorphoses*, Arruns from the *Pharsalia*, and finally Manto from the *Aeneid*.[33] Because of her connection to his natal city, introduced by the verse "poscia si puose là dove nacqu' io" ("then she settled in the place where I was born" [*Inf.* XX, 56]), Vergil has more to say about Manto than about the others, and so begins the lengthy account of Mantova's pre-history for which this canto is famous. Carefully tracing the movement of the waters in northern Italy from Lake Garda to the swampy area in which Mantova was built, he describes the arrival of the "vergine cruda" (the phrase echoes "Eritón cruda" from *Inferno* IX) to the chosen spot, her settling there, living there, and dying

---

(as compared to Lucan's text, which he considered historical, and Ovid's, which he considered fictional) corresponds to my formulation of the *Aeneid*, in Dantesque terms, as a "truthful lie" (see "Dante *Theologus-Poeta*," p. 63). On Dante's deliberate revisionism of Vergil's text, see Hollander's *Il Virgilio dantesco*, chap. II.

[33] Although both Tiresias and Manto appear in more than one of these poems, and Manto is mentioned only briefly in the *Aeneid*, it is evident that Dante intends to associate each diviner with a particular text, and that Manto is associated with Vergil's; E. G. Parodi recognizes the correspondences between sinners and texts in "La critica della poesia classica nel ventesimo canto dell'*Inferno*," *Atene e Roma*, 11 (1908), 183-195 and 237-250, writing "Dante ha voluto che fosse rappresentato con un suo personaggio ciascuno dei quattro massimi poeti latini che conosceva" (p. 194), and noting that these poets are evoked in *Inferno* XX in order to be corrected. For a detailed analysis of Dante's "misreadings" of these texts, see Hollander's "The Tragedy of Divination in *Inferno* XX"; for a reading that focuses more on the canto's early events than on the later corrections of classical texts, see Marino Barchiesi, "Catarsi classica e 'medicina' dantesca (del canto XX dell'*Inferno*)," *Letture classensi* (Ravenna: Longo, 1973), vol. IV, pp. 11-124.

there: "e visse, e vi lasciò suo corpo vano" ("and she lived [there], and left there her empty body" [87]). Because the settlers from the surrounding regions noticed that the swamps formed a natural bulwark, they moved in after her death, and they—not she—built the city: "Fer la città sovra quell' ossa morte" ("they built the city over those dead bones" [91]). The binary structure of line 91—the men who make the city on one side, and those dead bones on the other—mimics the line with which Vergil began this discussion, "poscia si puose là dove nacqu' io," whose two halves succinctly express an insuperable barrier: Manto may have settled there, but Vergil was born there.

The disjunction thus established between Manto's squalid resting-place and Vergil's beloved birthplace is underscored by an even more profound disjunction between the story as Vergil now tells it and the story in the *Aeneid*, where the prophetess bears a child, Ocnus, who founds the city and gives it his mother's name: "qui muros matrisque dedit tibi, Mantua, nomen" ("who gave you walls and the name of his mother, O Mantua" [*Aeneid* X, 200]).[34] Such a revision of the *Aeneid* is particularly

[34] The text of the *Aeneid* is from *P. Vergili Maronis Opera*, ed. F. A. Hirtzel (1900; repr. Oxford: Clarendon, 1966). On Dante's use of *Aeneid* X in *Inferno* XX, see Ettore Paratore, "Il canto XX dell'*Inferno*," *Studi danteschi*, 52 (1979-1980), 149-169. In my "True and False See-ers in *Inferno* XX," *California Lectura Dantis*, ed. Allen Mandelbaum (U. of California Press, forthcoming), I further develop thematic correspondences between *Aeneid* X and *Inferno* XX as well as showing that Dante's revision of the *Aeneid* in canto XX goes far beyond the Latin poem's content to invest the crucial issue of its style: rather than compose Vergil's most personal speech in the poem in a way that would approximate his renowned seamlessness of line, Dante inverts his master's style by granting him a particularly long and clumsy string of end-stopped *terzine*. Returning to the *Comedy*'s revision of the *Aeneid*'s content, I would like to draw attention to the related issue of Vergil's and Dante's ethnic origins. By denying, implicitly, the existence of Manto's son Ocnus, Dante also denies Manto's relation with the river god Tiber, Ocnus' illustrious father: "fatidicae Mantus et Tusci filius amnis" ("the son of prophetic Manto and of the Etruscan river" [*Aen*. X, 199]). Vergil's reference to the Tiber as the "Etruscan river" (the same expression for the Tiber is used in *Aeneid* VIII, 473) serves to emphasize Mantova's Etruscan origins and political affiliations. Vergil's insistence on this issue is such that he proceeds to tell us that the people of Mantova

Vergil: "Poeta fui"

noteworthy in the light of Vergil's closing injunction to the pilgrim to disregard all other accounts of Mantova's founding. Since the only true story is the one Vergil has just taught him, the pilgrim must "let no lie defraud the truth," i.e. he must reject all other accounts as falsehoods:

> Però t'assenno che, se tu mai odi
> originar la mia terra altrimenti,
> la verità nulla menzogna frodi.

> Therefore I charge you that, if you ever hear it said that my city originated otherwise, let no lie defraud the truth.
> (*Inf.* XX, 97-99)

But in what source could Dante find the story of "mia terra" told "altrimenti," if not in the *Aeneid*? According to Vergil's own statement then, the *Aeneid* is a text that—like the false prophets of this *bolgia*—is capable of defrauding the truth. The language of line 99, with its harsh juxtaposition of *verità* and *menzogna*, as well as the appearance in line 113 of *tragedìa*, the *Comedy*'s second genre term, indicate the close ties which bind this episode to that of canto XVI: Vergil's poem, defined as a *tragedìa*, is, at least at times, a lie that defrauds the truth, while Dante's poem is a truth that sometimes bears the face of

---

are not all of one stock, but of three races, each of which is subdivided into four peoples; however, the city's strength derives from its Etruscan blood: "Tusco de sanguine vires" (*Aen.* X, 203). In this way, Vergil lets his readers know that Mantova, although north of the Po, belonged to the Etruscan confederacy that came to Aeneas' aid, thus insuring his city a place in the founding of the Roman Empire. The *Aeneid*'s intentions are reversed in *Inferno* I, 68, where Vergil's identification of his Mantuan parents as "lombardi" implies that they are not Etruscans, and again in *Inferno* XX, where the Tuscan connection is removed, with Ocnus, from the account of Mantova's founding. This excision of Mantova's Tuscan roots is particularly intriguing in the light of Dante's references, throughout the *Comedy*, to himself as a Tuscan and to Vergil as a Lombard. Upon perusal of Dante's uses of *tosco* and *lombardo* throughout the *Comedy*, I am convinced of what I cannot now take the space to demonstrate: namely that these terms have been endowed with programmatic political connotations carefully developed over the course of the poem, and that the association of Vergil with Lombardy is actually in the spirit of the Latin poet's own earlier association of himself with Tuscany, since Lombardy is the region Dante links to Italy's imperial hopes.

a lie. Such a poetic truth is, as we already know, a *comedìa*, a term Dante will now use for the last time in the opening verses of canto XXI. We note the progressive unfolding of information: first the implicit association of the *Aeneid* with *menzogna* in XX, 99; then Vergil's reference to his poem as "l'alta mia tragedìa" in XX, 113, which results in the alignment of *menzogna* and *tragedìa*; and finally, safely distanced from the tragedies of the ancients by the boundary between cantos XX and XXI, the reference to Dante's poem as "la mia comedìa" in XXI, 2, which confirms that his poem is the opposite of the *Aeneid* and therefore also of *menzogna*.

If Vergil's text is capable of falsehood, Dante, by revising it, restores truth to it. And, as exegetes of canto XX have claimed from D'Ovidio on, Dante not only restores Vergil's text, but—by allowing Vergil to vociferously condemn and thus dissociate himself from the diviners he sees here—rescues Vergil himself from any guilt by association.[35] Thus, when the pilgrim weeps, Vergil lacerates him with the question "Ancor se' tu de li altri sciocchi?" ("Are you still among the other fools?" [*Inf.* XX, 27]), implying that he, unlike Dante, is completely unmoved by the vision that has so shaken his charge. Throughout his presentation of the soothsayers Vergil uses the language of prophecy, relying on strong imperatives and verbs of sight, linguistic markers that the *Comedy*'s author hands his character

---

[35] This thesis was put forth by D'Ovidio in "Dante e la magìa" and "Ancora Dante e la magìa," *Studii sulla Divina Commedia*, pp. 76-112 and 113-149. Padoan points out that of the three possible explanations for Aeneas' descent to the underworld available to Dante (he went in a mental vision, he went corporally through the agency of necromancy, he went corporally through the agency of divine grace), Dante chose the latter and most radical ("Enea," *Enciclopedia Dantesca*, vol. II, pp. 677-679); not only is such an explanation necessary if the classical hero is to serve as an antecedent of the pilgrim, but it also serves to further distance the *Aeneid* from necromantic practices. An interesting corollary to this issue is provided by Giuseppe Bolognese, "Fra i maghi danteschi: Michele Scoto," *Alighieri*, 17 (1976), 71-74, who suggests that Vergil's damning assertion regarding Michael Scot, "che veramente / de le magiche frode seppe 'l gioco" ("who truly knew the game of magic frauds" [*Inf.* XX, 116-117]), is motivated by the Scot's inclusion of Vergil as a great magician in his astrology manual, the *Liber Introductorius*.

Vergil: "Poeta fui"

deliberately: because what Vergil sees is the truth, such language is legitimate. He may speak as a prophet, because he is in a world where his prophecy is guaranteed true, because he is no longer a *vates*—a term used for Vergil in the *Monarchia*, and significantly omitted from the *Comedy*—but a *scriba*. In this way, Dante works to rehabilitate his preferred *auctor* and his text. And yet, his methods are typically double-edged. Is not Vergil, rather than the pilgrim, one of the "altri sciocchi," to the extent that he passively submitted to Erichtho's evil will? His informed tirade against the diviners is thus bought at a heavy price. Analogously, Vergil's text is preserved, but only at the cost of being revealed false. If Dante had simply wanted to distance his Vergil from the necromancer of medieval legend, the best course would surely have been to ignore completely any such insinuations, not to feed them by inventing a posthumous connection between the sage and so infamous a practitioner of the black arts as Erichtho.[36] His behavior suggests

[36] Dante could surely have found a way to give his guide prior knowledge of Hell without associating him with the most bloodcurdling scene in Latin literature. On the legends surrounding Vergil, see Comparetti, *Virgilio nel medio evo*, and John Webster Spargo, *Virgil the Necromancer* (Cambridge: Harvard U. Press, 1934). Far from being Neapolitan folktales as Comparetti thought, Spargo shows that these legends originate outside of Italy in the twelfth century, in learned authors like John of Salisbury. By Dante's time they were circulating in Italy and it seems reasonable to assume that Dante was aware of them, since Cino draws on the legend of the bronze fly fabricated by Vergil to keep all other flies out of Naples (first mentioned by John in the *Policraticus*; see Spargo, p. 8 and pp. 70-79) in his canzone-satire on Naples, where he rebukes Vergil as follows:

O sommo vate, quanto mal facesti
(non t'era me' morire
a Piettola, colà dove nascesti?),
  quando la mosca, per l'altre fuggire,
in tal loco ponesti

O supreme seer, how much evil you did (was it not better for you to die in Pietola, where you were born?) when you put in such a place the fly, in order to drive the others away

("Deh, quando rivedrò 'l dolce paese," 13-17)

These verses, most likely composed late in Cino's career (he was in Naples in 1330-1331), show that, despite his devotion to Dante, Cino was capable of

Epic Resolution

that he had a different goal in mind, that of distinguishing between three kinds of prophet: the utterly false prophet, housed in the fourth *bolgia* and exemplified by its inhabitants; the unwitting prophet, who is unknowingly a carrier of both truth and falsehood, a type exemplified by Vergil, whom Dante both accepts and corrects according to his perception of whether he is dealing with *verità* or *menzogna*; and the unconditionally true prophet, whose vision is divinely sanctioned, exemplified by Dante himself.[37]

---

adopting a very different, and more current, attitude toward his friend's guide. Extremely suggestive is his ironic reference to Pietola, mentioned reverently as Vergil's birthplace in *Purgatorio* XVIII, 82-83, and his use of the expression "O sommo vate"; perhaps Dante's avoidance of *vate* in the *Comedy*, for Vergil and even for himself (the word is never used), reflects his belief that in the popular mind *vate* is associated more with witchcraft than with the providential calling it describes in the *Monarchia*.

[37] Dante's view of himself as a true prophet is evidenced by his Epistle to the Florentines, where his warning of imminent destruction begins with the claim to have a "prophetic mind"—"presaga mens"—instructed by "truth-telling signs": "Et si presaga mens mea non fallitur, sic signis veridicis sicut inexpugnabilibus argumentis instructa prenuntians . . ." ("And if my prophetic mind does not err, that announces the future instructed both by truth-telling signs and by unassailable arguments" [*Epistola* VI, 17]). Interestingly, the commentaries to the Epistles point to a passage from none other than *Aeneid* X as the source for Dante's "presaga mens," thus indirectly relating this prophetic moment in the Epistle to Dante's gloss on *Aeneid* X and chief text on prophecy: *Inferno* XX. As I show in "True and False See-ers in *Inferno* XX," canto XX is enormously important for Dante's views on textuality, since prophecy is for Dante essentially a textual issue: a *profeta* is one who fore-tells, who reads in the "magno volume" of God's mind (*Par.* XV, 50) and deciphers the book of the future. The chief concern of *Inferno* XX is thus precisely the truth or falsity—*verità* or *menzogna*—of a statement, reading, or text; this problematic is then focused on two representative texts: the *Aeneid* and the *Comedy*. For more general discussions of Dante and prophecy, see: Bruno Nardi, "Dante profeta," in *Dante e la cultura medievale*, pp. 336-416; Joseph Anthony Mazzeo, "Dante's Conception of Poetic Expression," in *Structure and Thought in the Paradiso* (1958; repr. New York: Greenwood Press, 1968), pp. 25-49; Nicolò Mineo, *Profetismo e apocalittica in Dante* (Catania: U. di Catania, 1968), esp. pp. 297-354; Marjorie Reeves, "Dante and the Prophetic View of History," in *The World of Dante*, pp. 44-60. Mineo points out that Vergil was in fact known in the Middle Ages as a *propheta nescius*, an unwitting prophet (p. 340).

Vergil: "Poeta fui"

Vergil thus inhabits a middle ground, a limbo of dialectical possibility, and the key to him seems to be his passivity: he can function *in malo*, working for Erichtho, or *in bono*, working for Beatrice. In *Inferno* XX Dante wants to teach us that Vergil is not an *auctoritas* whose statements can be unquestioningly accepted, and so he revises Vergil's text first regarding the founding of Mantova and secondly regarding the status of Eurypylus, a minor character from the *Aeneid* presented as an augur in canto XX. The episode belongs to the *Aeneid*'s second book: in order to persuade the Trojans to take the fateful horse into their city, Sinon invents his deceitful tale, claiming that the Greeks were going to offer him in sacrifice to Apollo; Eurypylus is the soldier who, according to Sinon, was sent to consult the oracle, which would respond by demanding a Greek life: "suspensi Eurypylum scitatum oracula Phoebi / mittimus" ("Uncertain, we send Eurypylus to consult the oracle of Phoebus" [*Aeneid* II, 114-115]). In canto XX Dante transforms this harmless messenger into a partner of the seer Calchas, responsible with Calchas for the sacrifice of Iphigenia at Aulis, and has Vergil insist on this identification by pointing to the *Aeneid* as its source and stressing Dante's thorough knowledge of that text, a poem that he is said to know in its entirety, "tutta quanta":

> Euripilo ebbe nome, e così 'l canta
> l'alta mia tragedìa in alcun loco:
> ben lo sai tu che la sai tutta quanta.

> Eurypylus was his name, and so my high tragedy sings of him in a certain passage—well do you know this, since you know the whole of it.
>
> (*Inf.* XX, 112-114)

Arguing that Dante knew full well that Eurypylus was not an augur in the *Aeneid* ("ben lo sai tu che la sai tutta quanta"), Hollander claims that Dante here shows himself "to be what poets have always been called, 'liar,' in order to better serve the truth."[38] Once more, then, the *Comedy* is "un ver c'ha faccia

---

[38] "The Tragedy of Divination in *Inferno* XX," p. 203. Regarding the problem

221

di menzogna." And, if the *Comedy*'s version of Eurypylus is true, then the *Aeneid*'s version is not, with the result that Vergil's text is reduced to being in this instance the equivalent of Sinon's story: a lie.

By the time we finish *Inferno* XX, Dante has presented us with all the key elements of his Vergilian strategy; indeed, the *Inferno* from this point on becomes in part a running commentary on Vergil, for which we are prepared by the episodes already discussed. Interestingly, the true/false opposition runs through this commentary, suggesting that it is an integral and essential component of the Vergilian problematic. Thus, in cantos XXI to XXIII, Malacoda's lie is tied to the issue of the *ruine*, which, as we have seen, function as a kind of yardstick by which Vergil is measured. Canto XXI contains all the ingredients of cantos IX and XII: upon seeing the devils who torment the *barattieri*, Vergil reassures Dante by reminding him that he has been here before, in a reference to his journey for Erichtho: "non temer tu, ch'i' ho le cose conte, / per ch'altra volta fui a tal baratta" ("Do not fear, for I have things under control, since I was in a similar fray once before" [*Inf.* XXI, 62-63]). As though oblivious of the events of canto IX, he shows excessive confidence in his ability to handle the devils, and, as though to underscore the fact that his success in canto XII was of a superficial nature, precisely the *ruine* will now prove his undoing.[39] Malacoda's lie consists in telling the travelers that there

---

of Eurypylus in *Inferno* XX, D'Ovidio suggests that, for Dante, Sinon's pairing of Calchas and Eurypylus in his story reflects their actual participation at Aulis; thus, Dante is not correcting the *Aeneid* but cleverly drawing out its intended but unstated meaning ("Ancora Dante e la magìa," *Studii sulla Divina Commedia*, pp. 147-149).

[39] Vergil's ignorance with regard to the devils, and the resulting overconfidence in his handling of them, are treated by C. J. Ryan, "*Inferno* XXI: Virgil and Dante: A Study in Contrasts," *Italica*, 59 (1982), 16-31. Sam Guyler discusses Vergil's insufficiencies in *Inferno* XXIII, the canto in which Dante and his guide are forced to flee Malacoda's troop, in "Virgil the Hypocrite—Almost: A Re-interpretation of *Inferno* XXIII," *Dante Studies*, 90 (1972), 25-42. (I disagree, however, with the thesis that Vergil's excessive confidence is part of a hypocritical attempt to preserve the façade of his authority.) In an article that concentrates on the critique of Vergil in *Purgatorio* XXX, Chris-

is a bridge still leading out of this *bolgia*, although the one ahead of them collapsed in the earthquake that accompanied the Crucifixion; he is able to deceive Vergil because the poet's first trip antedates the earthquake, and because he accompanies his lie with a great truth, the date of the death of Christ. We could stretch a point to say that Malacoda's truthful lie is a lie that has the appearance of truth—"una menzogna c'ha faccia di vero"—and that Vergil is susceptible to it because he is himself a teller of truthful lies. And Vergil, of course, knows nothing about devils—those lying truths—as is evident from the truism with which the hypocrite Catalano apprises him of Malacoda's deceit (the extent of Vergil's ignorance of Christian truths is emphasized in this very *bolgia*, where we see him marvel over the crucifixion of Caiphas); using the key word which has figured in all these Vergilian passages, *menzogna*, Catalano explains that devils are liars: "ch'elli è bugiardo e padre di menzogna" ("for he is a liar and the father of lies" [*Inf*. XXIII, 144]).

If cantos XXI through XXIII revive the theme of Vergil's failure in the face of Christian devils and Christian ruins, cantos XXIV and XXV return to the revision and outdoing of classical authors. The famous vaunts of canto XXV, in which Dante boasts that his metamorphoses are superior to those of Lucan and Ovid, emerge from the *Comedy*'s fundamental polemic vis-à-vis ancient texts: they fail to deal in truth. The metamorphoses of canto XXV are part of a series of perverted religious motifs that runs through lower Hell, moving from "nostra imagine . . . sì torta" ("our image so twisted" [*Inf*. XX, 22-23]), to the "crucifixion" of Caiphas, the "resurrection" of Vanni Fucci, the "Eucharist" of Ugolino, and culminating in Lucifer, a perverse image of God Himself. Canto XXV fits into this scheme by way of the Christological focus of the metamorphoses, a focus that

---

topher J. Ryan begins by demonstrating that the events of *Inferno* VIII and XXI are examples of "the limitation in Virgil's knowledge with respect to evil" (p. 5); see "Virgil's Wisdom in the *Divine Comedy*," *Medievalia et Humanistica*, 11 (1982), 1-38. Giuseppe Baglivi and Garrett McCutchan have written on Malacoda and the *ruine* in "Dante, Christ, and the Fallen Bridges," *Italica*, 54 (1977), 250-262.

Epic Resolution

is rendered linguistically through the canto's insistence on the motif of "two in one";[40] while the miracle of Christ is to be simultaneously two *and* one, this infernal inversion results in a creature that is neither two nor one: "Vedi che già non se' né due né uno" ("You see that you are already neither two nor one" [*Inf*. XXV, 69]), remarks a thief, whose observation is confirmed by the poet's subsequent comment, "due e nessun l'imagine perversa / parea" ("both two and nothing the perverse image seemed" [77-78]). Also connected to Christ is the key word that Dante uses for the second of his two metamorphoses; while for the first he uses *mutare*, for the second he uses *trasmutare*, a verb that strongly suggests a higher kind of transfiguration: the prefix *tras*, which stands at the threshold of Paradise in Dante's coinage *trasumanar*, is linked in the *Comedy* to the *Paradiso*, where it is used insistently, and thus with religious transmutation. Moreover, Dante's criticism of Ovid—"ché due nature mai a fronte a fronte / non trasmutò sì ch'amendue le forme / a cambiar lor matera fosser pronte" ("for he never transmuted two natures front to front so that both forms were ready to change their substance" [100-102])—will be echoed by the description of Christ in the purgatorial procession, where the pilgrim marvels at the griffin's ability to be still while simultaneously being transformed: "ne l'idolo suo si trasmutava" ("in its image it was changing" [*Purg*. XXXI, 126]). In short, the superiority of Dante's metamorphoses derives from that which they parody; as negative versions of one of the greatest of Christian mysteries, the dual nature of Christ, they resonate with a power not available to their classical counterparts.[41]

[40] Paratore notes the importance of this motif in his reading, "Il canto XXV dell'*Inferno*," in *Tradizione e struttura in Dante*, pp. 250-280.

[41] Piero Floriani, "Mutare e trasmutare: alcune osservazioni sul canto XXV dell'*Inferno*," *Giornale storico della letteratura italiana*, 149 (1972), 324-332, notes in the canto "una religiosità non neoplatonica, anche sentimentalmente fondata sopra la resurrezione *della carne*" (p. 327, n. 8). Although Dante's vaunted superiority over Lucan and Ovid is generally viewed as a reference to purely technical mastery (see, for instance, Richard Terdiman, "Problematical Virtuosity: Dante's Depiction of the Thieves," *Dante Studies*, 91 [1973], 27-45), the Christological underpinnings of the metamorphoses are noted by James

Vergil: "Poeta fui"

Also noteworthy about the apostrophes to Lucan and Ovid is that Dante concentrates his criticism on the latter, specifying that Ovid was never able to transmute two natures into new substances. Dante makes much of Ovid as the poet of metamorphosis throughout this section of the *Inferno*: in canto XXIV the description of the phoenix, "che . . . more e poi rinasce" ("that dies and is then reborn" [107]), derives primarily from the *Metamorphoses*; in canto XXV Ovid is one who "converts by poetizing" ("converte poetando" [99]); in canto XXIX Dante invokes Ovid's story of the Myrmidons, according to which the dead population of Aegina, "le genti antiche" (62), destroyed by Juno's plague, is miraculously replaced by ants transformed into men: "si ristorar di seme di formiche" ("they were restored from seed of ants" [64]). The verbs that Dante associates with Ovid in each of these passages—*rinascere, convertire, ristorarsi*—are all verbs that adumbrate the Christian mystery of true metamorphosis: rebirth. Because the poet of transformations did not, however, deal with the ultimate transformation, Dante envelops each of Ovid's metamorphoses in expressions of doubt, indicating that they fell short: in canto XXIV the phoenix is introduced with "Così per li gran savi si confessa" ("So by the great sages it is stated" [106]); in canto XXV Ovid's transformations of Cadmus into a serpent and Arethusa into a fountain are countered by Dante's explicit "io non lo 'nvidio" ("I do not envy him" [99]); in canto XXIX the creation of the Myrmidons is prefaced by the subtly distancing "secondo che i poeti hanno per fermo" ("as the poets hold for certain" [63]). Not only is Dante here throwing doubt on the veracity of classical legend, but he is using classical material to suggest a type of negative or infernal metamorphosis that leads nowhere, that is repetitive rather than redemptive. Thus, the Ovidian tale of the Myrmidons serves as a term of comparison for the diseased inhabitants of the tenth *bolgia*, who will *not* be revived, and

---

Thomas Chiampi, *Shadowy Prefaces: Conversion and Writing in the Divine Comedy* (Ravenna: Longo, 1981), chap. 2, esp. pp. 96-98. For a complementary reading of the "Ovidian *poesis*" of *Inferno* XXIV-XXV, see Peter S. Hawkins, "Virtuosity and Virtue: Poetic Self-Reflection in the *Commedia*," *Dante Studies*, 98 (1980), 1-18.

Epic Resolution

whose movements are rendered by a perverse and nonrestorative use of *trasmutare*: "e qual carpone / si trasmutava per lo tristo calle" ("and some on all fours moved along the sad path" [68-69]). Particularly suggestive is the positioning of "secondo che i poeti hanno per fermo" immediately after "le genti antiche"; this last phrase will recur in *Paradiso* VIII, where the error of "le genti antiche ne l'antico errore" is precisely their belief in classical myth. Given that in *Convivio* IV, xxvii Dante recounts the story of King Aeacus and the Myrmidons with evident sympathy, explaining that Aeacus wisely turned to God ("esso saviamente ricorse a Dio" [17]), and that as a result his people were restored to him ("lo suo popolo ristorato li fu" [17]), it would seem that *Inferno* XXIX rehearses the same transition that we find in *Paradiso* VIII: here too the *Convivio*'s classical truth has become the *Comedy*'s falsehood.

Besides implying that classical metamorphoses, because they hide no Christian mysteries of consubstantiation, are less true than Dantesque transmutations, canto XXV also presents us—albeit less spectacularly—with another installment in the ongoing story of Vergil correcting his own text. Cacus the fraudulent centaur who stole Hercules' cattle is among the thieves in this *bolgia*; whereas in the *Aeneid* the hero strangles the thief, Vergil here recounts that Hercules beat him to death, thus following Ovid's version instead of his own.[42] By substituting a Vergilian story with an Ovidian one shortly before announcing his definitive primacy over Ovid, Dante may be implying his primacy over Vergil as well. A final infernal revision of the *Aeneid* may be found in *Inferno* XXXI, where the travelers view the giants before being placed by one of them on the floor of the lowest circle. These creatures are introduced as "li orribili giganti, cui minaccia / Giove del cielo ancora quando tuona" ("the horrible giants, whom Jove still threatens from heaven when he thunders" [*Inf.* XXXI, 44-45]), which is to say that

---

[42] Paratore notes the use of Ovid instead of Vergil, calling it "tanto più notevole in quanto il ricordo dell'episodio è posto proprio in bocca a Virgilio" ("Il canto XXV dell'*Inferno*," p. 257).

Vergil: "Poeta fui"

they are introduced as classical figures. In fact, except for Nimrod, whose origin is Biblical, all Dante's giants come from his classical *auctores*; he emphasizes their classical background from the start in the periphrasis about Jove, who still threatens them with his thunderbolts on account of their ill-fated attack on Mount Olympus. (*Giove* is referred to again in line 92, thus adding to the canto's classical flavor.) But, as he did earlier with Capaneus, who also invokes the battle of Phlegra, Dante reduces the giants by destroying the fabulous aura that surrounds them in classical literature, treating them rationally as nothing but enormous hulks of brute matter. This strategy involves the poet in complicated attempts to describe the size of the giants in natural terms—thus the face that is the size of Saint Peter's bronze pine cone, and the ostentatiously "mathematical" expressions such as "trenta gran palmi" ("thirty great palms" [65]), and "ben cinque alle" ("a good five ells" [113]); it also involves him in a correction of the *Aeneid*, where the giant Briareus is described as a creature having one hundred arms and fifty heads. In the *Comedy*, Briareus is described by Vergil as identical to the other giants, although somewhat more ferocious in appearance: "ed è legato e fatto come questo, / salvo che più feroce par nel volto" ("and he is bound and shaped like this one, except that his face seems more ferocious" [104-105]). This canto's reduction of Briareus to huge but natural proportions is part of a strategy of mathematical precision that Dante uses to point—as always—to the reality or truth of his characters as compared to those of his classical precursors.[43]

[43] As Dante earlier follows Ovid instead of Vergil, here he follows Statius, who describes Briareus simply as "immensus" (*Thebaid* II, 596). Two further examples of Dante's transposition of his classical sources in order to achieve greater "realism" involve Geryon and Cacus: while in the *Aeneid* Geryon is described as "threefold" or "three-bodied" (VIII, 202), in the *Comedy* he has one body articulated in three species; while in the *Aeneid* Cacus breathes flames from his jaws (VIII, 252), in the *Comedy* flames are provided by the dragon that sits on his shoulders. It would not be surprising were Dante to connect these two figures, since Vergil explicitly does so: Hercules enters the fray against Cacus as a recent victor over Geryon; indeed the cattle stolen by Cacus was part of Hercules' prize after defeating Geryon (*Aen.* VIII, 201-204). In drawing

Epic Resolution

There are two further episodes in the *Inferno* that undermine the status of Vergil's text; although they operate more subtly than actual revisions, I hope to show that they are in fact continuations of *Inferno* XX, since they share the same goal: these episodes are intended to disturb the attentive reader, to make him doubt the established value of terms like *tragedìa* and *comedìa*, and ultimately to make him suspect that here the context has dictated new meanings, whereby the humble *comedìa* is viewed as superior to the *alta tragedìa*. The first of these episodes is marked precisely by the use of the adjective *alto*, which we have seen referred to Vergil throughout the *Inferno*: he is the *altissimo poeta*, his poem an *alta tragedìa*. We are in the *bolgia* of the fraudulent counselors, where Vergil tells the pilgrim to let him address Ulysses and Diomedes—"Lascia parlare a me"—because, being Greeks, they may disdain Dante's speech: "ch'ei sarebbero schivi, / perch' e' fuor greci, forse del tuo detto" ("for perhaps, because they were Greeks, they would be disdainful of your speech" [*Inf.* XXVI, 74-75]). Vergil then breaks into the *Inferno*'s most explicit example of his *parola ornata*, a *captatio benevolentiae* modeled on the epic style and replete with anaphora, translation from the *Aeneid*, and a reference to his own "alti versi," and to which moreover Dante draws attention by noting that *"in questa forma lui parlare audivi"* ("in this form I heard him speak" [78; italics mine]):[44]

"O voi che siete due dentro ad un foco,
s'io meritai di voi mentre ch'io vissi,
s'io meritai di voi assai o poco
quando nel mondo li alti versi scrissi . . . "

---

on and revising two Vergilian monsters both slain by Hercules, a figure of Christ, Dante may be reminding us of Vergil's first great failure at the gates of Dis, an event surrounded by classical monsters and marked by the evocation of Hercules.

[44] H. D. Goldstein discusses the language of *Inferno* XXVI in "Enea e Paolo: A Reading of the 26th Canto of Dante's *Inferno*," *Symposium*, 19 (1965), 316-326, concluding that "Canto XXVI employs pagan 'high verse' to achieve anti pagan high verse and becomes, in this way, Dante's 'anti epic' " (p. 320).

Vergil: "Poeta fui"

"O you who are two within one fire, if I deserved from you while I lived, if I deserved from you much or little when in the world I wrote the high verses . . . "
(*Inf.* XXVI, 79-82)

To speak to Ulysses, a hero of epic poetry, Vergil has recourse to epic language, the language of his own "alti versi," suggesting that the pilgrim's language is not appropriate because it is not sufficiently lofty. A stylistic disjunction between Dante and Vergil is thus established, and will be reemphasized in the following canto, where Vergil instructs Dante to speak to Guido da Montefeltro; because Guido is a contemporary Italian, rather than a Greek hero, he does not merit an address in the high style, and so Dante can approach him on his own.

The canto of Guido da Montefeltro functions in many ways as an unmasking of the canto of Ulysses, following a rule that is fairly constant throughout the *Inferno*, whereby a sinner who is treated in a particularly metaphorical key is offset by one who is treated with a harsher literalism: thus, Francesca is followed by Ciacco, Pier della Vigna by Capaneo, and—turning to characters who committed the same sin—Brunetto is followed by the three noble Florentines. In the same way that the canto of Brunetto goes far beyond the issue of literal sodomy to invest a metaphorical sterility, caused by predicating the eternity of one's soul upon a text, so the Ulysses canto goes beyond the issue of fraudulent counsel into the nexus of ideas subsumed under the heading of "il trapassar del segno" (*Par.* XXVI, 117). As *Inferno* XVI serves to demythologize *Inferno* XV, pointing to the political and social consequences of corruption among society's elite, and focusing on the physical suffering of the sinners in a way that compensates for the comparative lack of such description in canto XV, so *Inferno* XXVII demythologizes *Inferno* XXVI: Guido's story clarifies the low and ignoble side of Ulysses' sin, the prosaic deceit practiced on his old companions, which the canto's high language—and the hero's "high" sin—had conspired to gloss over. The difference between Dante's treatment of Ulysses and his treatment of Guido is immediately apparent; the travelers are beginning to move off after Ulysses has finished speaking, when another flame comes after them, emitting a "confuso suon" (*Inf.* XXVII, 6): instead of Vergil's lengthy *captatio benevolentiae*, here the sinner begs them to remain, and instead of Ulysses' sonorous exordium, here there is only a confused sound. Dante now elaborates on the *modus operandi* of this speaking flame, something he chose not to do in canto XXVI, and there follows the graphic horror of the simile of the Sicilian bull, the bronze bull in which the tyrant Phalaris would roast his victims, whose shrieks would be transformed by the machine into the bellowing of a bull; as the tortured victims in the bull attempt to speak, but have their speech transformed into bellowing, so the soul within the flame attempts to speak, but can find no outlet for his voice. Only now do we understand that Ulysses' voice, like Guido's, must have been physically degraded by the effort of speaking; we learn the full import of the description "gittò voce di fuori" ("he threw forth a voice" [*Inf.* XXVI, 90]) and realize that Ulysses' eloquence, like Pier della Vigna's, was accompanied by great pain.[45]

The simile of the Sicilian bull functions as a transforming medium stationed at the outset of canto XXVII in order to "lower" the discourse, to accomplish the transition from high to low. This transition is articulated at the level of language, a key thematic concern in this *bolgia* inhabited by tongues of fire.[46] The simile stresses the transition from speech, in this context a "high" sound, to the "low" sound of the bull's bellows; the verb *mugghiare* is used twice, first in the simile's incipit ("Come 'l bue cicilian che mugghiò prima" "As the

[45] On the pairing of Ulysses and Guido, see James G. Truscott, "Ulysses and Guido: *Inferno* XXVI and XXVII," *Dante Studies*, 91 (1973), 47-72, and Richard Kay, "Two Pairs of Tricks: Ulysses and Guido in Dante's *Inferno* XXVI-XXVII," *Quaderni d'italianistica*, 1 (1980), 107-124.

[46] Dante plays on the metaphor of the fraudulent counselors as tongues of fire; thus, the *bolgia* itself is a throat ("la gola / del fosso" [XXVI, 40-41]), and the movement of Ulysses' flame is likened to that of a tongue ("come fosse la lingua che parlasse [XXVI, 89]).

Vergil: "Poeta fui"

Sicilian bull which bellowed first" [*Inf.* XXVII, 7]), and then in the line that points to the transformation from voice to bellow: "*mugghiava* con la *voce* de l'afflitto" ("it *bellowed* with the *voice* of the afflicted one" [10; italics mine]). The simile's second term describes the "conversion" of Guido's struggling words into "its language," i.e. the sounds of the flame as they actually come forth:

> così, per non aver via né forame
> dal principio nel foco, *in suo linguaggio
> si convertïan le parole* grame.

So, because at first they could find no way or outlet in the fire, his sorrowful *words converted themselves into its language*.
(Inf. XXVII, 13-15; italics mine)

This passage is followed by another *terzina* describing the mechanics of Guido's speech act, and then, finally, by his first words, which are addressed to Vergil and refer to the *maestro's* recent dismissal of Ulysses. If it is surprising to learn that Vergil, who had addressed the hero with such respect, should dismiss him with the words "Go away now," it is nothing short of shocking to hear that these words were spoken—far from the high style of the *captatio benevolentiae!*—in a coarse Lombard dialect, faithfully reproduced by Dante, and explicitly noted by Guido da Montefeltro: "O tu a cu' io drizzo / la voce e che parlavi mo lombardo, / dicendo 'Istra ten va, più non t'adizzo' " ("O you to whom I raise my voice, and who were just now speaking Lombard, saying 'Go away now, I urge you no more' " [19-21]). We now see what transformation the Sicilian bull has prepared us to accept: Vergil's "S'io meritai di voi" has become "Istra ten va"; the high style has been converted to the low style.[47]

---

[47] Commentators have been distracted from the main point of Guido's subversive apostrophe by the issue of language, attempting to ascertain what they will never know, i.e. in what language Vergil spoke to Ulysses. Although linguistic diversity is a fictional premise of Dante's afterlife, inhabited by people

Epic Resolution

Vergil is associated with Ulysses and the high style; Dante is associated with Guido and the low style, so much so that Vergil orders Dante to speak to Guido, saying "Parla tu; questi è latino" ("You speak, this one is Italian" [*Inf.* XXVII, 33]). And, as already noted, the pilgrim's conversation, beginning with his lack of awe or hesitation and his use of the simple periphrasis "O anima che se' là giù nascosta" ("O soul that are hidden down there" [36]), will result in a revelation regarding the previous episode. For, while in canto XXVI Vergil's *alti versi* set the tone for a discourse that enables Ulysses to mask

who speak "Diverse lingue, orribili favelle" ("Different languages, horrible tongues" [*Inf.* III, 25]), it is not a narrative premise, in that almost everyone speaks in the language in which the poem is written. Dante frequently approximates the speech of his characters in his Italian (a gallicism for Hugh Capet, regional dialectisms where appropriate), and occasionally employs other languages (Provençal for Arnaut Daniel, Latin for Cacciaguida), but, as Pagliaro points out: "si tratta di caratterizzazione di ordine, non linguistico, ma stilistico" ("Dialetti e lingue nell'oltretomba," in *Ulisse*, vol. II, p. 451; on this topic, see also Braccini, "Paralipomeni al 'Personaggio-Poeta' "). A stylistic issue is precisely what is at stake in *Inferno* XXVII as well; for although we do not know in what language Vergil originally spoke to Ulysses (i.e. whether Guido's reference to Vergil's "Lombard" applies only to his last remark, or to his previous address as well), we do know that he originally spoke in a high style, and is now represented as speaking in a low one. A similar point of view is that of Angelo Lipari, "Parla tu; questi è latino," *Italica*, 23 (1946), 73-81; see also Benvenuto Terracini, "Il canto XXVII dell'*Inferno*," in *Letture dantesche: Inferno*, ed. Giovanni Getto (Florence: Sansoni, 1955), pp. 517-545. Pagliaro's contribution to the question of Vergil's speech in *Inferno* XXVII is to place it in an ethnic and historical context, suggesting that Vergil is designated a Lombard because as such he is less offensive to Ulysses than is Dante, a Tuscan, i.e. a member of that race which came to Aeneas' aid; although I do not consider this thesis a solution to the problems posed by the opening of *Inferno* XXVII, I believe that it has interesting implications for other aspects of Dante's treatment of Vergil, as demonstrated above in note 34. Finally, on the question of language, in Chapter II, note 83, I indicated my fundamental agreement with Paratore, who suggests that Vergil would speak, according to Dante, a vernacular form of the *gramatica* in which he wrote, i.e. a vernacular form of Latin (see "Il latino di Dante"). I therefore suggest that Vergil's "Lombard" is a reference to the vernacular Latin he would have spoken while alive, a "Lombard Latin" as it were. The argument that, for Dante, Roman Vergil spoke the Lombard dialect of the thirteenth century contradicts, as Pagliaro points out, Dante's expressly stated views on the mutability of language.

Vergil: "Poeta fui"

his sin, enveloping it in rhetoric, in canto XXVII the low conversation between Dante and Guido cuts through the high rhetoric, just as Guido previously pierced the cocoon of Vergil's high language.[48] In other words, the low style reveals the truth, while the high style hides it. By initiating a rhetorical style that Ulysses will exploit, Vergil abets the propagation of grandiloquent falsehoods; in fact, his very use of the expression *alti versi* paves the way for Ulysses' reliance on the opposition "high" vs. "low" (converted by him to "high" vs. "small"), terms that function as the key semantic underpinnings of his discourse: whatever it serves his purpose to discount is called "small," while whatever he desires is "high." Thus, on the one side we find his small group of companions ("quella compagna / picciola" [*Inf.* XXVI, 101-102]), the brief life span that is all that remains to them ("questa tanto picciola vigilia / d'i nostri sensi ch'è del rimanente" [114-115]), and the little oration with which he seduces them ("con questa orazion picciola" [122]); on the other, we find the deep open sea ("l'alto mare aperto" [100]), their glorious enterprise ("l'alto passo" [132]), and his goal, which promises to be the first conquest that will finally satisfy all his desires, because it is "higher" than anything he has ever seen before: "una montagna . . . alta tanto / quanto veduta non avëa alcuna" (133-135). To the extent that Vergil's *alti versi* lay the rhetorical premise of this discourse, he partakes in its lies, and the fraudulent nature of Vergil's speech—as well as of Ulysses'—is therefore revealed in canto XXVII, where Dante once more makes the connection between high verses and *menzogna*. The transition from "S'io meritai di voi" to "Istra ten va" is thus the transition from a heroic mythos to a quotidian Logos, from *tragedìa* to *comedìa*, and—returning to the leitmotif of these episodes—from falsehood to truth.

The last infernal episode we shall consider is also marked by the juxtaposition of a classical with a contemporary figure, the classical figure being, not coincidentally, that same Sinon to

---

[48] Mazzotta discusses the stress in *Inferno* XXVI on rhetoric as that which hides, as "thievery," in *Dante, Poet of the Desert*, pp. 90-96.

whose lying story the *Aeneid* is implicitly compared in *Inferno* XX. Sinon is presented by the counterfeiter, maestro Adamo, in his full classical regalia as " 'l falso Sinon greco di Troia" ("false Sinon, the Greek from Troy" [*Inf.* XXX, 98]), where the contradiction inherent in the expression "greco di Troia" neatly summarizes the duplicity of Sinon's position. Sinon's violent reaction to maestro Adamo's description of him leads to an exchange of insults between the two sinners that is similar to the earlier exchange between the pilgrim and Filippo Argenti; both altercations are regularly invoked as examples of the *Comedy*'s low style, inherited from the *tenzone* with Forese Donati. It has, in fact, been suggested that the events of canto XXX serve as a palinode of the *tenzone*, that Vergil's rebuke to the pilgrim for his interest in the altercation reflects the poet's uneasiness at this own poetic past.[49] In my opinion, such a reading, while appropriate in the Forese cantos of the *Purgatorio*, is less appropriate here, in *Inferno* XXX, where the altercation between Sinon and maestro Adamo functions not as a pointer to Dante's personal poetic history (like the meeting with Forese), but as an important moment in the reader's ongoing reeducation. As a sequel to canto XXVII, canto XXX poses the same issues regarding the low style and the new value that is being assigned to it; therefore, the opening of *Inferno* XXX rehearses, in compressed form, the same shift from classical/high to Dantesque/low that we saw in the shift from canto XXVI to canto XXVII. Moreover, the quarrel at the canto's end is marked by precisely that terminology which we have seen to be associated with the issue of *comedìa* vs. *tragedìa* throughout the *Inferno*: the terms "true" and "false" are used insistently, hurled at each other by the injured participants of this dispute with the obsessive repetition that characterizes abusive medieval genres both inside and outside of the *Comedy*.

[49] Bosco comments on Vergil's rebuke: "Ciò sembra importare un ripudio di quella giovanile poesia" (*Inferno*, p. 426). Contini, while including "il *trobar clus* sulla feccia di Sinone e maestro Adamo" among the textual sins for which *Purgatorio* XXIII makes amends, focuses on Forese as the center of palinodic energy: "Forese è una liquidazione per tutti" ("Dante come personaggio-poeta della *Commedia*," pp. 52-53).

Vergil: "Poeta fui"

If the canto ends on a "low" note, it begins on a "high" one: in preparation for the madness visited upon the impersonators (one of the four types of falsifier to be found in this *bolgia*), Dante devotes the first twenty-one lines of canto XXX to two classical examples of madness, one Theban and the other Trojan. The first is Athamas who, driven insane by Juno as part of her revenge on Semele, is responsible for the deaths of his wife Ino, Semele's sister, and their two sons (1-12); the second is Hecuba, reduced to barking like a dog by the loss of her home, husband, and children (13-21). These exempla are executed in a deliberately high style: in each case the protagonist, Athamas or Hecuba, is presented only in the fourth line of the exemplum, after an initial *terzina* of background material. Thus, the canto opens with a great mythological panorama, which sets the madness of Athamas within the ongoing narrative of Jove's amours and Juno's anger: "Nel tempo che Iunone era crucciata / per Semelè contra 'l sangue tebano" ("In the time when Juno was irate because of Semele against the Theban blood" [1-2]); and Hecuba is preceded by a sweeping evocation of the fall of Troy: "E quando la fortuna volse in basso / l'altezza de' Troian che tutto ardiva" ("And when Fortune brought low the pride of the Trojans that dared all" [13-14]). The canto thus moves progressively forward in time: from remote Thebes, to less distant Troy, and finally to the present, in which the pilgrim sees "due ombre smorte e nude, / che mordendo correvan di quel modo / che 'l porco quando del porcil si schiude" ("two pale and naked shades, who were running and biting like the pig when it is let out of the pigsty" [25-27]). Here Dante presents the *bolgia*'s first sinners in a *terzina* whose style is in intentional opposition to the canto's extraordinarily literary exordium;[50] the unmediated realism of the brief simile of the pig loosened from the pigsty contrasts sharply with the elaborate Ovidian exempla. We note, moreover, that the introduction of low language, such as *porco* and *porcil*, corresponds to the moment in which the

---

[50] Contini discusses the literary quality of this exordium in "Sul XXX dell'*Inferno*," *Un'idea di Dante*, pp. 159-170, where he suggests that Dante composed it with Ovid open before him (p. 160).

canto reaches "reality": i.e. the sinners, the events of this *bolgia*. This fact is stressed by the transitional verses, placed between the Trojan vignette and the arrival of Gianni Schicchi, which make the point that nothing in the classical accounts—"Ma né di Tebe furie né troiane" ("But neither the furies of Thebes nor of Troy" [22])—can equal what the pilgrim sees in Hell.

The high style of the canto's opening thus gives way to the low style in which the sinners are presented, and ultimately to the low style of the quarrel at the canto's end. Within the sequence of insults exchanged by Sinon and maestro Adamo, we shall focus on the passage in which *ver* and its opposite—here not *menzogna*, but *falso*—are featured, since these terms are connected to the issue of genre throughout the *Inferno*. In response to Sinon's taunt that maestro Adamo's hands were less agile while he was being led to the stake than while he was coining money, the counterfeiter replies first by acknowledging that the Greek speaks the truth in this—"Tu di' ver di questo" (112)—and then by reminding Sinon of his great untruth, that most notorious of literary lies, the lie that drove Hecuba mad, to the very condition in which we find her at this canto's beginning: "ma tu non fosti sì ver testimonio / là 've del ver fosti a Troia richesto" ("but you were not so true a witness there at Troy where the truth was requested from you" [113-114]). To this insistence on the *ver* that he did not tell, and on his role as a non-true witness, Sinon throws back the generic falsification for which both are damned, further noting that maestro Adamo's crimes, unlike his own, were multiple. While maestro Adamo stresses the word *ver*, Sinon stresses *falso*:

"S'io dissi falso, e tu falsasti il conio,"
  disse Sinon; "e son qui per un fallo,
  e tu per più ch'alcun altro demonio!"

"If I spoke falsely, you falsified the coin," said Sinon, "and I am here for a single sin, and you for more than any other demon!"

(*Inf.* XXX, 115-117)

Vergil: "Poeta fui"

In response maestro Adamo again returns to Troy, the scene of Sinon's single but supremely infamous crime, recalling not only the horse—"Ricorditi, spergiuro, del cavallo" ("Remember, perjurer, the horse" [118])—but in particular the fact that the whole world knows Sinon's sin: "e sieti reo che tutto il mondo sallo!" ("and let it be a torment for you that the whole world knows it!" [120]).

The whole world knows what Sinon did because it is recounted in a poem that the whole world reads: the *Aeneid*. Vergil has already been to some extent implicated in the figure of Sinon; in *Inferno* XX he is made to retell the story of Eurypylus, which is Sinon's story. In canto XX the *Aeneid* is, by implication, denied the status of a "ver testimonio," to use maestro Adamo's expression; like Sinon, the *Aeneid* is—on occasion—a falsifier of the historical truth. The alignment of the *Aeneid* with " 'l falso Sinon" is marked enough to suggest that the following correspondences may not be entirely fortuitous: on one side we find the classical figure, Sinon, textually connected to the word *falso* ("S'io dissi *falso*, e tu *falsasti* il conio") and, on the other, the contemporary figure, maestro Adamo, textually connected to the word *ver* ("Tu di' *ver* di questo: / ma tu non fosti sì *ver* testimonio / là 've del *ver* fosti a Troia richesto"). These alignments suggest that whereas Sinon from the *tragedìa* is related to falsehood, maestro Adamo from the *comedìa* is related to truth. Such correspondences, it should be noted, have nothing whatever to do with a hierarchy of moral values; I am not suggesting that the counterfeiter is less evil than the liar, but that Dante has structured into the quarrel between these souls a metaphorical statement regarding the status of the genres *comedìa* and *tragedìa*. Maestro Adamo is related to "truth" in the same way as is Guido da Montefeltro, not because he is "better" than Sinon, but because he is "comedic": drawn not from the literary world of the classical *tragedìa*, but from the observed world of contemporary reality. A further implication of this reading regards Vergil's rebuke at the end of canto XXX. Having severely reprimanded his charge for listening too fixedly to the altercation, Vergil explains in the canto's last line that

Epic Resolution

the urge to listen to such a quarrel is a base one: "ché voler ciò udire è bassa voglia" ("for to want to hear that is a base wish" [148]). This verse has traditionally been interpreted along the palinodic lines mentioned earlier, as representing Dante's explicit condemnation of the low style. I would suggest, instead, that this passage constitutes not a palinode but a vindication of the low style, which a poet *should* use if it is appropriate to do so; the term *bassa* is the opposite of *alta*, and therefore must be viewed not negatively, but positively: the *bassa comedìa* stands in opposition to the *alta tragedìa*.[51] In other words, Vergil is wrong in chastising the pilgrim, whose intuitive behavior (as previously with the devils) is correct; confirmation of this may be found in the fact that Vergil is caught in a contradiction: here he reprimands Dante for merely listening, while earlier he complimented him for actually participating in the quarrel with Filippo Argenti. Far from being wrong, the pilgrim's wish to listen is right, for his is the comedic desire to confront evil and to bear witness to all of reality, including Hell.

The positive or affective strand of the Vergilian thematic is more subtle than the intellective erosion on which we have been concentrating; it is to a great extent a function of time—the longer Vergil is present, the more he is loved—and therefore more difficult to demonstrate. We shall begin our presentation of this "other" story with a passage from *Inferno* XXIV, a canto that begins with the drawn-out simile of the *villanello* who despairs at the sight of frost, exchanging it for snow. The simile relates back to the end of the preceding canto, where Vergil has just learned of Malacoda's deceit, a revelation that leaves him,

[51] *Alto* and *basso* were explicitly juxtaposed in this canto's classical exordium ("E quando la fortuna volse in *basso* / *l'altezza* de' Troian che tutto ardiva" [13-14; italics mine]), where the negative valence of *alto* is evident. I do not wish to imply that the word *alto* bears exclusively negative connotations in the *Comedy*, or to suggest that for Dante the high style is always wrong, but rather to point out that in these episodes he goes out of his way to disabuse us of the prejudice with which we most likely began his poem, namely that the high style is the best. Dante's ambivalence regarding the high style, depending on who is using it and for what purposes, is further suggested by his use of *altissimo* in the poem: after referring to Vergil and Homer in *Inferno* IV, it is used only to refer to God, "l'altissimo lume" of *Paradiso* XXXII, 71.

Vergil: "Poeta fui"

in a notable departure from the Stoic equilibrium displayed on the countenances of Limbo, "turbato un poco d'ira nel sembiante" ("disturbed somewhat by anger in his look" [*Inf.* XXIII, 146]). His anger eventually gives way to a look of tenderness directed at his charge: "lo duca a me si volse con quel piglio / dolce ch'io vidi prima a piè del monte" ("my leader turned to me with that sweet look which I first saw at the foot of the mountain" [*Inf.* XXIV, 20-21]). What is remarkable about this passage is not so much the tenderness of Vergil's regard per se as the author's specification that he first saw such a "sweet look" at the foot of the mountain, i.e. in *Inferno* I, where Dante tries to climb the *colle* and fails. At that point in the narrative there is no indication of any loving demonstration on Vergil's part toward Dante, or of any sweetness in his look; indeed, the meeting between the two poets is described, as we noted previously, in stiff and formal terms, as is their relationship throughout the early cantos of the *Inferno*. Therefore, in specifying that Vergil's "piglio / dolce" (where the enjambement puts *dolce* into relief) is first seen "a piè del monte," Dante is retrospectively rewriting the original meeting of *Inferno* I, instituting an affective tie which at the time was not there; not only are we forced to revisualize the episode of canto I, but also to conjure up many another sweet glance that the narrative has not seen fit to mention. Thus, in two lines Dante inscribes a new thread of affectivity into the texture of the *Inferno*, casting a long sweet light all the way back to canto I.

These two lines do not occur in canto XXIV fortuitously, but as part of a subtle strategy of counterbalancing that dictates most of the moves in Dante's Vergilian narrative; he is forced, by the dialectical principles of the structure he is creating, to rehabilitate what he has himself undone. At the outset of *Inferno* XXIV, Vergil has just emerged severely tarnished from a test that spans three cantos: he has been lied to by Malacoda, and humiliated by the discovery. Precisely at this moment of intellectual defeat, Dante tightens the affective screws; if Vergil is to function as a paradox at the heart of the poem, the reader must not be allowed easily to dismiss him, but instead must be forced, with the pilgrim, into the dilemma of loving and respecting that which is fallible, corruptible, and transitory—i.e. into the human experience par excellence. This is accomplished rhetorically by the insinuation of affective language into the narrative at the moments of greatest intellective stress. Thus, at the end of canto XXIII, after Catalano has informed Vergil that devils are liars, Vergil walks off with great strides in evident anger, and the author concludes the canto as follows: "ond' io da li 'ncarcati mi parti' / dietro a le poste de le care piante" ("so I departed from those burdened ones, behind the prints of the beloved feet" [*Inf.* XXIII, 147-148]). The reference to Vergil's "care piante" at this juncture represents an escalation in the tension of the Vergilian dialectic; although the great sage has been treated like a fool by a hypocrite in Hell, his charge loves him not less, but more. The "beloved feet" are in fact an element in an affective crescendo that peaks with the "sweet look" of canto XXIV, and that begins with the simile in which Vergil is compared to the mother who rescues her son from a burning house, a simile that has the effect of neutralizing the event it is illustrating. We remember that in the opening sequence of canto XXIII the pilgrim's fears regarding the pursuit of the devils are realized, and that he and Vergil must make a rapid escape down the slope into the sixth *bolgia*. Although Vergil, due to his lack of foresight, must be considered responsible for this situation, and although Dante has gone to considerable lengths to create an episode which will reveal Vergil's weaknesses, at the episode's dénouement his tactics shift, and he concentrates on the selfless devotion Vergil demonstrates toward the pilgrim: his concern is like that of a mother who flees with her son dressed not even in her shift, "avendo più di lui che di sé cura" ("caring more for him than for herself" [*Inf.* XXIII, 41]). This redirection of the author's emphasis is stressed by the line that caps the sequence, in which Vergil is said to carry the pilgrim on his breast, "come suo figlio, non come compagno" ("like his son, not like his companion" [51]). By picking up one of the key terms of the simile, *figlio*, this line serves notice that a new affective tie has in fact been created, and that its existence is not confined to figures of speech.

Vergil: "Poeta fui"

A similar strategy is employed in the initial cantos of the *Purgatorio*, where Vergil receives from Cato, a fellow Roman, his first explicit corrections.[52] If Vergil's severity toward Dante at the end of *Inferno* XXX may be seen as a reflection of his ignorance rather than of the pilgrim's error, no such view may be applied to Cato's corrections of Vergil: in canto I Cato repudiates Vergil's *captatio benevolentiae* involving Marcia, calling it flattery; in canto II his general chastisement of all the souls gathered to listen to Casella's song falls with particular weight on Vergil, who feels responsible for the behavior of his charge. Canto II ends with Cato's rebuke and the dispersal of the souls like doves rising in flight; canto III therefore begins with a countermovement: although the others react to Cato with a "subitana fuga" ("sudden flight" [*Purg*. III, 1]), the pilgrim draws nearer to his guide, "la fida compagna" ("the faithful companion" [4]). This demonstration of the pilgrim's continued faith in his guide, even in the face of an opposing and higher authority, is then stunningly elaborated by the poet, who breaks in to comment in his own voice on Vergil's unique capacities: "e come sare' io sanza lui corso? / chi m'avria tratto su per la montagna?" ("And how could I have proceeded without him? Who would have brought me up the mountain?" [5-6]). These rhetorical questions are ideally suited to pointing up the underlying ambiguity: while, theoretically, we must acknowledge that Vergil is not irreplaceable, emotionally he is perceived as such. In the subsequent *terzina* Dante recapitulates the rhetorical strategy of lines 4-6, where a simple statement ("I drew near to my faithful companion") is followed by two questions, markers of affectivity; in lines 7-9, a one-line statement (regarding Vergil's self-recriminations) is again followed by two emotive lines, this time in the form of an exclamatory apostrophe to Vergil's conscience: "o dignitosa cosc̈ienza e netta, / come t'è picciol fallo amaro morso!" ("O noble conscience and

[52] The fact that Cato was a pagan has enormous implications for Vergil, since it shows that all pagans are not *ipso facto* damned, and thus shifts the burden of responsibility for his damnation to Vergil himself. This issue will be further examined with respect to Ripheus at the end of this section.

pure, how bitter a bite is a small fault to you" [8-9]). Again with the authority conveyed by his own voice, the poet places Cato's rebuke into perspective, minimizing as a "picciol fallo" the error that Cato so harshly reprimanded.[53]

At this point the episode is essentially finished; Vergil has ceased running, leaving the pilgrim free to look about him. There is, however, an inserted line of little seeming importance on the undignified effects of running, which subtly begins the swing of the Vergilian pendulum away from the "pro" side back to the "con," or, more accurately, from the affective back to the intellective; Vergil's haste has temporarily deprived his actions of their "onestade" (11). Vergil's mistakes are frequently marked by a temporary loss of decorum: in *Inferno* XXIII he avoids the devils by sliding down the *ruina* on his back; here he is compelled to run. Nor can such physical duress be undervalued, since it is an intimate component of nobility that it be marked by a decorous physical bearing; Vergil shows himself highly sensitive to this fact in *Inferno* XVI, where his respect for the former high stations of the three noble Florentines is such that he warns the pilgrim to be more courteous than usual, adding the following remarkable *terzina*:

E se non fosse il foco che saetta
la natura del loco, i' dicerei
che meglio stesse a te che a lor la fretta.

And were it not for the fire that the nature of the place darts down, I would say that haste would befit you more than them.

(*Inf.* XVI, 16-18)

The haste of the sodomites is caused by the raining fire that falls down on them; in suggesting that haste is more appropriate to Dante than to them, Vergil is close to forgetting who is damned and who is not, so dazzled is he by earthly greatness.

---

[53] Vergil seems to feel a new anxiety about his role as a result of these events, an anxiety expressed in his question "non credi tu me teco e ch'io ti guidi?" ("Do you not believe that I am with you and that I guide you?" [*Purg.* III, 24]).

Vergil: "Poeta fui"

His peculiar attitude becomes apparent again shortly thereafter, when the poet recalls that he was tempted to jump down among the sodomites, to pay them homage, "e credo che 'l dottor l'avria sofferto" ("and I believe that my teacher would have allowed it" [48]). Vergil's susceptibility to earthly fame is a leitmotif of his character, dating from Beatrice's original *captatio benevolentiae* of *Inferno* II, which appeals to him on the basis of his lasting fame, and surfacing intermittently from then on, although rarely in as aggravated form as in *Inferno* XVI. It is essentially an infernal characteristic, a trait that he shares with many other damned souls.[54] By forcing Vergil to run, by depriving him of his physical dignity, the outward manifestation of his earthly greatness, Dante underlines his dependence on earthly greatness for his authority, and his similarity in this regard to other denizens of Hell.

On the other hand, Vergil is so inspired a teacher that he learns how to put even his bad qualities to good use;[55] thus, in *Inferno* XXIV his belief in fame issues into a resounding exhortation which, for all its pagan basis and infernal connotations, serves the proper present purpose of infusing the pilgrim with much needed vigor. Finding Dante exhausted after his climb out of the *bolgia* of the hypocrites, Vergil reminds him that fame cannot be acquired under a coverlet, and that without fame no traces of our existence will remain:

sanza la qual chi sua vita consuma,
   cotal vestigio in terra di sé lascia,
   qual fummo in aere e in acqua la schiuma.

and he who consumes his life without it [fame] leaves such vestige of himself on earth as does smoke in air or foam in water.

(*Inf.* XXIV, 49-51)

[54] See Silvio Abbadessa, "Trame dantesche: onore e fama," *Italianistica*, 8 (1979), 465-489.

[55] See Fernando Cento, "Il Virgilio dantesco tipo ideale dell'Educatore," in *L'Umanesimo in Dante*, ed. Giovannangiola Tarugi (Florence: Olschki, 1967), pp. 1-19.

Epic Resolution

Although Vergil is undoubtedly deluded, since there is no meaningful life but that of the immortal soul, his remarks form part of a statement whose total effect is positive; his success is demonstrated by Dante's rising and saying "Va, ch'i' son forte e ardito" ("Go on, for I am strong and resolute" [60]). In difficult moments or in moments of transition—climbing onto Geryon, or up Lucifer—Vergil successfully draws on his Roman and Stoic convictions to encourage the pilgrim. Another element of his guidance that perhaps derives from his pagan background is his concern with the passing of time, which we first note in *Inferno* XI, where a pause is required to adjust their olfactory senses to lower Hell. Although in this scene it is the pilgrim who first requests that time not be lost while they wait, as the poem progresses the role of timekeeper falls more and more to Vergil; he has found an aspect of their journey that he can handle correctly without Christian knowledge, on the sole basis of his Roman identity. In Purgatory in particular, one feels that Vergil's insistence on time is his attempt to operate within the spiritual context of the second realm; he senses the importance of time here, and although he cannot participate in its true purpose by growing spiritually, he mimics its purpose by insisting on their tardiness.

The use of the word *dolce*, which we may take as a marker of the affective story-line, occurs with increasing frequency as the journey proceeds and as Vergil's return to Limbo becomes more imminent. Such affective terminology makes its first conspicuous appearance, in accordance with our rule regarding its insertion into the text at moments of intellective stress, immediately preceding Vergil's discomfiture by the devils in *Inferno* IX.[56] Thus in *Inferno* VIII we find Dante's first reference

---

[56] In retrospect, we can see that a pattern based on the application of this formula has been in operation since the beginning of the poem: the first tiff between the pilgrim and his guide (*Inf.* III, 76-81) is followed by Vergil's first "Figliuol mio" (*Inf.* III, 121); the intellectual errors inherent in Vergil's characterization of Limbo are followed by the affective marker "Dimmi, maestro mio, dimmi, segnore" (*Inf.* IV, 46), where the use of the personal pronoun contrasts with the earlier "tu duca, tu segnore e tu maestro" (*Inf.* II, 140).

244

Vergil: "Poeta fui"

to his guide as *padre*, in an expression whose affective resonance is compounded by his use of *dolce* as well; when Vergil leaves the pilgrim to negotiate secretly with the devils, the poet comments as follows: "Così sen van, e quivi m'abbandona / lo dolce padre" ("And so he goes away, my sweet father, and leaves me there" [*Inf.* VIII, 109-110]). In this highly charged and emotional context, we are not surprised to find *caro* applied to Vergil too; in line 97 of canto VIII the pilgrim calls his guide "O caro duca mio." Both of these adjectives, *dolce* and *caro*, reappear in cantos XXIII and XXIV, in the aftermath of Vergil's mishandled dealings with Malacoda ("care piante" [XXIII, 148], "piglio / dolce" [XXIV, 20-21]), but they do not occur in the *Inferno* with great frequency: *caro* is used to refer to Vergil only on the two occasions mentioned here, and *dolce* is applied to the Roman poet four times in all (besides the two cases referred to above, also " 'l dolce duca" [XVIII, 44] and "dolce poeta" [XXVII, 3]). In the *Purgatorio*, on the other hand, Vergil is called *dolce* twelve times: "O dolce padre" (IV, 44), "O dolce segnor mio" (IV, 109), " 'l dolce duca" (VI, 71), " 'l dolce maestro" (X, 47), "il dolce pedagogo" (XII, 3), "dolce padre" (XV, 25), "O dolce padre mio" (XV, 124), "Dolce mio padre" (XVII, 82), "dolce padre caro" (XVIII, 13), "O dolce padre" (XXIII, 13), "lo dolce padre mio" (XXV, 17), "Lo dolce padre mio" (XXVII, 52). We note the crescendo in intensity as the travelers approach the moment of Vergil's departure, rendered by the increased use of the possessive adjective *mio*, and such double-adjectival phrases as "dolce padre caro." The care with which Dante has arranged these expressions is confirmed by his final touch: the first and only use of *dolcissimo* to modify a person in the *Comedy* applies to Vergil in the moment of his disappearance, when he is called "Virgilio dolcissimo patre" (XXX, 50).[57]

[57] Giovanni Getto points to this passage in *Purgatorio* XXX as the high point in Dante's use of tender language for his guide; see "Dante e Virgilio," *Il Veltro*, 3 (1959), 11-20. *Dolcissimo* is used twice more in the *Comedy*, for the milk of the Muses (*Par.* XXIII, 57), and for the song that marks the completion of the pilgrim's exams (*Par.* XXVI, 67).

The *Purgatorio* works less at gradually undermining Vergil than at gradually replacing him; not only is his authority already effectively shattered by Cato, but Vergil himself admits his ignorance to the newly arrived souls of canto II, saying "noi siam peregrin come voi siete" ("we are pilgrims like you" [63]). One of Vergil's most endearing characteristics at this stage of the journey, and one of the major changes in his behavior, is his ability to openly acknowledge his insufficiencies and yet keep on trying. In *Purgatorio* III, the travelers reach an impasse, not knowing how to find a way up the steep face of the mountain; Vergil looks down to think, while the pilgrim looks around and sees a group of souls approaching. He therefore informs his mentor that help is on its way; now that the guide needs to be guided, they must rely on such encounters with more informed travelers. Linguistically, a change is registered by the fact that the pilgrim addresses his teacher with an imperative, telling him to look up, in a reversal of all the many orders Vergil has given him:

"Leva," diss' io, "maestro, li occhi tuoi:
  ecco di qua chi ne darà consiglio,
  se tu da te medesmo aver nol puoi."

"Master," I said, "raise your eyes; over here are some
who will give us counsel, if you cannot have it from yourself."

(*Purg.* III, 61-63)

The imperative of his own with which Vergil replies—"Andiamo in là, ch'ei vegnon piano; / e tu ferma la spene, dolce figlio" ("Let us go over there, for they come slowly; and you strengthen your hope, sweet son" [65-66])—is a good example, along with the precept on time that he offers to the souls when they meet ("ché perder tempo a chi più sa più spiace" "for loss of time displeases most him who knows most" [78]), of the type of Stoic advice in which he now specializes. The same pattern recurs in cantos IV and V: in canto IV Vergil gives the pilgrim a long lesson on astronomy, at the end noting that they

Vergil: "Poeta fui"

have reached the limits of his understanding ("Più non rispondo, e questo so per vero" "I will answer no more, and this much I know for true" [96]); in canto V Vergil takes advantage of Dante's involvement with the souls who have gathered around to issue one of the *Comedy*'s most famous dicta: "sta come torre ferma, che non crolla / già mai la cima per soffiar di venti" ("Stand like a firm tower, which never shakes its summit because of blowing winds [14-15]).[58] Pathos accrues to Vergil's stern speech because we can see in it his diligent attempt to imitate Cato; he has learned his lesson regarding purgatorial priorities, but to what—other than this one-time journey—can he apply his knowledge?

Canto VI contains the first correction of the *Aeneid* in the *Purgatorio*, vis-à-vis the efficacy of prayer and the immutability of justice; the pilgrim, noting the prayers of the souls they have encountered, reminds his guide of the passage in the *Aeneid* where the Sibyl answers Palinurus' supplications with the harsh injunction: "desine fata deum flecti sperare precando" ("cease to hope that heaven's decrees may be bent by praying" [VI, 376]).[59] Although Vergil responds that his writing is easily understood, his explanation is not comprehensive, and he concludes by invoking someone who will be able to answer more fully, Beatrice:

> Veramente a così alto sospetto
>   non ti fermar, se quella nol ti dice
> che lume fia tra 'l vero e lo 'ntelletto.
> Non so se 'ntendi: io dico di Beatrice . . .

Nonetheless you should not remain in so profound a doubt, but she should tell you about it who will be a light

---

[58] The Stoic flavor of these lines may be due to the fact that they derive in part from Brutus' tribute to Cato in *Pharsalia* II, 242-244, as Felicina Groppi points out in *Dante traduttore*. Other possible influences on these lines are the passages in Vergil and Seneca cited by Sapegno, *Purgatorio*, p. 48.

[59] Hollander discusses the revisionist impulses of this passage in *Il Virgilio dantesco*, pp. 113-115.

between the truth and the intellect. I do not know if you
understand: I speak of Beatrice . . .

(*Purg.* VI, 43-46)

In the *Inferno* Vergil was the "sol che sani ogne vista turbata"
("sun that heals every troubled vision" [XI, 91]); earlier in the
Purgatorio he was "quel condotto / che speranza mi dava e facea
lume" ("that leader who gave me hope and made light" [IV,
29-30]). Now Vergil's ability to "make light" is eclipsed by
Beatrice, who is herself a *lume*. This passage, which further
underscores Vergil's limits by naming the guide who will ul-
timately take over from him, prepares us for the imminent
usurpation of Vergil's role, on a smaller scale, by Sordello. The
meeting with Sordello is typical of Dante's Vergilian strategy.
Simultaneous with the first formal takeover of Vergil's role as
guide, his first explicit demotion from the position he has oc-
cupied for so long, comes one of the text's greatest tributes to
Vergil as poet and as inspiration for later poets: the scene at
the beginning of *Purgatorio* VII in which Sordello, on discov-
ering Vergil's identity, humbly embraces him "where the in-
ferior embraces" (15), calling him the glory of the Latins. Sor-
dello's attention is so exclusively dedicated to Vergil that he
never notices that the pilgrim is alive, thus differing from both
infernal and purgatorial predecessors; he learns this only in
canto VIII, two cantos after his initial meeting with the travelers,
when the pilgrim explains his situation to his friend Nino Vis-
conti. Even then, while Nino calls to Currado Malaspina to come
see what God has brought about, Sordello returns his gaze to
Vergil, for him an object of even greater wonder.[60]

[60] See *Purgatorio* VIII, 61-66. In "Le tre guide," *Italianistica*, 7 (1978), 499-533, Giuliana Nuvoli comments as follows on the meeting with Sordello: "Il legame emotivo con Virgilio, l'accompagnarsi nel cammino ai protagonisti, la partecipazione al dialogo, sono elementi che, rendendo il suo intervento [di Sordello] molto simile a quello di Stazio, contribuiscono al processo di 'estenua-zione' della figura di Virgilio" (p. 501, n. 10). The most marked similarity between Vergil's encounter with Sordello and his later encounter with Statius is that both poets attempt to embrace him: Sordello succeeds; Statius fails. The pattern of embraces in the *Purgatorio* indicates Dante's willingness to manip-

Vergil: "Poeta fui"

Between the meeting with Sordello and the meeting with Statius, the same patterns continue to operate, albeit somewhat more self-consciously: in *Purgatorio* XII, when Vergil reminds his charge that this day never dawns again, Dante comments on how accustomed he is to these admonitions ("Io era ben del suo ammonir uso / pur di non perder tempo" "I was well used to these warnings not to lose time" [85-86]); in *Purgatorio* XIII we return to the theme of Vergil the apt learner, when he correctly turns to the right and prays to the sun for guidance (13-21); in *Purgatorio* XV the theme of his inadequacies is raised once more. Here we encounter the first of the great discourses that take up the central cantos of the canticle, discourses that function like all other features of the Vergilian problematic, pointing simultaneously in two directions: in that these discourses are put in Vergil's mouth, they are a tribute to his unique wisdom and status; in that he must admit his insufficiencies in the course of delivering them, they underscore his intellectual limitations. One of the signs of Vergil's tentativeness in the discourse of canto XV is his recourse to similes as a means of explanation; later, in canto XXV, when the pilgrim inquires into the relation between man the physical entity and man the metaphysical being, Vergil is able to answer him only with analogies, and must refer him to Statius for a more rigorous logical presentation. Although in canto XV Vergil is still on surer footing than he will be in canto XXV, his use of two brief similes in lines 69 and 75 anticipates his later dependence on analogy. And, although in canto XV he does not need to turn to a purgatorial soul for assistance, he does refer the pilgrim to Beatrice at the end of his speech, as he had in discussing the efficacy of prayer in canto VI. In the last of his great speeches, that of canto XVIII, Vergil refers the pilgrim to Beatrice not once but twice, for the first time at the beginning of his discourse as well as at the end; here he explicitly describes his limited

ulate the laws of his afterworld in order to achieve his ends (as with the sinners in Hell, whose hair can be pulled if the occasion demands): the pathos of Statius' failure to embrace his master is assured by contrast with the unproblematic earlier embrace enjoyed by Sordello.

capacities as compared to hers: "Quanto ragion qui vede, / dir ti poss' io; da indi in là t'aspetta / pur a Beatrice, ch'è opra di fede" ("As far as reason sees here, I can tell you; from there on wait only for Beatrice, for it is a matter of faith" [*Purg.* XVIII, 46-48]).[61] As though to compensate for these disclaimers, the author follows up by paying homage to Vergil, still in canto XVIII, both as poet and as guide; if, to the world, he is "quell' ombra gentil per cui si noma / Pietola più che villa mantoana" ("that noble shade because of whom Pietola is named more than the city of Mantova" [82-83]), for the pilgrim he remains "quei che m'era ad ogne uopo soccorso" ("the one who was my succor in every need" [130]).

These tributes prepare us for the meeting with Statius, the episode that recapitulates all the above, furnishing—with respect to Vergil's persona—simultaneous accolade and displacement, and—with respect to his text—simultaneous citation and revision. For the moment, since *Purgatorio* XXI and XXII will be discussed in greater detail in the next section, we shall confine ourselves to noting what happens as a result of this meeting at the level of plot, in terms of Vergil's ongoing story. As we have seen, Vergil will require Statius' assistance in *Purgatorio* XXV, to explain the generation of the body and soul; thus the last great purgatorial discourse belongs to Statius rather than to Vergil. Statius' preceptorial role is anticipated in canto XXI, where he instructs the pilgrim and his guide as to the reason

---

[61] Margherita De Bonfils Templer discusses Vergil's inadequacies and the insufficiencies of reason with respect to the pilgrim's second purgatorial dream, that of the *femmina balba*, in "Il Virgilio dantesco e il secondo sogno del *Purgatorio (Purg.* XIX)," *Italica*, 59 (1982), 41-53. Vergil has a tendency, as the embodiment of *ratio*, to "rationalize" away that which he cannot explain or understand; particularly notable in this regard is the discrepancy between the violent ec-stasis of the pilgrim's first dream and Vergil's serene narrative account of the same events. Discrepancies between Vergilian expectations and purgatorial realities are noted by Christopher J. Ryan, "Virgil's Wisdom in the *Divine Comedy*," and by Jennifer Petrie ("Dante's Virgil: *Purgatorio* XXX," in *Dante Soundings: Eight Literary and Historical Essays*, ed. David Nolan [Dublin: Irish Academic Press, 1981], pp. 130-145); both point to Vergil's mistaken forecasts regarding Beatrice's behavior at the top of the mountain.

Vergil: "Poeta fui"

for the earthquake and regarding the miraculous nature of purgatorial weather. And, toward the end of canto XXII, after the two poets have been introduced and when Statius is no longer a novelty, the author manufactures a doubt for Vergil, simpler than the one that assails him in canto XXV, but enough to underscore the importance of Statius' presence. Suddenly Vergil is not sure how to proceed up the mountain; despite the many times he has faced this decision before and the fact that he resolved it correctly as far back as canto XIII, he is once more tentative: "*Io credo* ch'a lo stremo / le destre spalle volger ne convegna, / girando il monte come far solemo" ("*I think* that we should turn our right shoulders to the edge, circling the mountain as we are accustomed to do" [*Purg.* XXII, 121-123; italics mine]). Vergil's hesitation is further emphasized by the poet, who notes that, although they let usage be their guide, they proceeded with less uncertainty because of Statius' assent:

Così l'usanza fu lì nostra insegna,
   e prendemmo la via con men sospetto
   per l'assentir di quell' anima degna.

And so usage was there our guide, and we took our way
with less doubt because of the assent of that worthy soul.
                      (*Purg.* XXII, 124-126)

Nonetheless, in canto XXIII Vergil is called "lo più che padre" ("my more than father" [4]), and his irreplaceable gifts as the pilgrim's personal mentor are celebrated in canto XXVII, where he alone knows how to induce Dante to pass through the wall of fire. Here, where he looks back over their journey and reminds the pilgrim of the past dangers they have overcome together ("E se io / sovresso Gerïon ti guidai salvo, / che farò ora presso più a Dio?" "And if on Geryon I guided you safely, what shall I do now nearer to God?" [22-23]), Vergil successfully faces his last great challenge as guide.

With this, our story nears its end. The complex intertextual resonance of *Purgatorio* XXX, where Vergil becomes the only poet, besides God, whose text is incorporated without translation

Epic Resolution

into Dante's own, has been much discussed and does not require further rehearsing here.[62] Canto XXX, in which Vergil is named five times in the course of being asked to appear by the pilgrim and caused to disappear by the poet, does not, however, constitute the final Vergilian touchstone of the *Comedy*; the Roman poet is also evoked in the poem's last canticle, where he is explicitly referred to on three occasions. Vergil is introduced to the *Paradiso* in terms of his greatness as a poet. The scene is the arrival of Cacciaguida, who presents himself to Dante in the same way that Anchises presented himself to Aeneas in the Elysian fields, according to the account given in *Aeneid* VI:[63]

Sì pïa l'ombra d'Anchise si porse,
se fede merta nostra maggior musa,
quando in Eliso del figlio s'accorse.

So lovingly did the shade of Anchises reach out, if our greatest muse merits belief, when in Elysium he recognized his son.

(*Par.* XV, 25-27)

[62] The incorporated phrase from the *Aeneid*, "manibus date lilia plenis" (VI, 883), immediately follows the famous "tu Marcellus eris" whose reading reportedly caused Octavia to faint (Suetonius, *Vita Vergili*, p. 475). The line appears in the *Comedy* as "*Manibus*, oh, *date lilïa plenis!*" ("Give lilies with full hands" [*Purg.* XXX, 21]), with the addition of "oh"; although Groppi, *Dante traduttore*, suggests that the interpolated *oh* is intended to bring the line to eleven syllables, it is worth noticing that its presence also insures that no intact textual fragment belonging to another poet makes its way into the *Comedy*. Other Vergilian moments in *Purgatorio* XXX include the translation of Dido's "agnosco veteris vestigia flammae" (IV, 23) with "conosco i segni de l'antica fiamma" ("I know the signs of the ancient flame" [48]), and the evocation of a passage in the *Georgics*: as Moore notes, the triple repetition of Vergil's name in lines 49-51 imitates the placement of Eurydices' name in *Georgics* IV, 525-527 (see *Scripture and Classical Authors in Dante*, p. 21). On these "deliberately skewed" Vergilian echoes of *Purgatorio* XXX, see the comments of John Freccero, in a letter to Harold Bloom cited in *The Anxiety of Influence*, pp. 122-123, and Christopher J. Ryan, "Virgil's Wisdom in the Divine Comedy."

[63] Cacciaguida's first words to Dante, "*O sanguis meus*" ("O my blood" [*Par.* XV, 28]), also evoke *Aeneid* VI in that they repeat Anchises' words to the shade of Caesar, in which Anchises begs Caesar to refrain from Civil War and calls him "sanguis meus" (VI, 835).

Vergil: "Poeta fui"

Whatever we wish to make of the caveat "se fede merta," which seems to allude to the issue of the *Aeneid*'s credibility first touched upon in *Inferno* XIII, the phrase "nostra maggior musa" confirms Vergil's position as the supreme author of the Latin world, echoing the earlier tributes of the *Convivio* and the *Comedy*. In this instance Vergil is evoked by the poet as part of a comparison, while in the next he is named by the pilgrim, who wants to know from his ancestor the meaning of the various prophecies about his future he has heard during his journey through Hell and Purgatory, "mentre ch'io era a Virgilio congiunto" ("while I was joined to Vergil" [*Par.* XVII, 19]). The shift of perspective evidenced in this passage, where Vergil is viewed in terms of his providential function vis-à-vis the pilgrim rather than in his own right, becomes even more marked in *Paradiso* XXVI, where Vergil is mentioned only as part of a periphrasis for Limbo, defined as "that place whence your lady moved Vergil": "Quindi onde mosse tua donna Virgilio" (118). Thus, from this higher vantage, Vergil is seen exclusively as Beatrice's deputy, a stance that reminds us of his passive role throughout the poem: Vergil is always a medium, never an agent. We note, moreover, that Dante deliberately evokes his guide for the last time in the context of Limbo, a locus from which Vergil can be moved, but which he of his own initiative can never leave.[64]

[64] Vergil's radical inactivity is, in a sense, both the *contrapasso* of his sin and, as he defines it, his sin itself, which consists precisely of *non fare*: "Non per far, ma per non fare ho perduto / a veder l'alto Sol che tu disiri" ("Not for doing, but for not doing, have I lost the sight of the high Sun that you desire" [*Purg.* VII, 25-26]). Although Vergil most likely expects this self-description to reflect positively on his character, the author of the *Comedy*, who knows that "the whole Catholic tradition taught . . . the culpability of sins of omission" (Foster, "The Two Dantes," p. 179), undoubtedly intends it as a self-condemnation. Foster further notes the appositeness of St. Thomas' views on grace to Dante's Vergil, citing a passage in which the angelic doctor holds that "a man may hinder himself from receiving grace," and that "they, and they alone, are deprived of grace who themselves put an obstacle to it" ("The Two Dantes," p. 252). A passive hindering, as compared to an active searching, is precisely what is conveyed by the words "Non per far, ma per non fare," when they are taken out of their original context of vice and virtue and put into the context of grace and salvation. It should be mentioned that

Epic Resolution

Thus we come back to Vergil's passivity, but also to the sense of mystery, reminiscent perhaps of the *mysterium fidei*, generated by Beatrice's promise to praise Vergil to her Lord. After all, Trajan was brought forth from Hell by the prayers of Gregory the Great, and Heaven boasts yet another saved pagan in the person of Ripheus the Trojan, whose dedication to justice is praised in the *Aeneid*.[65] But the presence of Ripheus is not a salutary one for Vergil, since it implies that Vergil's exile is not simply the result of an impartial dogma. Dante could have reduced the tension surrounding Vergil by tacitly excluding all pagans from Heaven, or at least by including only those whose salvation, like Trajan's, was buttressed by medieval legend.[66]

---

this point is made, and these passages from St. Thomas are cited, in G. Busnelli, "La colpa del 'non fare' degl' infedeli negativi," *Studi danteschi*, 23 (1938), 79-97. One further point: Vergil's ostentatiously monasyllabic *verso tronco*, "e per null' altro rio / lo ciel perdei che per non aver fé" (*Purg.* VII, 8; italics mine) would seem to offer a stylistic correlative to his condition of being eternally cut off, *tronco*.

[65] Ripheus is mentioned three times in *Aeneid* II, as part of a carefully orchestrated crescendo of events: he is seen first with a group of young Trojan warriors around Aeneas, among whom is Coroebus, in love with Cassandra (II, 339); then, at Coroebus' instigation, they don the weapons of some fallen Greeks and sally forth among their enemies (II, 394); finally, still in their Greek spoils, they rush to rescue Cassandra and are killed. Only now does Vergil describe Ripheus, in a way intended to heighten the pathos of his premature death: "cadit et Rhipeus, iustissimus unus / qui fuit in Teucris et servantissimus aequi / (dis aliter visum)" ("Ripheus too falls, the most just among the Trojans and most observant of the right—the gods willed otherwise" [II, 426-428]). Paratore has noted that, by saving Ripheus, Dante undoes Vergil's *dis aliter visum*, and corrects the pagan gods' callous indifference to Ripheus' virtue; see "Il canto XX del *Paradiso*," *Tradizione e struttura in Dante*, pp. 281-314, and also Marguerite Chiarenza, "Boethian Themes in Dante's Reading of Virgil," *Stanford Italian Studies*, 3 (1983), 25-35.

[66] The total omission of pagans from Paradise would not have been problematic, since, according to Foster, contemporary theologians tended to ignore the doctrine of implicit grace: "Catholic theology by and large did not much concern itself with the ultimate destiny, in God's sight, of the pagan world whether before or since the coming of Christ. . . . The concept itself of *fides implicita* was not lacking . . . but it was hardly a central preoccupation of theologians, nor, in particular, do its implications for an assessment of the spiritual state of the world outside Christendom seem to have been taken very seriously" ("The

Vergil: "Poeta fui"

By placing in Heaven a bit player from Vergil's text, on the sole recommendation of Vergil's text, while excluding the author of that text, Dante does the opposite: he draws attention to the intentionality of Vergil's exclusion.[67] Ripheus' appearance is intended to shock; the Trojan hero is presented last among the six souls who make up the eye of the eagle, and he is the only one of the six to be introduced with a question:

> Chi crederebbe giù nel mondo errante
> che Rifëo Troiano in questo tondo
> fosse la quinta de le luci sante?
>
> Who down in the erring world would believe that Ripheus the Trojan was the fifth of the holy lights in this circle?
> (*Par.* XX, 67-69)

This is a nonrhetorical rhetorical question, for few indeed would expect that Ripheus could be saved while his *auctor* was damned. Ripheus functions in this respect like an arrow pointing directly at Vergil, a function Dante makes even more explicit in his explanation of Ripheus' miraculous baptism. The Trojan was baptized by the three theological virtues, who are specifically referred to as the same three ladies seen by the pilgrim at the

---

Two Dantes," pp. 171-172). In other words, Dante's personal concern with this issue is such that he actively courts difficulties by including pagans in heaven, when it would have been far easier, and theologically not unorthodox, to have bypassed the question of pagan salvation altogether.

[67] The intentionality of Vergil's exclusion becomes an overt issue with the appearance of the saved Cato in *Purgatorio* I; the issue is kept alive by the reference to the salvation of Trajan in *Purgatorio* X, 74-75, and—after the crucial encounter with Statius—it culminates with the presence of Ripheus in heaven. This is a cause of concern to Henri Hauvette, "Les Païens appelés par Dante au Paradis: Pourquoi Virgile en est exclu," *Nouvelle Revue d'Italie*, 18 (1921), 48-54; in order to account for Vergil's inexplicable exclusion from the roster of saved pagans, Hauvette hypothesizes that Dante conceived of saving some pagans only after writing the *Inferno*, and that it was by then too late to save Vergil. Regarding Paratore's claim that Dante's treatment of Ripheus is "l'ultimo e altissimo omaggio tributato da Dante al suo Virgilio" ("Il canto XX del *Paradiso*," p. 281), I would agree only with the caveat that it is the greatest of Dante's *double-edged* tributes to Vergil.

right wheel of Beatrice's chariot in the Earthly Paradise: "Quelle tre donne li fur per battesmo / che tu vedesti da la destra rota" ("Those three ladies stood for his baptism whom you saw by the right wheel" [*Par.* XX, 127-128]). This reference is designed to take us back mentally to the allegorical procession in the Earthly Paradise, to the place where "Tre donne in giro da la destra rota / venian danzando" ("Three ladies around the right wheel came dancing" [*Purg.* XXIX, 121-122]). At this point in *Purgatorio* XXIX, the virtues dance about the empty chariot awaiting Beatrice's arrival; somewhat earlier in the same canto, we see Vergil for the last time, as the pilgrim, awed by the marching candelabras, turns to his guide: "Io mi rivolsi d'ammirazion pieno / al buon Virgilio" ("I turned around full of amazement to the good Vergil" [55-56]). But Vergil, no longer *duca* or *maestro*, has no advice or comment to offer, since his amazement is as great as the pilgrim's: "ed esso mi rispuose / con vista carca di stupor non meno" ("and he looked back at me with a face laden with no less wonder" [56-57]). The evocation of the purgatorial procession in the heaven of justice thus establishes a last Vergilian paradox: Vergil is a sage, and Ripheus is not, but Vergil's ignorance—his *stupor*—stands in eternal contrast to Ripheus' grace-given knowledge, the knowledge that led him away from Limbo, to baptism and ultimate salvation.

Statius: "Per te poeta fui"

There is no episode that dramatizes the tensions of Vergil's predicament more fully than that of Statius, the Silver Latin poet who appears to the travelers as a newly liberated soul at the beginning of *Purgatorio* XXI. There are, moreover, few issues that have puzzled scholars more than that of Statius' Christianity: "many wonder why our very Christian poet places Statius, a non-Christian, here," says Benvenuto, who offers the explanation that "the poet could conjecture from many signs—

Statius: "Per te poeta fui"

ex multis indiciis—that Statius was a Christian."[68] Benvenuto's indicia include the fact that Statius witnessed the persecution of the martyrs, along with their miracles (and, the argument goes, if Vergil who lived before Christ sensed something about Him from the songs of the Sibyl, how much more would Statius have felt, living in the time of Domitian); he further adduces a line from the *Thebaid*, and the fact that Statius was "honestissimus et moralissimus in omnibus suis dictis." The pattern that Benvenuto establishes has prevailed into our century, with critics either pointing to the propitious climate in which Statius lived, or, more frequently, searching the *Thebaid* for passages that Dante may have construed as witnesses to his latent Christianity.[69] Some, but not all, follow Benvenuto's analysis to its

[68] Benvenuto's remarks on Statius, as cited here and below, are from Lacaita, vol. IV, pp. 3-4.

[69] The line pointed to by Benvenuto, "primus in orbe deos fecit timor" ("fear first created gods in the world" [III, 661]), is not particularly appropriate, not least because it is spoken by Capaneus. Scevola Mariotti, "Il cristianesimo di Stazio in Dante secondo il Poliziano," in *Letteratura e critica: Studi in onore di N. Sapegno* (Rome: Bulzoni, 1975), vol. II, pp. 149-161, surveys both the critics who have sought clues in the *Thebaid* and the passages on which they have concentrated. Mariotti himself, who begins as an elucidator of Poliziano rather than Dante, concludes that Poliziano's solution to the problem of Statius' Christianity is the best and should be reinstated: Poliziano points to the passage in Book IV in which Tiresias invokes a "triplicis mundi summum" ("the supreme being of the triple world" [516]), and finds in Tiresias' words a covert declaration of Statius' own faith. A slightly different approach is that of C. S. Lewis, "Dante's Statius," *Medium Aevum*, 25 (1956), 133-139, who claims that the *Thebaid* is spiritually more akin to the Christian Middle Ages than the *Aeneid*; he points to Jupiter's almost monotheistic power, the poem's fundamental pessimism regarding human nature, its sexual prudery, the invective against divination, and the contrast between the ethical personifications (*Virtus, Pietas, Clementia*) on the one side and the diabolical Olympians on the other. Finally, there is the argument that connects Statius' Christianity to an allegorical commentary of the *Thebaid* attributed to Fulgentius, vigorously sustained by Giorgio Padoan in "Teseo 'figura Redemptoris' e il cristianesimo di Stazio"; in the absence of any indication that Dante knew this commentary, Padoan makes much of Dante's Fulgentian reading of the *Aeneid* in the *Convivio*. My problems with this argument are twofold: (1) the allegorical reading of the classics found in the *Convivio* is replaced, in the *Comedy*, with a historical approach; (2) if an allegorical commentary were of such import in Dante's assessments, would

Epic Resolution

conclusion, in which the commentator puts his earlier arguments to one side in order to arrive at a purely textual reason for Statius' Christianity: "but whether he was a Christian, or whether he was not, I care little, since subtly and by necessity the poet feigns this because of the many issues he could not treat without a Christian poet, as will appear in canto XXV and elsewhere."[70] In this remarkable passage Benvenuto goes, as he so often does, to what I believe is the heart of the matter, which is that Dante's fiction at this point *requires* a figure just like Statius. In fact, Dante needs a foil to Vergil, a role for which the Christianized Statius is carefully tailored, as the character who can best bring out the ambivalence of Vergil's situation: whereas Statius the epic poet is Vergil's inferior, his disciple, the Statius who became Christian is Vergil's superior, his teacher.

While Vergil was chosen for the *Comedy* for himself, because of the hold he exerted over Dante's imagination, Statius was chosen for Vergil, because of his mathematical suitability for the equation Dante is establishing. If one thinks of the group

---

he not have saved Vergil, whom he explicitly reads in an allegorical key in the *Convivio*, rather than Statius? Padoan also discusses the tradition of Theseus as a *figura Christi* in the light of the fact that Theseus is the peacemaker at the end of the *Thebaid*; this argument, along with the others mentioned above, could in my opinion have been used by Dante to support an *a priori* decision to make Statius Christian, but would not by itself have induced him to do so. In fact, Padoan's demonstration regarding the frequency with which classical authors were Christianized in the Middle Ages, so that biographies like the one Dante ascribes to Statius became veritable topoi, seems to support my arguments in favor of a purely textual solution to the problem: the question is why did Dante choose specifically Statius, and the answer lies not in the usual texts that were available to him but not to us, but in the economy of his poem.

[70] Critics who have affirmed the arbitrary nature of Statius' Christianity include Pézard, who calls it "une invention arbitraire" in "Rencontres de Dante et de Stace," *Bibliothéque d'Humanisme et Renaissance*, 14 (1952), 10-28, and Renucci, *Dante, Disciple et Juge du Monde Gréco-Latin*, who writes: "ce n'est pas assez dire que le Stace du *Purgatoire* est un personnage historique retouché, interpreté, refondu: il est proprement créé" (p. 334). Renucci's position is endorsed by Alessandro Ronconi, "L'incontro di Stazio e Virgilio," *Cultura e scuola* 4, nos. 13-14 (1965), 566-571, and Giorgio Brugnoli, "Stazio in Dante," *Cultura neolatina*, 29 (1969), 117-125, who considers Statius' redemption to be "attuata da Dante coscientemente contro tutta la tradizione" (p. 119).

Statius: "Per te poeta fui"

of poets in Dante's earlier texts from whom Statius was picked for the undertaking of *Purgatorio* XXI and XXII, he seems by far the most plausible.[71] He lived during the alleged religious persecutions of Domitian, which Dante has him cite as an incentive to his conversion, a conversion whose basis in fact Dante neatly avoids confronting by having Statius declare that he was a secret Christian, who outwardly practiced paganism: "ma per paura chiuso cristian fu'mi, / lungamente mostrando paganesmo" ("but for fear I was a hidden Christian, long making show of paganism" [*Purg.* XXII, 90-91]); for this Dante, buttressing his inventions with the invented reality of his poem, has him spend four hundred years on the terrace of sloth. The prodigality that confines Statius to the fifth terrace for half a millennium is a sin that serves many Dantesque purposes: it allows Dante to revise the *Aeneid* to Christian ends, by having Statius construe a Vergilian attack on avarice as though it were an appeal to moderation; and, by inserting the Aristotelian scheme of the golden mean into the theological scheme based on the seven deadly sins, it allows him to further accentuate the thematics of the Golden Age—seen as a period of balance and due measure in all things—which he is at pains to develop in these cantos.[72] Prodigality is, moreover, a suitable sin to

---

[71] Brugnoli points out that no other member of the *regulati poetae* was available for Statius' role, since Lucan was a suicide and Ovid was "Venus' clerk" ("Stazio in Dante," p. 119).

[72] Statius' translation of "quid non mortalia pectora cogis, / auri sacra fames!" ("To what do you not drive mortal hearts, accursed hunger for gold!" [*Aen.* III, 56-57]) as "Per che [Perché] non reggi tu, o sacra fame / de l'oro, l'appetito de' mortali?" (*Purg.* XXII, 40-41) has traditionally divided commentators into two camps: while one attempts to bring Statius' Italian into line with the original, the other accepts the changed significance of the Italian as intentional. In recent times, the first camp has been represented by Sapegno, whose suggested reading "per quali opere, a quali malvagità, non conduci tu, o esecranda fame dell'oro, l'appetito dei mortali?" (*Purgatorio*, p. 242) requires not only the shift from "Perché" to "Per che," but also that the terms "reggi" and "sacra" be assigned highly uncharacteristic meanings: *reggere* for Dante normally means "to direct" or "to govern," not "to lead," and *sacro* never means "accursed" in Italian (see the articles on *reggere* and *sacro* in the *Enciclopedia Dantesca*, respectively by Luigi Blasucci and Alessandro Niccoli). Singleton and Petrocchi

assign to a poet one respects: like Bertran's liberality in the *Convivio*, it has a poetic flavor, and, from a theological point of view, it is less offensive than avarice;[73] Dante may also have felt justified in his choice of sins by a passage describing Statius' extreme poverty in Juvenal, a poet he goes out of his way to associate with Statius in canto XXI.[74] But, finally, the best reason

---

both follow Sapegno (with the result that Petrocchi's edition reads "Per che" instead of "Perché") because they are reluctant to accept a deliberate misreading of Vergil's text on Dante's part. I find more critically sophisticated the oft-quoted remark written by Francesco da Buti à propos of this passage: "li Autori usano l'altrui autorità arrecarle a loro sentenzia quando commodamente vi si possano arrecare, non ostante che colui che l'ha ditta l'abbia posta in altra sentenzia" (*La Divina Commedia nella figurazione artistica e nel secolare commento*, vol. II, p. 450). Among the moderns, this position is sustained by Renucci, *Dante, Disciple et Juge du Monde Gréco-Latin*, who claims that Vergil's "auri sacra fames" is "providentiellement prise à contresens" (p. 334); further endorsers include Ronconi, "L'incontro di Stazio e Virgilio," Esposito, "Dante traduttore di Virgilio," and Hollander, *Il Virgilio dantesco*. Conclusive arguments in favor of this reading are presented by R. A. Shoaf, " 'Auri sacra fames' and the Age of Gold (*Purg.* XXII, 40-41 and 148-150)," *Dante Studies*, 96 (1978), 195-199, who places Dante's "sacred hunger for gold" within the context of the Golden Age, in which, as Dante specifies at the end of canto XXII, hunger made even acorns savory. The notion of a moderate and virtuous hunger is thus attested to by Dante within this canto; far from being the peculiarity some modern critics have suggested (the early commentators have no difficulty interpreting "sacra fame" in terms of the golden mean), "the entire setting is one of properly regulated 'hungering' " (H. D. Austin, "*Aurea Justitia*: A Note on *Purgatorio*, XXII, 40 f.," *MLN*, 48 [1933], 327-330). Indeed, the theme of the Golden Age finds its purgatorial focus in this very canto by way of the quotation of Vergil's fourth Eclogue: the souls on Mount Purgatory are engaged precisely in returning to a new "primo tempo umano" (*Purg.* XXII, 71), and thus in establishing a new Golden Age.

[73] In *Summa Theologiae*, 2a2ae. q. 119, a. 3, St. Thomas asks whether prodigality is a more serious sin than avarice, and concludes that it is less serious.

[74] In the seventh Satire, Juvenal describes Statius as so poor that he had to sell his play *Agave* to keep from starving (82-87). Although Juvenal's point is that all poets are poor, Benvenuto comments that this passage may have led Dante to believe that Statius was prodigal with his means, since he knew of Statius' popularity. Brugnoli argues for Dante's knowledge of this satire in "Stazio in Dante"; he finds especially telling Dante's use, in a nearby canto, of the verb *esurire*, "to desire to eat," "be hungry," used by Juvenal with

Statius: "Per te poeta fui"

for using Statius as a testimonial to Vergil in the *Comedy* is provided by the historical Statius himself, who not only imitated the *Aeneid* throughout the *Thebaid*, but who (perhaps uniquely) ends his major work with a closing apostrophe to his text, in which he draws attention to the revered forerunner that will always eclipse it: "vive, precor; nec tu divinam Aeneida tempta, / sed longe sequere et vestigia semper adora" ("Live, I pray, nor rival the divine *Aeneid*, but follow at a distance and always revere its footsteps" [*Thebaid* XII, 816-817]).[75] The Statius of the *Comedy* is only speaking with the same self-effacement as the original when he says that to have lived while Vergil was alive he would consent to an extra year of purgation (*Purg.* XXI, 100-102); indeed, the closing passage of the *Thebaid* almost seems to give Dante proleptic license to treat its author as a secondary figure with respect to the author of the *Aeneid*, and in this spirit to make whatever biographical or historical alterations are required to throw the character of Vergil into greater relief.

---

reference to Statius' potential starvation, and by Dante in his paraphrasing of the beatitude "Beati qui esuriunt et sitiunt iustitiam" ("Blessed are they who hunger and thirst for justice"). (We note, in passing, that Dante's rendering, "esurïendo sempre quanto è giusto" ["hungering always as much as is right" (*Purg.* XXIV, 154)], is an apt gloss on the "sacra fame / de l'oro" of *Purgatorio* XXII, since it speaks precisely of a controlled, and therefore "sacred," hunger.) Dante goes out of his way to introduce Juvenal into the problematic by having Vergil tell Statius that he first learned of his affection through the author of the *Satires*, who told him of Statius' admiration when he arrived in Limbo (*Purg.* XXII, 13-15). On Statius' prodigality and Juvenal, see also Maurizio Bettini, "Fonti letterarie e modelli semiologici in Dante: come Dante utilizzò alcuni autori latini," *Studi danteschi*, 52 (1979-1980), 189-211. In "Dante and the Latin Poets," Wicksteed notes that "Juvenal is the only contemporary author who mentions Statius, and he speaks of the *dulcedo* of his verse" (p. 177); once more, then, Dante constructs a variant of real life in his afterlife.

[75] Chaucer's imitation of the ending of the *Thebaid* in *Troilus and Criseyde* (V, 1786-1792) is mediated through the closing passages of the *Filocolo*: like Boccaccio, Chaucer refers to a general canon of classical precursors, whereas the *Thebaid* is concerned solely with its one great rival. Padoan points out that Statius' reference to the *Aeneid* as a "divina fiamma" (*Purg.* XXI, 95) echoes the *Thebaid*'s "divinam Aeneida" ("Il canto XXI del *Purgatorio*," *Nuove letture dantesche* [Florence: Le Monnier, 1970], vol. IV, pp. 327-353).

Epic Resolution

If Statius, who never in the past was treated as different from any of the other *regulati poetae*, is now differentiated from his peers in so important a respect as his Christian faith, it is because he is composed, as Renucci puts it, *"ad majorem Vergilii gloriam."*[76] But, as we know, whatever works to Vergil's advantage in Dante's poem also works simultaneously to his detriment, and so it is that Statius' presence both glorifies Vergil and undercuts him. Statius quotes the *Aeneid* only in a providential mistranslation, and prefaces his more correct rendition of the fourth Eclogue with the simile of Vergil as the light-bearer, which specifies that he was unable to benefit from his own intuition: "che porta il lume dietro e sé non giova, / ma dopo sé fa le persone dotte" ("who carries the light behind him and helps not himself, but makes those who come after him wise" [*Purg*. XXII, 68-69]). Statius is both a living tribute to Vergil, and a means of putting the *maestro* into perspective; since he exists in the poem as a function of Vergil, the encounter with Statius serves retrospectively to clarify the value assigned to Vergil, not least in the original encounter with the pilgrim. The language with which Statius introduces himself is intended to echo Vergil's language of *Inferno* I; the parallels between the two encounters are exact.[77] Vergil's first words, we remember, are entirely circumscribed by human experience and endeavor: "Non omo, omo già fui" ("Not a man, a man I once was" [*Inf*. I, 67]) he begins, and continues by locating himself as an individual in time, fashioning his historical coordinates with respect to genealogy, place of origin, political setting, domicile, religion, and vocation. Statius, on the other hand, says "O frati miei, Dio vi dea pace" ("O my brothers, may God grant you peace" [*Purg*. XXI, 13]), and does not address the topic of his earthly identity until Vergil specifically requests, sixty-nine lines later, that he do so.[78] In reply, Statius identifies himself with

---

[76] *Dante, Disciple et Juge du Monde Gréco-Latin*, p. 333.

[77] Paratore speaks in general terms of parallelisms between *Inferno* I and *Purgatorio* XXI; see *Tradizione e struttura in Dante*, p. 72.

[78] On the importance of Statius' initial greeting, see Denise Heilbronn, "The Prophetic Role of Statius in Dante's Purgatory," *Dante Studies*, 95 (1977), 53-67.

the time of Titus, who, he says, with God's help avenged the death of Christ; " 'l buon Tito" (*Purg.* XXI, 82) echoes " 'l buono Augusto" (*Inf.* I, 71). But whereas the conquests of Titus are presented within a providential context, Vergil places the reign of Augustus "nel tempo de li dèi falsi e bugiardi" ("in the time of the false and lying gods" [72]). The presentation of the two Emperors thus forecasts the essential difference between the two poets, a difference further reflected in the sharp contrast between the only two occurrences of the adjective *famoso* in the poem: on the one hand is Vergil, "famoso saggio" (*Inf.* I, 89); on the other is Statius, "famoso assai, ma non con fede ancora" ("famous enough, but not yet with faith" [*Purg.* XXI, 87]). With its strong caesura and adversative, this line retrospectively qualifies and limits the value of Vergil's earthly fame.

Purgatorio XXI is for Statius what *Inferno* I is for Vergil: a debut canto, containing the drama of first presentation and recognition. Its sequel, *Purgatorio* XXII, is a more technical canto, in that the dramatic impact is muted and the emphasis is placed instead on making relations more precise and tightening the focus. In this sense, *Purgatorio* XXII corresponds to *Inferno* IV, where Vergil's identity is clarified with respect to his peers; it should not surprise us, therefore, to find that canto XXII bears all the hallmarks of a second Limbo. Thus, when Vergil tells Statius that he has loved him ever since Juvenal arrived in Limbo with the news of his affection ("da l'ora che tra noi discese / nel limbo de lo 'nferno Giovenale" "from the hour in which Juvenal descended among us in the Limbo of Hell" [*Purg.* XXII, 13-14]), he is not only naming the first new classical poet to be introduced into the poem since canto IV, but also using the word *limbo*, which occurs only here and in the fourth canto of the *Inferno*. A few lines later, Vergil questions Statius about his presumed avarice, asking how such a sin could reside in Statius' breast, "tra cotanto senno" ("amid such wisdom" [23]); his use of the expression "tra cotanto senno" echoes its only other appearance in the poem, in the celebrated verse of *Inferno* IV in which Dante marks his inclusion by the great poets of antiquity: "sì ch'io fui sesto tra cotanto senno" ("so that I was sixth amid such wisdom" [102]). As the canto progresses, its characteristics as a purgatorial Limbo become more marked. In line 97 Statius begins questioning Vergil as to the whereabouts of their fellow poets, and the result is the only long list of classical poets and personages from their poems outside of *Inferno* IV, a catalogue that comprises both Latin and Greek dramatists and poets.[79] In his reply, Vergil specifies that those whom Statius has mentioned are to be found in the first circle of Hell, "con quel Greco / che le Muse lattar più ch'altri mai" ("with that Greek whom the Muses suckled more than any other" [101-102]); this reference to Homer is another signpost linking this canto to Limbo, where Homer is first described. Finally, we should note that in both these cantos poetry is discussed as a craft by its practitioners: in *Inferno* IV, the *bella scola* discusses matters that Dante prefers not to relate, but which were appropriate to the place and the company, while in *Purgatorio* XXII he walks behind his guides, listening to the discourses "ch'a poetar mi davano intelletto" ("which gave me understanding in the making of poetry" [129]).

If *Inferno* IV defines Vergil as *l'altissimo poeta*, *Purgatorio* XXII defines Statius as a poet who is less high, but more Christian. In fact, one of the functions of this purgatorial Limbo is to present Statius as the one classical poet in the poem who does not belong to the real Limbo; his uniqueness in this regard becomes more striking as the canto proceeds and we realize that all his peers are in the first circle of Hell. Dante stresses the contrast between this re-created Limbo and the original: when Vergil asks Statius by what means Christianity was revealed to him, he asks "qual sole o quai candele / ti stenebraron" ("what sun or what candles took you from the shadows" [*Purg.* XXII, 61-62]); the use of the verb *stenebraron* reminds us of Limbo, where the *tenebre* are barely kept at bay by a light "ch'emisperio di tenebre vincia" ("that conquered a hemisphere of shadows"

---

[79] Paratore refers to this section of the dialogue between Vergil and Statius as "un'appendice del c. IV dell'*Inferno*" (*Tradizione e struttura in Dante*, p. 38); on this aspect of *Purgatorio* XXII, see Roberto Mercuri, "Terenzio nostro antico," *Cultura neolatina*, 29 (1969), 84-116.

Statius: "Per te poeta fui"

[*Inf*. IV, 69]). Statius has come out of the shadows, and out of Limbo, as he says in his reply, because of that luciferous text, the fourth Eclogue, whose apposite passage regarding earthly renewal at the hands of a celestial progeny he now cites, concluding with the great declaration of his indebtedness to Vergil: "Per te poeta fui, per te cristiano" ("Through you I was a poet, through you a Christian" [73]). In these words, Statius not only defines himself in relation to Vergil, but also becomes the first character in the poem after Vergil to appropriate the noun *poeta*, which heretofore has referred almost exclusively to the author of the *Aeneid*. In fact, the word makes its first appearance in the poem in *Inferno* I, when Vergil says "Poeta fui" (73); after that, it is applied once to Homer, "poeta sovrano" (*Inf*. IV, 88), and once, in lower Hell, to classical poets in general.[80] Otherwise, it is used only for Vergil; indeed, *poeta* gives the appearance of being little more than an alternate for *duca* or *maestro*, rather than a term whose use Dante is so carefully monitoring. In *Purgatorio* XXII, however, this Vergilian tag is adopted by Statius, to whom it will continue to refer in the succeeding cantos, and Vergil is—if not quite displaced—certainly joined. Where there had been one *poeta* guiding the pilgrim, suddenly there are two, a fact that is duly registered by some simple but telling phrases that appear toward the end of canto XXII: "Tacevansi ambedue già li poeti" ("Already both the poets were silent" [115]), and "Li due poeti a l'alber s'appressaro" ("The two poets approached the tree" [139]). *Poeta*, the term used to refer to Vergil for fifty-five cantos, is now replaced by *li due poeti* as part of a textual design intended to reflect the historical realities of poetic influence and appropri-

[80] The reference, "secondo che i poeti hanno per fermo" (*Inf*. XXIX, 63), although generic, regards Ovid in particular, since it is in the context of the legend of the Myrmidons. Interestingly, the *Inferno*'s one use of *poetare*, which functions according to the same rules as the noun, also applies to Ovid ("converte poetando" [XXV, 99]). If *poeta* is a badge of honor in the *Comedy*, Dante has accorded it to Ovid in a backhanded way that typifies his treatment of this poet; he singles out Ovid only under the generic cover of "i poeti."

ation: Vergil, a supreme but non-Christian poet, is replaced by Statius, a lesser poet but a Christian.

Poeta is not the only Vergilian term from *Inferno* I that Dante now assigns to Statius in order to mark the watershed in Vergil's status brought about by the advent of Christianity. *Saggio* and *savio*, used as both nouns and adjectives, observe a similar pattern within the *Comedy*: both forms are associated with Vergil from the beginning of the poem, where Vergil is called a *saggio* in canto I, and *savio* in canto II. In *Inferno* IV the term is shared with the other classical poets, who as a group are called "questi savi" (110). The term is then applied only to Vergil throughout the *Inferno* until canto XXIV, where there is a general reference to poets and authorities of antiquity as "li gran savi" (106).[81] In the *Purgatorio* there are two indeterminate references ("scorta saggia" [IV, 39], "fatene saggi" [V, 30]), and two references to non-poets who are singled out for displays not of wisdom but of its contrary; otherwise, *saggio* and *savio* pertain only to Vergil, until the arrival of Statius.[82] At that point, Dante uses the terms to suggest a subtle counterpoint in emotional and intellectual allegiances: for instance, he chooses the moment immediately after Statius' speech on the weather, his first bravura performance as wise man and potential guide, to remind us of the wisdom of the guide who has served so well until now; thus, we find not a commendation of Statius at the end of his speech, but an emphatic return to Vergil: "E 'l savio duca . . ." (*Purg.* XXI, 76). This bow to Vergil is only a temporary

---

[81] Again the generic reference "li gran savi" hides a specific reference to Ovid, whose text was most likely Dante's chief source of information regarding the phoenix. Thus Ovid is accorded both badges of honor, *poeta* and *savio*, both times generically.

[82] "Savia non fui" ("I was not wise" [*Purg.* XIII, 109]), says Sapia of herself, while Averroes is described as someone wiser than Dante who made the same mistake regarding the formation of the human soul: "quest' è tal punto, / che più savio di te fé già errante" ("this is such a point that it already caused a wiser than you to err" [*Purg.* XXV, 62-63]). Thus, the two non-poets to be modified by this adjective are both *non savi*. The *Paradiso*'s two uses of *savio / saggio* are both generic. See also Michele D'Andria, "Dell'uso di 'savio' e 'saggio' nella *Divina Commedia*," *Aspetti letterari*, 8 (1968), 9-18.

Statius: "Per te poeta fui"

postponing of reality, however, for, like *poeta, savio* is now an appellation Vergil must share. In the same way that *il poeta* becomes *li due poeti*, *'l savio* becomes the plural "i savi" (XXIII, 8), referring, of course, to Vergil and Statius. On the other hand, when the three travelers reach the wall of fire that separates the last terrace from the Earthly Paradise, it is Vergil, not Statius, who knows how to persuade the recalcitrant pilgrim, reminding him of the beloved who waits, like Thisbe, on the other side of the wall. We note that Vergil now asks Statius, who had been between him and Dante, to go behind the pilgrim, with the result that Vergil is once more the pilgrim's sole guide; moreover, Vergil's wisdom in dealing with his charge is marked by a last emphatic testimonial: on hearing Beatrice's name, Dante turns "al savio duca" (*Purg.* XXVII, 41). The term is used only twice more: again in canto XXVII, where we find "li miei saggi" (69), and finally in canto XXXIII, where Beatrice beckons to her companions: "me e la donna e 'l savio che ristette" ("me and the lady and the sage who remained" [15]). This last appearance of *'l savio* is emblematic of Statius' role; for although he is "the sage who remained," the phrasing points to the sage who does not remain—to Vergil. Thus, words that literally refer to Statius work to eclipse him and to conjure up Vergil, showing us one more time that Statius exists in the poem less for himself than for another.[83]

Statius, then, is a mediated figure, whose triumphs are less his successes than someone else's failures. Perhaps this fact is best clarified by those Vergilian terms from *Inferno* I that his

[83] Thus, Padoan writes of *Purgatorio* XXI and XXII that although they are "per antonomasia, i canti di Stazio;" nonetheless "il personaggio centrale non è Stazio, è Virgilio" ("Il canto XXI del *Purgatorio*," p. 353), and J. H. Whitfield considers it the task of these cantos, having first created a gap between Vergil and Statius, "to afford to Virgil the most flattering of compensatory poetic homage" ("Dante and Statius: *Purgatorio* XXI-XXII," in *Dante Soundings*, pp. 113-129). We note, moreover, a suggestive inversion in Dante's handling of the recognition scenes of *Inferno* I and *Purgatorio* XXI: while in the *Inferno* the poet being introduced (Vergil) receives the tribute (from Dante), in the *Purgatorio* the poet being introduced (Statius) pays the tribute (to Vergil). The result is that both times attention is focused on Vergil.

Epic Resolution

successor is not allowed to appropriate, the key terms *volume* and *autore*. Both belong to the pilgrim's initial accolade to his newly found guide, in which he speaks of the love with which he has searched "lo tuo volume" (84), and declares "Tu se' lo mio maestro e 'l mio autore" ("You are my master and my author" [85]). As compared to *poeta* and *saggio*, terms that describe a trajectory or progression, *volume* and *autore* are used in only two contexts: in *Inferno* for Vergil, and in *Paradiso* for God. The transition is so immense that it both heightens Vergil, the only poet who is an *autore* and whose book is a *volume*, and shrinks him by comparison with that other *autore*, Who is God, and that other *volume*, which is God's book (*volume* is used variously in the last canticle, but always with relation to texts "written by" God, for instance the book of the future, the book of justice, the universe gathered into one volume).[84] Moreover, when God is termed an author, He is not " 'l mio autore," but the "verace autore" (*Par.* XXVI, 40). It can hardly be coincidental that God should be called the *verace autore* precisely in *Paradiso* XXVI, where language and textuality are such prominent issues, and where Vergil's name last appears as part of a periphrasis for Limbo.[85] The lesson inherent in such a juxtaposition is obvious, but at the same time that Vergil will ulti-

---

[84] Robert Hollander discusses *autore* and *volume* in "Dante's Use of *Aeneid* I in *Inferno* I and II," *Comparative Literature*, 20 (1968), 142-156. On the image of the universe "legato con amore in un volume" ("bound by love into one volume" [*Par.* XXXIII, 86]), see John Ahearn, "Binding the Book: Hermeneutics and Manuscript Production in *Paradiso* 33," *PMLA*, 97 (1982), 800-809.

[85] *Paradiso* XXVI constructs a discourse based on the juxtaposition of human versus divine authority in the realm of textuality; thus, in the same way that Vergil, " 'l mio autore," gives way to God, the "verace autore," so the "grande autorità" of the poets and philosophers of Limbo yields to the "autorità che quinci scende" ("the authority that descends from here" [*Par.* XXVI, 26]), i.e. Scripture. *Paradiso* XXVI's double reference to divine authorities (the "autoritadi" of line 47 are also scriptural) is intended to contrast with the only other use of *autorità* in the poem, that of *Inferno* IV, 113, cited above. On canto XXVI and the *De Vulgari Eloquentia*, see Pier Vincenzo Mengaldo, "Appunti sul canto XXVI del *Paradiso*," in *Linguistica e retorica di Dante* (Pisa: Nistri-Lischi, 1978), pp. 223-246.

mately be reduced to a grammatical aside by the *verace autore*, we should remember that he is unique in being chosen for so extreme—and dangerous—a compliment. He is the only poet considered worthy of being compared and being found wanting, his are the only poetic shoulders strong enough to fail to carry such a burden. There is, in the *Comedy*, only one *autore* besides God, even if he is not a true one, and only one earthly author's *volume*. Statius and his text have no place in this world of extreme compliments, and extreme failures; Statius serves Dante's purpose precisely in that he is always secondary, never primary, and as a figure in the *Comedy* he is therefore always mediated, modified, and deflected: a *per te poeta, 'l savio che ristette*.

Dante: "ritornerò poeta"

If Statius replaces Vergil in *Purgatorio* XXII when he appropriates for himself (albeit in modified form) the name *poeta*, the final displacement is accomplished by Dante, when he becomes the only *poeta* of the last canticle, announcing in *Paradiso* XXV that he shall return as poet to Florence to receive the laurel crown.[86] Although that hope was never fulfilled, the impact of the phrase "ritornerò poeta" remains undiminished at a textual level, since it reveals the arc Dante has inscribed into his poem through the restricted use of the word *poeta*: the poetic mantle passes from the classical poets, essentially Vergil, to a transitional poet, whose Christianity is disjunct from his poetic practice (and hence the verse with its neat caesura: "Per te poeta fui, per te cristiano"), to the poet whose Christian faith is a *sine qua non* of his poetics. This is Dante himself, the *poeta* of *Paradiso*, a label that also carries some implications of a technical nature, for Dante's restricted use of seemingly generic termi-

[86] *Poeta* occurs in a general sense in the invocation of *Paradiso* I, in a context which clearly points to Dante; he is deploring the rarity with which either rulers or poets—"o cesare o poeta" (29)—seek the laurel crown. It is used again only in the celebrated opening of *Paradiso* XXV. *Poetare* occurs only once (*Par.* XXX, 32) and refers to Dante.

nology has rendered its application highly significant.[87] Thus, we note that no lyric poet is called *poeta* in the *Comedy*, just as none is ever called *saggio* or *savio*, an omission that gains in interest if we consider that Guinizzelli is a *saggio* in the *Vita Nuova*. In the *Comedy*, such terminology is reserved for the figures to whom Dante also assigns the responsibilities of teaching and guiding the pilgrim, narrative responsibilities analogous to the poetic tasks undertaken by these poets, who dared to confront the historical and social problems of their times. In the poem, as in life, the social orientation of these poets is rewarded by badges of honor not conferred on those whose poetry is more self-concerned. Both the poets whom Dante distinguishes in this way are epic poets, and although Dante does not use this terminology, his treatment of Vergil and Statius demonstrates his careful differentiation of them from the vernacular lyric poets of his own day. By calling himself *poeta*, Dante links himself to them, establishing himself as their fulfillment, his poem as their poems' completion, and underscoring the message of *Inferno* I and IV, where he invokes Vergil as the *only* source of his beautiful style and is admitted by the fraternity of classical poets as one of their own. When I say, then, that Dante claims to be an "epic" poet in the *Paradiso*, I do not mean to compare the *Comedy* to national epics like the *Chanson de Roland*, or to claim technical epic status for it, but to draw the conclusion to which Dante is pointing when he says "ritornerò poeta": he is an "epic" poet in that he sees himself as fulfilling and completing a poetic itinerary that begins with

[87] The intentionality with which Dante restricts the term *poeta* in the *Comedy* is more striking if it is remembered that in the *Vita Nuova* he goes out of his way to appropriate for vernacular poets, *dicitori*, the term traditionally used only for Latin authors, *poeti*. Thus, Dante first clears the way for vernacular *dicitori* to be recognized as *poeti*, and then, in the *Comedy*, imposes new restrictions of his own fabrication. On Dante's use of these terms, see Angelo Jacomuzzi, *L'imago al cerchio* (Milan: Silva, 1968), pp. 37-40, and Francesco Tateo, *Questioni di poetica dantesca* (Bari: Adriatica, 1972), pp. 65-68; on the history of such terminology, see Alfredo Schiaffini, " 'Poesis' e 'poeta' in Dante," in *Studia philologica et litteraria in honorem L. Spitzer* (Bern: A. Francke, 1958), pp. 379-389.

Dante: "ritornerò poeta"

the *Aeneid* and that finds in the *Comedy*—also a long narrative with social, historical, and prophetic pretensions—its last and highest form of expression.[88]

We have already seen how, in the *Inferno*, Dante takes care to educate his readers with respect to the true value of the term *comedìa* as he is using it; having time and again seen him demonstrate the superiority of the *bassa comedìa* over the *alta tragedìa*, we should not now be surprised to see the humble scribe appropriate the name *poeta* for himself, displacing the great poets of antiquity. Within the discourse of Dante's poem the conventions to which he subscribes in the Epistle to Cangrande, whereby the poem is called a comedy because it proceeds from a foul beginning to a happy ending and is written in the vernacular, do not hold; here Dante has evolved a transcendental poetics, which alters the significance of *comedìa* by rendering it paradoxical.[89] Thus, although Dante twice calls his poem a

---

[88] I wish to emphasize that I am not bolstering the pretensions of patriotic scholars to an Italian national epic (see, for instance, Giulio Natali, "A qual 'genere letterario' appartiene la *Divina Commedia?*," *Il Giornale dantesco*, 26 [1923], 147-152, who writes "non potremo più negare, come tanti hanno fatto, all'Italia una epopea nazionale"); in fact, I share Curtius' opinion that the *Comedy* "can be assigned to no genre" (*European Literature and the Latin Middle Ages*, trans. Willard R. Trask [1948; repr. Princeton: Princeton U. Press, 1973], p. 361). Dante deliberately set out, in my opinion, to write a poem that would be unclassifiable; to this end, he mimics not only epic conventions (the invocations, the catalogue of ships in Cacciaguida's listing of Florentine families), but also those of every other major genre in circulation.

[89] In the article "Comedìa," Franco Ferrucci argues that the terms *comedìa* and *tragedìa* are used in the poem "in una accezione personalissima e inedita" (p. 40); he too claims that *comedìa* ultimately surpasses *tragedìa*. The fact that I do not think the terminology of the Epistle reflects the situation of the *Comedy* does not affect my belief in the Epistle's authenticity, since such disjunctions between the poet and the exegete are common in Dante. Moreover, the Epistle does allude to the *Comedy*'s new poetics, albeit in more veiled fashion than the poem: enormously significant is the presence of the same Psalm, "In exitu Israel de Aegypto," used by Dante in two other key passages (*Convivio* II, i, 6 and *Purg*. II, 46); also, as Curtius demonstrates, Dante's list of the *Comedy*'s *modi tractandi* is carefully chosen in order to claim for the poem "the cognitional function which Scholasticism denied to poetry in general" (*European Literature and the Latin Middle Ages*, p. 225). From a purely rhetorical perspective,

Epic Resolution

comedìa, he does so only in the *Inferno*, and he embeds this fallen terminology in contexts that are intended to explode its conventional significance; in the *Paradiso*, the conventions of earthly language and of the rhetorical treatises no longer apply, and Dante therefore makes it clear that the usual distinctions between *comedìa* and *tragedìa* are irrelevant:

> Da questo passo vinto mi concedo
> più che già mai da punto di suo tema
> soprato fosse comico o tragedo

> By this enterprise I concede myself beaten more than ever comic or tragic poet was overpowered by a point in his theme

(Par. XXX, 22-24)

In this passage Dante declares himself poetically bankrupt by Beatrice's beauty, which has reached a pitch he says he can no longer describe; he is more defeated than any "comico o tragedo," i.e. any poet at all, has ever been defeated by what he was writing. But if Dante here invokes such distinctions, he does so in order to underscore the fact that they belong to an unredeemed world, a linear world of hierarchized schematization, and that whereas such poets, existing within the limitations of conventional genres, in fact could not attempt such a description, he—the poet whose method cancels the old oppositional distinctions between tragedy/comedy and high/low in an

---

Alfredo Schiaffini points to the appositeness of Horace's dictum, in a passage of the *Ars Poetica* cited in the Epistle, stipulating that comedians may occasionally use tragic diction and vice versa; see "A proposito dello 'stile comico' di Dante," in *Momenti di storia della lingua italiana*, 2d ed. (Rome: Editrice Studium, 1953), pp. 43-56. Regarding the Epistle's authenticity, résumés of the controversy are provided by: Arsenio Frugoni, "Le Epistole," in *Cultura e scuola* 4, nos. 13-14 (1965), 739-748; Manlio Pastore Stocchi, in "Epistole," *Enciclopedia Dantesca*, vol. II, pp. 706-707; Giorgio Brugnoli in his introduction to *Epistola* XIII in the 1979 Ricciardi edition. In "La 'mirabile visione' di Dante e l'Epistola a Cangrande," orig. 1965, repr. *Il pio Enea, l'empio Ulisse*, pp. 30-63, Giorgio Padoan clarifies and dissipates the differences between the two chief modern debaters on this issue, Francesco Mazzoni (who accepts the Epistle in its entirety) and Bruno Nardi (who accepts only the opening paragraphs).

Dante: "ritornerò poeta"

all-embracing circularity—can and does undertake it. The paradox of the method, whereby one does what one says one cannot do, precisely by saying that one cannot do it, corresponds to the paradox of the genre that surpasses and eliminates genre: the *comedìa* that is higher than the highest *tragedìa*.

In the *Paradiso*, where Dante invokes the old categories of the *comico* and *tragedo* only to show how they fail with respect to him, he also clarifies the new significance assigned to *comedìa*, not through contextual implications, as in the *Inferno*, but by explicitly redefining it in his new language, according to the new system. Matching the double use of *comedìa* in the *Inferno*, we find the double use of the new appellation: in *Paradiso* XXIII, after having proclaimed the absolute disjunction between himself and all previous poets, Dante calls his poem "lo sacrato poema" (62), and in the great opening prayer of *Paradiso* XXV, he calls it " 'l poema sacro" (1). Given that these two occurrences constitute the only appearances of *poema* in the *Comedy*, it would seem that—paradoxically—only a scribe can write a poem.[90] The passage of canto XXIII, in particular, dwells on the dissimilarity between Dante's poetic undertaking and all others; here it is stated that if all those tongues to whom Polyhymnia and her sisters gave their sweetest milk were to come to Dante's aid in describing Beatrice's smile, they would not succeed in expressing a thousandth part of the truth: "al millesmo del vero / non si verria" (58-59). Because of the failure of poetic language at such a juncture, he goes on to say, his poem too must yield to the exigencies of describing Paradise in figurative terms: "e così, figurando il paradiso, / convien saltar lo sacrato poema" ("and so, in figuring Paradise, the sacred poem is obliged to leap" [61-62]). Again the technique is to surpass paradoxi-

---

[90] *Scriba* is used only with reference to Dante, in "quella materia ond' io son fatto scriba" (*Par.* X, 27), while the only "writers" in the *Comedy* are "li scrittor de lo Spirito Santo" (*Par.* XXIX, 41), i.e. the composers of the Bible. In a context in which terms such as "writer" and "author" have been assimilated to God, to be a scribe is no degradation; indeed, it is to be the greatest of poets. On *poeta* and *scriba* in Dante, see Jacomuzzi, "Ond'io son fatto scriba," in *L'imago al cerchio*, pp. 31-100.

Epic Resolution

cally, conveying the true stature of the *comedìa* by pointing to the *vero* that it must needs fail to express, a truth that would elude the combined expressive powers of all mankind's greatest poets; only now, when the task of rendering his own limits has succeeded in nullifying his precursors, and when he has effectively surpassed his own limits by rendering them, does Dante reveal the true meaning of *comedìa*, telling us that it is a *sacrato poema*. And, lest we fail to grasp the full significance of this expression, and the completeness with which it cuts this poem off from all others, from those that owe their existence solely to human hands, we learn in canto XXV that a sacred poem is one in whose creation all reality—heaven and earth—participates: " 'l poema sacro / al quale ha posto mano e cielo e terra" ("the sacred poem to which both heaven and earth have set hand" [1-2]).[91]

These verses deserve a special prominence in the history of Western literature, for they bring the concept of mimesis full circle: rather than claiming that he has described both heaven and earth, which he has, this poet claims that heaven and earth have helped to describe themselves. The origins of this paradoxical inversion of the mimetic principle, in the name of a higher mimesis, are to be found in *Purgatorio* X, where Dante stands the tradition on its head by positing a form of art that would put to shame not only the greatest of human artists, but even nature herself; the engravings he sees on the terrace of pride are such that "non pur Policleto, / ma la natura lì avrebbe scorno" ("not only Polycletus, but nature would there be shamed" [32-33]). In that these engravings are in fact God's handiwork, the contrast between these lines and the traditional principle as set forth in *Inferno* XI is only an apparent one; nature is said in *Inferno* XI to take its course from the divine intellect and from its art ("dal divino 'ntelletto e da sua arte" [100]), in the same way that human art in turn follows nature, so that the scenario of *Purgatorio* X—whereby nature would imitate God

---

[91] Dante's use of the expressions *sacrato poema* and *poema sacro* is particularly significant in light of the fact, noted by Alfredo Schiaffini, that Macrobius refers to the *Aeneid* as a *sacrum poema* ("A proposito dello 'stile comico' di Dante," p. 53).

Dante: "ritornerò poeta"

if she could—is in fact perfectly orthodox. But Dante has gone out of his way to suggest something else; by having nature put to scorn by God's art, rather than by His reality, he has brought into play the notion of an art that is more real than the real, where mimesis is perfected to the point that it is inverted upon itself, as the imitator achieves a greater reality than that possessed by what he is imitating. Moreover, in *Purgatorio* X the imitator is ultimately Dante himself: having posited a kind of supreme realism that is God's art, Dante must then attempt to imitate God's realism with his own, which is essentially what he does when he tries to describe what he saw—God's art—with the only means available to him, the words of his poem. The verbal tableaux of *Purgatorio* X, Dante's emphasis on the confusion of his senses, and the fast-paced dialogue between Trajan and the poor widow—all are attempts to re-create the engravings' *visibile parlare* in words, to find a way to project his art, like God's, into the fourth dimension. The situation of *Purgatorio* X thus generates one of those contradictions with which the *Comedy* is rife: although Dante is here dedicated to showing that God's art is greater than that of any other artist, the result is an enhancement of his own art, which dares to imitate the divine mimesis.[92] The exaltation of divine art at the expense of human art paradoxically leads to the exaltation of that human artist who most closely imitates divine art, who writes a poem to which heaven and earth contribute, and who by way of being only a scribe becomes the greatest of poets.

Dante's counterpart in *Purgatorio* X, the figure who embodies the contradiction in Dante's daringly humble imitation, is David, "l'umile salmista" (65), who by publicly dancing before the arc

---

[92] In stressing the paradoxical implications inherent in Dante's depiction of God's depicting, I do not intend to disagree with those who concentrate on the presence of divine art in canto X as a means of humbling human pride; see, for instance: Maria Sampoli Simonelli, "Il canto X del *Purgatorio*," *Studi danteschi* 33, fasc. 2 (1955-56), 121-145; Francesco Tateo, "Teologia e 'arte' nel canto X del *Purgatorio*," in *Questioni di poetica dantesca*, pp. 139-171; Philip R. Berk, "Some Sibylline Verses in *Purgatorio* X and XII," *Dante Studies*, 90 (1972), 59-76; James Thomas Chiampi, *Shadowy Prefaces: Conversion and Writing in the Divine Comedy*, chap. 3, esp. pp. 69-85.

Epic Resolution

of the covenant shows himself to be both "more and less than king": "e più e men che re era in quel caso" (66). In the same way, Dante's *poema sacro*, his *comedìa*, is both more and less than the king of poems, the *tragedìa*; as David's humility makes him more glorious, so the *comedìa*'s lowly standing makes it more sublime.[93] The connection between Dante and David becomes more explicit in the *Paradiso*, where the humble Psalmist, composer of sacred poetry, is present in the canto where Dante most strikingly proclaims his own *poema sacro*: in *Paradiso* XXV David is again the poet of the Psalms, "sommo cantor del sommo duce" ("supreme singer of the supreme leader" [72]). The term *cantore* is always used in the *Comedy* for a divinely inspired artist; thus, Vergil is the "cantor de' buccolici carmi" ("singer of the bucolic songs" [*Purg.* XXII, 57]), in a reference to the prophetic fourth Eclogue, and David is a *cantor* throughout *Paradiso*: as the pupil in the center of the eagle's eye in the heaven of justice, he is called (in a passage whose combined reference to the Psalms and the arc of the covenant echoes *Purgatorio* X) "il cantor de lo Spirito Santo, / che l'arca traslatò di villa in villa" ("the singer of the Holy Spirit, who transferred the arc from town to town" [*Par.* XX, 38-39]); and in canto XXXII Ruth is named by periphrasis as the great-grandmother of David, the "cantor che per doglia / del fallo disse '*Miserere mei*'" ("singer who for sorrow of his sin said '*Miserere mei*'" [11-12]).[94] The central passage of this Davidic triptych is that

[93] David articulates the paradox of his glorious humility in the Biblical account, when he says to Michal that as a result of making himself more vile, he will appear more glorious; see the passage from Kings quoted in Singleton, *Commentary* to the *Purgatorio*, pp. 206-207, who also provides the apposite commentary from Gregory's *Moralium libri*. In "Some Sibylline Verses in *Purgatorio* X and XII," Philip Berk discusses Augustine on "the paradox of Christian humility" whereby "less is really more," a doctrine that illuminates not only the behavior of David but also the relation between Vergil and Statius.

[94] The other uses of *cantore* in the *Comedy* are minimal and do not contradict its usage as we have defined it: it refers to Cacciaguida, who takes his place among the lights of the cross and shows the pilgrim what kind of artist he is among the "cantor del cielo" (*Par.* XVIII, 51); it occurs in a simile that compares the movements of Trajan and Ripheus, synchronized with the voice of the eagle, to the relation between a "buon cantor" and a "buon citarista" (*Par.* XX, 142).

Dante: "ritornerò poeta"

of canto XXV, the canto in which Dante implicitly aligns his poetry with David's by calling his poem a *poema sacro*; here, as part of his examination on hope, Dante translates word for word from David's ninth (now tenth) Psalm: " 'Sperino in te,' ne la sua tëodia / dice, 'color che sanno il nome tuo' " (" 'Let them hope in Thee,' he says in his *tëodia*, 'who know Thy name' " [73-74]). The term *tëodia*, "divine song," coined to describe the Psalms, is easily transferred to Dante's own *poema sacro*: needing a new descriptive term for his new genre, Dante invents it with the rest of the *Comedy*'s basic poetic baggage, its structure, form, and meter. True to his fundamental procedural principles of appropriation and revision, he first appropriates a standard rhetorical term, *comedìa*, and then—having redefined it from within as a *poema sacro*—replaces the original term with a new one: *tëodia*.[95]

If all of the *Paradiso*'s three references to David, "cantor de lo Spirito Santo," seem designed to contribute to the identification of the inspired Biblical poet with the inspired Italian poet, the last reference, by echoing the pilgrim's first words to Vergil, gives us a sense of the distance Dante has traveled to become the author of the new *tëodia*. David is last named, in *Paradiso*

[95] *Tëodia* is coined on the basis of terms like *comedia* and *tragedìa*; interestingly, the only other such term in the *Comedy*, *salmodia*, also refers to David in the context of a direct citation from a Psalm (*Purg.* XXXIII, 2). Gian Roberto Sarolli, "Dante Scriba Dei," in *Prolegomena alla Divina Commedia*, treats these issues from a similar perspective; rather than establishing a direct parallel between Dante and David, however, Sarolli identifies Dante with Nathan, the prophet who reproved David for his adulterous love for Bathsheba, and identifies David, whom he views solely as king, with the Emperor Henry VII (see pp. 189-246). A direct analogy between Dante and David is suggested by Robert Hollander, who thinks that Dante "may have thought of his own poem as being like one of David's" ("Dante *Theologus-Poeta*," p. 66). Vincent Truijen, in the entry "profeta" of the *Enciclopedia Dantesca*, points out that Dante frequently uses the term to refer to David, calling him simply "il Profeta" (vol. IV, p. 694); thus David is "the prophet" in the same way that Aristotle is "the philosopher." Indeed, the *Convivio* refers to the Psalm "In exitu Israel de Aegypto" as "quello canto del Profeta che dice che, ne l'uscita del popolo d'Israel d'Egitto, Giudea è fatta santa e libera" ("that song of the Prophet which says that, in the departure of the people of Israel from Egypt, Judea is made holy and free" [II, i, 6]).

XXXII, as the singer who said "Have mercy on me"; Dante, in *Inferno* I, uses a hybrid form of the Psalm's "Miserere mei" when he cries to Vergil, in a mixture of Latin and Italian, "*Miserere* di me" (65).[96] The reference to David at the end of the *Paradiso* is intended to function as a recall of the meeting with Vergil, because the divine singer is seen as providing the model that enables Dante to decisively surpass his Roman precursor. The events of *Purgatorio* X provide an emblem for just such a transcendence: after the pilgrim has studied the first bas-relief, detailing the Annunciation, he looks forward at his guide's prompting and discovers "un'altra storia ne la roccia imposta" ("another story set in the rock" [52]); this discovery leads him to go beyond his guide—"per ch'io varcai Virgilio" ("so that I went past Vergil" [53])—in order to view the second engraving. The phrase "per ch'io varcai Virgilio" is emblematic of the effect that David's art will have on Dante, for the result of "going beyond Vergil" in *Purgatorio* X is to see, in the second engraving, the *umile salmista*, composer of the *tëodia*, i.e. of an art form that certainly, from Dante's point of view, transcends Vergil's. Indeed, to go beyond a great model—to get past Vergil—Dante requires a humble model, on whose example he can forge his own humbly superior poetics. Once more we see the value of Benvenuto's celebrated circular assertion, whereby "divine language is smooth and plain, not high and proud like the language of Vergil and the poets."[97] Benvenuto's distinction between a style that is *divinus* because it is *planus*, as compared

---

[96] Hollander notes the parallel between these two passages in "Dante's Use of the Fiftieth Psalm"; he sees David's penitence as a prefiguration of Dante's penitence in the *selva oscura* (p. 111).

[97] Benvenuto's magisterial comment (Lacaita, vol. I, p. 90) was noted by Auerbach, who rightly made much of it in his discussion of Dante's *sermo humilis*. Auerbach's thesis regarding a Christian discourse, the *sermo humilis*, that encompasses the sublime (elaborated in *Literary Language and Its Public in Late Latin Antiquity and in the Middle Ages*, trans. Ralph Manheim [1958; repr. Princeton: Princeton U. Press, 1965], chap. I) finds its perfect exponent in the *Comedy* because Dante deliberately set out to situate his text within a paradoxical framework, whose emblem—the description of David as "più e men che re"—is entirely appropriate as an emblem for the *Comedy* itself.

Dante: "ritornerò poeta"

to a style that is *altus* and *superbus*, precisely adumbrates the distinction between the *comedìa-tëodìa* on the one hand, and the *tragedìa* on the other.

And yet Vergil is, as Dante tells us, the original source of his poetic style, of "lo bello stilo che m'ha fatto onore," a fact that allows us to assume that the paradoxical nature of the Vergilian problematic is related to the *Comedy*'s most basic textual strategies, as it is also related to its key thematic concerns. If, on a thematic level, we may say that Vergil embodies the paradoxical relation of human knowledge to divine grace, on a textual level we may say that the true/false dialectic that is at the heart of Dante's Vergil is also at the heart of Dante's poem—as it would have to be at the heart of any fiction that proclaims itself to be true.[98] A fiction that claims to be nonfiction must deal squarely with problems of credibility, and one of Dante's tactics in this regard involves his treatment of his peers: in the same way that Dante tells us that his was the only love poetry directly inspired by Love, so he informs us that his is the only narrative poem to tell the truth and nothing but the truth, even if that truth sometimes has the face of a lie. This claim is the burden of the many episodes that deal, like *Inferno* XX, with Dante's narrative precursors. In other words, the credibility of the *Comedy* is achieved, in part, by establishing the incredibility of its forebears. As Dante's treatment of Vergil's text repeatedly demonstrates, the classical *tragedìa* participates in fiction, also known as falsehood—*menzogna*—while the *comedìa*, based on the conviction that the real is more valuable

[98] Particularly emblematic of this true/false dialectic, as well as an apt gloss on the "ver c'ha faccia di menzogna," are certain lines spoken by Statius to Vergil regarding his alleged avarice: "Veramente più volte appaion cose / che danno a dubitar falsa matera / per le vere ragion che son nascose" ("Truly many times things do appear which, because their true reasons are hidden, present false matter for doubting" [*Purg.* XXII, 28-30]). Regarding the role of the *Aeneid* in this problematic, Hollander notes that Dante learns from it "to compose a fiction that is intended to be taken as historically true" ("Dante Theologus-Poeta," p. 71); see also the brief note by Enzo Noè Girardi, "Virgilio nella poetica di Dante," in *Dante e Roma: Atti del Convegno di Studi* (Florence: Le Monnier, 1965), pp. 237-241.

than the beautiful, deals exclusively in truth. The *comedìa* is faithful to Augustine's dictum "in verbis verum amare, non verba" ("in words to love the truth, not the words");[99] as a genre that is devoted to the truth, rather than to the *parola ornata*, it may exploit any register—high or low—but depends entirely on none, since it must always be free to adopt the stylistic register that most accurately reflects the truth of the situation at hand.[100] We may say, then, that Dante would approve of St. Thomas' distinction between poetry, which employs

---

[99] The quotation is from *De Doctrina Christiana Liber Quartus*, comm. and trans. Sister Thérèse Sullivan (Washington: Catholic U. of America, 1930), 4, 11, 26. Augustine stresses the issue of a text's truth or falsity from the beginning of Book IV, noting that "per artem rhetoricam et vera suadeantur et falsa" ("through the art of rhetoric both truths and falsehoods are pleaded" [4, 2, 3]), and commenting later that the teacher's aim should be "veritas pateat, veritas placeat, veritas moveat" ("that the truth be clear, that the truth be pleasing, that the truth be persuasive" [4, 28, 61]). Dante's inheritance of Augustine's verbal epistemology is discussed by Marcia L. Colish, *The Mirror of Language: A Study in the Medieval Theory of Knowledge* (New Haven and London: Yale U. Press, 1968), pp. 224-341.

[100] The potential equivalence between *parola ornata* and *menzogna* is established in *Inferno* XVIII, where Beatrice's instructions to Vergil from *Inferno* II—"Or movi, e con la tua parola ornata . . . l'aiuta" ("Now move, and with your ornate speech . . . help him" [67-69])—are ominously echoed in the story of how Jason (a classical hero by whom Vergil is particularly entranced) deceived Hypsipyle: "Ivi con segni e con parole ornate / Isifile ingannò" ("There, with signs and with ornate words, he deceived Hypsipyle" [91-92]). These are the only other *parole ornate* in the poem (as though to underscore the point, Dante here indulges in a bit of ornate wordplay himself, echoing "ingannò" [92] with "ingannate" [93] and "inganna" [97]). If the point is the alignment of beautiful language with deception, in retrospect we can see that this issue was already broached in *Inferno* II, as part of that canto's overall concern with the value of discourse; there, Vergil's "parola ornata" finds its corrective in the "vere parole" of line 135, words belonging—of course—to Beatrice. (A nagging question nonetheless remains regarding Beatrice's own language in canto II: can her words promising to praise Vergil to her lord be classified as *parole vere*, and if not, are they *parole ornate?*) We should also note that the only other words in the poem specifically labeled true are the pilgrim's, whose words to Nicholas III are called "parole vere" (*Inf.* XIX, 123). Thus, two sets are constituted: in one (*parole ornate*) we find Vergil and Jason; in the other (*parole vere*) we find Beatrice and Dante.

Dante: "ritornerò poeta"

metaphor "propter repraesentationem," and "sacra doctrina," which employs metaphor "propter necessitatem et utilitatem," with the caveat that his poem, not for nothing called a *poema sacro*, functions more like *sacra doctrina* in this respect than like "poetry."[101] In elaborating the category of *comedìa*, as this term is used in the *Comedy*, Dante has not simply availed himself of current rhetorical theory, but has invented a new category, in order to accommodate a new kind of textuality, whose employment of figurative language "propter necessitatem et utilitatem" distinguishes it from all *belle menzogne*, whether they be his own, in the *Convivio*, or those of his classical antecedents. The hallmark of this textuality is the ability to say, with Cacciaguida, "Io dirò cosa incredibile e vera" (*Par.* XVI, 124), or, like Dante in an eclogue to Giovanni del Virgilio: "mira loquar, sed vera tamen" ("I tell of marvels, but they are nonetheless true"). The unbelievable but true—*mira vera*—is precisely the province of what, in another eclogue, Dante calls his *comica verba*.[102]

---

[101] *Summa Theologiae*, 1a. q. 1, a. 9.

[102] The *Paradiso*'s "cosa incredibile e vera," with reference to one of the gates of ancient Florence, glosses the *Inferno*'s "cosa incredibile," namely a speaking thornbush derived from the *Aeneid* (*Inf.* XIII, 50); the parallel between the mythological content of the infernal episode and Cacciaguida's sober fact further clarifies the difference between *comedìa* and *tragedìa*. The phrase "mira loquar, sed vera tamen" is from Dante's second Eclogue, line 40; particularly suggestive is the fact that the narrator is here preparing to describe the "true marvel" of the singing flute, a verbal marvel reminiscent of others in Dante's canon: from the miraculous speech that leads to the creation of "Donne ch'avete," to the *visibile parlare* of *Purgatorio* X. In the first Eclogue, Tityrus (Dante) had explained to his friend that Mopsus (Giovanni del Virgilio) disapproves of his use of "Comica . . . verba," i.e. the vernacular, because it sounds on the lips of women and is spurned by the Muses (52-54); the similarity between this passage and the Epistle to Cangrande, where Dante claims that his poem is written in the "locutio vulgaris in qua et muliercule comunicant" ("vernacular discourse that even women use" [*Epistole* XIII, 31]), has been noted. The *Eclogues* also provide valuable insights regarding Dante's relation to Vergil, whose *buccolici carmi* Dante is here openly—and prophetically—imitating, and whose pastoral name he adopts (Vergil uses the name Tityrus for himself in *Eclogues* I and VI; on the decidedly non-Vergilian pastoral tradition before Dante, see Carlo Battisti, "Le Egloghe Dantesche," *Studi danteschi* 33, fasc. 2 [1955-56], 61-

Dante gives us two basic signs that his text is to be considered "true." One is his appropriation of real people, historical lives, a historicity that functions dialectically: the text "takes life" from some and "gives life" to others. The appropriation of a major figure, like Vergil, gives life to the text, allowing the text in turn to give life to all the minor figures, like Francesca, who crowd its pages. The distinction between text and life—text and truth—is thus deliberately blurred, and never more so than when Cacciaguida invests Dante with his poetic mission, telling him that, in order to assure his poem its exemplary powers of persuasion, he has been introduced only to famous souls, "anime che son di fama note" ("souls who are known to fame" [*Par.* XVII, 138]), even though this is patently untrue: most of the souls Dante meets we would never have heard of were it not for his poem. They are famous now because the text has given them life, making them into the kinds of exemplary figures whom Cacciaguida describes; Cacciaguida's assertion, untrue when it was written, is true now, because the text has made it true. Besides articulating the principle of the exemplum, with its necessary contamination between life and text, Cacciaguida further tells his descendent to make manifest all that he has seen ("tutta tua visïon fa manifesta" [128]), having first set aside all falsehood ("rimossa ogne menzogna" [127]), for although Dante's voice will be unpleasant at first taste, it will

---

111, who demonstrates precise textual echoes of Vergil in Dante). Regarding our earlier discussion of the relation between *virga* and *Virgilio*, it is perhaps not insignificant that, in these poems written under the sign of Vergil, Dante should coin the term "virgiferi" ("staff-bearers" [IV, 92]) to refer to his poet-shepherds (on this use of *virgiferi* for "poets," see Battisti, "Le Egloghe Dantesche," p. 109). Finally, we note that Dante seems to accept Giovanni's terminology, according to which he—like Vergil—is a *vates*; he uses the term for himself and others in II, 36 (this constitutes the only occasion in which Dante applies the term, even indirectly, to himself). If, in the *Eclogues*, Dante accepts the standard terminology dictated by Latin usage, his avoidance of *vates* in the *Comedy* would appear to be related to that text's disjunction of itself from its forebears in the name of a new poetics, in which a *poeta* is a *vates* by implication. On the identity established by Dante between the terms *poeta* and *profeta*, see Mineo, *Profetismo e apocalittica in Dante*, pp. 303-307.

Dante: "ritornerò poeta"

leave vital nourishment when digested (130-132);[103] he then transforms "la voce tua" of line 130 into the more potent *grido* of line 133, the cry that will smite the great of the earth: "Questo tuo grido farà come vento, / che le più alte cime più percuote" ("This cry of yours will do as the wind, which strikes most on the highest peaks" [133-134]). If Cacciaguida's injunction to leave aside all falsehood—"ogne menzogna"—seems to steer Dante's text away from its classical antecedents, his other remarks work to align it with more worthwhile precursors; the text's "vital nodrimento" reminds us that it is written "per utilitatem," and the emphasis on making truth manifest anticipates the description of the Gospel of John as "l'alto preconio che grida l'arcano / di qui là giù sovra ogne altro bando" ("the high announcement that more than any other heralding cries out the mystery of here down there" [*Par.* XXVI, 44-45]). The duty of a text is to be a proclamation, revealing secrets that should be made manifest, to be, like the Gospel, a "preconio che grida l'arcano"; the use of *gridare* here, with reference to the Gospel, is linked to Cacciaguida's definition of Dante's own text as *questo tuo grido*.[104] The importance of *gridare* for the

---

[103] The stress on the text as nourishment seems connected to the placement of one of the *Purgatorio*'s most notable poetic discourses on the terrace of gluttony. Whereas Bonagiunta and the other souls on the terrace of gluttony pray to the Lord to open their mouths in a song of praise, in the *Paradiso* we witness a poet whose mouth *has been* opened: the *Purgatorio*'s "Labïa mëa, Domine" (XXIII, 11) is answered by St. Peter's "apri la bocca, / e non asconder quel ch'io non ascondo" ("Open your mouth, and do not hide what I do not hide" [*Par.* XXVII, 65-66]).

[104] On the prophetic implications of the term *grido*, see Gian Roberto Sarolli, "Dante's Katabasis and Mission," in *Prolegomena alla Divina Commedia*, pp. 381-419. It may be recalled that Guittone too is associated with the term *grido*, albeit negatively; he is one whose praises were passed on from cry to cry, until finally the ill-founded *grido* was overcome by the truth: "di grido in grido pur lui dando pregio, / fin che l'ha vinto il ver con più persone" (*Purg.* XXVI, 125-126). There is a passage in *Paradiso* XIII, in which St. Thomas cautions the pilgrim not to make hasty judgments, that contains the verbal imprints of the Guittone passage of *Purgatorio* XXVI: here the *stolti* (used twice, in 115 and 127) are those who, because they do not discriminate, are bent in the wrong direction by "current opinion," and then fixed there by their vanity (*Par.* XIII,

283

poet's mission is expressed as early as the *Convivio*, where, regarding the composition of his first didactic poem, "Le dolci rime," Dante says: "proposi di gridare a la gente che per mal cammino andavano, acciò che per diritto calle si dirizzassero" ("I decided to cry out to the people who were going on the wrong path, so that they would straighten themselves onto the right way" [*Convivio* IV, i, 9]).

If Dante's poem is a *visïon*, it is the same kind of vision afforded Saint John in the Apocalypse, the vision of one who

---

118-120). The echoing, in "l'oppinïon corrente" (119), of the "oppinïone" of *Purgatorio* XXVI, which tied people to the rumor of Guittone's greatness ("A voce più ch'al ver drizzan li volti, / e così ferman sua oppinïone / prima ch'arte o ragion per lor s'ascolti" [121-123]), finally issues forth in a condemnation that contains two more key terms from *Purgatorio* XXVI, *vero* and *arte*. Using the implied metaphor of sailing, which is linked to poetry throughout the *Comedy*, St. Thomas explains that he who leaves the shore ill-equipped does so at his peril: "Vie più che 'ndarno da riva si parte, / perché non torna tal qual e' si move, / chi pesca per lo vero e non ha l'arte" ("Far worse than in vain does he leave the shore, because he returns not the same as he sets out, he who fishes for the truth and has not the art" [121-123]). Given the insistent use of terms from the Guittone passage of *Purgatorio* XXVI—*stolti, oppinïone, vero, arte*—it seems not farfetched to suggest that the phrase "chi pesca per lo vero e non ha l'arte" is intended (although by no means exclusively) to describe Guittone, who certainly was "fishing for the truth," and who—according to Dante—had not the art to do so. If this is so, the passage confirms Dante's sense of Guittone as a poet whose aspirations were much like his own. Finally, let me conclude this excursus on the lyric subtext of *Paradiso* XIII by pointing out that if Guittone provides the negative term for Thomas' remarks, showing us what not to be, Guinizzelli provides the substance of his discourse: in his sonnet to Bonagiunta, "Omo ch'è saggio non corre leggero" ("A wise man does not run lightly"), Guinizzelli advocates the same intellectual caution and discrimination enjoined upon us by the saint. Indeed, the likelihood that Dante had Guinizzelli's poem in mind while composing canto XIII seems confirmed by the fact that the sonnet contains another highly pertinent verse: line 5, "Foll'è chi crede sol veder lo vero" ("He is mad who thinks that he alone sees the truth"), could stand as a rubric for the entire heaven of the Sun in which *Paradiso* XIII is situated. If Dante here raises the shadows of his lyric precursors, it is because the passage at hand deals implicitly with the very core of his paradoxical poetics; he is the poet who judges all while admonishing us not to judge, the poet—as witness to a sole and unimpeachable truth—can dramatize its many facets.

Dante: "ritornerò poeta"

is in a waking sleep, like the old man who personifies the Apocalypse in the allegorical procession and who comes forward "dormendo, con la faccia arguta" ("sleeping, with a keen face" [*Purg.* XXIX, 144]).[105] It is in a waking sleep, with perfect consciousness, that Dante decides on his radical handling of textuality's fundamental issue, the question of its truth or falsity, and that he decides to make a text which attempts to obliterate the boundaries between art and life. With equal deliberateness, Dante chooses his title, making it a sign of the text's marginal status, its self-imposed difference, its newness. The title, which has generated controversy from the beginning of the exegetical tradition to the present because of its seeming unsuitability, is the pivotal element of the poet's revisionist poetics:[106] the *alto preconio* announcing his decision to adopt a solution to the problem of fiction that would be simple, totally effective, and so radical that it would place his text in a condition of outsideness, eternal liminality with respect to both past and future, the traditions that exist in a normal genealogical flow

---

[105] Indeed, Dante openly aligns himself with John earlier in this canto, where he cuts short the description of the four animals surrounding the chariot with the injunction to read Ezekiel; however, on the question of the number of their wings, "Giovanni è meco e da lui si diparte" ("John is with me, and departs from him," i.e. Ezekiel [*Purg.* XXIX, 105]). Thus the poet is one of the prophets, who—although they may differ on details—share knowledge of the truth. The strategy here is typically Dantesque: because it is embedded within the pedantry of the discussion (six wings or four?), the enormous claim seems unremarkable. We don't even notice the hubris of "Giovanni è meco": Dante is not saying that he agrees with John, but that John agrees with him!

[106] Benvenuto devotes the last pages of his Introduction to the question of the *Comedy*'s title, claiming that the text contains all three basic styles, and that it could as correctly be entitled "satyra, quam tragoedia, vel comoedia" (vol. I, p. 19). He goes on to suggest that the poem's happy ending may have induced Dante to choose its perplexing title. On this issue, see: Pio Rajna, "Il titolo del poema dantesco," *Studi danteschi*, 4 (1921), 5-37; Manfredi Porena, "Il titolo della *Divina Commedia*," *Rendiconti della Reale Accademia Nazionale dei Lincei*, classe di scienze morali, storiche e filologiche, 9 (1933), 114-141; Amilcare A. Iannucci, "Dante's Theory of Genres and the *Divina Commedia*," *Dante Studies*, 91 (1973), 1-25; and, from an entirely different perspective, Giorgio Agamben, "Comedìa: la svolta comica di Dante e la concezione della colpa," *Paragone* 29, fasc. 346 (1978), 3-27.

on either side of it. All texts end with the *Comedy*, but none come out of it, for the price of inimitability is not to be imitated, as Dante knew full well when he inscribed one of the *Comedy*'s great *forse* verses at the outset of the *Paradiso*: "forse di retro a me con miglior voci / si preghera perché Cirra risponda" ("perhaps after me better voices will pray that Cyrrha may respond" [*Par.* I, 35-36]). No "better voices" will follow in this tradition, for the very desperation that gives the *Comedy* its certainty is also the index of its emargination. Dante knows that there will be no *di retro a me* and signifies as much in his title, whose paradoxical mixture of pride and humility will not be available to the poets of a later time, for whom the appropriation of reality is no longer a viable textual option. Dante's title is not intended to work in a conventional context, but to point the way out of it; precisely because it eludes conventional understanding, it was altered in the Venice edition of 1555 by Lodovico Dolce, who added the adjective *divina* and thereby unwittingly rendered it redundant.[107] But Dolce's apparent oxymoron has at least the merit of preserving the paradoxical nature of the original, which serves as the key to a paradoxical hermeneutics: as a title that embodies the principle of conversion, *Comedia* contains in itself the dialectic of the poem's totalitarian instability, its volatile peace.

[107] Rajna demonstrates that Dolce's most likely source for the adjective *divina* was Claudio Tolomei's *Cesano*, published by Gabriele Giolito at the same time as Dolce's edition of the *Comedy*; see "L'epiteto 'divina' dato alla *Commedia* di Dante," *Bullettino della Società Dantesca*, 22 (1915), 107-115 and 255-258. Besides its descriptive function, the adjective also possesses an apt if unintentional intertextual resonance in its echo of the *Thebaid*'s reference to Vergil's poem as "divinam Aeneida."

APPENDIX

DANTE'S POETS

This Appendix provides, for each of the *Comedy*'s chief poets, the locations in which Dante names or refers to him throughout his oeuvre. These summaries can be used synchronically, as indices of the poets who most interested Dante at a particular stage in his development, or diachronically, as charts of his developing attitudes toward a specific poet. Thus, one can verify the impression that Arnaut Daniel and Juvenal would, before intersecting in the *Comedy*, trace very different itineraries through Dante's texts: Arnaut is represented in the *De Vulgari Eloquentia*, while Juvenal figures in the *Convivio* and *Monarchia*. The decision to list only those instances in which a poet is named or mentioned (so that both "Stazio poeta" and "lo dolce poeta" are included), omitting those in which he is quoted or echoed without being explicitly referred to, results in certain lacunae of which the reader should be aware. For instance, Giacomo da Lentini is not named until the *Comedy*, but he was most likely in Dante's mind in *Vita Nuova* XXV, where he writes of "li primi che dissero in lingua di *sì*" ("the first who composed in Italian" [5]), and a canzone of Giacomo's is cited in the *De Vulgari Eloquentia*. By the same token, since the citations from the *Aeneid* and the *Pharsalia* in *Epistola* VII are not registered, only Vergil, who is explicitly named, appears as a classical authority of that Epistle. The entries are divided into three groups—Provençal, Italian, and classical—and each group is arranged alphabetically.

Appendix

Arnaut Daniel

Rime

Vita Nuova

De Vulgari Eloquentia   II, ii, 8
                                   II, vi, 6
                                   II, x, 2
                                   II, xiii, 2

Convivio

Monarchia

Epistole

Commedia   *Purg.* XXVI (appears)

Bertran de Born

Rime

Vita Nuova

De Vulgari Eloquentia   II, ii, 8

Convivio   IV, xi, 14

Monarchia

Epistole

Commedia   *Inf.* XXVIII (appears)

Dante's Poets

Folquet de Marselha

Rime	
Vita Nuova	
De Vulgari Eloquentia	II, vi, 6
Convivio	
Monarchia	
Epistole	
Commedia	Par. IX (appears)

Giraut de Bornelh

Rime	
Vita Nuova	
De Vulgari Eloquentia	I, ix, 3
	II, ii, 8
	II, v, 4
	II, vi, 6
Convivio	IV, xi, 10
Monarchia	
Epistole	
Commedia	Purg. XXVI (mentioned)

Appendix

Sordello

Rime	
Vita Nuova	
De Vulgari Eloquentia	I, xv, 2
Convivio	
Monarchia	
Epistole	
Commedia	*Purg.* VI–*Purg.* IX (appears)

Bonagiunta da Lucca

Rime	
Vita Nuova	
De Vulgari Eloquentia	I, xiii, 1
Convivio	
Monarchia	
Epistole	
Commedia	*Purg.* XXIV (appears)

Dante's Poets

Cino da Pistoia

Rime	"Perch'io non trovo chi meco ragioni," 12
	"Io mi credea del tutto esser partito," 2
Vita Nuova	
De Vulgari Eloquentia	I, x, 2
	I, xiii, 4
	I, xvii, 3
	II, ii, 8
	II, v, 4
	II, vi, 6
Convivio	
Monarchia	
Epistole	III, 1
Commedia	

Giacomo da Lentini

Rime	
Vita Nuova	
De Vulgari Eloquentia	
Convivio	
Monarchia	
Epistole	
Commedia	*Purg.* XXIV (mentioned)

Appendix
Guido Cavalcanti

Rime	"Guido, i' vorrei che tu e Lapo ed io"
Vita Nuova	III, 14 XXIV, 3, 6 XXV, 10 XXX, 3 XXXII, 1
De Vulgari Eloquentia	I, xiii, 4 II, vi, 6 II, xii, 3 II, xii, 8
Convivio	
Monarchia	
Epistole	
Commedia	Inf. X (mentioned) Purg. XI (mentioned)

Guido Guinizzelli

Rime	"Amore e 'l cor gentil sono una cosa," 2
Vita Nuova	XX, 3 ("Amore e 'l cor gentil sono una cosa," 2)
De Vulgari Eloquentia	I, ix, 3 I, xv, 6 II, v, 4 II, vi, 6 II, xii, 6
Convivio	IV, xx, 7
Monarchia	
Epistole	
Commedia	Purg. XI (mentioned) Purg. XXVI (appears)

Dante's Poets

GUITTONE D'AREZZO

Rime

Vita Nuova

De Vulgari Eloquentia   I, xiii, 1
                                             II, vi, 8

Convivio

Monarchia

Epistole

Commedia   Purg. XXIV (mentioned)
                                             Purg. XXVI (mentioned)

HOMER

Rime

Vita Nuova   II, 8
                                             XXV, 9

De Vulgari Eloquentia

Convivio   I, vii, 15
                                             IV, xx, 4

Monarchia   I, v, 5
                                             II, iii, 9

Epistole

Commedia   Inf. IV (appears)
                                             Purg. XXII (mentioned)

Appendix

HORACE

Rime	
Vita Nuova	XXV, 9
De Vulgari Eloquentia	II, iv, 4
Convivio	II, xiii, 10
	IV, xii, 8
Monarchia	
Epistole	XIII, 30, 32
Commedia	Inf. IV (appears)

JUVENAL

Rime	
Vita Nuova	
De Vulgari Eloquentia	
Convivio	IV, xii, 8
	IV, xxix, 4 (mentioned twice), 5
Monarchia	II, iii, 4
Epistole	
Commedia	Purg. XXII (mentioned)

LUCAN

Rime	
Vita Nuova	XXV, 9
De Vulgari Eloquentia	II, vi, 7
Convivio	III, iii, 7
	III, v, 12
	IV, xi, 3
	IV, xiii, 12
	IV, xxviii, 13
Monarchia	II, iv, 6
	II, vii, 10
	II, viii, 7, 9, 12
	II, ix, 17
Epistole	XIII, 63
Commedia	*Inf.* IV (appears)
	Inf. XXV (mentioned)

Appendix

OVID

Rime	
Vita Nuova	XXV, 9
De Vulgari Eloquentia	I, ii, 7
	II, vi, 7
Convivio	II, i, 3
	II, v, 14
	II, xiv, 5
	III, iii, 7
	IV, xv, 8
	IV, xxiii, 14
	IV, xxvii, 17, 19
Monarchia	II, vii, 10
	II, viii, 4
Epistole	III, 7
Commedia	*Inf.* IV (appears)
	Inf. XXV (mentioned)

STATIUS

Rime	
Vita Nuova	
De Vulgari Eloquentia	II, vi, 7
Convivio	III, viii, 10
	III, xi, 16
	IV, xxv, 6, 8, 10
Monarchia	
Epistole	
Commedia	*Purg.* XXI–*Purg.* XXXIII (appears)

Dante's Poets

VERGIL

Rime	
Vita Nuova	XXV, 9
De Vulgari Eloquentia	II, iv, 10
	II, vi, 7
	II, viii, 4
Convivio	I, iii, 10
	II, v, 14
	II, x, 5
	III, xi, 16
	IV, iv, 11
	IV, xxiv, 9
	IV, xxvi, 8, 11, 13, 14
Monarchia	I, xi, 1
	II, iii, 6, 8, 10, 11,
	12, 14, 15, 16
	II, iv, 8
	II, v, 11, 12, 13
	II, vi, 9
	II, vii, 11
	II, viii, 11
	II, ix, 14
Epistole	VII, 6
Commedia	*Inf.* I–*Purg.* XXIX (appears)

INDEX

Abbadessa, S., 243n
Abrams, R., 52n
Accardo, S., 58n, 62n
Adamo, maestro, 49, 49n, 234, 236-237
Adonis, 151, 153
Adrastus, 193, 193n
Aeacus, 195-196, 226
Aeneas, 24n, 191n, 194-195, 198, 218n, 254n
Aesop, 191n
Agamben, G., 285n
Ahearn, J., 32n, 268n
Aimeric de Belenoi, 92, 93n
Aimeric de Pegulhan, 92, 93n
Albertus Magnus, 144n, 191n
Alderotti, Taddeo, 191n
Alfraganus, 191n
Algazel, 191n
Alì, 166, 169
allegory, 9n, 16, 19-31, 35-37, 80-84, 90-91, 195, 202n, 206n, 212, 257n, 258n
Alpetragus, 191n
Amphiaraus, 215
Anaxagoras, 191n
Anchises, 252, 252n
Andreas Capellanus, 5, 5n, 11
Anonimo fiorentino, 49n, 127n, 128n
Ante-Purgatory, 46, 170
antithesis, 50, 56
Appel, C., 158n
Arethusa, 225
Argia, 193

Aristotelianism, 67n, 144n, 145n; golden mean, 259, 260n; tripartite division of soul, 185-186
Aristotle, 23, 191, 191n, 199, 277n
Arnaut Daniel, 13, 92, 93n, 96-100, 107n, 108, 112-114, 115n, 117n, 154, 164, 174, 176-179, 185-186, 287, 288; Provençal speech of, 113n, 117n, 118n, 232n
Arno, the, 47, 47n
Arruns, 215
Ascanius, 194
Athamas, 235
Auerbach, E., 278n
Augustine, St., 4, 4n, 19, 20n, 191n, 280, 280n; *De Doctrina Christiana*, 280n
Augustus, 198, 263
Austin, H. D., 260n
autore, 268-269
Avalle, D. S., 5n, 6n, 158n
Averroes, 145n, 266n
Averroism, 54n, 144, 144n
Avicenna, 191n

Baglivi, G., 223n
Baldelli, I., 95n, 137n
Baldi, A., 102n
ballata, 137-138, 152, 152n
Barbi, M., 20-21, 30n, 48n, 53n, 77n
Barchiesi, M., 215n
Barolini, T., 154n, 216n, 220n
Barral, lament for. *See* Folquet de Marselha

Index

Bathsheba, 277n
Battaglia, S., 69n
Battisti, C., 281n, 282n
Beatrice, 7-8, 10, 16-19, 21n, 22, 25, 30-31, 36-38, 42, 44, 48, 52-58, 67, 67n, 69-71, 75-79, 82-83, 123, 137n, 138-139, 145, 146n, 151n, 152, 174, 202, 205, 221, 243, 247-250, 253, 256, 267, 272-273, 280n; promise to Vergil, 9, 205n, 254, 280n
Benvenuto da Imola, 9n, 127n, 128n, 204, 204n, 256-258, 260n, 278, 278n, 285n
Bergin, T., 154, 154n, 158n
Berk, P. R., 275n, 276n
Bernart de Ventadorn, 114n
Bertalot, L., 93n
Bertran de Born, 108, 126n, 131, 153-154, 157-159, 164-173, 175, 179, 185-186, 260, 288; laments for Prince Henry, 158-159, 167; *razos* of, 164; *vidas* of, 164-165, 168-169
Bettini, M., 261n
Biagi, G., 9n, 127n
Bible, 201, 201n; books referred to: Psalms, 34, 51, 51n, 52n, 271n, 276-278; Proverbs, 27, 27n; Luke, 207, 207n; John, 283; Apocalypse, 284-285
Biscaro, G., 173n
Blacatz, lament for. *See* Sordello
Blasucci, L., 259n
Bloom, H., 175n, 252n
Boccaccio, 65; *Filocolo*, 261n
Boethius, 4, 19, 20n, 36-37, 191, 191n, 197n; *Consolatio Philosophiae*, 19-20
Bolognese, G., 102n, 218n
Bolognese poets, 92-93, 95, 130, 174
Bonagiunta da Lucca, 13, 40-42, 45, 48, 51-52, 56-57, 65n, 85-87, 90, 92n, 95, 98n, 154, 179, 283n, 284n, 290
Boni, M., 113n, 156n, 185n
Boniface VIII, 135n
Bosco, U., 45n, 48n, 54n, 62, 149n, 154n, 234n
Boutière, J., 119n
Bowra, M., 112n, 155n
Boyde, P., 8n, 14n, 21, 26n, 27n, 30n, 67, 67n, 77n, 81, 82n, 100n, 101n, 102n, 109, 109n, 129n, 137n, 176
Braccini, M., 113n, 114n, 118n, 177n
Brandeis, I., 91n
Briareus, 227, 227n
Brugnoli, G., 190n, 199n, 258n, 259n, 260n, 272
Brunetto Latini, 92n, 95, 154, 229
Brutus, 247n
Buondelmonte, 166
Busnelli, G., 254n

Cacciaguida, 60, 154, 232n, 252, 252n, 271n, 276n, 281-283
Cacus, 226, 227n
Cadmus, 225
Caesar, 166, 182, 252n
Caiphas, 223
Calchas, 221, 222n
Camilli, A., 20n
canso, 151n
Capaneus, 211, 211n, 227, 229, 257n
captatio benevolentiae, 202, 228, 230-231, 241, 243
Caretti, L., 5n
Casella, 12-13, 31-40, 55, 59, 62-66, 201n, 241
Casella, M., 145n
Cassandra, 254n
Cassata, L., 53n
Castelvetro, L., 9n
Catalano, 104, 223, 240

Index

Cato, 34-35, 37, 191n, 195-196, 202, 241-242, 246-247, 255n
Cattaneo, M. T., 102n
Cavalcanti, Cavalcante de', 101n, 126, 145, 147-148, 160
Cavalcanti, Guido, xiii, 8n, 42n, 52, 53n, 54n, 89, 93, 93n, 101, 123-153, 175-179, 292; *ballata* in, 137, 152, 152n; manner of, 42, 129n; poems referred to:
  "A me stesso di me pietate vene," 42n
  "Biltà di donna e di saccente core," 139-142, 148
  "Da più a uno face un sollegismo," 133-134
  "Di vil matera mi conven parlare," 135, 177-178
  "Donna me prega," 125, 133, 138, 142-146, 148
  "Era in penser d'amor quand' i' trovai," 138, 138n
  "Fresca rosa novella," 148
  "In un boschetto trova' pasturella," 8n, 148-152
  "Io non pensava che lo cor giammai," 178n
  "I' vegno 'l giorno a te 'nfinite volte," 53n
  "Poi che di doglia cor conven ch'i' porti," 125
  "Una giovane donna di Tolosa," 138
Cento, F., 243n
Cerberus, 205, 210, 210n
Cerisola, P. L., 146n
Cesari, A., 128n
Chanson de la Croisade, 119n
Chanson de Roland, 270
Charles I of Anjou, 65, 157n, 167, 185, 185n
Charles Martel of Anjou, 13-14, 57-60, 62-68, 70-71, 73, 76, 116, 185

Charon, 210n
Chaucer, *Troilus and Criseyde*, 261n
Chaytor, H. J., 99n
Chiampi, J. T., 225n, 275n
Chiarenza, M., 254n
Chiaro Davanzati, 103
Chimenz, S. A., 199n
Christ, 22, 139, 208-209, 214, 223-224, 257
Ciacco, 168, 229
Ciccuto, M., 86n, 128n, 134n
Cicero, 191, 191n, 197, 197n; *De Amicitia*, 19, 19n, 201n; *De Finibus*, 54n; *De Senectute*, 195
Cielo d'Alcamo, 92n
Cino da Pistoia, 76n, 89, 93-94, 108, 125, 125n, 129-130, 135-136, 162, 173n, 174, 186, 219n, 220n, 291; poems referred to: "Deh, quando rivedrò 'l dolce paese," 219n
Cioffari, V., 58n, 62n
Clemence, 58n, 66, 66n
Cocytus, 74n, 211
Colish, M. L., 280n
comedìa, 213-214, 218, 228, 233, 237-238, 271-281; as title, 285-286
Commager, S., 200n
Comparetti, D., 203n, 219n
consolare, 36, 37n
Consoli, D., 190n, 191n
Contini, G., 3n, 5n, 6, 6n, 24n, 30n, 86n, 100n, 102n, 111n, 126n, 132n, 133n, 136n, 146n, 148n, 179n, 234n, 235n
contrapasso, law of, 166
Coroebus, 254n
Corti, M., 136n, 145n
Crescini, V., 167n
Croce, B., 160n
Cudini, P., 49n
Cunizza da Romano, 64, 67-68, 69n, 185, 185n

301

Index

Cupid, 61, 72-73, 75
Curato, B., 5n
Curio, Gaius Scribonius, 166
Curtius, E. R., 271n

D'Alverny, M. T., 20n
D'Andria, M., 266n
Dante, texts referred to:
  Commedia, 288-297; cantos discussed:
    Inf. I, 199, 202, 239, 262-270, 278-279;
    II, 7-12, 149, 152, 202, 205n, 243, 280n;
    IV, 171, 189, 199, 200, 202, 202n, 263-270;
    V, 4-12, 33;
    VI, 168, 170;
    VIII, 203-204, 207-208, 223n, 244-245;
    IX, 203-210, 244;
    X, 126-127, 142, 145-148, 160-161, 168-170;
    XII, 208-210;
    XIII, 212;
    XIV, 139-140, 211;
    XVI, 213-214, 217, 242-243, 279n;
    XX, 214-222, 237;
    XXI, 222-223;
    XXIII, 222n, 223, 245;
    XXIV, 223-225, 243-245;
    XXV, 223-226;
    XXVI, 228-233;
    XXVII, 229-233;
    XXVIII, 164-172;
    XXIX, 225-226;
    XXX, 233-238;
    XXXI, 226-227;
  Purg. II, 12-13, 31-40, 241;
    III, 241-242, 246;
    IV, 246-247;
    V, 246-247;
    VI, 100n, 101n, 155, 157, 159-163, 168-171, 179-184, 247-248;
    VII, 139-141, 157, 162-163, 170-171, 248;
    VIII, 47, 184, 247;
    X, 274-276, 278, 281n;
    XI, 127-129, 177;
    XXI, 250-251, 256, 259-269;
    XXII, 250-251, 259-269;
    XXIII, 40-57;
    XXIV, 40-57, 85-90, 96, 113, 177, 178n;
    XXVI, 85-89, 95-100, 112-114, 117, 117n, 283n, 284n;
    XXVIII, 148-153;
    XXIX, 152, 256;
    XXX, 202, 244, 250-252;
  Par. VIII, 57-84, 226;
    IX, 68, 115-117, 120-121;
    XIII, 283n, 284n;
    XVII, 282-283;
    XX, 255-256;
    XXIII, 273;
    XXV, 269, 273-274, 276-277;
    XXVI, 268;
    XXX, 272;
  Convivio, 3n, 4n, 10, 14-17, 19-20, 22-25, 26n, 27n, 30, 37-38, 58, 68-70, 72-74, 75n, 79, 84, 104n, 111n, 116n, 131-132, 164, 166, 186, 190-199, 201n, 226, 253, 257n, 258n, 260, 271n, 277n, 284, 287-297;
  De Vulgari Eloquentia, 30, 44-45, 86n, 89, 91-100, 108, 111, 114-115, 121, 124-126, 130, 133n, 135, 136n, 161-162, 164, 166, 174-177, 185-186, 190, 268n, 287-297;
  Egloge, xiii, 281, 281n, 282n;
  Epistole, 288-297; VI, 220n; VII, 197n, 287; XIII (to Cangrande della Scala), 4n, 24, 214n, 271, 271n, 272n, 281n;
  Fiore, 24n;

Index

Monarchia, 30, 197-198, 219, 220n, 287-297;
Rime, 15, 54, 77, 288-297; *petrose*, 101, 112; poems referred to:
"A ciascun'alma presa e gentil core," 101
"Al poco giorno e al gran cerchio d'ombra," 44n
"Amor, che movi tua vertù da cielo," 44n
"Amor che ne la mente mi ragiona," 13, 18, 20-21, 27, 29, 31-40, 66, 82, 84
"Amor, da che convien pur ch'io mi doglia," 76n
"Amore e 'l cor gentil sono una cosa," 6, 129
"Amor, tu vedi ben che questa donna," 44n, 177
"Ballata, i' vòi che tu ritrovi Amore," 137, 137n
"Bicci novel, figliuol di non so cui," 49n
"Cavalcando l'altr'ier per un cammino," 136
"Ciò che m'incontra, ne la mente more," 42
"Con l'altre donne mia vista gabbate," 42
"Doglia mi reca ne lo core ardire," 26, 44n, 102, 107n, 108-110, 187
"Donna pietosa e di novella etate," 44n
"Donne ch'avete intelletto d'amore," 13, 15, 31, 37-38, 40-57, 58n, 62, 79, 82, 84-85, 114, 129-130, 132, 137n, 281n
"Gentil pensero che parla di vui," 16-17, 36
"Guido, i' vorrei che tu e Lapo ed io," 123-125
"Io sono stato con Amore insieme," 76n
"Le dolci rime d'amor ch'i solia," 25, 28-29, 33, 35, 80-83, 107, 284
"O dolci rime che parlando andate," 27-29
"Oltre la spera che più larga gira," 17-18, 36, 77n
"Parole mie che per lo mondo siete," 27-29, 77-78, 81
"Per quella via che la bellezza corre," 77n
"Poscia ch'Amor del tutto m'ha lasciato," 26, 44n, 110n
"Spesse fiate vegnonmi a la mente," 42
"Tanto gentile e tanto onesta pare," 132
"Traggemi de la mente amor la stiva," 44n
"Tre donne intorno al cor mi son venute," 103
"Tutti li miei penser parlan d'Amore," 129n, 137n
"Voi che 'ntendendo il terzo ciel movete," 13-14, 16-21, 24, 26n, 27-28, 31, 36-37, 57-84, 111n
"Voi che savete ragionar d'Amore," 27
Vita Nuova, 3n, 4n, 6, 10, 14-17, 19n, 20-22, 25, 36-37, 42-44, 51, 51n, 53n, 58, 67, 69, 79, 82n, 84, 101, 123-124, 126, 129-132, 136-139, 152, 175, 178n, 188-189, 199, 270, 270n, 287-297; two redactions of, 21n
Dante da Maiano, 100-101; *tenzone del duol d'amore*, 100n
Dardanus, 198
David, 275-278
Davis, C. T., 197n
De Bartholomaeis, V., 157n
De Bonfils Templer, M., 250n

Index

Deianira, 209
Deipyle, 193
Del Lungo, I., 66n
Del Monte, A., 46n, 48n, 91n, 102n
De Lollis, C., 90n, 91n, 102n, 110n, 112n, 113n, 115n, 155n, 167n
Democritus, 191n
De Robertis, D., 19n, 20n, 21n, 26n, 41n, 78n, 125n, 133n, 136n, 137n
De Sanctis, F., 102n
devils, 203, 223. See also Malacoda
Devoto, G., 104n
dicitori, 270n
Dido, 24n, 61, 115, 194, 252n
Diomedes, 228
Dionysius (Academico), 191n
Di Pino, G., 128n
dolce, 245, 245n
Dolce, L., 286, 286n
dolce stil novo. See *stil novo*
Dominic, St., 101n, 119
Domitian, 257n, 259
Donati, Corso, 65
Donati, Forese, 13, 45-57, 59, 62, 62n, 65-67, 234, 234n. See also *tenzone*, Dante and Forese
Donati, Piccarda, 57, 154
Donatus, Aelius, 207n
donna gentile, 15-17, 19-22, 24, 29-30, 36-37, 40, 53n, 54, 71, 75-77, 81-82, 111n
D'Ovidio, F., 49n, 53n, 155n, 199n, 202n, 205n, 206n, 218, 218n, 222n
Dragonetti, R., 5n

Earthly Paradise, 47, 47n, 49, 55, 256
Egidi, F., 100n, 103n
Egidio Romano, 191n
Empedocles, 209
Epicurus, 191n
Erichtho, 205-206, 219, 221-222
Esposito, E., 116n, 201n, 260n

Euclid, 191n
Eurydice, 252n
Eurypylus, 221, 222n, 237
Eve, 48, 57
exemplum, principle of, 282
Ezekiel, 285n
Ezzelino III da Romano, 69n, 185n

fabbro, for poets, 100, 113, 176-177
Fallani, G., 3n, 58n
Farinata degli Uberti, 126, 147-148, 153, 160-161, 168-170, 203n
Favati, G., 41n, 133n, 144, 144n, 155n, 178n
Ferdinand III of Castile and León, 157n
Ferrante, J. M., 47n
Ferrers Howell, A. G., 98n, 110n
Ferrucci, F., 214n, 271n
Figurelli, F., 144n
Filippo Argenti, 207, 234, 238
Folena, G., 93n, 94n, 96n, 112n, 118n, 121n, 154n
folle amore, 60-62, 68, 74, 76, 115
Folquet de Marselha, 61-62, 64, 67-68, 69n, 83, 92, 93n, 104, 114-122, 154, 176, 179, 184-185, 187, 289; lament for Barral, 119-120; *razos* of, 121, 121n; *vidas* of, 119, 119n
Forti, F., 199n, 202n
Foster, K., 8n, 14n, 21, 26n, 27n, 30n, 67, 67n, 77n, 81, 82n, 100n, 101n, 129n, 137n, 202n, 253n, 254n, 255n
Fra Dolcino, 166
Francesca da Rimini, 5-7, 10, 12, 58n, 126, 126n, 154, 229, 282
Francesco da Buti, 127n, 128n, 260n
Francis, St., 101n
Fratia Gaudenti, 103-105
Freccero, J., 4n, 5n, 31n, 34, 34n, 36n, 252n

304

Index

Frederick II, Emperor, 126, 126n, 157n
Frugoni, A., 272n
Fubini, M., 167n
Fulgentius, reading of *Aeneid* of, 24, 257n
Furies, 205, 210n

gabbo, episode of in *Vita Nuova*, 42-43, 136, 137n
Galen, 191n
Gallo of Pisa, 92n
Gardner, E. G., 94n
Garrod, H. W., 193n
Gentile, G., 160n
Gentucca, 57, 65n
Geryon, 213, 214n, 227n, 244
Getto, G., 160n, 232n, 245n
Ghibellines, 183n
Ghislieri, Guido, 92n
Giacomo da Lentini, 86, 92n, 287, 291
giants, 226-227
Gilson, E., 54n, 67n
Giolito, G., 286n
Giovanna, 138
Giovanni del Virgilio, xiii, 281, 281n, 282n
Girardi, E. N., 95n, 279n
Giraut de Bornelh, 92-93, 96-100, 108-112, 121-122, 130-131, 164, 175, 186, 289
Gmelin, H., 196n
Golden Age, 153, 259, 260n
golden mean. *See* Aristotelianism
Goldin, F., 158n
Goldstein, H. D., 228n
Gorni, G., 124n, 125n, 132n, 136n
Grayson, C., 197n
Gregory the Great, 70-71, 254; *Moralium libri*, 276n
Groppi, F., 201n, 247n, 252n
Guelphs, 103, 183n
Guerri, D., 48n, 49n

Guglielminetti, M., 3n, 19n, 20n
Guido da Montefeltro. *See* Montefeltro, Guido da
Guido del Duca, 47, 47n
Guido delle Colonne, 92, 92n, 93n
Guilhem de Montanhagol, 113, 113n
Guillem de Berguedà, 117n
Guinizzelli, Guido, 6-8, 13, 36n, 59n, 87-89, 92, 92n, 93n, 94, 96, 98n, 100, 112, 112n, 125-136, 139, 142, 153, 154, 164, 170, 174-176, 178-179, 185, 270, 284n, 292; poems referred to:
"Al cor gentil rempaira sempre amore," 6, 130, 132, 136n, 192n
"Di fermo sofferire," 130
"Io voglio del ver la mia donna laudare," 8n, 132, 139
"[O] caro padre meo, de vostra laude," 98n, 133
"Omo ch'è saggio non corre leggero," 98n, 284n
"Tegno de folle 'mpres', a lo ver dire," 130
"Vedut' ho la lucente stella diana," 8n
Guittone d'Arezzo, 6n, 86, 88, 92n, 94-98, 100-112, 122-123, 128n, 129, 131, 133-135, 137n, 174-176, 178-184, 283n, 284n, 293; *Lettere*, 104, 104n, 123n, 184n; manner of, 15, 133, 177; poems referred to:
"Ahi lasso, or è stagion de doler tanto," 100n, 101n, 103, 103n
"Ahi, quant'ho che vergogni e che doglia aggio," 105
"Altra fiata aggio giá, donne, parlato," 106-110
"Comune perta fa comun dolore," 103n, 131
"Gente noiosa e villana," 103
"Giudice de Gallura, en vostro amore," 184

Index

Guittone d'Arezzo (*cont*).
"Magni baroni certo e regi quasi," 103n, 179-184
"Meraviglioso beato," 101n
"Messer Marzuccho Scornigian, sovente," 184n
"Ora parrà s'eo saverò cantare," 103n, 106, 122, 122n
"Padre dei padri miei e mio messere," 105
"Poi male tutto è nulla inver peccato," 106
"Tuttor, s'eo veglio o dormo," 103n, 128n
"Vergogna ho, lasso, ed ho me stesso ad ira," 105
Guyler, S., 222n
Guzzardo, J., 202n

harrowing of Hell, 208
Hatcher, A., 5n
Hauvette, H., 98n, 112n, 255n
Hawkins, P. S., 225n
Hecuba, 235-236
Heilbronn, D., 262n
Henry VII of Luxembourg, Emperor, 277n
Henry Plantagenet, the Young King, 157-158, 164, 164n, 169; laments for, *see* Bertran de Born
Henry II, King of England, 164
Henry III, King of England, 157n
Henry, King of Navarre, 157n
Hercules, 115, 209-210, 226, 227n, 228n
heredity, 64-65
Hero, 151, 153
Highet, G., 207n
Hill, R. T., 158n
Hippocrates, 191n
Hirtzel, F. A., 216n
Hoepffner, E., 98n, 112n, 154n
Hollander, R., 5n, 22n, 31n, 34, 34n, 36n, 52n, 58n, 202n, 207n,
214n, 215n, 221, 221n, 247n, 260n, 268n, 277n, 278n, 279n
Homer, 175n, 188-190, 196, 197n, 199, 238n, 264, 293
Horace, 188-190, 196, 294; *Ars Poetica*, 189-190, 272n
Housman, A. E., 206n
Hugh Capet, 232n
Hypsipyle, 280n

Iacopo del Cassero, 183
Iannucci, A. A., 4n, 199n, 285n
"Infra gli altri difetti del libello," 173-175
Ino, 235
Iphigenia, 221
Isolde, 24n

Jacobus de Pistorio, 144n, 145n
Jacoff, R., 59n
Jacomuzzi, A., 270n, 273n
Jacopo della Lana, 127n, 128n
James I of Aragon, 157n
Jason, 24n, 280n
Jeanroy, A., 98n
Jerome, St., 191n
John of Salisbury, *Policraticus*, 219n
John, St., 284, 285n
John the Baptist, 139, 153
Joshua, 68, 120
Jove, 227, 235. *See also* Jupiter
Juno, 225, 235
Jupiter, 198, 257n. *See also* Jove
Justinian, 24n
Juvenal, 189n, 190, 196, 197n, 260, 260n, 261n, 263, 287, 294; *Satires*, 260n

Kastner, L. E., 158n
Kay, R., 230n
Ker, W. P., 112n
Kolsen, A., 109n
Kristeller, P. O., 144n

Index

Lacaita, J. P., 9n, 257n, 278n
Lambertazzi, Fabruzzo de', 92n
Lamberti, Mosca de', 166, 168
Lancelot du Lac, 5, 9
language. *See* Latin; Lombard dialect; Provençal; Romance languages; *vulgare illustre*
languages spoken in *Comedy*, 231n, 232n
Lanza, A., 49n
Lapo Gianni, 89
Latin, 163n, 232n
Lazar, M., 114n
Leander, 151, 153
Leo, U., 192n, 194, 194n
Lethe, 211
Lewis, C. S., 257n
Limbo, 171, 199-200, 202, 202n, 239, 244, 244n, 253, 256, 261n, 263-264, 268, 268n
Lipari, A., 232n
Lisetta, 77n
Livy, 167, 191n, 197, 197n
Loderingo, 104-105
Lombard dialect, spoken by Vergil, 231, 232n
Lombard origins, Vergil's, 216n, 217n
Louis IX, King of France, 157n
Lucan, 182, 188-190, 192, 195-197, 205, 206n, 215, 215n, 223, 224n, 225, 259n, 295; *Pharsalia*, 189, 195, 201n, 205, 206n, 215, 247n, 287
Lucifer, 223, 244

McCutchan, G., 223n
MacLennan, L. J., 4n
Macrobius, 274n
MacVay, A. P., 205n, 206n
maestro Adamo. *See* Adamo, maestro
Maggini, F., 48n, 77n
Malacoda, 208, 222-223, 238-239, 245

Malaspina, Currado, 248
Malaspina, Moroello (Marchese), 204n
Mandelbaum, A., 216n
Manto, 215-216
Mantova, 160-161, 250; founding of, 205n, 215-217, 221
Marcellus, 182
Marcia, 13, 35, 191n, 195, 241
Marco Lombardo, 76, 89n
Margueron, C., 102n, 103n
Marigo, A., 93n
Mariotti, S., 257n
Mars, 143-144
Martellotti, G., 190n, 196n
Marti, M., 21n, 31, 32n, 49n, 53n, 86n, 88n, 92n, 94n, 100n, 125n, 128n, 132n, 146n, 173n, 201n
Martinez, R. L., 86n, 91n
Mary, 57
Masciandaro, F., 47n
Matelda, 47, 148, 149n, 151-153
Mattalia, D., 5n
Mazzaro, J., 4n
Mazzeo, J. A., 54n, 75n, 220n
Mazzoni, F., 199n, 272n
Mazzotta, G., 5n, 47n, 91n, 233n
Medea, 24n
Medusa, 205-206, 208
Melli, E., 113n
Mengaldo, P. V., 93n, 94n, 121n, 125n, 131n, 136n, 161n, 162n, 186n, 268n
Mercuri, R., 190n, 264n
Meriano, F., 184n
metamorphosis, 223-226
Michael Scot, *Liber Introductorius*, 218n
Michal, 276n
Milites Beatae Virginis Mariae. *See* Frati Gaudenti
mimesis, 274-275
Mineo, N., 220n, 282n
Mino Mocato, 92n, 95

307

Index

Minos, 210n
Minotaur, 208-210
Misenus, 194
Mohammed, 166, 168
Moleta, V., 36n, 59n, 102n, 136n, 137n
Montanari, F., 20n, 26n
Montaperti, 103
Monte Andrea, 103
Montefeltro, Bonconte da, 183
Montefeltro, Guido da, 229-233, 237
Monteverdi, A., 96n
Moore, E., 54n, 196, 196n, 201, 252n
Moore, O. H., 158n, 164n
Mopsus, 281n
Murari, R., 20n
Musa, M., 5n, 52n, 88n, 205n
Muscetta, C., 59n, 62n
Mustard, P., 193n
Myrmidons, 225-226, 265n

Nardi, B., 20n, 21n, 54n, 69n, 77n, 144, 144n, 220n, 272n
Natali, G., 271n
Nathan, 277n
nature, 141, 141n, 274
Nebuchadnezzar, 211
Nella, 56-57
Neoplatonism, 144n
Nessus, 209
Niccoli, A., 259n
Nicholas III, 280n
Nimrod, 227
Noakes, S., 5n
Nolan, D., 250n
Nuvoli, G., 248n

Ocnus, 216, 216n
Octavia, 252n
Oderisi da Gubbio, 128
Old French poets, 92n, 93, 93n
Old Man of Crete, 47, 47n, 211, 211n

Onesti, Onesto degli, 86n, 92n, 173n, 174
Orlandi, Guido, 86n, 135, 177-178; poems referred to: "Amico, i' saccio ben che sai limare," 177n
Orosius, 191n, 197, 197n
Ottakar II, King of Bohemia, 157n
Ottimo Commento, 127n, 128n
Ovid, 61-62, 73-74, 178, 188-190, 192, 195-197, 215, 215n, 223-226, 227n, 235n, 259n, 265n, 266n, 296; *Metamorphoses*, 74, 74n, 195, 215, 225; *Remedia Amoris*, 189

Paasonen, A. A.-M., 123n
Paden, W. D., 158n
Padoan, G., 199n, 210n, 218n, 257n, 258n, 261n, 267n, 272n
Pagliaro, A., 5n, 146n, 232n
Palinurus, 247
Panvini, B., 93n
Paoletti, L., 206n
Paparelli, G., 4n, 199n
Pappalardo, F., 145n
Paratore, E., 126n, 163n, 189n, 196n, 211n, 216n, 224n, 226n, 232n, 254n, 255n, 262n, 264n
Parducci, A., 99n
pargoletta, 48, 54, 54n
Parodi, E. G., 155n, 199n, 215
parola ornata, 7, 228, 280, 280n
Pasquali, G., 203n
Pastine, L., 98n
pastorela, 138, 138n, 153
Pastore Stocchi, M., 272n
pasturella, 151n
Paterson, L. M., 110n, 111n, 113n, 177n
Peire d'Alvernhe, 91, 91n
Peire Vidal, 158n
Peirone, L., 99n
Pellegrini, S., 91n, 95n, 104n, 114n
Pellizzari, A., 102n, 104n

Index

Pépin, J., 22n
Perella, N. J., 5n
Pernicone, V., 20, 30n, 38n, 77n
Perugi, M., 98n, 112n, 117n
Peter III of Aragon, 157n
Peter, St., 283n
Petrarch, 51, 65, 128n
Petrie, J., 250n
Petrocchi, G., 20n, 32n, 142n, 201, 201n, 259, 260n
Pézard, A., 58n, 61n, 258n
Philip III, King of France, 157n
Philosophy, Lady, 19-21, 24-25, 27, 27n, 29-30, 34, 36-39, 58, 67, 69, 76
Phlegethon, 211, 211n
phoenix, 225, 266n
Phyllis, 115
Pia de' Tolomei, 183
Piattoli, R., 183n
Picone, M., 109, 109n, 111n, 113n, 128n, 138n, 167n
Pier da Medicina, 65n, 166, 168-169
Pier della Vigna, 126, 126n, 201n, 212, 229-230
Pietola, 220n, 250
Pietrobono, L., 21n
Pietro di Dante, 127n
Pirot, F., 99n
Plato, 76, 191n
Pluto, 151, 153
Plutus, 210n
poema, 273
poema sacro, 274, 274n, 276-277, 281
poeta, 265-271, 273n, 275, 282n
Poggioli, R., 5n
Poliziano, 257n
Polydorus, 212
Polyneices, 193
Popolizio, S., 5n
Porena, M., 285n
praise-style, 38, 52, 52n, 132
Primavera, 138, 148

Prince Henry. *See* Henry Plantagenet
Principalities, 70-71, 75
prodigality, 259-260
prophecy, 198, 218-220, 276, 282n, 283-284, 285n
Proserpina, 47, 151, 153
prosimetrum, 20, 104n
Proto, E., 196n
Provençal, as language, 161-162; poetry, 87, 92; poets, 92n, 93, 93n, 98n; spoken in *Comedy*, see Arnaut Daniel
Provenzan Salvani, 128n
pseudo-Dionysius, the Areopagite, *De Coelesti Hierarchia*, 70
Ptolemy, 24n, 191n
Pythagoras, 191n

Quaglio, A. E., 86n, 94n, 102n
Quint, D., 205n

Raab, 68, 120
Raimon VII of Toulouse, 157n
Raimon Bérenger IV of Provence, 157n
Rajna, P., 285n, 286n
Ransom, D. J., 75n
razos, Provençal. *See* Bertran de Born; Folquet de Marselha
Reeves, M., 220n
Reggio, G., 46n
Renaudet, A., 196n, 199n
Renucci, P., 195n, 196n, 258n, 260n, 262, 262n
rhyme, equivocal, 178; Sicilian, 142n; *caras rimas*, 117
Rinaldo d'Aquino, 92n
Ripheus, 241n, 254-256, 276
Robert of Anjou, 65
Robson, A., 197n
Rocca, L., 58n
Rolfe, J. C., 207n
Romance languages, 163, 163n

309

Index

Roman de la Rose, 24n
Roncaglia, A., 96n, 112n, 113n, 168, 168n
Ronconi, A., 19n, 190n, 196n, 198n, 201n, 258n, 260n
Rudolf I, Emperor, 157n
Ruggieri, R. M., 155n
ruine, 208, 210, 222, 223n, 242
Ruth, 276
Russo, V., 32n, 46n, 48n, 49n, 88n
Ryan, C. J., 222n, 223n, 250n

Sabbadini, R., 207n
Saffiotti Bernardi, S., 183n
saggio/savio, 6, 11, 90, 266-270
Salinari, C., 104n
Salverda de Grave, J.-J., 110n, 111n
Santagata, M., 53n
Santangelo, S., 14n, 98, 98n, 104n
Santoro, M., 191n
Sapegno, N., 8n, 50n, 62, 66n, 117n, 128n, 173n, 247n, 259n, 260n
Sapia, 266n
Sarolli, G. R., 4n, 31n, 277n, 283n
savio. See saggio
Sayers, D., 200n
Scherillo, M., 115n, 164n, 167n
Schiaffini, A., 270n, 272n, 274n
Schicchi, Gianni, 236
Schoder, R. V., 206n
Schutz, A.-H., 119n
Scornigiani, Gano, 183, 183n
Scornigiani, Marzucco, 183-184
Scott, J. A., 5n, 51n, 203n
screen ladies, Folquet's use of, 117, 117n
scriba, 90, 106, 219, 273n
Segre, C., 104n
Selvaggia, 173n, 174
Semele, 235
Semiramis, 11
Seneca, 191, 191n, 197n, 247n

sestina, 100, 176; double sestina, 177
Shakespeare, 175n
Shapiro, M., 167n
Shaw, J. E., 20n, 86n, 144n
ship, poem as, 106
Shoaf, R. A., 260n
Sibyl, 194, 247, 257
Sicilian bull, simile of, 230-231
Sicilian poets, 86, 86n, 92-93, 95, 126
Sicilian Vespers, 65
Siculo-Tuscan poets, 86
Sigier of Brabant, 24n
Simonelli, M., 6n, 21n, 25n, 86n, 275n
Singleton, C. S., 22n, 32n, 90, 142n, 149n, 167n, 259n, 260n, 276n
Sinon, 49, 49n, 221-222, 233-234, 236-237
Sirago, V., 196n
Sirens, 54n
Smith, N. B., 118n
Socrates, 24n, 191n
Solomon, 24n
sonnet, double, 137n
Sordello, 13, 69n, 153-157, 159-163, 169-174, 176, 179, 184-185, 187, 248-249, 290; Ensenhamens d'onor, 155n, 159; lament for Blacatz, 155, 158-159, 179
Spargo, J. W., 219n
Spengemann, W. C., 3n
Spitzer, L., 126n
Spongano, R., 131n
Statius, xiii, 13, 153, 170-172, 190, 190n, 192-196, 200, 206n, 215, 227n, 248n, 249-251, 255n, 256-270, 279n, 296; Agave, 260n; Thebaid, 193, 193n, 211, 215, 227n, 257, 257n, 258n, 261, 261n, 286n
Stäuble, A., 111n, 121n
Stephany, W. A., 126n

Index

stil novo/stilnovisti, 5-6, 9, 26, 41, 41n, 48, 48n, 52, 53n, 56, 67, 82, 84, 86n, 87-89, 93, 101, 101n, 113, 113n, 124-125, 133n, 137n, 152, 152n, 173n, 176-179
stilo de la loda. See praise-style
stilus planus, 9, 278
Stoicism, 239, 244, 246, 247n
Stroński, S., 115n, 116n, 117n, 119n, 121n, 185n
Suetonius, *Vita Vergili*, 207n, 252n
Suitner, F., 86n, 98n, 115n, 119n, 167n
Sullivan, Sister Thérèse, 280n
synonymic reduplication, 8, 8n

Tartaro, A., 102n
Tarugi, G., 243n
Tateo, F., 20n, 270n, 275n
Taylor, K., 5n
tenzone: Dante and Forese, 48-49, 53, 53n, 56, 77n, 234; question of attribution, 48n, 49n
tenzone del duol d'amore. See Dante da Maiano
tëodia, 277-279
Terdiman, R., 224n
Terracini, B., 232n
Thaïs, 201n
Thebes, 235
Theseus, 205, 209-210, 258n
Thibaut de Champagne, King of Navarre, 92, 92n, 130, 157n
Thomas Aquinas, St., 191n, 253n, 254n, 260n, 280-281, 283n, 284n; *Summa Theologiae*, 260n, 281n
Thomism, 67n
Thrones, 70-72, 74-75
Tiber, 216n
time: in *Purg.*, 46, 244; Vergil as timekeeper, 244, 246
Tiresias, 215, 215n, 257n
Titus, 263
Tityrus, 281n

Toja, G., 113n, 114n, 121n, 177n
Tolomei, C., *Cesano*, 286n
Torraca, F., 102n, 115n, 155n
Tower of Babel, 162
Toynbee, P., 4n
tragedìa, 214, 216, 218, 228, 233, 237-238, 271-281
Trajan, 254, 255n, 276n
traviamento morale, 48, 54n, 56
Tristan, 24n
trobar clus, 117n
trobar leu, 110, 110n
Troccoli, G., 199n
Trojans, 194, 221, 254n
Troy, 198, 198n, 235, 237
Truijen, V., 277n
Truscott, J. G., 230n
Tuscan poets, 86, 92, 92n, 95-96; manner of, 129n
Tydeus, 193
Typhoeus, 73-74

Ugolino della Gherardesca, 179-180, 182-184, 223
Uguccione da Pisa, 191n
Ulysses, 54n, 228-233

valley of the princes, 39, 140-141, 148, 155, 171, 184
Vallone, A., 191n
Vance, E., 141n
Vanni Fucci, 223
Vanossi, L., 24n
vates/vate, 197-198, 219, 220n, 282n
Vaturi, V., 58n, 63
Vellutello, S., 128n
Venus, 60-62, 72-75, 151, 153
Véran, J., 98n, 112n
Vergil, xiii, 4, 7-10, 35, 52, 55-57, 61-62, 72-74, 112, 146n, 153-155, 157, 159-160, 162-163, 170-172, 175n, 188-270, 276, 278-283, 286n, 287, 297; *Aeneid*, 24, 61,

311

Index

Vergil (cont.)
73-74, 189, 192, 198, 201-202, 206n, 211-212, 214-218, 220n, 221, 222n, 226, 227n, 234, 237, 247, 252, 252n, 254, 254n, 257n, 259, 259n, 261-262, 271, 274n, 279n, 281n, 287; *Eclogue* IV, 197, 260n, 262, 265, 276; *Georgics*,252n
Vettori, V., 116n
vidas, Provençal. *See* Bertran de Born; Folquet de Marselha
villanello, simile of, 238
Villani, G., 14n
virga, 207, 207n, 282n
virtuous pagans, 241n, 253n, 254-256
Viscardi, A., 6n

Visconti, Nino, 179-180, 182-184, 248
volume, 268-269
vulgare illustre, 125, 162, 162n, 163n

Whitfield, J. H., 201, 201n, 267n
Wicksteed, P. H., 196n, 261n
Wilhelm, J. J., 158n
Wilkins, E. H., 98n
William Montferrat, 157n

Zeno, 191n
Zenocrates, 191n
Zingarelli, 115n, 117n, 121, 121n, 173n
Zumthor, P., 3n

LIBRARY OF CONGRESS CATALOGING IN PUBLICATION DATA

Barolini, Teodolinda, 1951-
Dante's poets.

Includes index.
1. Dante Alighieri, 1265-1321. Divina commedia.
2. Dante Alighieri, 1265-1321—Characters—Poets.
3. Poets in literature. I. Title.
PQ4409.P64B37 1984   851'.1   84-42586
ISBN 0-691-06609-4 (alk. paper)

Teodolinda Barolini is Associate Professor in the
Department of French and Italian at New York University